The Originality Standard of Photographic Works in EU Copyright Law

The Originality Standard of Photographic Works in EU Copyright Law

Marián Jankovič

Wolters Kluwer

Citation:
MARIÁN JANKOVIČ, *The Originality Standard of Photographic Works in EU Copyright Law* (Kluwer Law International, 2024).

Published by:
Kluwer Law International B.V.
PO Box 316
2400 AH Alphen aan den Rijn
The Netherlands
E-mail: lrs-sales@wolterskluwer.com
Website: www.wolterskluwer.com/en/solutions/kluwerlawinternational

Sold and distributed by:
Wolters Kluwer Legal & Regulatory U.S.
920 Links Avenue
Landisville, PA 17538
United States of America
E-mail: customer.service@wolterskluwer.com

Reviewers:
Ivana Kunda, University of Rijeka
Philipp Homar, Johannes Kepler Universität Linz

ISBN print 9789403514192
MI# 10125369-0001
e-ISBN 9789403514291
MI# e-Pub 10125370-0001
Web PDF ISBN 9789403514390
MI# Web PDF 10125371-0001

This book is the result of a project funded by the Grant Agency of the Czech Republic [Copyrighted Works and the Requirement of Sufficient Precision and Objectivity (GA22-22517S)].

CONTENTS

ABOUT THE AUTHOR

Marián Jankovič is a Slovak legal expert with an extensive background in intellectual property law and data protection. He currently serves as the Deputy Head of Public Performance Licensing and a Data Protection Officer at the Slovak Performing and Mechanical Rights Society (SOZA) and has previously held positions as a Licensing and Privacy Specialist within the same organization. *Jankovič* is also affiliated with *Masaryk University* in Brno as a researcher at the *Institute of Law and Technology*, and he lectures on intellectual property law at the *Academy of Fine Arts and Design in Bratislava*. His academic pursuits include an LLM study in Law and Technology program from Tilburg University and a PhD study in Intellectual Property Law doctoral program from Masaryk University, complemented by research stays at the Institute for Information Law of University of Amsterdam and the Max Planck Institute for Innovation and Competition in Munich. *Marián's* research focuses on copyright law, with particular emphasis on the originality standard of photographic works in the European Union. His publications include analyses of how landmark cases have influenced the originality standard for photographic works and studies on copyright ownership under private international law in Czech and Slovak contexts. His work has been published in respected journals such as *Masaryk University Journal of Law and Technology* and *Review of Central and East European Law*.

PREFACE

With the advent of photography in the 19th century, legal systems across the world were confronted with a novel challenge—how to categorize photographs, which, at first glance, appeared to be mere mechanical reproductions of reality. The central question that arose was whether a photograph, created through a largely automated process, could possess the necessary elements of creativity and originality to warrant protection under copyright law.[1] This dilemma was not merely a technical issue, but a profound philosophical debate about the nature of art and creativity. Could the mechanical capture of an image reflect the personal, intellectual effort required for something to be deemed original?

Over time, the evolution of legal thought recognized that photography, while mechanically facilitated, involves significant human intervention and creative decision-making. The choices a photographer makes—such as the framing of a shot, the manipulation of light, the selection of angles, and the moment of capture—imbue the photograph with personal expression. These artistic choices raise the photograph from a mere technical reproduction to an original work of authorship, deserving of copyright protection.[2]

This book is the culmination of comprehensive research conducted by Marián Jankovič, both as part of his dissertation and within a broader research project funded by the Czech Grant Agency, '*Díla chráněná autorským právem a požadavek dostatečné přesnosti a objectivity*' (Copyrighted Works and the Requirement of Sufficient Precision and Objectivity; Project No. GA22-22517S). While the project itself centres on the requirements of precision and objectivity in copyrighted works, it also addresses the deeper, interconnected issue of *originality*—a foundational criterion for copyright protection.

Originality, as defined in European Union law and interpreted by the Court of Justice of the European Union (CJEU), has evolved through numerous landmark rulings (such as *Painer case*)[3] which have shaped our understanding of what qualifies a work as an *original* creation deserving of protection.

---

1 Christine Haight Farley, The Lingering Effects of Copyright's Response to the Invention of Photography, 65 *U. Pitt. L. Rev.* 385 (2003), pp. 385–456; Kathy Bowrey 'The World Daguerreotyped: What a Spectacle!' Copyright Law, Photography and the Economic Mission of Empire' In: Brad Sherman & Leanne Wiseman, *Copyright and the Challenge of the New* (Wolters Kluwer, 2012), p. 12 ff.

2 André Lucas et al., *Traité de la propriété littéraire et artistique* (LexisNexis, 5e édition ed. 2017), p. 142; Michel Vivant & Jean-Michel Bruguière, *Droit d'auteur et droits voisins* (Dalloz, 4. ed. 2019), p. 329 ff.; Ilva Johanna Schiessel, *Reichweite und Rechtfertigung des Einfachen Lichtbildschutzes gem. § 72 UrhG* (Nomos, 2020).

3 CJEU, Case C-145/10, *Eva-Maria Painer v Standard VerlagsGmbH and Others*, 1 Dec. 2011, ECLI:EU:C:2011:798.

The research team behind this project, which included *Marián Janković*, *Matěj Myška*, and myself, has extensively examined and published on the complex interrelations between precision, objectivity, and originality. Our work delves into the implications of CJEU case law on various categories of creative output—from visual arts to functional designs highlighting how these judicial decisions influence the copyrightability of diverse types of works.[4]

This book advances the existing research by focusing on one of the most critical aspects of copyright protection: originality. Through a detailed exploration of the originality requirement, *Jankovič* emphasizes the importance of understanding how this concept fits into the larger framework of conditions for copyright protection. His approach underscores that originality cannot be considered in isolation, but must be understood in conjunction with other requirements for copyright protection.

One of the key contributions of this book is its comparative analysis of how different jurisdictions interpreted and applied the originality standard, especially in the context of photographic works. *Jankovič* carefully examines the impact of the harmonization of originality standards across selected European jurisdictions—specifically France, Germany, the Czech Republic, and Slovakia. By looking at how these countries' legal systems have responded to the CJEU's harmonized interpretation of originality, the book sheds light on both the successes and challenges of integrating European-wide standards into national frameworks.

For instance, the French legal system, with its rich tradition of protecting artistic works, has generally been more receptive to the CJEU's concept of originality, incorporating it relatively smoothly into its national jurisprudence. In contrast, countries like the Czech Republic have displayed a more cautious and sometimes resistant attitude, with courts often struggling to align domestic rulings with the CJEU's harmonized standards. These differences in reception across jurisdictions illustrate the broader legal and cultural dynamics that shape copyright law in Europe.

In addition to exploring these national variations, the book provides a historical perspective on why certain jurisdictions may be more resistant to the adoption of CJEU rulings. The influence of national traditions, legal scholarship, and varying interpretations of what constitutes creativity and authorship all play significant roles in how courts approach the issue of originality. By analysing these factors, *Jankovič* offers a nuanced understanding of why harmonization in copyright law, while beneficial, is not always straightforward or fully reflected in national court decisions.

Ultimately, this book makes a significant contribution to the field by providing a clear and accessible exploration of how the concept of originality, particularly in photography, has been shaped by both European and national legal frameworks. It offers valuable insights for legal scholars, practitioners, and anyone interested in understanding how the evolving standards of creativity and originality are applied

4 *Project information: Díla chráněná autorským právem a požadavek dostatečné přesnosti a objektivity* (1 Nov. 2024), https://www.muni.cz/en/research/projects/64428.

in copyright law. By linking the theoretical foundations of originality to real-world judicial outcomes, the book enriches the ongoing discourse on the harmonization of copyright standards in Europe, particularly in relation to the photographic industry.

Brno, December 2024 Pavel Koukal

LIST OF ABBREVIATIONS

Act of 11 March 1957
Loi n°57-298 du 11 mars 1957 sur la propriété littéraire et artistique
Act of 3 July 1985
Loi n° 85-660 du 3 juillet 1985 relative aux droits d'auteur et aux droits des artistes-interprètes, des producteurs de phonogrammes et des producteurs de vidéogrammes, et aux droits des entreprises de communication audiovisuelle
AG
Advocate General
AutZ 1965
Zákon č. 35/1965 Sb., o dílech literárních, vědeckých a uměleckých
AutZ 2000
Zákon č. 121/2000 Sb., o právu autorském, o právech souvisejících s právem autorským a o změně některých zákonů
AZ 1997
Zákon č. 383/1997 Z. z., autorský zákon
AZ 2003
Zákon č. 618/2003 Z. z., o autorskom práve a právach súvisiacich s autorským právom
AZ 2015
Zákon č. 185/2015 Z. z., autorský zákon
Berne Convention
Berne Convention for the Protection of Literary and Artistic Works
BGH
Bundesgerichtshof
CJEU
Court of Justice of the European Union
Copyright, Designs and Patents Act 1988
An Act to restate the law of copyright, with amendments; to make fresh provision as to the rights of performers and others in performances; to confer a design right in original designs; to amend the Registered Designs Act 1949; to make provision with respect to patent agents and trade mark agents; to confer patents and designs jurisdiction on certain county courts; to amend the law of patents; to make provision with respect to devices designed to circumvent copy-protection of works in electronic form; to make fresh provision penalising the fraudulent reception of transmissions; to make the fraudulent application or use of a trade mark an offence; to make provision for the benefit of the Hospital for Sick Children, Great Ormond Street, London; to

enable financial assistance to be given to certain international bodies; and for connected purposes (1988, Chapter 48)

CPI
Code de la propriété intellectuelle, Loi n° 92-597 du 1 juillet 1992 relative au code de la propriété intellectuelle

Database Directive
Directive 96/9/EC of the European Parliament and of the Council of 11 March 1996 on the legal protection of databases, OJ L 77, 27. 3. 1996

Digital Single Market Directive
Directive (EU) 2019/790 of the European Parliament and of the Council of 17 April 2019 on copyright and related rights in the Digital Single Market and amending Directives 96/9/EC and 2001/29/EC, OJ L 130, 17. 5. 2019

EU
European Union

GbU
Gesetz, betreffend das Urheberrecht an Werken der Literatur, Kunst und Photographie, RGBl. 197/1895

InfoSoc Directive
Directive 2001/29/EC of the European Parliament and of the Council of 22 May 2001 on the harmonisation of certain aspects of copyright and related rights in the information society, OJ L 167, 22. 6. 2001

KUG
Gesetz betreffend das Urheberrecht an Werken der bildenden Künste und der Photographie, vom 09. 01. 1907 (RGBl. 1906, s. 7)

LG
Landgericht

Member State
Member State of the European Union

OGH
Oberster Gerichtshof Österreich

OLG
Oberlandesgericht

Painer case
Case C-145/10, Eva-Maria Painer v. Standard VerlagsGmbH and Others, 1 December 2011, ECLI:EU:C:2011:798

PG
Gesetz, betreffend den Schutz der Photographien gegen unbefugte Nachbildung, vom 10. Januar 1876 (RGBl. 1876, 8)

Software Directive
Directive 2009/24/EC of the European Parliament and of the Council of 23 April 2009 on the legal protection of computer programs (Codified version), OJ L 111, 5. 5. 2009

Statutory Article 1884
: 1884. évi XVI. törvénycikk a szerzői jogról

Term Directive I
: Council Directive 93/98/EEC of 29 October 1993 harmonizing the term of protection of copyright and certain related rights, OJ L 290, 24. 11. 1993

Term Directive II
: Directive 2006/116/EC of the European Parliament and of the Council of 12 December 2006 on the term of protection of copyright and certain related rights (codified version), OJ L 372, 27. 12. 2006

TFEU
: Consolidated version of the Treaty on the Functioning of the European Union signed on 13 December 2007, 2012/C 326/01, OJ C 326, 26. 10. 2012

TRIPS Agreement
: Agreement on Trade-Related Aspects of Intellectual Property Rights

UG
: Gesetz, betreffend das Urheberrecht an Schriftwerken, Abbildungen, musikalischen Kompositionen und dramatischen Werken, vom 11. Juni 1870 (Bundesgesetzblatt des Norddeutschen Bundes Band 1870, Nr. 19, 339)

UrhG
: Gesetz über Urheberrecht und verwandte Schutzrechte, vom 9. September 1965 (BGBl. I S. 1273)

WIPO Copyright Treaty
: World Intellectual Property Organization Copyright Treaty

ZoPA 1926
: Zákon č. 218/1926 Sb. o původcovském právu k dílům literárním, uměleckým a fotografickým (o právu autorském)

ZoPA 1953
: Zákon č. 115/1953 Sb., o právu autorském

LIST OF CASES

Judgments of the CJEU and Opinions of the AG

Decisions of the German Courts

Decisions of the French Courts

Decisions of the Czech Courts

Decisions of the Slovak Courts

1. Constitutional Court, II. ÚS 647/2014, 30. Sep. 2014. | pp. 293, 294
2. Regional Court in Žilina, 7 Co 335/2015, 23 Sep. 2015. | p. 295
3. Constitutional Court, III. ÚS 651/2016, 28. Nov. 2017. | pp. 293, 295, 296
4. Regional Court in Bratislava, No. 5Co/239/2019, 10 Dec. 2019. | pp. 296, 297
5. Regional Court in Žilina, 40C/176/2015, 20 Apr. 2021.

Other Decisions

1. Chancery Division, University of London Press v University Tutorial [1916] 2 Ch 601, 26 Jul. 1916. | p. 32
2. Tribunal de Commerce de Bruxelles, St Gobain v. SVPC, 1924. | p. 94
3. Schweizerisches Bundesgericht, 4 C.117/2003, 5. Sep. 2003, 'Bob Marley-Foto'. GRUR Int 2004. | p. 69
4. OGH, 4Ob170/07i, 11. Mar. 2008. | p. 208

1 INTRODUCTION

1.1 The Position of Photographic Products

Photographic products have always been a special subject-matter and thus have always created problems for copyright law.[1] These problems were, and to a certain extent still are, related to their ambiguous position as subject-matter capable of being protected by copyright. In this respect, the matter of clear and sufficient distinguishing between protectable (original) and unprotectable (non-original) photographic products is referred to by some as the single most important dispute in matters of copyright.[2] To this day, the status of photographic products as products eligible for copyright protection remains fragile.[3] This is due to their necessary association with technical and/or chemical equipment, through which such photographic products are produced, and without the said association with which their existence would not be possible. It is the necessity of this association that fuels the scepticism regarding the recognition of photographic products as works of art, their position among other traditional works of art, and especially their equality among those other works of art.

1.2 The Need for a Harmonized Originality Standard

Prior to the initiation of the harmonization process in the field of copyright within the EU, national copyright frameworks varying as a result of the unique historical and social developments of each Member State, did not ensure uniformity in the copyright protection of photographic products. As a result, the traditional ambiguity of photography as a medium within the context of its position in the realm of copyright law carried over into the copyright framework of the EU. Depending on which qualities the photographic product possesses, it may be protected by a corresponding type of protection or left altogether unprotected. Photographic products have been recognized as capable of being affiliated with both the creative/artistic as

1 Hugh I. L. Laddie, Peter Prescott & Mary Vitoria, *The Modern Law of Copyright and Designs* (LexisNexis, 4th ed. 2011), p. 253.

2 Michel Vivant & Jean-Michel Bruguière, *Droit d'auteur et droits voisins* (Dalloz, 4th ed. 2019), p. 236.

3 Mélanie Clément-Fontaine, Synthèse. 70 *Revue Lamy Droit de l'immatériel* (2011), p. 136.

well as the information domains.[4] The medium itself is not primarily viewed as an art form; however, its capacity to transform objects/subjects into artistic products gives it a twofold perception.[5] Neither EU legislation, nor the jurisprudence of the CJEU, have been able to eliminate this Janus view of the photographic medium. So far, the CJEU has only managed to mitigate this dilemma.

The intended achievement of harmonization is the establishment of a relationship between dissimilar parts based on balance and harmony.[6] Obviously, if national regulation was already relatively harmonious, no harmonization activities and subsequent enforcement by the respective authorities would be necessary in the first place. In this respect, the field of copyright, and especially the medium of photography, can be seen as a natural field for harmonization. Harmonization can be also defined as a process that aims to replace existing individual national provisions by common content rules for all Member States.[7] As such, it can be therefore considered of paramount importance to create common notions, concepts, definitions and methods in many areas, copyright notwithstanding.

The dissimilar parts of regulation to be eliminated by harmonization are represented by the various (different) national approaches to different types of photographic products, and connected with that, their potential copyrightability, or other corresponding type of protection. The hypothetical bouquet, as *Haimo Schack* described it, representing the various national approaches to the protection of photographic products by copyright, or other corresponding types of protection, became less colourful through the process of harmonization, but nonetheless more compact.[8]

Therefore, it is necessary, especially considering the aforementioned ambiguous and fragile position of photographic products, that any decision regarding copyrightability is not based on an unconscious, intuitive, unclear, and unjustified decision, however challenging this task might sound. It is for this reason that the copyrightability of every photographic product must be assessed on a case-by-case basis and in accordance with the harmonized guidelines. These harmonized guidelines must stipulate which particular circumstances, steps, and choices of a photographer, conducted in connection with the production process of a photographic product, possess significance and potential for its copyrightability.

---

4 Alain Strowel, *Le droit d'auteur européen en transition numérique: de ses origines à l'unification européenne et aux défis de l'intelligence artificielle et des Big Data* (Larcier, 2022), p .95.

5 Susan Sontag, *On Photography* (Penguin Books 2008), p. 149.

6 Claudia Schlüter. 'Harmonisierung ohne Harmonie? Das Infopaq v. DDF-Urteil des EuGH und der europäische Werkbegriff' In: Horst-Peter Götting, Dieter Stauder, & Claudia Schlüter (eds.), *Nourriture de l'esprit: Festschrift für Dieter Stauder zum 70. Geburtstag* (Nomos 2011), p. 239.

7 Petrus S. R. F. Mathijsen, *A Guide to European Union Law* (Sweet & Maxwell, 9th ed 2007), p. 379.

8 Haimo Schack, *Urheber- und Urhebervertragsrecht* (Mohr Siebeck, 10th ed. 2021), p. 86.

1.3 The Initiation of Harmonization Process

Applicable EU legislation also officially acknowledged the aforementioned fragmentation of the national copyright frameworks of Member States, initially in Recital 17 of Term Directive I. It stated that

'the protection of photographs in the Member States is the subject of varying regimes'.[9]

From the perspective of the intended creation of a harmonized internal market,[10] the outlook of probable inconsistent decisions of national courts operating under individual copyright frameworks of Member States was not a desirable one. Nonetheless, copyright came into the *harmonization focus* of the EU at rather late stage.

Factors obstructing earlier initiation of harmonization of copyright included the differing cultural traditions of each Member State and language barriers, both of which had made transborder exploitation of copyrighted works rather unimportant economically.[11] However, the situation changed with the rapid emergence of new copyright-protectable subject-matter, such as computer programs and databases, which can be used irrespective of cultural background or language, as well as across borders. Expansion of new communication technologies by which copyright-protectable subject-matter can be exploited has also brought new urgency to the harmonization process.[12]

For the purposes of this book, the harmonization process as such will be divided into two phases. The first phase will be represented by harmonization conducted via EU legislation, while the second phase consists of harmonization conducted via jurisprudence of the CJEU. These two phases of copyright harmonization have resulted in two developments particularly worthy of more detailed assessment: the adopted standardized definition of *work* and the standard of originality to be applied to works, photographic or otherwise.

9 Recital 17 of the Council Directive 93/98/EEC of 29 October 1993 harmonizing the term of protof copyright and certain related rights, OJ L 290, 24. 11. 1993.

10 Sauter, W. Vos, E. 'Harmonisation under community law: the comitology issue' In: Paul p. Craig & Carol Harlow (eds.), *Lawmaking in the European Union* (Kluwer Law International 1998), p. 169.

11 Annette Kur, Thomas Dreier & Stefan Luginbühl, *European Intellectual Property Law: Text, Cases and Materials* (Edward Elgar Publishing, 2nd ed. 2019), p. 243.

12 Mireille van Eechoud, 'The European Concern with Copyright and Related Rights' In: Mireille van Eechoud (ed.) *Harmonizing European copyright law: the challenges of better lawmaking* (Kluwer Law International 2009), p. 7.

1.4 The First Harmonization Phase

The instruments of the first harmonization phase that EU used in the field of copyright law were numerous directives.[13] In order to harmonize the various aspects of copyright, 11 directives have been introduced by the EU so far. Directives which refer to a protectable subject-matter are unified in terms of providing protection only to original works which are intellectual creations of the author. Due to their relevance to photographic products, only three of these 11 Directives will be substantially assessed: Term Directive I,[14] Term Directive II,[15] and the Digital Single Market Directive.[16]

Term Directive II, currently in force and the most relevant for photographic products, defines photographic products eligible for copyright as *photographic works* in Article 6. The said copyrightability is subject to the condition of being the *author's own intellectual creation.*[17] However, Recital 16 formulates an additional requirement to that of the *author's own intellectual creation.* Here, any photographic product to qualify for copyright protection must also *reflect the personality of its author*, the photographer.[18] One can then deduce that meeting the standard of originality according to Term Directive II is the determining factor in whether a photographic product is to be recognized as a photographic work according to the meaning of Term Directive II and subsequently eligible for copyright protection.

1.5 The Second Harmonization Phase

In terms of Directives, no other guidance on application of the formulated originality standard to photographic products in practice exists. Turning to other sources, the Berne Convention, to which all Members States are contracting parties, might provide further answers. The official guide to the Berne Convention leaves the question of originality to be answered by (national) courts.[19] In light of this, copyright law on the EU level must rely on further interpretation of the Article 6 and Recital 16

13 Thomas Margoni, *The Harmonisation of EU Copyright Law: The Originality Standard* (1. Sep. 2024), https://papers.ssrn.com/sol3/papers.cfm?abstract_id=2802327.

14 Council Directive 93/98/EEC of 29 October 1993 harmonizing the term of protection of copyright and certain related rights, OJ L 290, 24. 11. 1993.

15 Directive 2006/116/EC of the European Parliament and of the Council of 12 December 2006 on the term of protection of copyright and certain related rights (codified version), OJ L 372, 27. 12. 2006.

16 Directive (EU) 2019/790 of the European Parliament and of the Council of 17 April 2019 on copyright and related rights in the Digital Single Market and amending Directives 96/9/EC and 2001/29/EC, OJ L 130, 17. 5. 2019.

17 Art. 6 of the Term Directive II.

18 Recital 16 of the Term Directive II.

19 Georg Hendrik Christiaan Bodenhausen (ed.), *Guide to the Berne Convention for the Protection of Literary and Artistic Works* (BIRPI 1968), p. 18.

of Term Directive II by the CJEU through its jurisprudence—individual decisions. Such additional interpretation of EU legislation by the CJEU represents the second phase of the harmonization process.[20] In other words, this phase consists of CJEU jurisprudence in applying and shaping the standard of originality formulated by the EU legislation.

Further interpretation of the originality standard by the CJEU runs through a string of case law. The *Painer* case can be considered the most relevant to photographic products. The CJEU described a number of ways through which a photographer could make free and creative choices at various points during the production process of a photographic product, through which originality can be demonstrated to the court,[21] thus demonstrating why a certain photographic product should be considered original, and therefore eligible for copyright protection. The manoeuvring room for this demonstration of free and creative choices that photographers can make throughout various stages of the production process has been set widely by the CJEU. As a result, in most Member States, copyright protection should be extended to photographic products which might not have been traditionally considered original in the past. It will be demonstrated, how through its decision in *Painer*, the CJEU lowered the threshold of the originality standard applicable to photographic products within most Member States' copyright frameworks, with the result that only a few photographic products would fail to satisfy it.[22]

1.6 Harmonized Treatment of Photographic Products by Member States

In practice, photographic products are not always easily indicated as original with sufficient precision and therefore eligible for copyright protection. On the Member-State level, the aforementioned traditionally problematic relationship between photographic products and copyright resulted in differing approaches to their treatment for the purposes of their copyrightability. As already mentioned, EU legislation has referred to such different treatments of photographic products as *varying regimes*. One assumption, which was further confirmed by the circumstances of the *Painer* case decision, is that some photographic genres are traditionally looked upon as non-original by the copyright frameworks of some Member States. By extension, photographic products affiliated with such genres are seen as non-original as well.

20 Thomas Margoni, *The Harmonisation of EU Copyright Law: The Originality Standard* (1. Sep. 2024), https://papers.ssrn.com/sol3/papers.cfm?abstract_id=2802327.

21 CJEU, Case C-145/10, *Eva-Maria Painer v Standard VerlagsGmbH and Others*, 1 Dec. 2011, ECLI:EU:C:2011:798, para. 90.

22 Marián Jankovič, 'The Development and Harmonisation of Originality Standard of Photographic Works in the Copyright Framework of the European Union' 20 *Jusletter IT 30. März 2023* (2023), p. 1.

Such generalized treatment of photographic products based on their assignment to a certain photographic genre was found to be problematic by the CJEU.

Nonetheless, in the *Painer* case, the CJEU left the final decision regarding the presence of originality to be determined by national courts of Member States.[23] Therefore, it is national courts which are to apply the harmonized originality standard in practice. This might prove to be problematic, since a clash of the harmonized requirements with any previously traditionally applied national requirements is inevitable. The magnitude of such a clash might depend on how different, or similar, the traditionally applied national requirements are to the harmonized ones.

1.7 Terminology

Due to the lack of officially standardized terminology related to the outcome of photographic process, this text uses the expression *photographic product* as an umbrella term of a purely technical nature, representing all results of all photographic and related processes, both original and non-original, and therefore without differentiating or taking into account their potential corresponding type of protection. The expression of a *photographic work* will be used throughout the text as an explicit referral only to original photographic products eligible for copyright protection as photographic works. Other terminology related to the outcomes of photographic processes applied at the EU and national levels of copyright frameworks of the selected Member States will be used in accordance with definitions and translations provided in each such dedicated chapter.

Due to the ambiguous usage of the notion of *work*, especially in connection with the subject-matter eligible for copyright protection, the notions of *product*, *subject-matter*, and *creation* are used throughout this text interchangeably, within the identical common meaning of the result of various types of production processes. Therefore, these expressions refer to any result of a production process, regardless of its status in terms of originality—in other words, the potential eligibility for a corresponding type of protection. Therefore, these expressions refer to both original, as well as non-original results. The expression *work* shall be used exclusively as a reference to an original product eligible for copyright protection.

1.8 General Outline of the Book

The following section outlines the structure of the following text with regard to the research conducted, its individual phases, and the formulated research questions.

[23] CJEU, Case C-145/10, *Eva-Maria Painer v Standard VerlagsGmbH and Others*, 1 Dec. 2011, ECLI:EU:C:2011:798, para. 99.

The goal is to structure the text such that it provides both a chronological and comprehensive overview of the chosen topic.

The first chapter serves as an initial introduction to the general issue, presenting the terminology applied, the methodology, and the research questions. The second chapter presents selected aspects related to the treatment and position of photographic products and originality internationally, within the framework set by the Berne Convention. The third chapter presents a general introduction to the topic of originality and its different understandings within continental and common-law systems. The fourth chapter presents preliminary remarks on the nature of the production process of photographic products, identifying the moment(s) of potential consideration for eligibility for protection, as well as the necessity of the incorporation of a technical device into the production process.

The fifth chapter presents an overview on the national copyright framework of Germany, with an initial focus on general requirements for copyrightability, followed by a special emphasis on photographic products. This *special* emphasis consists of a presentation of historical developments related to the position of photographic products within the German copyright framework, as well as their eligibility for a corresponding type of protection. The sixth, seventh, eighth and ninth chapters focus on the national copyright framework of France and Czechoslovakia (including the Czech and Slovak Republics), respectively, following the structure established in the fifth chapter.

The tenth chapter presents the outlook on the legislative and jurisprudential harmonization activities within the copyright framework of the European Union divided into two phases, with an initial focus on the general requirements for eligibility of products for copyright protection, followed by special emphasis on photographic products. This *special* emphasis consists of a presentation of the legislative and jurisprudential development of originality standard and its application to photographic products in practice. The eleventh, twelfth, and thirteenth chapters explore harmonization efforts within the national copyright frameworks of Germany, France, the Czech Republic, and Slovak Republic, with a particular focus on photographic works. Finally, the fourteenth and fifteenth chapters summarize the research findings and offer concluding remarks.

1.9 The Proposed Hypotheses and Subsequent Research Questions

The hypotheses and subsequent related research questions below were formulated and chosen with the aim of determining the potential change in the position of photographic products in the copyright frameworks of the EU and those of the selected Member States. To show this, I conduct an assessment of the requirements and criteria for the copyright protection eligibility of photographic products resulting from legislation of the EU and case law of the CJEU, as parts of two harmonization phases. This thus required formulating the following hypotheses and research questions:

Hypothesis No. 1

I assume that as part of both harmonization phases, new requirements and criteria were introduced and formulated for the protection of photographic products by copyright, known as the originality standard. These requirements and criteria are intended to be applied throughout the EU's copyright framework, notwithstanding the national copyright frameworks of the Member States. I therefore assume, that as a result, the diverse traditional national requirements and criteria for eligibility of photographic products for copyright protection applicable within copyright frameworks of the Member States were replaced by the harmonized ones, via a combination of these two phases of harmonization.

In light of Hypothesis No. 1, I have formulated the following research question:

A: What requirements, in terms of originality, must a photographic product meet to be eligible for copyright protection within the entirety of the copyright framework of the EU?

Hypothesis No. 2

I assume that the national copyright frameworks of the Member States have not formally adjusted to the conclusions and subsequent intended effects of either harmonization phases, meaning through amendments to their national copyright legislation. Rather, given the requirement of an EU-conforming interpretation, Member States reinterpret their traditional national requirements and concepts affected by the harmonization to give them a new, EU-conforming meaning. I therefore assume that as a result, the adjustment of national copyright frameworks of the Member States is a primarily informal process.

In light of Hypothesis No. 2, I formulate the following research question:

B: Are the implications of the conclusions and subsequent intended effects of both harmonization phases on the traditional requirements and concepts within the national copyright frameworks of the Member States such that Member States make these adjustments to their national frameworks informally, via an EU-conforming (re)interpretation?

Hypothesis No. 3

I assume that the newly introduced requirements and criteria resulting from both phases of harmonization for the copyrightability of photographic products (known as the originality standard) have had the effect of lowering the threshold for their copyrightability. I therefore assume that as a result, the number of photographic products potentially eligible for copyright protection has increased within the entirety of the copyright framework of the EU.

In respect to Hypothesis No. 3, I thus formulate the following research question:

C: Are the implications of the newly introduced originality standard resulting from both harmonization phases such that the threshold for the eligibility of photographic products for copyright protection has been lowered, and thus the number of photographic products potentially eligible for copyright protection has increased within the entirety of the copyright framework of the EU?

1.10 Methodology Applied

This research is primarily based on understandings of *copyright* and *work* according to how these terms are applied in the continental EU. As opposed to common-law copyright frameworks, copyright protection in the continental EU focuses primarily on the person of the creator, rather than on their creation—the work.[24] In respect to this, the copyright therefore serves the purpose of protecting authors, rather than their investments, as is the case in the common-law copyright frameworks. The first research question above was formulated in such a manner as to presume that this approach is also applicable to photographic products when being assessed for their originality via the harmonized requirements and subsequently determining their copyrightability. The second research question was formulated in such a manner so as to confirm the manner in which this approach is accepted and implemented into practice within national copyright frameworks of the selected Member States. Finally, the third research question was formulated in such a manner so as to determine whether the emphasis on authors' *personality* in photographic products has led to an increase in the copyrightability of photographic products possessing such a *manifestation*, and thus also resulting in an increase in the number of protected authors.

I used a normative research framework due to its specific capabilities, which enable the provision of standards for evaluation.[25] My research progresses in the following three steps:

1.10.1 The First Step

As part of the first step, I assess general requirements for copyrightability in the national copyright frameworks of the selected Member States, focusing on the development of the position of photographic products and their gradual recognition

[24] Andreas Rahmatian, Originality in UK Copyright Law: The Old 'Skill and Labour' Doctrine Under Pressure. 44 *IIC* 4 (2013), p. 4.

[25] Sanne Taekema *Theoretical and Normative Frameworks for Legal Research: Putting Theory into Practice* (1 Sep. 2024), https://papers.ssrn.com/sol3/papers.cfm?abstract_id=3123667.

as a subject-matter capable of being protected by copyright. Specific features of the national copyright frameworks of each selected Member State will be highlighted.

1.10.2 The Second Step

In the second step, I assess the legislative and judicial harmonization phases related to the standard of originality, with a special emphasis on photographic products. Here too, specific features of the developed EU harmonized approach towards copyrightability will be highlighted.

1.10.3 The Third Step

In the third step, I assess the potential effects of both harmonization phases on the national copyright frameworks of the selected Member States. Again, I give special attention to photographic products.

The intended aim of the three research steps is to provide the most comprehensive and structured possible understanding of the sources, developments, and effects of the EU's harmonization process on the position of photographic products (in terms of their copyrightability) within the copyright framework of the EU.

The copyright framework of Each Member State under review has specific features that warrant deeper investigation. The German copyright framework has been chosen due to its specific twofold treatment of photographic products in terms of their potential protectability, either by copyright or by a related type of protection. The French copyright framework has been chosen for its assumed similarities with outcomes of EU harmonization, particularly its use of an *originality* requirement. I chose the Czechoslovak, Czech, and Slovak copyright frameworks due to their traditional employment of a specific requirement for copyrightability: the need to demonstrate *statistical uniqueness*.

In sum, my goal is to elaborate on, as well as confirm , whether the EU harmonization process has had the potential of starting a revolution in terms of understanding of the notion of a *photographic product*, and through it position in terms of originality within the EU's copyright framework.[26] Specifically, the research will assess the different approaches to the application of the *originality standard* to photographic products—those traditionally applicable within the national copyright frameworks of the selected Member States, as well as the harmonized standard introduced by the EU. Finally, I assess the potential effects that harmonization has had on the selected national copyright frameworks of the Member States.

[26] Martin Husovec, Judikatórna harmonizácia pojmu autorského diela v únijnom práve. 12 *Bulletin slovenskej advokácie* (2012), p. 16.

2 PRELIMINARY REMARKS ON PHOTOGRAPHY

Given the chosen topic, the author considers it important to provide the reader with several selected preliminary remarks on the medium of photography. These remarks have been chosen for their relevance to the field of copyright and their intersections with it. The remarks cover topics related to the nature of photographic products, the particularities of the production process, and the protection of these in detail. Therefore, the purpose of the following section is to provide a basic philosophical and technical overview about the medium of photography, which will in turn allow the reader to better understand the role and context of copyright law within the EU and its Member States.

2.1 What is Photography?

One might be under the impression that in the current age of constant technological and digital development, the definition of photography itself would require constant redefinition and readaptation. However, the traditional concept of a photographic product does not pose any practical issues in this sense.[27] Two sources have long influenced the definition of photography: one the one hand, those formed by history of art, philosophy, and technology; on the other, those formed by legislation.

It was *Hubert Damisch*, who cited a traditional definition of photography, according to which it is nothing but a process of recording, a technique of writing a permanent image caused by light rays (onto a suitable medium).[28] This definition remains very simple and refers to only two necessary components of the *photographic equation.* The first is light and its rays, which possess the capability of *writing* an image. The second is a suitable medium onto or into which the image can be *written.* It is presumed that out of this combination, a photographic product will emerge. The definition does not consider it necessary to incorporate any kind of technical equipment into the equation. In fact, as will be demonstrated later in this text, the involvement of technical equipment is not categorically necessary, although its omnipresence does support this incorrect assumption.

---

[27] Hartwig Ahlberg, 'Geschützte Werke' In: Philipp Möhring et al. (eds.), *Urheberrecht: UrhG, KUG, UrhWahrnG, VerlG; Kommentar* (C.H. Beck, 3rd ed. 2014), p. 56.

[28] Hubert Damisch 'Pět poznámek k fenomenologii fotografického obrazu'. In: Karel Císař, *Co je to fotografie?* (Herrmann & synové 2004), p. 47.

In terms of the latter, legislative definition, copyright legislation in general avoids formulating a definition of photography or its results (photographic products), and merely resorts to universal references signifying the applicability of copyright-eligible subject-matter, especially its origin, in a photographic production process.[29] However, there is a variety of production processes from which a photographic product might emerge, and it is also potentially impossible to unambiguously classify such production processes as purely photographic. For this reason, other products are also recognized as *photographic products* eligible for copyright protection when they are produced by processes similar, or analogous to that of photography.[30]

Nonetheless, some national copyright frameworks have taken it upon themselves to formulate such a definition and have also incorporated it into their national copyright acts. Some refer to the capture of an image by means of a photographic technical device;[31] some to the recording of light or other radiation on any medium (on which an image is produced or from which an image may be produced).[32] The former considers the combination of capturing an image and using photographic device to be determinative for the classification of a product originated from such combination as photographic. The latter considers the combination of recording of light or other radiation and suitable medium to be determinative for the classification of a product originated from such combination as photographic. However, such an approach might seem short-sighted considering the variety of variables that can be included into the production process of photographic products.

For the purposes of dealing with the nature of the *recorded* or *captured* image, it must be noted that an image must therefore be static.[33] This static nature is crucial for the purposes of differentiating photographic products from other subject-matter, especially films. It must be also noted that an image does not have to be *recorded* or *captured* in a permanent form for it to be considered a photographic product.

Still, both of the two approaches above and their corresponding formulated definitions show three recurring ideas in connection with photography: light (or other radiation), a photographic technical device, and a suitable receiving medium. Such concepts, or components, can therefore be considered crucial for the production of photographic products. The reliance on these three concepts simply renders any considerations related to the technological process of production of photographic products unimportant, with one exception—the process itself these are incorporated into must to be of a photographic or similar nature.[34] Focusing on the photographic

---

29 Such as the German UrhG, the French CPI, or the Czech AutZ 2000.

30 Such as the German UrhG, the French CPI, or the Czech AutZ 2000, as well as, on the international level, the Berne Convention.

31 Such as Sec. 3 (5) of the Slovak AZ 2015.

32 Such as Sec. 4 (2) b) of the Copyright, Designs and Patents Act 1988.

33 Zuzana Adamová & Branislav Hazucha, *Autorský zákon: komentár* (C.H. Beck 2018), p. 27.

34 Fedor Seifert & Thomas Wirth, 'Das Werk'. In: Jan Eichelberger, Thomas Wirth, & Fedor Seifert (eds.), *UrhG Urheberrechtsgesetz: UrhG, UrhDaG, VGG : Handkommentar* (Nomos, 4. ed. 2022), p. 75.

nature of the production process and the subsequent light (radiant) energy therein with its effects and results should be the decisive factor for the characterization of a product as *photographic*. This approach can broadly and fully adapt to technological developments and innovations in the area of photography.[35] Due to the relevance of the research conducted, only the first two concepts—the need for light and the need for a technical device—will be given attention in the text below.

2.2 On the Importance of the Radiation Source

The term *photography* is formed from two Greek words. The first one is *phos*,[36] meaning *light*. The second one is *graphein*,[37] meaning *to write*. Put together in a translated form, the term *photography* therefore means *written by light*.[38] The very content of the term itself presupposes the existence of light and its significance for the production process of a photographic product. After all, as *František Drtikol* put it, it was light that created photography.[39] The radiation source itself also fulfils a distinguishing role between *standard* photographic products on one hand, and *other* photographic products produced by similar or analogous processes to that of standard photography. Only the light itself can be the constituent of the former type of a photographic product, whereas all other radiant energies can only be constituents of later photographic products.[40] However, the different ways in which radiation is employed throughout the production process may also create a deviation from a *standard* (but analogous) photographic product.[41]

In light of this line of argument, to even begin considerations related to extending any kind of protection to photographic products, one must still first deal with the question of the existence of a radiation source, before the use of even digital photographic equipment. To be more precise, we must answer the questions of whether a radiation source was used in the production process of the product in question, and if that radiation source was responsible for the production of the image displayed in the photographic product.

---

35 Axel Nordemann, *Die künstlerische Fotografie als urheberrechtlich geschütztes Werk* (Nomos 1992), p. 65.

36 Robert Beekes & Lucien van Beek, *Etymological Dictionary of Greek* (Brill 2010), p. 1602.

37 Robert Beekes & Lucien van Beek, *Etymological Dictionary of Greek* (Brill 2010), p. 287.

38 Antoine Latreille. 'Images numériques et pratique du droit d'auteur'. 34 *LEGICOM* 51, p. 51.

39 František Drtikol, *Oči široce otevřené* (Svět 2002), p. 61.

40 Thomas Platena, *Das Lichtbild im Urheberrecht: Gesetzliche Regelung und Technische Weiterentwicklung* (Petr Lang 1998), p. 120.

41 Melanie Overbeck, *Der Lichtbildschutz gem. § 72 UrhG im Lichte der Digitalfotografie* (Lit 2018), p. 62.

2.3 The Role of Technical Equipment

It is true that photographic products depict what already exists; however, it is only through photographic equipment, most frequently a camera, that such depiction is possible.[42] It is well established that the use and employment of technical equipment throughout the production process of a photographic product does not preclude its copyrightability as an original photographic work.[43] However, what is determinative for the purposes of copyrightability is the extent to which the author manages to maintain control over the technical equipment and therefore over the creative process itself.[44] If the technical equipment employed in the production process of a photographic product assumes a dominant role at the expense of the author, one cannot speak of an *original photographic work*. Still, under no circumstances can photographic equipment, such as a camera, assume the position of an author.[45] However, if the technical equipment is fully controlled by the author and used only as an aid throughout the production process, then photographic products eligible for copyright protection can be produced (and only in such circumstances).[46] In the simplest of terms, the author cannot give up or renounce the possibilities which can be taken advantage of during the production process of a photographic product.

According to *Lucia Moholy*, the three components of which the production process of a product consists of are the author's mind, their hands, and whatever equipment the author decides to incorporate.[47] Within the realm of a production process of traditional works of art, it is the mind, first and foremost, that governs the hands and only after that the equipment. Within such a setting, it is the equipment which is of least importance. However, within the realm of the production process of photographic products, it is still the mind which governs, but the hands swap places in order of importance with the (technical) equipment. Within such a setting, it is therefore the technical equipment that gains importance at the expense of the hands. For example, *František Drtikol* considered the photographic lens as a tool better suited to the submission of the photographer's creative thought than the tools of painters or sculptors, due to its ability to preserve the nature of the creative moment better and faster.[48]

The determinative role of technical equipment within the context of the production of photographic products as well as the relationship equipment had with the

42 Susan Sontag, *On Photography* (Penguin Books 2008), p. 122.

43 Pierre Sirinelli, Antoine Latreille & Julie Groffe-Charrier. *Code de la propriété intellectuelle: annoté et commenté* (Dalloz 2023), p. 32.

44 André Lucas et al., *Traité de la propriété littéraire et artistique* (LexisNexis, 5th ed. 2017). p. 79.

45 Axel Nordemann, *Die künstlerische Fotografie als urheberrechtlich geschütztes Werk* (Nomos 1992), p. 118.

46 Gunda Dreyer. 'Geschützte Werke' In: Gunda Dreyer et al., *Urheberrecht: Urheberrechtsgesetz, Verwertungsgesellschaftengesetz, Kunsturhebergesetz* (C.F. Müller, 4th ed. 2018), p. 171.

47 Lucia Moholy, *Sto let fotografie: 1839-1939* (Kunsthalle 2024), p. 27.

48 František Drtikol, *Oči široce otevřené* (Svět 2002), p. 7.

photographer was also described by *Vilém Flusser*. *Flusser* described the medium of photography as a constant competition, struggle or a fight between man (the photographer) and technology (the technical device in use).[49] The sole challenge is for the photographer to enable the camera's capacity to subjectivize reality, rather than use it to objectivize it.[50]

For example, if the photographer assumes a dominant role over the technical equipment during the production process of a photographic product, this production process can be characterized as following two main phases. The first one involves the decision of the author regarding the initiation of the production process itself, while the second one involves decisions regarding the characteristics of the design that the photographic product should have.[51] This second phase involves numerous interventions, and the author's capability of directing them is limited only by the constraints imposed by the technological nature of the production process of the photographic product itself.

When looking at technical equipment, and cameras in particular, *Peter Rezek* introduced the concept of an *animated camera*,[52] as well as its counterpart, the *dead camera*. From a phenomenological point of view, the decisive criterion between the two is the involvement of the photographer in the actual act, the moment, of production of a photographic product. Regarding the relationship between the production process and the photographer, the former considers the production process an internal event, while the latter considers it an external event. In other words, the photographer is being present and responsible at each moment in which the actual photographic product is produced with the *animated camera*.[53] On the other hand, with the latter, the photographer is detached from the said moment and merely documents the scene around them.[54]

Therefore, regardless of what technical equipment is used throughout the production process of a photographic product, its role must remain auxiliary to the photographer and the creative steps they take. Moreover, the nature of the production process as such is irrelevant, as long as it remains creative, photographic and controlled by the photographer. Within the French copyright framework, for example, the technical equipment must be controlled throughout the production process by the photographer's creative intelligence to the extent and result that it takes a form of an imprint of their personality.[55] In other words, throughout the production process of a photographic product, the photographer must depart from the technology

---

49 Vilém Flusser et al., *Za filosofii fotografie* (Fra, 2nd ed. 2013), p. 53.

50 Susan Sontag, *On Photography* (Penguin Books 2008), p. 178.

51 Thomas Platena, *Das Lichtbild im Urheberrecht: Gesetzliche Regelung und Technische Weiterentwicklung* (Peter Lang 1998), p. 32.

52 Animated in the sense of *brought to life*; from Latin *anima,* breath.

53 Petr Rezek, *Tělo, věc a skutečnost v umění šedesátých a sedmdesátých let* (Jan Placák-Ztichlá klika, 2nd ed. 2010), p. 254.

54 *Ibid.*

55 Antoine Latreille. 'Images numériques et pratique du droit d'auteur'. 34 *LEGICOM* 51, p. 51.

as such, and approach art, as *Nordemann* quoted French case law.[56] However, as will be shown later in the text, photographers' approach of creativity suffices. The extent to which the photographer does so precisely corresponds to the assessment of originality.

Photographic equipment, especially the camera itself, has shaken the foundations of the traditional artistic creative process and its understandings, especially in connection to copyright law. Generally, two assumptions have been clearly considered certain—that only a person can be regarded as *the creator* and that the spheres of *creation* and *reproduction* can be clearly delimited.[57] Initially, however, the role of the person operating the camera was seen as supplementary to the camera and for that reason, the camera itself was seen as the *creator*. Moreover, differentiating between the original and a copy was seen as impossible, due to the possibility of creating an endless number of identical prints from the negative. Therefore, questions regarding copyrightability sprang up from the involvement of a technical device as well as from the mechanical and chemical nature of the processes necessary for the fixation and subsequent visualization of the exposed image.

The technical part of the photographic process, especially the fixation/exposure part, was considered determinative for the entire production of a photographic product. However, critics claimed that it was in this precise moment of execution where the personal intellectual involvement of the author was lacking.[58] According to them, for that moment, the photographer figuratively shifts the responsibility for the fixation to the technical device. In other words, the fixation is not directly executed by the photographer.

As quoted by *Walter Koschatzky*, it was *Jules Janin* who, in 1839, stated that even though the light is the one that does the work, the photographer is the one who remains its master.[59] In other words, the light does the job, however it is still done under the supervision of a human being. In simplified terms, this quote demonstrates the ideal circumstances for the production of a protected photographic product. It is the photographer who, through their various inputs into the production process, influences it to such an extent that its output will reflect their intentions, ideas, and expectations regarding the appearance of the final photographic product. *Janin* continued by adding that no photographic product is produced mindlessly, since the image resided in the photographer's mind prior to its capture and materialization by the photographic process.[60] *František Drtikol* made a very similar statement, claiming that the image must be ready in the photographer's mind long before it is

[56] Axel Nordemann, *Die künstlerische Fotografie als urheberrechtlich geschütztes Werk* (Nomos 1992), p. 53.

[57] Frederich, K. Fromm, Der Apparat als geistiger Schöpfer. *GRUR.* 1964, p. 304.

[58] René Gouriou, *La photographie et le droit d'auteur*. (Pichon et Durand-Auzias 1959), p. 63.

[59] Walter Koschatzky, *Die Kunst der Photographie: Technik, Geschichte, Meisterwerke* (Dt. Taschenbuch-Verl. 1987), p. 68.

[60] Walter Koschatzky, *Die Kunst der Photographie: Technik, Geschichte, Meisterwerke* (Dt. Taschenbuch-Verl. 1987), p. 23.

reflected in the camera's viewfinder.[61] *Jean-Luc Daval* quoted photographer *Alfred Stieglitz*, who claimed that every picture was the exact staging of an idea.[62] *Susan Sontag* quoted *Ansel Adams*, who characterized photography as a *concept and not an accident.*[63] It is true that without an imaginary conceptualization of the image in a photographer's mind prior to its actual production, one would not even know where or how to point the photographic apparatus.[64] One might think, that such described process might happen without the photographer even consciously thinking about it, and therefore labelled as automatic. However, nothing could be further from the truth—and it is true from comprehensively thought-out photographic products to mere snapshots.

The purpose of the aforementioned quotes is to demonstrate the way photographers themselves see the production process of photographic products, the way they place and involve themselves into the process, and the way they influence the production process through this active physical and intellectual (mental) participation. The result of this is a photographic product that has qualities and features that they expected and anticipated. This presence of the photographer during the production process, not only physically, but primarily intellectual, is therefore determinative for understanding its outcomes in the form of a photographic product as a potential subject-matter eligible for copyright protection. Nonetheless, the place of photographic products within the realm of copyright is still easily challenged based on the potential lack of a photographer's intellectual presence. It is exactly for this reason that the photographer's intellectual *presence* is subject to thorough assessment by copyright law and subsequently serves as the basis for determining the copyrightability of a given photographic product.

The emphasis that these photographers put on their intellectual involvement within the production process signifies its importance. However, this importance is not only an abstract desire for the photographers themselves, but also for law. It plays a determinative role in the potential eligibility of a photographic product for protection by copyright. The opposite of intellectual involvement is chance. If chance itself is not deliberately (i.e., with intellectual/mental involvement) incorporated into the production process, a photographic product is of no significance to copyright law. According to *Robin Kelsey*, *'chance valorizes neither the photographic product, nor the photographer'*.[65]

It was *Henri Desbois* who first clearly delimited the technical nature of the photographic process from the contributions of the photographer. According to him, it was critical to disregard the mechanical and chemical features of a photographic process altogether, and focus on other phases of the creative process, during

61 František Drtikol, *Oči široce otevřené* (Svět 2002), p. 7.

62 Jean-Luc Daval, *Photography: History of an Art* (Skira/Rizzoli, R. F. M. 1982), p. 135.

63 Susan Sontag, *On Photography* (Penguin Books 2008), p. 117.

64 Axel Nordemann, *Die künstlerische Fotografie als urheberrechtlich geschütztes Werk* (Nomos 1992), p. 93.

65 Robin Earle Kelsey, *Photography and the Art of Chance* (Belknap press 2015), p. 2.

which the personality of the photographer could manifest itself.[66] According to this opinion, the remaining parts of the photographic process were therefore seen as purely mechanical, impersonal, and uninfluenceable by the photographer, as *Heitland* quoted *Desbois*.[67] Such an approach towards the assessment of originality was necessary due to the fact that the actual act of fixation of an image onto a selected medium was considered to be dependent on circumstances and processes that were uninfluenceable by the photographer. Another point of criticism in the early stages of establishing photography as an artistic craft was the opinion that photography is only capable of reproducing reality given in nature, whereas art reproduces the idea of an author, as *Pohlhausen* quoted *Riezler*.[68]

Of course, such statements must be understood in the context of the times they were made, especially in connection with the challenges of mastering the photographic process and its general uncommonness. Nonetheless, they can still be very well applied even to contemporary photography, for example when assessing the amount of intellectual involvement, a photographer has, which is crucial for determining the eligibility of a photographic product for copyright protection. Indeed, *František Drtikol* used the involvement of the heart and mind as opposed to the mere involvement of the photographic lens as a distinguishing criterion between *artistic* photographic products and *artisan* photographic products.[69]

The necessary involvement of a technical device and the subsequent chemical processes for the creation of the image also became a source of criticism of photography in the late 19th century in connection with its possible establishment as a form of art, as *Heitland* quoted *Allfeld*.[70] Given the need to cooperate with the technical device, the photographer was seen as someone whose artistic ideas could not be communicated to their potential audience to their full extent, as *Pohlhausen* quoted *Klosterman*.[71] Communication of the author's artistic ideas or statements was therefore seen as restricted by the necessity of employing a technical device. The dominance of the technical device, and technology as such, in the early stages of photography overshadowed the role and importance of the individually formed intellectual input of the author for years thereafter.[72] As the use and recognition of photography continued to grow, it became acknowledged the necessary use of the

66 Henri Desbois, *Le droit d'auteur en France* (Dalloz, 3rd ed. 1978), p. 81.

67 Horst Heitland, *Der Schutz der Fotografie im Urheberrecht Deutschlands, Frankreichs und der Vereinigten Staaten von Amerika* (C.H. Beck 1995), p. 139.

68 Philine Pohlhausen, *Das Original in der Fotografie im Lichte des Urheberrechts* (Nomos 2021), p. 194.

69 František Drtikol, *Oči široce otevřené* (Svět 2002), p. 8.

70 Horst Heitland, *Der Schutz der Fotografie im Urheberrecht Deutschlands, Frankreichs und der Vereinigten Staaten von Amerika* (C.H. Beck 1995), p. 27.

71 Philine Pohlhausen, *Das Original in der Fotografie im Lichte des Urheberrechts* (Nomos 2021), p. 194.

72 Stefan Ricke, *Entwicklung des rechtlichen Schutzes von Fotografien in Deutschland unter besonderer Berücksichtigung der preußischen Gesetzgebung* (Lit 1998), p. 164.

technical device does not automatically preclude the intellectual involvement of the author—and therefore the potential existence of originality.

In the traditional (critical) analogy of a photographic product to a painting, the photographic process is referred to as having an impersonal and mechanical character, as opposed to traditional artistic processes, which allow for natural (i.e., human) errors.[73] Within this context, photography is seen as being too precise to give opportunities for the employment of one's personal preferences and the manifestation of one's personality. If one is to continue making analogies to painting, the differences can also be found in the fixation/recording processes. The fixation of an image through painting is seen as a free and personal depiction of reality surpassed by human perception, whereas with photography, the fixation process is seen as solely governed by external factors of a technical nature, as *Heitland* quoted *Desbois*.[74]

Photographic equipment, especially the camera, can (quite correctly, with the ever-increasing level of technological development) be considered as *perfect* or even *automatic*, and thus restraining the photographer's wilful creative interventions into its functioning. For this reason, a creative result in the form of an intellectual creation might become more and more difficult to achieve. Nonetheless, if the author still has the opportunity to intellectually influence the process, the result of which will be an intellectual creation, the role of the technical equipment is still considered secondary to the person of the author—the photographer, as *Heitland* quoted *Ulmer* and *Nordemann*.[75]

Within the context of the employment of technical equipment, it is necessary to separate the purely mechanical process and photographer's creative wilful inputs. One must clearly delimit and define spaces in which the creation of the image itself results from a purely mechanical point of view, and in which the photographer has possibilities to creatively influence the content and appearance of the photographic product itself. The creative influence of the photographer, along with the creative possibilities, lie outside of and surrounding the mechanical process of creating/fixing an image.[76] The mechanical process might in itself be seen as a necessary act, which concludes and delimits the initial phase of preparation of the to-be-fixed photographic image, but at the same time it allows the photographer to move on to other phases, during which they can continue the creative (post)process.

Nonetheless, the necessary role that photographic equipment plays in the production process of a photographic product, and also its irreplaceability, came to be gradually accepted and recognized as the *conditio sine qua non* of photography, as

73 Henri Desbois, *Le droit d'auteur en France* (Dalloz, 3rd ed. 1978), p. 81.

74 Horst Heitland, *Der Schutz der Fotografie im Urheberrecht Deutschlands, Frankreichs und der Vereinigten Staaten von Amerika* (C.H. Beck 1995), p. 139.

75 Horst Heitland, *Der Schutz der Fotografie im Urheberrecht Deutschlands, Frankreichs und der Vereinigten Staaten von Amerika* (C.H. Beck 1995), p. 33.

76 Ekkehard Gerstenberg, 'Fototechnik und Urheberrecht' In: Georg Herbst (ed.) *Festschrift für Rainer Klaka* (J. Schweitzer Verlag 1987), p. 122.

Pohlhausen quoted *Hamann*.[77] Therefore, it became crucial to separate the technology used to depict the image and through it the author's statement, and rather focus on the production process and its nature.[78] This separation allows us to distinguish between a *true expression* and *photography conceived*.[79] The former concept represents a photographic product in a production process that the photographer was intellectually involved with. The latter concept, in contrast, represents a photographic product that merely faithfully depicts and therefore its production process lacked the intellectual involvement of the photographer.

2.4 The Moment of Protection of Photographic Products

The final materialization of a photographic product in a form that allows it to be visually perceived by its potential audience is the result of a complex technical, chemical/electronic process. This process involves several consecutive phases, which must be completed in a given order, or otherwise the production of a photographic product will not be possible. The standing of these individual phases of the production process in terms of copyright thus merits further exploration.

In this respect, especially in connection with the said necessary perceptibility of a photographic product by the senses of the potential audience, there have been debates regarding the moment from which the protection of a photographic product is possible, especially of the image contained within such product. Here, I present two approaches that differ in their opinions regarding the moment a photographic product becomes copyrightable. The first approach is based on the moment of fixation, whereas the second approach on the moment of visualization.

Keeping in mind the different necessary technological production processes, hypothetical questions regarding the protection of a recorded image can be raised.[80] Some claim the production of a photographic product does not begin with the exposure of the analogue film or the electronic sensor, but rather with the first fixation of the captured image, as *Hertin* quoted *Hamann*.[81] In case of analogue film photography, an exposed, light-sensitive layer with the recorded image must be first

[77] Philine Pohlhausen, *Das Original in der Fotografie im Lichte des Urheberrechts* (Nomos 2021), p. 379.

[78] Axel Nordemann, *Die künstlerische Fotografie als urheberrechtlich geschütztes Werk* (Nomos 1992), p. 92.

[79] Susan Sontag, *On Photography* (Penguin Books 2008), p. 118.

[80] Thomas Platena, *Das Lichtbild im Urheberrecht: Gesetzliche Regelung und Technische Weiterentwicklung* (Peter Lang 1998), p. 135.

[81] Paul W. Hertin, 'Schutz der Lichtbilder'. In: Wilhelm Nordemann et al. *Urheberrecht: Kommentar zum Urheberrechtsgesetz und zum Urheberrechtswahrnehmungsgesetz: Mit den texten der Urheberrechtsgesetze der Früheren DDR, Österreichs und der Schweiz* (W. Kohlhammer, 8th ed. 1994), p. 462.

developed in order for it to become fixed and truly perceptible by human senses. Further production of prints only can be implemented after the development of the film. In case of digital photography, an exposed light sensitive sensor records the image and stores it electronically within the memory of a storage device. It is only after this stored image is electronically retrieved and visualized that it becomes perceptible to human senses. A certain similarity can be drawn between an image fixed on an undeveloped analogue film and an image electronically stored within a memory of a storage device—both require certain additional, albeit different, processes for the perceptible visualization of the *fixed* image. According to this view, the decisive moment for possible consideration of a photographic product for copyright protection is its perceptibility by the senses, and its fixation is precisely what makes it perceivable in this way.

The perceptibility of a photographic product is in this view closely connected to its eligibility for copyright protection. Considerations regarding the conferral of this protection can only be initiated after a photographic product has reached such a form that makes it possible for third parties to exploit it.[82] Naturally, no third party would be able to exploit a photographic product if it were not perceptible by their senses. It is therefore at the transformation of an image from its fixed, but yet imperceptible form, to a form perceptible by human senses where considerations regarding the appropriate type of protection must be initiated.

However, the second approach argues against eligibility starting at the moment of visualization of the fixed image. Provided that the development of analogue film or the electronic visualization process results in a perceptible work, copyrightability should begin *ex tunc*, from the moment of the successful exposure. In other words, from the moment of the fixation of the image itself. In this respect, such visualization processes, mostly automatic, only reveal what was already and previously fixed by the author. The following processes can be therefore performed by a person different from the author and achieve the same result as if it were done by the author themselves. If we keep in mind possible exploitation by third parties (and therefore the need for protection), exposed analogue film or an image stored within electronic storage media as data is already in a suitable form for future processing and exploitation. The intellectual activity of the author is most often involved in the exposure and the following formation and fixation of the image. All subsequent activities, such as developing the film or electronically retrieving and visualizing an image, do not necessarily have an effect on the previously fixed image, except for making this visualization perceptible by human senses. However, if a third party wishes to, they can employ creative inputs into the development process itself as well, thus affecting the appearance of the initially exposed image.[83] For this reason,

[82] BGH, I ZR 118/60, 27. Feb. 1962, 'AKI' *GRUR*. 1962, p. 470.

[83] Dana Ferchland, *Fotografieschutz im Wandel: Auswirkungen technischer, künstlerischer und rechtlicher Veränderungen auf den Urheberrechtsschutz von Fotografien* (Verlag Dr. Kovač 2018), p. 77.

Thomas Platena has claimed that protection must begin at the very moment of the fixation of the image through the exposure.[84] Similarly, *Horst Heitland* has asserted that the moment of exposure is when the formation of the image takes place.[85]

An image that is exposed but not yet not developed and materialised can be referred to as *latent*, since its nature precludes it from being seen by a human eye, which also reinforces its vulnerability, as *Ferchland* quoted *Adams*.[86] Such images, however latent and prone to destruction, could still be exploited by third parties, as described above. However, one would have to work according to the (dubious) assumption that the image was indeed, and still is, successfully fixed in whatever material, and when materialized the photographic product will meet the requirements for copyrightability set by the applicable standard of originality.

As an example of this, Germany's BGH[87] also spoke in favour of the protection of a fixed but not yet developed/visualized, image. In its *AKI*[88] decision, the BGH stated the visualization of the fixed image was not determinative for its copyrightability status. The court's reasoning in the decision was that copyright provides protection to intellectual assets; the tangible form of these assets is not required for such protection.[89]

Claims in favour of the second approach are in fact also supported by the wording of Article 7 (4) of the Berne Convention, which sets the term of protection of *photographic works* to 25 years *'from the making of such a work'*.[90] Such a clearly delimited period of protection from the instant of its creation is designed to prevent situations where the protection period could be artificially extended by purposely not developing a roll of analogue film or by not viewing the content of storage media after an image was exposed and fixed (although the second example would be highly questionable in practice). The approach of Article 7 (4) therefore suggests the protection period must be calculated from the moment of the exposure and fixation of the image, not the visualization through development of analogue film or via electronic technology in a computer, for example.

An approach similar to that of the BGH was formulated in the French *Code de la propriété intellectuelle* (CPI). Under this legislation, even if one considers a photographic product unfinished, meaning if only the image is fixed/exposed on the selected medium and is not yet perceptible by human senses, Article L111-2 of the CPI can still be conveniently employed. According to the said Article:

---

84 Thomas Platena, *Das Lichtbild im Urheberrecht: Gesetzliche Regelung und Technische Weiterentwicklung* (Peter Lang 1998), p. 139.

85 Horst Heitland, *Der Schutz der Fotografie im Urheberrecht Deutschlands, Frankreichs und der Vereinigten Staaten von Amerika* (C.H. Beck 1995), p. 36.

86 Dana Ferchland, *Fotografieschutz im Wandel: Auswirkungen technischer, künstlerischer und rechtlicher Veränderungen auf den Urheberrechtsschutz von Fotografien* (Verlag Dr. Kovač 2018), p. 84.

87 In English, 'Federal Court of Justice'.

88 BGH, I ZR 118/60, 27. Feb. 1962, 'AKI' *GRUR*. 1962, p. 470.

89 BGH, I ZR 118/60, 27. Feb. 1962, 'AKI' *GRUR*. 1962, p. 470.

90 Art. 7(4) Berne Convention.

L'œuvre est réputée créée, indépendamment de toute divulgation publique, du seul fait de la réalisation, même inachevée, de la conception de l'auteur.'[91] *('A work shall be deemed to have been created, irrespective of any public disclosure, by the mere fact of realization of the author's concept, even if incomplete.').*[92]

This indicates that a fixed/exposed image that is not yet finished, is still covered by the wording of Article L111-2. It is generally accepted within the French copyright framework that a photographic product becomes a work as soon as the composed image is fixed/exposed on the selected medium.[93] Moreover, the perceptibility of the image within a photographic product by human senses does not have to be immediate.[94]

According to the approach set out in German and French copyright law, it suffices for the fixed image to become perceptible by human senses at some point in the future for the photographic product which bears the said fixed image to become potentially eligible for copyright protection. Although based on a refutable assumption, such an approach towards copyrightability nonetheless ensures maximum (copyright) protection for photographers, given that additional requirements for a photographic product's copyrightability will be met.

2.5 Conclusion to Chapter 2

This section has looked at four key topics related to the medium of photography and their relevance for copyright law. They lay the groundwork as a knowledge base for the future considerations related to photography in this text.

First, it is critical to note that a radiation source must be employed in order for a photographic product to be produced. Depending on the nature of this radiation source, we can further differentiate between *standard* or *other* photographic products. The production process most often also entails certain technical equipment, but the use of this does not preclude the copyrightability of a photographic product. The use of technical equipment also does not preclude, per se, the granting of author status to the individual operating it. Finally, the moment decisive for the commencement of potential copyrightability is the moment of the fixation of an image—even if it remains undeveloped (in the case of analogue film) or stored unseen and unretrieved in electronic media (in the case of an electronic photographic image).

91 Art. L111-2 of the CPI.

92 *Intellectual Property Code* (1. Sep. 2024), https://wipolex-res.wipo.int/edocs/lexdocs/laws/en/fr/fr467en.html.

93 Ysolde Gendreau, Axel Nordemann, & Rainer Oesch (eds.), *Copyright and photographs: an international survey* (Kluwer Law International 1999), p. 24.

94 Ysolde Gendreau, Axel Nordemann, & Rainer Oesch (eds.), *Copyright and photographs: an international survey* (Kluwer Law International 1999), p. 35.

3 THE DEVELOPMENT OF INTERNATIONAL PROTECTION OF PHOTOGRAPHIC PRODUCTS

Before I present how photographic products fit in the copyright frameworks of Member States and the EU, we first will look at the international copyright framework. This will hopefully provide some insight into international minimum standards concerning photographic products. Indeed, as will be evident from the following text, these Member States played a key role in helping to shape international standards and requirements for copyrightability. Nevertheless, for reasons of space I focus on the relevant provisions of the Berne Convention and omit any major discussion of the subsequent WIPO Copyright Treaty and the TRIPS Agreement.

3.1 The Berne Convention and Photographic Products

The Berne Convention is the oldest international treaty still in effect concerning intellectual property law. As such, it sets minimum standards and requirements for the eligibility of photographic products for copyright protection, to which its contracting parties, the countries of the Union, must adhere. However, it was not always as such. The initial ambiguous approach towards copyright eligibility of photographic products, and the lack of priority vis-à-vis other categories of works at the national level, meant a corresponding level of ambiguity and dismissiveness at the international level.[95] Therefore, the first codified wording of the 1886 version of the Berne Convention did not include photographic products as a protectable subject-matter. The situation changed with the 1896 amendment, which included *photographic works and works produced by an analogous process*. However, these were not protected as artistic works. Also, no explicit term of protection was provided by the said amendment, and any protection was to be governed by the national laws of each country of the Union. By 1908, mandatory protection of photographic products was introduced. Again, no information concerning the term of any protection was given. Finally, the uncertain position of photographic products was remedied by the 1948

[95] Michael M. Walter & Silke von Lewinski (eds.) *European Copyright Law: A Commentary* (Oxford Univ. Press 2010), p. 584.

Brussels amendment. This amendment officially included *photographic works and works produced by a process analogous to photography* among the protected works specified in Article 2 of the Berne Convention. Nonetheless, the amendment still failed to specify any term of protection.

Before photographic products could officially be included into the wording of the Berne Convention in 1948, it was up to the Subcommittee for Photography and Cinematography to discuss the necessity and details. One such consideration, on which no agreement could be reached, touched on the necessity of specifying that only photographic products which were *personal creations* could be copyrightable in accordance with the Berne Convention. The subcommittee concluded that formulating such a specification and accompanying the term of a *photographic work* with it, would in fact be unnecessary, since the specification applied to all categories of works falling under the Berne Convention, not only photographic works.[96] The additional specification was rejected not because it failed to reflect the actual position of the Berne Convention regarding the *personal* character of photography, but because including that wording would seem redundant. From the aforementioned, a conclusion can be drawn that only products which are *personal creations* can qualify for copyright protection according to the Berne Convention. Therefore, any photographic product according to the Berne Convention must also be considered a *personal creation.*

It was Germany that proposed that the extent of protection of *photographic works* would be determined by each country of the Union separately.[97] France played a key role in that it proposed that protection only be extended to

'photographic works which constitute intellectual creations, in order to exclude mere mechanical reproductions.'[98]

Finally, the former Czechoslovakia proposed that only *photographic works which constitute intellectual creations* would qualify for copyright protection.[99] This settled the issue that for the Berne Convention, the term (photographic) *work* already presupposed an *intellectual creation.*[100]

---

96 Rapport de la sous-commission pour la photographie et la cinématographie. *Documents de la conférence de Bruxelles 5-26 Juin 1948* (Imprimerie Atar 1951), p. 111.

97 Rapport de la sous-commission pour la photographie et la cinématographie. *Documents de la conférence de Bruxelles 5-26 Juin 1948* (Imprimerie Atar 1951), p. 167.
Art. 2(1) Berne Convention.

98 Rapport de la sous-commission pour la photographie et la cinématographie. *Documents de la conférence de Bruxelles 5-26 Juin 1948* (Imprimerie Atar 1951), p. 168.

99 Rapport de la sous-commission pour la photographie et la cinématographie. *Documents de la conférence de Bruxelles 5-26 Juin 1948* (Imprimerie Atar 1951), p. 169.
Art. 2(1) of the Berne Convention.

100 Ramon Casas Vallés. 'The requirement of originality' In: Estelle Derclaye (ed.), *Research Handbook on the Future of EU Copyright* (Edward Elgar Publishing 2009), p. 105.

As a result of the 1948 Conference in Brussels, photographic products were included into the Berne Convention via Article 2 (1), but still without any further explicit specification or qualification.[101] The quality of being *personal* or intellectual remained implicit. The wording of Article 2 (1) still only provides a list of examples of *literary and artistic works* and is therefore neither exhaustive nor definitive.[102] Article 2 only included the following reference to photographic products:

'The expression "literary and artistic works" shall include every production in the literary, scientific and artistic domain, whatever may be the mode or form of its expression, such as ... photographic works to which are assimilated works expressed by a process analogous to photography... '[103]

By acceding to the Berne Convention, the individual countries of the Union agreed to provide protection by copyright to *literary and artistic works*, including *photographic works to which are assimilated works expressed by a process analogous to photography*. As contracting parties to the Berne Convention, Member States received status of countries of the Union. As parties of the Berne Convention, Member States already had some common copyright notions and concepts on a multinational level even prior to the initiation of the harmonization processes within the EU. Although the EU itself is not a contracting party to the Berne Convention itself, it acceded to the TRIPS Agreement in 1995. Article 9 of the TRIPS Agreement subjects its contracting parties to comply with Article 1 through 21 of the Berne Convention and its Appendix.[104] In this respect, the EU can be considered an indirect contracting party to the Berne Convention.

The Berne Convention itself does not refer to intellectual creations, let alone an *author's own intellectual creation*; but only to *works*. However, as is evident from references in EU Directives and jurisprudence of the CJEU to the *works within the meaning of the Berne Convention*, a link can clearly be made between the two notions. Therefore, we can deduce that the protection of certain objects, referred to as *works* within the meaning of the Berne Convention, presupposes that these *works* also constitute *intellectual creations* according to harmonized EU law.[105] Therefore, both terms—a *work* and an *intellectual creation*—should be considered synonyms for the purposes of copyright law. Further evidence from this with respect to photographic products can be seen in the remarks by the French delegation in 1948.

[101] Sam Ricketson & Jane C. Ginsburg, *International Copyright and Neighbouring Rights. 2* (Oxford Univ. Press, 2nd ed. 2006), p. 451.

[102] Antoine Latreille, 'From Idea to Fixation: A View of Protected Works' In: Estelle Derclaye (ed.), *Research Handbook on the Future of EU Copyright* (Edward Elgar Publishing 2009), p. 134.

[103] Art. 2(1) of the Berne Convention.

[104] Art. 9 of the TRIPS Agreement.

[105] Alain Strowel, *Le droit d'auteur européen en transition numérique: de ses origines à l'unification européenne et aux défis de l'intelligence artificielle et des Big Data* (Larcier 2022), p. 71.

The notion of *production* can also be interpreted as referring to a work of the mind and as such can be further interpreted as the *author's own intellectual creation* according to harmonized EU law.[106] This indicates, that the protectable product originated in the mind of a human being, and must become perceptible by senses of others, its potential audience, through its externalization by the production process.[107] The notion of *production* itself is therefore intended to be understood as broadly as possible, such that it covers as many production processes as possible.

In 1968, the Berne Convention was amended to define the applicable term of protection to photographic products to a minimum length. *Photographic works and works produced by a process analogous to photography* were to be protected for 25 years from their creation. The current wording the Article 7 (4) is as follows:

'It shall be a matter for legislation in the countries of the Union to determine the term of protection of photographic works and that of works of applied art in so far as they are protected as artistic works; however, this term shall last at least until the end of a period of twenty-five years from the making of such a work.'[108]

This minimal term of protection represents a base level below which the countries of the Union may not pass within their national copyright frameworks. As will be evident from the text below, the EU's harmonization processes have extended the said minimum term significantly.

3.2 The Berne Convention and Originality

The Berne Convention stays silent on matters of originality, more specifically, it does not stipulate any conditions or requirements a product must meet in order for it to be considered *original* in the hypothetical eyes of copyright law. The dearth of regulation therefore leaves countries of the Union with a correspondingly wide margin of discretion for defining not only the conditions and requirements of originality, but basically also the entire originality framework.[109] However, the said margin is not without limitations. It is true that the Berne Convention does leave the particularities of the originality to its contractual parties, but nonetheless still sets certain general boundaries which limit national originality frameworks.[110]

106 Silke von Lewinski, *International Copyright Law and Policy* (Oxford University Press 2008), p. 122.

107 Eleonora Rosati, *Copyright and the Court of Justice of the European Union* (Oxford University Press 2019), p. 92.

108 Art. 7(4) of the Berne Convention.

109 Sam Ricketson & Jane C. Ginsburg, *International Copyright and Neighbouring Rights. 2* (Oxford Univ. Press, 2nd ed. 2006), p. 406.

110 Sam Ricketson & Jane C. Ginsburg, *International Copyright and Neighbouring Rights: The Berne Convention and Beyond* (Oxford University Press, 3rd ed. 2022), p. 406.

Photographic products can actually be used as a fitting example for existence of general boundaries. Article 2 (1) of the Berne Convention lists

'photographic works to which are assimilated works expressed by a process analogous to photography'

as a protected subject-matter. This limitation is drafted in a way that obliges all countries of the Berne Union to bear in mind that their national originality standard should not be set in a way that excludes all such subject-matter from copyrightability, due to being excessively high. Nonetheless, as stated above, the official guide to the Berne Convention leaves the question of originality to be answered by (national) courts.[111]

As mentioned above, the membership of all Member States in the Union significantly affects copyright framework of the EU. This has been repeatedly confirmed by EU legislation as well as the CJEU.[112] While the Berne Convention is not an EU legal document as such, its role in the general framework of EU copyright law in connection with photographic products makes it a crucial element of analysis in this text.

[111] Georg Hendrik Christiaan Bodenhausen (ed.), *Guide to the Berne Convention for the Protection of Literary and Artistic Works* (BIRPI 1968), p. 18.

[112] In relation to photographic products, for example Rec. 16 of the Term Directive II, and Case C-145/10, *Eva-Maria Painer v. Standard Verlags GmbH and Others*, 1 Dec. 2011, ECLI:EU:C:2011:798, para. 5.

4 ORIGINALITY

We have seen how the requirement of originality has not sufficiently been elaborated (or even defined) by the Berne Convention on the international level. For this reason, we must therefore turn to other sources. This chapter begins with a general overview of originality, followed by a focus on EU conceptualizations of the term.

4.1 General Remarks on Originality

Originality has long served as a prerequisite for copyrightability in all modern legal systems.[113] However, its suitable height, serving as an imaginary threshold that a product must overcome to be eligible for copyright protection was not unanimously agreed upon for a considerable period of time.[114] One major reason for this ambiguity has been the lack of a legislative definition, which has left further interpretation to courts.[115]

Traditionally, *originality* has been approached from two main perspectives, an objective and a subjective. The former has been characteristic for common law countries, the latter for civil law countries, including the continental EU.[116] According to the subjective perspective, the assessment process focuses on examining the creative input of the author into the final appearance and features of the product as a form of their personality. In other words, the assessment process focuses on the demonstration of a certain amount of creativity by the author.[117] In other words, the originality test as applied in continental Europe is traditionally author-oriented, providing protection to the author's personality as manifested in their creation, by protecting the creation (expression) itself.[118]

---

113 Irini A. Stamatoudi, 'Originality under EU Copyright Law' In: Paul Torremans (ed.) *Research Handbook on Copyright Law* (Edward Elgar Publishing 2017), p. 57.

114 Jonathan Griffiths, 'The role of the Court of Justice in the development of European Union copyright law' In: Irini A. Stamatoudi & Paul Torremans (eds.) *EU Copyright Law: A Commentary* (Edward Elgar Publishing 2014), p. 1102.

115 Daniel J. Gervais, *(Re)Structuring Copyright: A Comprehensive Path to International Copyright Reform* (Edward Elgar Publishing 2017), p. 94.

116 Nicolas Berthold, 'L'harmonisation de la Notion D'originalité en Droit D'auteur,' 16 *Journal of World Intellectual Property* 58 (2013), p. 58.

117 *Ibid.*

118 Stef van Gompel, 'Creativity, Autonomy, and Personal Touch' In: Mireille van Eechoud, Jostein Gripsrud & Lionel Bently, *Work of Authorship* (Amsterdam University Press, 2015), p. 103.

On the other hand, the objective perspective entails an approach, that the baseline requirement for granting copyright protection is that the product directly originates with the author and demonstrates *'skill, labour, and judgement'* performed directly by the author in the process of that work's creation.[119] In other words, the author of a product must be able to demonstrate that their investment, or labour, into its creation meets certain minimum standards of conscious effort. Also, the product must not be copied from another product—that is, it should directly originate from the author.[120] It is evident the traditional approach to originality in common-law countries is connected more to the actual physical labour part of the author's investment into the final creation than to the intellectual part of it. Labour—rather than creativity—is considered the basis for copyrightability in such countries.

The core concept of *originality* is not *novelty*, with which it is often confusingly associated. The significance of novelty lies in its reference to how an idea has been transformed into a solution for a technical issue, whereas originality relates to expression, specifically how such expression compares to other already known expression.[121] In other words, *novelty* refers to idea, while the *originality* refers to expression. The various specific features of national understandings of originality stem from different ways of assessing how *expression* compares or does not compare to previous expression.[122]

4.2 Originality in the context of the EU

Within the context of the EU, the issue of originality was discussed by the Commission in the Staff Working Paper on the Review of the EC Legal Framework in the Field of Copyright and Related Rights. The paper provided the following definition of the concept:

The notion of originality is one of the key concepts in copyright law and forms part of the underlying justification for the statutory system of copyright protection for authors. Originality corresponds to the independent creativity of the author as reflected in his or her literary or artistic creation.[123]

[119] William R. Cornish & David Llewelyn, *Intellectual Property: Patents, Copyright, Trade Marks and Allied Rights* (Sweet & Maxwell, 6th ed. 2007), p. 417.

[120] Chancery Division, *University of London Press v University Tutorial* [1916] 2 Ch 601, 26 Jul. 1916.

[121] Irini A. Stamatoudi. 'Originality under EU Copyright Law' In: Paul Torremans (ed.) *Research Handbook on Copyright Law* (Edward Elgar Publishing 2017), p. 57.

[122] *Ibid.*

[123] *Commission staff working paper on the review of the EC legal framework in the field of copyright and related rights.* SEC (2004) 995. Brussels 2004.

It has been traditionally assumed that whenever a concept (such as originality) has not been uniformly defined on the EU level that the Member States should proceed with an interpretation according to their own applicable national laws.[124] However, this practice is no longer viable for the concept of *originality*. If the concept of *originality* is to be harmonized, then it also means that it needs to be construed in an autonomous and uniform manner that would ensure its universal applicability throughout the legal (copyright) framework of the EU.[125] This approach has been confirmed by the CJEU on numerous occasions. According to the CJEU, if a certain provision of the EU law makes no direct reference to the laws of the Member States with the intention of establishing its meaning, the provision must be given an independent and uniform interpretation.[126]

Moreover, interpretation should be made in a way that not only takes its wording into account, but most importantly the context in which it occurs and the objectives pursued by the legislation of which it is a part.[127] In other words, Member States must refrain from interpreting the concept of originality according to their own national laws. The generalized and harmonized originality standard adopted by the CJEU is designed to make the EU copyright framework more comprehensible and harmonization done in this area removes any ambiguities related to the assessment of works in individual Member States.[128]

Originality itself, as well as how harmonization of this concept developed will be further discussed in a later chapter. However, the main characteristics of the harmonized originality standard can be summed up in the following five points:

First, the crucial point of originality lies within the relationship between the author and their created product—the work.[129] This relationship serves as a foundation for originality to further develop. Second, originality itself must be manifested in the manner in which the work is expressed.[130] In other words, expression, rather than idea, is what must be assessed to define something as *original*. Third, the nature of the originality requirement does not preclude protection of derivative works.[131] If a particular work derives from or is based on another, it can still attract copyright protection, regardless of the protectability of the work that served as inspiration. Fourth, the threshold a product must pass in order for it to be considered as original

124 *Ibid.*

125 Irini A. Stamatoudi, 'Originality under EU Copyright Law' In: Paul Torremans (ed.) *Research handbook on copyright law* (Edward Elgar Publishing 2017), p. 63.

126 Case C-128/11, *UsedSoft GmbH v Oracle International* Corp, 3 Jul. 2012, ECLI:EU:C:2012:407, para. 39.

127 Case C-306/05, *Sociedad General de Autores y Editores de España (SGAE) v Rafael Hoteles SA*, 7 Dec. 2006, ECLI:EU:C:2006:764, para. 34.

128 Lionel Bently et al., *Intellectual Property Law* (Oxford University Press, 6th ed. 2022), p. 106.

129 Lionel Bently et al., *Intellectual Property Law* (Oxford University Press, 6th ed. 2022), p. 100.

130 Lionel Bently et al., *Intellectual Property Law* (Oxford University Press, 6th ed. 2022), p. 101.

131 *Ibid.*

is relatively low.[132] However, it is not non-existent.[133] Fifth, the understanding of originality and its subsequent assessment still largely depends on various contexts within the Member State in which the assessment process takes place.[134]

132 *Ibid.*

133 Opinion of AG Maciej Szupnar in case C-683/17, from 2 May 2019 in the matter C-683/17, *Cofemel – Sociedade de Vestuário SA v G-Star Raw CV*, 12. 9. 2019, ECLI:EU:C:2019:721, para. 57.

134 Lionel Bently et al., *Intellectual Property Law* (Oxford University Press, 6th ed. 2022), p. 102.

5 THE DEVELOPMENT OF THE ORIGINALITY STANDARD IN THE COPYRIGHT FRAMEWORK OF GERMANY

The first national framework of a Member State this text will examine is Germany. As stated in the introduction, the German copyright framework is particularly relevant because of its twofold approach to photographic products. In practice, this approach consists of a distinction between *original* and *non-original* photographic products and with it connected eligibility for either copyright or a related type of protection.

However, before assessing the development, position, and treatment of photographic products, it is helpful to first outline the general characteristics of the German copyright framework. To do so, I start with the notion of a *work* and its definition. After the definition and assessment of the notion of a *work*, I then move on to other related concepts relevant for Germany's copyright framework. After this general foundation has been laid down, I then turn the focus toward photographic products specifically.

5.1 The Chapter's Relationship to the Selected Hypotheses and Research Questions

The purpose of this chapter is to present some theoretical knowledge on the development of Germany's traditional approach to the protection of photographic products, either by copyright or a related right type of protection. This theoretical framework will then serve to structure the subsequent answers to Research Questions B and C, confirming or refuting them in the chapter dedicated to the effects of harmonization on the German copyright framework.

5.2 The Concept of a Work

Given its long-lasting usage and significance, the concept of a *work* may serve as the point of departure for an examination of the German copyright framework.[135] Although some copyright legislation was adopted before the 19th century's processes of unification in Germany, this chapter takes its starting point as the concept of a *work* in German copyright legislation from the UG adopted in 1870.[136] The UG provided copyright protection to works in selected areas of creative and productive activities. The single term used throughout the UG to refer to protectable products of creative and productive activities was a *work*. The term itself has remained in use by the German legislation ever since. Its position and meaning have remained unchanged even in the most recent and currently effective legislation regulating the German copyright framework, the UrhG, which was adopted in 1965.[137]

The UrhG provided the German copyright framework with a new list of protectable products, or *works*. Section 2 (1) contains a list of seven categories of protectable works from three domains: literature, science, and art.[138] However, these three domains are to be interpreted broadly.[139] They only represent approximate regions in which a product should reside in order for it to be eligible for copyright protection. The list itself and the types of protectable works it contains only serve as examples. The list deliberately leaves room for a flexible and adaptive application of its content in practice, which is necessary due to the constant development and introduction of new production techniques.[140] The consequence of this is that the UrhG can directly include new types of products eligible for copyright protection without any amendment of its wording by the German legislator.[141] If a new type of product appears within the German copyright framework seeking copyright protection, it can be included into one of the three categories, or as an additional type of a protectable work.[142] Section 2 (2) of the UrhG provides clarification of what can be considered a protectable work. According to this clarification, only works which are *persönliche geistige Schöpfungen* (*personal intellectual creations*) may be

[135] Axel Nordemann. 'Das Werk'. In: Axel Nordemann et al., *Urheberrecht: Kommentar zum Urheberrechtsgesetz, Verlagsgesetz, Urheberrechtswahrnehmungsgesetz*, (W. Kohlhammer, 11th ed. 2014). p. 128.

[136] In English: 'Law concerning copyright in written works, illustrations, musical compositions and dramatic works'.

[137] Act on Copyright and Related Rights (1. Sep. 2024), https://www.gesetze-im-internet.de/englisch_urhg/index.html.

[138] Sec. 2 (1) of the Act on Copyright and Related Rights (1. Sep. 2024), https://www.gesetze-im-internet.de/englisch_urhg/index.html.

[139] Ulrich Loewenheim, 'Geschützte Werke' In: Ulrich Loewenheim et al., *Urheberrecht: UrhG, KUG, VGG: Kommentar*, (C.H. Beck, 6th ed. 2020), p. 55.

[140] Haimo Schack, *Urheber- und Urhebervertragsrecht* (Mohr Siebeck, 9th ed. 2019), p. 103.

[141] *Ibid.*

[142] Gernot Schulze, 'Das Werk' In: Thomas Dreier & Gernot Schulze, *Urheberrechtsgesetz: Verwertungsgesellschaftengesetz, Kunsturhebergesetz: Kommentar* (C.H. Beck, 6th ed. 2018), p. 82.

protected.[143] We can therefore deduce that the notion of a *work* is a key concept of the UrhG.[144] The wording of Section 1 (2) of the UrhG and the prescribed requirement for copyright has not changed since.

The traditional premise of the German copyright law regarding the eligibility of products for copyright protection consists of the cumulative fulfilment of two conditions. For a product to be eligible for copyright protection, it must fall somewhat within the seven categories of products in literature, science, or art; at the same time, it must also be a *personal intellectual creation.* However, if a product has sufficiently distinct features to be classified as belonging to one of the seven categories of works, any further classification to the realm of literature, science, or art is irrelevant.[145] In other words, the legal effects and consequences of copyright protection do not depend on the specific classification of a work into one of the three main categories.[146] The determining factor is whether a certain product can be considered a *work* and therefore being copyrightable, since only a *work* can trigger the rights and obligations contained in provisions of the UrhG.[147]

These two cumulative conditions for copyright protection must be seen holistically. To be eligible for copyright protection, it is not enough for a product to belong to one of the seven categories alone. Nor it is enough for a product to be a personal intellectual creation. Not every product belonging to the areas of literature, science, or art is a personal intellectual creation and vice versa. Only by cumulatively meeting both of the conditions set out by the UrhG can a product be considered a work. It is safe to say that the German copyright framework, through the currently effective UrhG, protects various types and categories of works which, despite their diversity, are nonetheless unified. This unifying factor is the uniform concept of a *work.*[148]

According to the German copyright framework, the concept of the *work* is purely neutral, in the sense of the work's purpose, quality, and effort.[149] A neutral assessment means that the purpose for which the product was created, the quality in which

[143] Sec. 2 of the of the Act on Copyright and Related Rights (1. Sep. 2024), https://www.gesetze-im-internet.de/englisch_urhg/index.html.

[144] Axel Nordemann 'Das Werk'. In: Axel Nordemann et al., *Urheberrecht: Kommentar zum Urheberrechtsgesetz, Verlagsgesetz, Urheberrechtswahrnehmungsgesetz* (W. Kohlhammer, 11th ed. 2014), p. 128.

[145] Axel Nordemann 'Das Werk'. In: Axel Nordemann et al., *Urheberrecht: Kommentar zum Urheberrechtsgesetz, Verlagsgesetz, Urheberrechtswahrnehmungsgesetz* (W. Kohlhammer, 11th ed. 2014), p. 129.

[146] Loewenheim, U. Geschützte Werke. In: Loewenheim, U. Geschützte Werke. In: Ulrich Loewenheim et al., Urheberrecht: UrhG, KUG, VGG: Kommentar, (C.H. Beck, 6th ed. 2020), p. 56.

[147] Gernot Schulze, 'Geschützte Werke' In: Thomas Dreier & Gernot Schulze, *Urheberrechtsgesetz: Verwertungsgesellschaftengesetz, Kunsturhebergesetz: Kommentar* (C.H. Beck, 6th ed. 2018), p. 82.

[148] Gernot Schulze, 'Geschützte Werke' In: Thomas Dreier & Gernot Schulze, *Urheberrechtsgesetz: Verwertungsgesellschaftengesetz, Kunsturhebergesetz: Kommentar* (C.H. Beck, 6th ed. 2018), p. 83.

[149] Thomas Dreier & Gernot Schulze, *Urheberrechtsgesetz: Verwertungsgesellschaftengesetz, Kunsturhebergesetz: Kommentar* (C.H. Beck, 6th ed. 2018), p. 134.

the product was created, and the effort spent by the person creating the product or invested into its creation have no effect on the work's copyrightability. Closely connected to the concept of neutrality is the concept of objectivity, meaning that each assessment of a work must be carried in an objective way and by employing objective criteria, a requirement originated also from the jurisprudence of the CJEU, as *Schack* points out.[150] However, in practice, a product can only be assessed based on criteria of the individual performing the assessment, which can be subjective.[151] That person can, therefore, only try to perform this task as objectively as possible.

Closely linked to the neutral nature of the concept is the need to base it on objective criteria.[152] As a result, it is not up to the creator to decide whether their product or creation may be regarded as a work according to the UhrG. On the basis of an author's subjective feelings and opinions, any of their creations could indeed be considered a work, but such a creation must nonetheless undergo an objective assessment in order to determine whether it indeed fulfils the characteristics prescribed by the law.

Nevertheless, the concept of a work, as applied in the German copyright framework, can be considered indefinite.[153] Some see the concept as extremely broad.[154] The consequences of this vagueness for legal practice, lie in the requirement for further interpretation of a given work by courts, according to factual and other circumstances connected to the contested product. On the other hand, as described above, the indefinite and flexible nature of the concept of a *work* makes it easier for new types of products whose authors seek copyright protection to be recognized as such.[155] The concept of a work does not undertake to define what art is, but neither does copyright itself.[156] Such attempts would prove contrary to the loose and relatively open definition of the concept of a work itself.

[150] Haimo Schack, *Urheber- und Urhebervertragsrecht* (Mohr Siebeck, 9th ed. 2019), p. 105.

[151] Gernot Schulze, 'Der Schutzumfang des Urheberrechts in Deutschland' In: Reto M. Hilty, Christophe Geiger, & Valérie-Laure Benabou (eds.), *Impulse für eine europäische Harmonisierung des Urheberrechts: Urheberrecht im deutsch-französischen Dialog* (Springer 2007), p. 119.

[152] Haimo Schack, *Urheber- und Urhebervertragsrecht* (Mohr Siebeck, 10th ed. 2021), p. 108.

[153] Axel Nordemann. 'Das Werk'. In: Axel Nordemann et al., *Urheberrecht: Kommentar zum Urheberrechtsgesetz, Verlagsgesetz, Urheberrechtswahrnehmungsgesetz* (W. Kohlhammer, 11th ed. 2014), p. 134.

[154] Ulrich Loewenheim & Matthias Leistner. 'Werkbegriff' In: Ulrich Loewenheim et al., *Urheberrecht: UrhG, KUG, VGG: Kommentar* (C.H. Beck, 6th ed. 2020), p. 69.

[155] Ulrich Loewenheim & Matthias Leistner. 'Werkbegriff' In: Ulrich Loewenheim et al., *Urheberrecht: UrhG, KUG, VGG: Kommentar* (C.H. Beck, 6th ed. 2020), p. 70.

[156] Ulrich Loewenheim & Matthias Leistner. 'Geschützte Werke' In: Ulrich Loewenheim et al., *Urheberrecht: UrhG, KUG, VGG: Kommentar* (C.H. Beck, 6th ed. 2020), p. 59.

5.3 The Concept of 'persönliche geistige Schöpfungen'

As stated above, Section 2 (2) of the UrhG defines in more detail what may be considered a work. The nature of paragraph (2) is supplementary, since in a way it serves as an addition to paragraph (1) of Section 2 and the list of categories of protectable works it contains. Moreover, there has never been a definition of the term *personal intellectual creation*[157] in the German legislation. Taking this step was ultimately left to German jurisprudence and academia, as *Nordemann* quoted *Möhring* and *Nicolini*.[158] To better understand the concept of the *author's own intellectual creation*, the following section systematically assesses, defines, and analyses the concept as well as its individual parts.

5.3.1 Own (Personal)

Only a product created by a person can be considered *personal*.[159] Therefore, in order for a product to be considered a work, it must be based on human creative activity[160]: Only a human being is capable of creating something that can be considered a work according to the UrhG. The personality materialized in the product (its *personal* feature) does not need to form or define the product itself.[161] What suffices for its eligibility for copyright protection is the expression of personality in the product. However, the concept of personality is not person-related, but rather work-related.[162] As a result, the relevant point is not to seek an answer to the question of whom the product can be attributed to, but rather whether the product bears any manifest signs of personality.

The idea behind the definition of *own (personal)* does not preclude the use of, for example, various technical aids or machines by a person throughout the production process. If the resulting form of a product is clearly planned and governed by

157 Hereafter, I use the official translation of *'author's own intellectual creation'*.

158 Axel Nordemann, 'Germany'. In: Ysolde Gendreau, Axel Nordemann, & Rainer Oesch (eds.), *Copyright and photographs: an international survey* (Kluwer Law International 1999), p. 137.

159 Gernot Schulze. 'Geschützte Werke'. In: Thomas Dreier & Gernot Schulze, *Urheberrechtsgesetz: Verwertungsgesellschaftengesetz, Kunsturhebergesetz: Kommentar* (C.H. Beck, 6th ed. 2018), p. 83.

160 Ulrich Loewenheim & Matthias Leistner. 'Geschützte Werke'. In: Ulrich Loewenheim et al., *Urheberrecht: UrhG, KUG, VGG: Kommentar* (C.H. Beck, 6th ed. 2020), p. 71.

161 Axel Nordemann. 'Das Werk'. In: Axel Nordemann et al., *Urheberrecht: Kommentar zum Urheberrechtsgesetz, Verlagsgesetz, Urheberrechtswahrnehmungsgesetz* (W. Kohlhammer, 11th ed. 2014), p. 137.

162 Hartwig Ahlberg, 'Geschützte Werke'. In: Philipp Möhring et al. (eds.), *Urheberrecht: UrhG, KUG, UrhWahrnG, VerlG; Kommentar* (C.H. Beck, 3rd ed. 2014), p. 66.

a human being, concerns as to whether it is a work should be unjustified.[163] On the other hand, if a photographic product was for example produced solely by a machine, this would preclude its eligibility for any type of protection according to the UrhG.[164] Nonetheless, if any issues connected to the identification of the presence of a personality in a product were to occur, a definitionally clarifying solution based on the aforementioned characteristics could be applied easily.[165]

5.3.2 Intellectual—Spiritual (content)

Not every product that results from human activity can be considered a work for the purposes of copyright law. Such activity must also add content of an intellectual or spiritual nature into the product. To be recognized as a work, the product's creation must be intentional and the product itself must be considered an expression of the creator's individual spirit.[166]

The idea of *spiritual/intellectual* in connection to content refers to being controlled by the mind, in the sense of expressing thoughts.[167] The presence of such characteristics serves as the first of the two determining factors of a work along with form.[168] Intellectual or spiritual content is also closely connected to the *personal* nature of a product; to an extent, it is a subset. Only if human expressions of thoughts radiate from the product or if content of an emotional nature is communicated through it, can such content be referred to as having an intellectual or spiritual nature.[169] In addition to thoughts, feelings and sensations may also be expressed as *spiritual* content, as *Heitland* quoted *Schricker* and *Loewenheim*.[170] It is within this context that one may also refer to the *aura* of a product, emanating as objective uniqueness.[171] However, such *emanating* content must be recorded and immediately recognizable in the structure of the assessed product.[172]

---

163 Ulrich Loewenheim & Matthias Leistner. 'Geschützte Werke'. In: Ulrich Loewenheim et al., *Urheberrecht: UrhG, KUG, VGG: Kommentar* (C.H. Beck, 6th ed. 2020), p. 71.

164 Thomas Platena, *Das Lichtbild im Urheberrecht: Gesetzliche Regelung und Technische Weiterentwicklung* (Peter Lang 1998), p. 94.

165 Marcel Bisges, *Die Kleine Münze im Urheberrecht: Analyse des ökonomischen Aspekts des Werkbegriffs* (Nomos 2014), p. 26.

166 Haimo Schack, *Urheber- und Urhebervertragsrecht* (Mohr Siebeck, 10th ed. 2021), p. 109.

167 Thomas Platena, *Das Lichtbild im Urheberrecht: Gesetzliche Regelung und Technische Weiterentwicklung* (Peter Lang 1998), p. 230.

168 Hartwig Ahlberg, 'Geschützte Werke'. In: Philipp Möhring et al. (eds.), *Urheberrecht: UrhG, KUG, UrhWahrnG, VerlG ; Kommentar* (C.H. Beck, 3rd ed. 2014), p. 66.

169 Axel Nordemann. 'Das Werk'. In: Axel Nordemann et al., *Urheberrecht: Kommentar zum Urheberrechtsgesetz, Verlagsgesetz, Urheberrechtswahrnehmungsgesetz* (W. Kohlhammer, 11th ed. 2014), p. 138.

170 Horst Heitland, *Der Schutz der Fotografie im Urheberrecht Deutschlands, Frankreichs und der Vereinigten Staaten von Amerika* (C.H. Beck 1995), p. 34.

171 Haimo Schack, *Urheber- und Urhebervertragsrecht* (Mohr Siebeck, 9th ed. 2019), p. 106.

172 BGH, Ib ZR 129/61, 27. Mar. 1963, 'Rechenschieber', *NJW*. 1963, p. 1877.

In case of photographic products, intellectual/spiritual content can be especially hard to conceptualize, interpret, and precisely express in words. As an image, it would necessarily require additional transformation into words. However, one transformation—from words into an image—was already performed by the author. Further (re)conceptualization requires reversing the transformation back into words. Even so, the intellectual/spiritual content added by the author into the photographic product can be read in different ways by the audience, possibly overlooking the original meaning of the content.[173] Nonetheless, different interpretations of a photographic product would not disqualify it from its status as a *work* since the presence of intellectual/spiritual content could not be disputed.

If one is to refer to a product as a work of intellect or intellectual creation, such reference should bear in mind the very nature of such reference. The content of such product must be emotional or have expression, which then must originate from the person who produced the product—the author.[174] The requirement of personal intellectual creation presupposes that only a human being can be considered the author of a work.[175] The said spiritual content itself finds its expression through the deliberate shaping and guidance of thoughts performed by the author, as *Bisges* concluded from German case law.[176] According to this definition, any photographic products accidentally produced by a photographer would be excluded from protection due to the lack of their deliberate actions, as *Ahlberg* quoted *Fromm* and *Nordemann*.[177] Moreover, the thought itself must be expressed, as *Bisges* quoted *Erdmann*.[178] In other words, the product must evoke a response beyond that of regular perception.[179]

This response beyond regular perception of a product should mentally stimulate its audience (readers, listeners, or viewers) in some way.[180] The overall impact depends on the type of the product. The senses of a spectator must be stimulated to such an extent that sensations beyond the product's physical existence are triggered.[181]

[173] Horst Heitland, *Der Schutz der Fotografie im Urheberrecht Deutschlands, Frankreichs und der Vereinigten Staaten von Amerika* (C.H. Beck 1995), p. 35.

[174] Gernot Schulze, 'Geschützte Werke' In: Thomas Dreier & Gernot Schulze, *Urheberrechtsgesetz: Verwertungsgesellschaftengesetz, Kunsturhebergesetz: Kommentar* (C.H. Beck, 6th ed. 2018), p. 85.

[175] Axel Nordemann, *Die künstlerische Fotografie als urheberrechtlich geschütztes Werk* (Nomos 1992), p. 118.

[176] Marcel Bisges, *Die Kleine Münze im Urheberrecht: Analyse des ökonomischen Aspekts des Werkbegriffs* (Nomos 2014), p. 27.

[177] Hartwig Ahlberg, 'Geschützte Werke'. In: Philipp Möhring et al. (eds.), *Urheberrecht: UrhG, KUG, UrhWahrnG, VerlG; Kommentar* (C.H. Beck, 3rd ed. 2014), p. 64.

[178] Marcel Bisges, *Die Kleine Münze im Urheberrecht: Analyse des ökonomischen Aspekts des Werkbegriffs* (Nomos 2014), p. 26.

[179] Ulrich Loewenheim & Matthias Leistner. 'Geschützte Werke'. In: Ulrich Loewenheim et al., *Urheberrecht: UrhG, KUG, VGG: Kommentar* (C.H. Beck, 6th ed. 2020), p. 73.

[180] Gernot Schulze, 'Geschützte Werke' In: Thomas Dreier & Gernot Schulze, *Urheberrechtsgesetz: Verwertungsgesellschaftengesetz, Kunsturhebergesetz: Kommentar* (C.H. Beck, 6th ed. 2018), p. 85.

[181] Haimo Schack, *Kunst und Recht: bildende Kunst, Architektur, Design und Fotografie im deutschen und internationalen Recht* (Mohr Siebeck, 3rd ed. 2017), p. 117.

These include effects that entertain, instruct, illustrate, edify or similar.[182] It must be highlighted that *intellectual* (*spiritual*) *content* is in no way connected to aesthetics of a product.[183] This means any considerations related to the protectability of a product based on the level of aesthetics are not relevant for copyright law. Products of art are not subject to ideals of beauty, and are known and recognized for also presenting repulsive and aesthetically displeasing objects.[184]

5.3.3 Perceptibility of a Product—Shaping—Expression

In order for the audience to perceive the mentally stimulating effect emanated by a product, such an effect must take a certain form of the expression given to it by the author.[185] The unprotected thoughts of the author need to transition from the realm of pure mental abstraction to a state where they can be perceived. In other words, the effect must be expressed in a way that makes it appreciable by the senses; the product must take a certain shape that makes this perception possible.[186] This definition also does not exclude products expressed in non-physical or non-permanent forms.[187] In this respect, one should not confuse the necessity of having a certain shape with the fixation requirement, which is of no relevance for purposes of copyrightability.[188] However, it is only through the specific form of expression that the content of the product becomes perceptible.[189] In this sense, the form serves as the second of the two determining factors of a work.[190] For example, the nature of photographic products poses no issues in terms of their perceptibility by the sense of sight.[191] Again, it is also important to emphasize that a photographic

---

182 Gernot Schulze, 'Der Schutzumfang des Urheberrechts in Deutschland'. In: Reto M. Hilty, Christophe Geiger, & Valérie-Laure Benabou (eds.), *Impulse für eine europäische Harmonisierung des Urheberrechts: Urheberrecht im deutsch-französischen Dialog* (Springer 2007), p. 118.

183 Haimo Schack, *Urheber- und Urhebervertragsrecht* (Mohr Siebeck, 9th ed. 2019), p. 106.

184 Haimo Schack, *Kunst und Recht: bildende Kunst, Architektur, Design und Fotografie im deutschen und internationalen Recht* (Mohr Siebeck, 3rd ed. 2017), p. 117.

185 Marcel Bisges, *Die Kleine Münze im Urheberrecht: Analyse des ökonomischen Aspekts des Werkbegriffs* (Nomos 2014), p. 28.

186 Gernot Schulze, 'Geschützte Werke'. In: Thomas Dreier & Gernot Schulze, *Urheberrechtsgesetz: Verwertungsgesellschaftengesetz, Kunsturhebergesetz: Kommentar* (C.H. Beck, 6th ed. 2018), p. 85.

187 Artur-Axel Wandtke, Winfried Bullinger & Michael Bohne, *Praxiskommentar Urheberrecht: UrhG, UrhDaG, VGG, InsO, UKlaG, KUG, EVtr, InfoSoc-RL, Portabilitäts-VO* (C.H. Beck, 6th ed. 2022), p. 54.

188 Haimo Schack, *Urheber- und Urhebervertragsrecht* (Mohr Siebeck, 10th ed. 2021), p. 110.

189 Philipp Möhring et al. (eds.), *Urheberrecht: UrhG, KUG, UrhWahrnG, VerlG; Kommentar* (C.H. Beck, 3rd ed. 2014), p. 66.

190 *Ibid.*

191 Axel Nordemann, 'Germany'. In: Ysolde Gendreau, Axel Nordemann, & Rainer Oesch (eds.), *Copyright and photographs: an international survey* (Kluwer Law International 1999), p. 138.

product does not necessarily need a permanently perceptible form in order to enjoy protection.[192]

5.3.4 Creation

Not just any type of creation will suffice in order for it to be considered for copyright protection. The creation must be of intellectual nature—an intellectual creation.[193] Only a creation of an intellectual/spiritual nature may result in a work according to the UrhG.[194] The core of this legal concept lies in the combination of the creator and their creation—the result of their thought process.[195] Another aspect that comes into play within this chain of the author and their creation is the inclusion of a technical device or aid in the creation process of a photographic product, for example. If the author is the one who determines the outcome of such process, and operates the employed technical device, the creation will still be considered as having an *intellectual* nature.[196]

5.3.5 Individuality

One of the features a *to-be-protected* product must possess is individuality, making it another necessary component forming an integral part of the concept of a work within the meaning of the UrhG.[197] Some consider it to be the most important criterion on which the quality of a work can be based in copyright law.[198] A product must have a sufficient degree of (creative) individuality, however of a creative nature.[199] Given the broad interpretation of the concept of a *work*, assessing the

---

192 Axel Nordemann, *Die künstlerische Fotografie als urheberrechtlich geschütztes Werk* (Nomos 1992), p. 119.

193 Gernot Schulze, 'Geschützte Werke' In: Thomas Dreier & Gernot Schulze, *Urheberrechtsgesetz: Verwertungsgesellschaftengesetz, Kunsturhebergesetz: Kommentar* (C.H. Beck, 6th ed. 2018), p. 87.

194 Thomas Platena, *Das Lichtbild im Urheberrecht: Gesetzliche Regelung und Technische Weiterentwicklung* (Peter Lang 1998), p. 230.

195 Philipp Möhring et al. (eds.), *Urheberrecht: UrhG, KUG, UrhWahrnG, VerlG; Kommentar* (C.H. Beck, 3rd ed. 2014), p. 64.

196 Horst Heitland, *Der Schutz der Fotografie im Urheberrecht Deutschlands, Frankreichs und der Vereinigten Staaten von Amerika* (C.H. Beck 1995), p. 33.

197 Ulrich Loewenheim & Matthias Leistner. 'Geschützte Werke'. In: Ulrich Loewenheim et al., *Urheberrecht: UrhG, KUG, VGG: Kommentar* (C.H. Beck, 6th ed. 2020), p. 76.

198 Artur-Axel Wandtke, Winfried Bullinger & Michael Bohne, *Praxiskommentar Urheberrecht: UrhG, UrhDaG, VGG, InsO, UKlaG, KUG, EVtr, InfoSoc-RL, Portabilitäts-VO* (C.H. Beck, 6th ed. 2022), p. 54.

199 BGH, I ZR 198/85, 10. Dec. 1987, 'Vorentwurf II' *GRUR*. 1988, p. 533.

individual creativity present in a product is key.[200] The core of this requirement lies in the fact that only a product which stands out amongst the mass of other similar or generically identical products deserves protection by copyright.[201] A product designated as possessing individuality must be shaped by the individual spirit of the author; it must be a personal creation of individual expressiveness.[202] In other words, individuality can be seen as an inseparable connection between the product and its creator.[203] For example, this connection can be seen as the way a creator—the photographer—transports an artistic message.[204] It is also worth noting that individuality can only exist in a work that allows its own development and emergence through the personal preferences of the author, as *Bisges* concluded from German case law.[205] The recognition of the author in the work resulting from the personal preferences reflected in it does not have to be immediate—even a significantly reduced level of such exhibited personal influence is still satisfactory for the purposes of individuality demonstration.[206] The existence of individuality can be demonstrated in a photographic product if it is possible to make an inference regarding the photographer from the image depicted.[207]

The clear superiority of a product in terms of its characteristics, surpassing the average known and available in the field is traditionally required for copyright protection.[208] In other words, simply being *different* in comparison with other products does not suffice.[209] One cannot speak of an individual product if its creator merely repeats or recreates already existing procedures without enriching them; the result of such procedures, the final product requires the addition of the author's personal characteristics—individuality.[210] This requirement of individuality must be

[200] Ulrich Loewenheim & Matthias Leistner. 'Geschützte Werke'. In: Ulrich Loewenheim et al., *Urheberrecht: UrhG, KUG, VGG: Kommentar* (C.H. Beck, 6th ed. 2020), p. 69.

[201] Axel Nordemann. 'Das Werk'. In: Axel Nordemann et al., *Urheberrecht: Kommentar zum Urheberrechtsgesetz, Verlagsgesetz, Urheberrechtswahrnehmungsgesetz* (W. Kohlhammer, 11th ed. 2014), p. 138.

[202] Ulrich Loewenheim & Matthias Leistner. 'Geschützte Werke'. In: Ulrich Loewenheim et al., *Urheberrecht: UrhG, KUG, VGG: Kommentar* (C.H. Beck, 6th ed. 2020), p. 76.

[203] Haimo Schack, *Urheber- und Urhebervertragsrecht* (Mohr Siebeck, 9th ed. 2019), p. 108.

[204] Axel Nordemann, 'Germany'. In: Ysolde Gendreau, Axel Nordemann, & Rainer Oesch (eds.), *Copyright and photographs: an international survey* (Kluwer Law International 1999), p. 138.

[205] Marcel Bisges, *Die Kleine Münze im Urheberrecht: Analyse des ökonomischen Aspekts des Werkbegriffs* (Nomos 2014), p. 30.

[206] Axel Nordemann, *Die künstlerische Fotografie als urheberrechtlich geschütztes Werk* (Nomos 1992), p. 72.

[207] Thomas Platena, *Das Lichtbild im Urheberrecht: Gesetzliche Regelung und Technische Weiterentwicklung* (Peter Lang 1998), p. 233.

[208] BGH, I ZR 52/83, 9. May 1985, 'Inkasso-Program', *GRUR.* 1985, p. 1041.

[209] Schulze, G. Geschützte Werke. In: Thomas Dreier & Gernot Schulze, *Urheberrechtsgesetz: Verwertungsgesellschaftengesetz, Kunsturhebergesetz: Kommentar* (C.H. Beck, 6th ed. 2018), p. 88.

[210] Artur-Axel Wandtke, Winfried Bullinger & Michael Bohne, *Praxiskommentar Urheberrecht: UrhG, UrhDaG, VGG, InsO, UKlaG, KUG, EVtr, InfoSoc-RL, Portabilitäts-VO* (C.H. Beck, 6th ed. 2022), p. 54.

understood and applied objectively, as the opposite of imitation.[211] In this sense, products that faithfully imitate other already existing products cannot be considered *individual*. However, given the requirement for an objective understanding, so-called *'Doppelschöpfungen'* (*double creations*) are permissible as individual.[212] Double creations include situations in which two or more authors, unaware of each other, create the same work. For the purposes of copyrightability, however, there is still the expectation that the author will follow a process of a creative nature; otherwise, an individual result recognized by copyright law cannot be expected to be achieved.

In the broadest terms, a product must be special, and different from other known products. However, it does not have to be absolutely new.[213] It suffices if the product itself is new to the author.[214] This subjective novelty derives from the function of copyright in continental Europe—protection of the individual creator. In this sense, copyright protection is based on individuality rather than on absolute novelty.[215] A product must possess individual characteristics that enable it to be differentiated from other, older works.[216] This approach is based on the nature of the production process itself, because the author may have based their product on other, previously known, products and processes. As a result, the term *new* can be seen as constituting a product which is a previously unknown combination of the known with addition of the *new* by the author, as *Nordemann* quoted *Hubmann*.[217] Such actions of the author must be subjective and of a creative nature.[218]

For an accurate and relevant assessment of individuality, it is necessary to compare the assessed product with the entirety of all existing products.[219] The purpose of such comparison and assessment is to determine and identify a moment at which the individuality of the assessed product reaches the point beyond which it becomes distinguishable from other existing products. The number of other products, along

[211] Horst Heitland, *Der Schutz der Fotografie im Urheberrecht Deutschlands, Frankreichs und der Vereinigten Staaten von Amerika* (C.H. Beck 1995), p. 38.

[212] Haimo Schack, *Kunst und Recht: bildende Kunst, Architektur, Design und Fotografie im deutschen und internationalen Recht* (Mohr Siebeck, 3rd ed. 2017), p. 14.

[213] Gernot Schulze, 'Der Schutzumfang des Urheberrechts in Deutschland'. In: Reto M. Hilty, Christophe Geiger, & Valérie-Laure Benabou (eds.), *Impulse für eine europäische Harmonisierung des Urheberrechts: Urheberrecht im deutsch-französischen Dialog* (Springer 2007), p. 119.

[214] Axel Nordemann, *Die künstlerische Fotografie als urheberrechtlich geschütztes Werk* (Nomos 1992), p. 72.

[215] Artur-Axel Wandtke, Winfried Bullinger & Michael Bohne, *Praxiskommentar Urheberrecht: UrhG, UrhDaG, VGG, InsO, UKlaG, KUG, EVtr, InfoSoc-RL, Portabilitäts-VO* (C.H. Beck, 6th ed. 2022), p. 54.

[216] *Ibid.*

[217] Axel Nordemann, *Die künstlerische Fotografie als urheberrechtlich geschütztes Werk* (Nomos 1992), p. 72.

[218] Horst Heitland, *Der Schutz der Fotografie im Urheberrecht Deutschlands, Frankreichs und der Vereinigten Staaten von Amerika* (C.H. Beck 1995), p. 39.

[219] Marcel Bisges, *Die Kleine Münze im Urheberrecht: Analyse des ökonomischen Aspekts des Werkbegriffs* (Nomos 2014), p. 54.

with knowledge one possesses about them, is crucial, because it is against these products that the individuality of the assessed product is evaluated. However, it is objectively unknown whether surpassing this abstract level of individuality in comparison to other products, must be minimal or significant.[220] Given the necessity to weigh each product on a case-by-case basis, the application of objective criteria is impossible and also precluded by the individual/subjective approach.

The UrhG itself, however, does not prescribe the level of individuality upon which the protectability of a product should be based. It can be nonetheless deduced that the greater the individuality the product displays, the more complex it is, the stronger its hypothetical stance against allegations connected to its protectability, or lack of, would be.[221] In respect to this, it can be stated in reverse, that the lower the level of individuality a work possesses, the lower the level of potential protection would be.[222]

Both the conception of the work as well as its form can give rise to individuality.[223] In practice, individuality may manifest itself in many ways and forms, depending on the type of product it emanates from. Attempts by the German legislator to at least approximately indicate these various examples of individuality have been manifested in the wording of Section 2 (1) of the UrhG. Although not definitive, the list provides us with various types of works that allow development of their *individual* traits.[224] Therefore, if this kind of development were not possible or allowed by the type of the work, one could not speak of an *individual* work; individuality would be precluded by the very nature of such work.

In this context, one type of connection between the product and its potential observer must be highlighted. The core of this metaphorical relationship is not the way that the product, by itself, is special or individual. It is only through human perception that the potential individuality of a product can be assessed and perceived.[225] Figuratively speaking, the source of individuality is the relationship between the product itself and a human being perceiving its effects. One can then speak about the *'Schutz der qualifizierte menschliche Kommunikation'* (*protection of qualified human communication*), as *Schulze* put it, quoting *Schricker*, rather than about the

220 Marcel Bisges, *Die Kleine Münze im Urheberrecht: Analyse des ökonomischen Aspekts des Werkbegriffs* (Nomos 2014), p. 60.

221 Artur-Axel Wandtke, Winfried Bullinger & Michael Bohne, *Praxiskommentar Urheberrecht: UrhG, UrhDaG, VGG, InsO, UKlaG, KUG, EVtr, InfoSoc-RL, Portabilitäts-VO* (C.H. Beck, 6th ed. 2022), p. 57.

222 Thomas Platena, *Das Lichtbild im Urheberrecht: Gesetzliche Regelung und Technische Weiterentwicklung* (Peter Lang 1998), p. 254.

223 Loewenheim U. Leistner, M. 'Geschützte Werke'. In: Ulrich Loewenheim et al., *Urheberrecht: UrhG, KUG, VGG: Kommentar* (C.H. Beck, 6th ed. 2020), p. 77.

224 Axel Nordemann, *Die künstlerische Fotografie als urheberrechtlich geschütztes Werk* (Nomos 1992), p. 73.

225 Schulze, G. Geschützte Werke In: Thomas Dreier & Gernot Schulze, *Urheberrechtsgesetz: Verwertungsgesellschaftengesetz, Kunsturhebergesetz: Kommentar* (C.H. Beck, 6th ed. 2018), p. 88.

protection of a product.[226] It must be therefore repeatedly stated, that for the purposes of (German) copyright law, a product can never be naturally individual in itself.[227] It is only through the author's creative and wilful involvement that such individuality is given space and potential fixation. This individuality is later maintained and affirmed by the audience of the product.

Since most of the traditional terminology used to refer to individuality in a work was devised before the invention of photography, its applicability to products in this genre was found to be problematic.[228] *Axel Nordemann* chose the term *'individuelle Geistestätigkeit'* from the jurisprudence of the BGH,[229] which he translated as *individual intellectual forming activity*, as amongst the most frequently used in order to refer to individuality in a photographic product.[230] Moreover, the presence of individuality must be inherent at the moment of the completion of a photographic product and cannot arise retrospectively.[231]

The assessment and demonstration of the requirement of individuality in connection with photographic products can prove to be problematic in practice. The original understanding and conceptualization of the requirement of individuality was built on traditional visual artists and their works. Because of this, the requirement did not take into account the specific features of photography. Photography quite simply was not yet considered as an artistic form, and its capabilities of displaying the individuality of its creators were questionable.[232] In addition, the assessment of a photographic product with respect to individuality must be done on a case-by-case basis, since no universal or blanket approach exists to identify *individuality* in photographic products.[233] The necessity of such approach, or its impossibility, may be based on the individuality of each person and their respective personality. With the figurative transfer of individuality of each person to their photographic product, an individual work is created. Therefore, each individual work requires a correspondingly individual assessment.

---

226 *Ibid.*

227 Haimo Schack, *Kunst und Recht: bildende Kunst, Architektur, Design und Fotografie im deutschen und internationalen Recht* (Mohr Siebeck, 3rd ed. 2017), p. 12.

228 Axel Nordemann, 'Germany'. In: Ysolde Gendreau, Axel Nordemann, & Rainer Oesch (eds.), *Copyright and photographs: an international survey* (Kluwer Law International 1999), p. 138.

229 BGH, I ZR 160/84, 20. Nov. 1986, 'Werbepläne'. *GRUR*. 1987, p. 360.

230 Nordemann, A. Germany. In: Ysolde Gendreau, Axel Nordemann, & Rainer Oesch (eds.), *Copyright and photographs: an international survey* (Kluwer Law International 1999), p. 138.

231 Ilva Johanna Schiessel, *Reichweite und Rechtfertigung des einfachen Lichtbildschutzes gem. § 72 UrhG* (Nomos 2020), p. 52.

232 Axel Nordemann, *Die künstlerische Fotografie als urheberrechtlich geschütztes Werk* (Nomos 1992), p. 80.

233 Horst Heitland, *Der Schutz der Fotografie im Urheberrecht Deutschlands, Frankreichs und der Vereinigten Staaten von Amerika* (C.H. Beck 1995), p. 41.

5.3.6 Creative Freedom

The availability and extent of creative freedom at one's (the author's) disposal throughout the production process of a product is determinative for its assessment of copyrightability.[234] Assessing whether the creative freedom available was taken advantage of to such an extent to make the product eligible for copyright protection must be made in respect to the individual nature of every product. Not every product provides the possibility to exercise creative freedom to the same extent. The product itself must, figuratively speaking, allow for individual traits to develop.[235] In practice, the more the form of a product is determined by its intended purpose or technical constraints, the narrower the scope of available creative freedom becomes.[236] Products offering a greater extent of creative freedom will more likely to be eligible for copyright without significant difficulties. If the copyright protection of a work is contested due to the lack of evidence of creative freedom, its author must prove that they have exercised creative freedom, however limited, and they were able to work their way around restrictions and exercise their creative freedom in an individual manner.

The creative process—the manifestation of creative freedom entails two main components: the composition of the depicted content and its realization.[237] In relation to photography, these two components can be described accordingly: during the first component, we can imagine the photographer envisioning compositions of a future, to-be-realised image; during the second one, the process entails the expression of the devised composition in a manner perceivable by senses (in this case the photographic product).

5.4 The Concept of Schöpfungshöhe, Gestaltungshöhe, or Werkhöhe

'Schöpfungshöhe' (*creativity doctrine*) describes the concept of setting up a threshold of originality for copyrightability.[238] Adopted in 1958 and applied in the German

---

[234] Schulze, G. In: Geschützte Werke. Thomas Dreier & Gernot Schulze, *Urheberrechtsgesetz: Verwertungsgesellschaftengesetz, Kunsturhebergesetz: Kommentar* (C.H. Beck, 6th ed. 2018), p. 93.

[235] Axel Nordemann. 'Das Werk'. In: Axel Nordemann et al., *Urheberrecht: Kommentar zum Urheberrechtsgesetz, Verlagsgesetz, Urheberrechtswahrnehmungsgesetz* (W. Kohlhammer, 11th ed. 2014), p. 143.

[236] Gernot Schulze, 'Geschützte Werke'. In: Thomas Dreier & Gernot Schulze, *Urheberrechtsgesetz: Verwertungsgesellschaftengesetz, Kunsturhebergesetz: Kommentar* (C.H. Beck, 6th ed. 2018), p. 93.

[237] Hartwig Ahlberg, 'Geschützte Werke'. In: Philipp Möhring et al. (eds.), *Urheberrecht: UrhG, KUG, UrhWahrnG, VerlG; Kommentar* (C.H. Beck, 3rd ed. 2014), p. 65.

[238] Lionel Bently & Brad Sherman, *Intellectual Property Law* (Oxford University Press, 4th ed. 2014), p. 99.

copyright framework, *Schöpfungshöhe* might seem rather recent.[239] Originally, the concept of *Schöpfungshöhe* was created for applied arts, where a certain, usually higher, level of creativity was expected in a work belonging to the genre.[240] Nonetheless, it does not matter if the term used is *'Schöpfungshöhe'*, *'Gestaltungshöhe'*, or *'Werkhöhe'*, the meaning remains identical: a threshold that represents the lower limit for a work's eligibility for copyright. The German copyright framework thus does not traditionally employ the term *originality*, but typically replaces it with the three aforementioned terms, while keeping the function of the terms the same.

It is similarly possible to closely connect the requirement of individuality and the three terms. Individuality itself must be evident or visible in a product to a certain minimum extent.[241] Whenever there is room for creativity in a product, regardless of how minimal, the question arises of whether it is sufficient for copyright protection. Performing an assessment helps answer whether or not the necessary prescribed level of creativity inheres in a product and thus merits protection.[242] Uniqueness or the difference from what is already known are among the most relevant assessment criteria to separate copyrightable products from common products.[243]

In practice, the sole purpose of the existence and assessment of the level of creativity is to prove and demonstrate the existence of the individuality in the assessed product.[244] The level of creativity is therefore used to quantitatively calculate the potential presence of individuality, as *Nordemann* quoted *Schricker* and *Loewenheim*.[245] The individuality requirement therefore does not serve as the criterion for evaluation of artistic value, of the author, or the overall quality of the work itself, as *Heitland* quoted *Schricker* and *Loewenheim*.[246] It is the intellectual and creative impression of the assessed design that is the decisive criterion; the level of creativity can be seen as an auxiliary means of proving the existence of a certain minimum degree or extent of individuality in a potentially protected work.

---

239 Paul Goldstein & Marketa Trimble, *International Intellectual Property Law: Cases and Materials* (Foundation Press, 5th ed. 2019), p. 220.

240 John A. L. Sterling, *World Copyright Law: Protection of Authors' Works, Performances, Phonograms, Films, Video, Broadcasts, and Published Editions in National, International, and Regional Law* (Sweet & Maxwell, 3rd ed. 2008), p. 345.

241 Axel Nordemann. 'Das Werk'. In: Axel Nordemann et al., *Urheberrecht: Kommentar zum Urheberrechtsgesetz, Verlagsgesetz, Urheberrechtswahrnehmungsgesetz* (W. Kohlhammer, 11th ed. 2014), p. 140.

242 Marcel Bisges, *Die Kleine Münze im Urheberrecht: Analyse des ökonomischen Aspekts des Werkbegriffs* (Nomos 2014), p. 31.

243 Marcel Bisges, *Die Kleine Münze im Urheberrecht: Analyse des ökonomischen Aspekts des Werkbegriffs* (Nomos 2014), p. 32.

244 Artur-Axel Wandtke, Winfried Bullinger & Michael Bohne, *Praxiskommentar Urheberrecht: UrhG, UrhDaG, VGG, InsO, UKlaG, KUG, EVtr, InfoSoc-RL, Portabilitäts-VO* (C.H. Beck, 6th ed. 2022), p. 55.

245 Axel Nordemann, *Die künstlerische Fotografie als urheberrechtlich geschütztes Werk* (Nomos 1992), p. 109.

246 Horst Heitland, *Der Schutz der Fotografie im Urheberrecht Deutschlands, Frankreichs und der Vereinigten Staaten von Amerika* (C.H. Beck 1995), p. 47.

If the level of creativity is used to determine the degree of uniqueness and overall intellectual and creative impression, it is necessary to conduct a comprehensive comparison of all previous designs in the corresponding area.[247] This process is identical to that of assessing individuality. The purpose of conducting such a comparison is to determine whether the product possesses features distinguishable from previously known and available types of designs. If the answer to the question is no, the product cannot be considered eligible for copyright protection due to it being common or average. In such cases, the said product could be considered for a protection under design law, for example.[248]

Here again, same as with individuality, no universal or blanket approach to assessing the level of creativity exists. This is due to actual differences between various types of products which can bear evidence of creativity and the extent to which these allow for the actual development and presence of individual creativity as such.[249] Without the existence of a *creativity height* concept and a corresponding precise indicator of creativity, it becomes necessary to resort to case-by-case assessment. German jurisprudence follows this and applies variously strict standards depending on the type of the product and its intended use.[250]

For photographic products, the core of the creativity height assessment lies in a quantitative determination of individuality within the photographic product itself by separating the protected and unprotected intellectual achievements of the author during the production process.[251] Therefore, a photographic product can be granted copyright protection only if the photographic product itself allows individual attributes to be developed and at the same time the author took advantage of the freedom to shape the photographic product itself through their choices.

The level of creativity therefore serves as a convenient tool for excluding products not eligible for copyright protection due to their lack of individuality. Such products can be defined as being *simple* or *common*. This may be caused either by the nature or characteristics of the product itself, which do not allow for individuality to form at all, or due to the omission of a conscious activity by the author during the production process of the product itself. Turning to *photographic products* again, if the appropriate level of creativity is lacking or absent altogether, it cannot

---

[247] Fedor Seifert & Thomas Wirth. 'Das Werk'. In: Jan Eichelberger, Thomas Wirth, & Fedor Seifert (eds.), *UrhG Urheberrechtsgesetz: UrhG, UrhDaG, VGG : Handkommentar* (Nomos, 4. ed. 2022), p. 67.

[248] Koray Güven, Eliminating *'Aesthetics'* from Copyright Law: The Aftermath of Cofemel, 71 *GRUR Int.* 213 (2022), p. 213.

[249] Horst Heitland, *Der Schutz der Fotografie im Urheberrecht Deutschlands, Frankreichs und der Vereinigten Staaten von Amerika* (C.H. Beck 1995), p. 47.

[250] Marcel Bisges, Der europäische Werkbegriff und sein Einfluss auf die deutsche Urheberrechtsentwicklung. *ZUM.* 2015, p. 357.

[251] Axel Nordemann. 'Das Werk'. In: Axel Nordemann et al., *Urheberrecht: Kommentar zum Urheberrechtsgesetz, Verlagsgesetz, Urheberrechtswahrnehmungsgesetz* (W. Kohlhammer, 11th ed. 2014), p. 141.

be considered a photographic *work*.[252] In such cases, the object or an event is simply *photographed* or *taken picture of*.[253]

However, here too, clearly and comprehensively identifying the point which determines the shift of the product from the realm of *common* to the realm of *individual* through its level of creativity, is impossible.[254] It is also worth mentioning that the required level of creativity is not uniform and varies from product to product, or work to work, depending on the type.[255] Therefore, any assessment must still be done on a case-by-case basis, with an emphasis on the type of the product in question and other related circumstances; no uniform and commonly accepted level of creativity currently exists.

5.5 The Concept of Kleine Münze—Small Coin

After creating a creativity threshold to separate products eligible for copyright protection from products of applied arts that are covered by design law, the German copyright framework included another concept, known as *kleine Münze* or *small coin*. Doing so ensured that products not meeting the aforementioned higher creativity threshold were still eligible for copyright protection. In the broadest of terms, the concept of *kleine Münze* includes all products at the lower end of copyright protection due to their very low level of individuality, as *Bisges* quoted *Ahlberg*.[256]

When an assessment is made regarding the type of protection for a product, the issue does not lie in defining what *kleine Münze* is, but rather in whether the product meets the requirements prescribed in legislation for personal intellectual creation.[257] This means always beginning with an assessment of the product for signs of personal intellectual creation. If the product does not contain such signs, it does not meet the criteria for copyright protection, and therefore is ineligible also for consideration as *kleine Münze*. Nonetheless, German courts have traditionally been willing to provide copyright protection in accordance with the *kleine Münze* concept to a relatively large number of works containing an extremely low degree of individuality.[258]

[252] BGH, Ib ZR 77/65, 4. Nov. 1966, 'Skai-cubana'. *GRUR* 1967, 315.

[253] Hartwig Ahlberg, 'Geschützte Werke'. In: Philipp Möhring et al. (eds.), *Urheberrecht: UrhG, KUG, UrhWahrnG, VerlG; Kommentar* (C.H. Beck, 3rd ed. 2014), p. 57.

[254] Marcel Bisges, *Die Kleine Münze im Urheberrecht: Analyse des ökonomischen Aspekts des Werkbegriffs* (Nomos 2014), p. 32.

[255] Artur-Axel Wandtke, Winfried Bullinger & Michael Bohne, *Praxiskommentar Urheberrecht: UrhG, UrhDaG, VGG, InsO, UKlaG, KUG, EVtr, InfoSoc-RL, Portabilitäts-VO* (C.H. Beck, 6th ed. 2022), p. 55.

[256] Marcel Bisges, *Die Kleine Münze im Urheberrecht: Analyse des ökonomischen Aspekts des Werkbegriffs* (Nomos 2014), p. 19.

[257] Gernot Schulze, 'Geschützte Werke'. In: Thomas Dreier & Gernot Schulze, *Urheberrechtsgesetz: Verwertungsgesellschaftengesetz, Kunsturhebergesetz: Kommentar* (C.H. Beck, 6th ed. 2018), p. 83.

[258] Haimo Schack, *Urheber- und Urhebervertragsrecht* (Mohr Siebeck, 10th ed. 2021), p. 162.

This approach has naturally resulted in an increase in the number of copyrightable, most often marginal, products. The *kleine Münze* subject-matter presents a counterpart to works with a very high level of individuality, but it nonetheless still legally remains under the auspices of copyright protection.[259] We can conceive them as two ends of a copyright spectrum. For the German copyright framework, it is therefore irrelevant whether a product is labelled as belonging on either end of this copyright spectrum, since it is considered to be eligible for copyright protection in any case.

The role of the *kleine Münze* concept is to create a conceptual border that creates a smooth transition between culturally significant and truly individual artistic works, and the massive number of less significant, minimally but sufficiently individual works.[260] However, the border figuratively dividing personal, *fully* intellectual creations and works of *kleine Münze* is only described visually and of no apparent significance.[261]

5.6 The Historical Development of Protection of Photographic Products in the German Copyright Framework

Throughout the 19th century, the level of explicit legal protection for photographic products varied amongst the individual German states to a significant extent. This was caused by inconsistent understandings of their status among traditional works of art, especially the process of their production and involvement of their respective author. Positive and welcoming opinions regarding the novel nature of the production process of photographic products were mixed with those that emphasized the limited possibilities and constraints of photography as opposed to traditional creative art.[262]

In the German state of Prussia, the willingness to provide protection to photographic products was equal to zero. The protection provision was governed by an act with the title of *das Königlich Preußischen Gesetzes vom 11. Juni 1837 zum Schutze des Eigenthums an Werken der Wissenschaft und Kunst gegen Nachdruck und Nachbildung*.[263] According to its wording, equal treatment with the most similar works

[259] Marcel Bisges, *Die Kleine Münze im Urheberrecht: Analyse des ökonomischen Aspekts des Werkbegriffs* (Nomos 2014), p. 19.

[260] Haimo Schack, *Urheber- und Urhebervertragsrecht* (Mohr Siebeck, 10th ed. 2021), p. 161.

[261] Gernot Schulze, 'Geschützte Werke'. In: Thomas Dreier & Gernot Schulze, *Urheberrechtsgesetz: Verwertungsgesellschaftengesetz, Kunsturhebergesetz: Kommentar* (C.H. Beck, 6th ed. 2018), p. 83.

[262] Horst Heitland, *Der Schutz der Fotografie im Urheberrecht Deutschlands, Frankreichs und der Vereinigten Staaten von Amerika* (C.H. Beck 1995), p. 5.

[263] In English: *'The Royal Prussian Law of 11 June 1837 for the Protection of Ownership of Works of Science and Art against Reprinting and Reproduction'*.

of art, illustrations,[264] was not possible. The justification for such refusal was that photography was seen as a mere craft, lacking any intellectual activity.[265] Therefore, photographic products could not be regarded as works of art.[266] The definition of a work of art according to Section 21 of the Prussian Act assumed the existence of an expression of an author's individual artistic idea, while a photographic product could only depict objects, as *Schiessel* quoted from the *Archiv für preußisches Strafrecht 1864*.[267] Some claimed that granting protection to photographic products would even violate the very nature of artistic authorship.[268] In spite of this, it was nonetheless recognized that a work of art identified as intellectual and artistic could be created through the photographic process; however, even after this recognition, the protection was still refused.[269] As a result of this treatment, photographic products were largely unprotected in Prussia.[270] This lack of willingness to provide photographic products with protection was also endorsed in a report by the *Artistic Expert Association* of 1855. Despite the fact that no photographer was amongst the members of this association, the content of its report described photography as a purely mechanical reproduction process and therefore not eligible for protection under Prussian law.[271]

In the German state of Saxony, photographic products were seen and treated differently. In Saxony, the protection provision was governed by the *Gesetz den Schutz der Rechte an literarischen Erzeugnissen und Werken der Kunst betreffend* dated 2 February 1844. Although the wording of this act did not explicitly include photographic products as a protectable subject-matter, the application of its provisions to photographic products in order to assure their protection was accepted. Photographic products were seen as having artistic character, and therefore were equal to other works of art and subject to copyright protection, as *Schiessel* quoted *Hoenisch*.[272] The only exceptions were photographic products of purely reproductive nature used for the reproduction of non-coloured graphic representations.[273]

264 Sec. 18 of Das Königliche Preußischen Gesetzes vom 11. Juni 1837 zum Schutze des Eigenthums an Werken der Wissenschaft und Kunst gegen Nachdruck und Nachbildung.

265 Axel Nordemann, *Die künstlerische Fotografie als urheberrechtlich geschütztes Werk* (Nomos 1992), p. 7.

266 Ilva Johanna Schiessel, *Reichweite und Rechtfertigung des einfachen Lichtbildschutzes gem. § 72 UrhG* (Nomos 2020), p. 25.

267 *Ibid.*

268 Stefan Ricke, *Entwicklung des rechtlichen Schutzes von Fotografien in Deutschland unter besonderer Berücksichtigung der preußischen Gesetzgebung* (Lit 1998), p. 38.

269 Börsenblatt für den deutschen Buchhandel und die ihm verwandten Geschäftszweige. 3. Jun. 1863, vol. 70, p. 1166.

270 Stefan Ricke, *Entwicklung des rechtlichen Schutzes von Fotografien in Deutschland unter besonderer Berücksichtigung der preußischen Gesetzgebung* (Lit 1998), p. 40.

271 Stefan Ricke, *Entwicklung des rechtlichen Schutzes von Fotografien in Deutschland unter besonderer Berücksichtigung der preußischen Gesetzgebung* (Lit 1998), p. 37.

272 Ilva Johanna Schiessel, *Reichweite und Rechtfertigung des einfachen Lichtbildschutzes gem. § 72 UrhG* (Nomos 2020), p. 26.

273 Stefan Ricke, *Entwicklung des rechtlichen Schutzes von Fotografien in Deutschland unter besonderer Berücksichtigung der preußischen Gesetzgebung* (Lit 1998), p. 41.

In the German state of Bavaria, the eligibility for copyright protection was governed by the *Gesetz zum Schutze der Urheberrechte an literarischen Erzeugnissen und Werken der Kunst*[274] of 1865. Article 28 of this law was the first in German history that expressly standardized the copyright protection of photographic products as works of art. At that time, the prevailing opinion in Bavaria was that photographic products could be regarded as a new form of art and therefore also of possible artistic origin, as *Schiessel* quoted *Vogel*.[275] This opinion was echoed by the Royal Bavarian Academy of Arts which, in its report on photography of 1865, stated that a photographer does indeed conduct artistic activities throughout the production process of a photographic product. These activities arise from their soul and include the conceptualization of the photographed object, along with selecting the right moment, a favourable position, and the right lighting to do so.[276] Here again, such eligibility for protection is not extended to photographic products of purely reproductive nature. However, the report itself caused quite a stir in the art community and its contents had to be restated to clarify that it did not designate photographic products themselves as works of art, but merely advocated for their protection as works of art.[277] Nonetheless, the Bavarian understanding and subsequent granting of corresponding protection against the copying of photographic products was considered very modern.[278] According to Section 12 of the said Act, photographic products were to enjoy protection for a duration of 30 years *post mortem auctoris*.[279] However, for a photographic product to enjoy the said term of protection, it had to possess an artistic character.

The first German-wide legislation explicitly mentioning the term *'Photographie'* and with it the provision of its official, legislatively codified protection, can be dated back to the year 1876, when the PG[280] was issued. At that time, the PG was to be applied uniformly throughout the whole German Empire.[281] The established terminology used in its wording in order to refer to the protected products of photography was *photographische Werk* (*photographic work*). With legislators bearing in mind the diversity of photographic craft, protection was to be granted not only to photographic works, but also to works produced by a process similar to photography.[282]

[274] In English: *'Act on the Protection of Copyright in Literary and Artistic Works'*.

[275] Ilva Johanna Schiessel, *Reichweite und Rechtfertigung des einfachen Lichtbildschutzes gem. § 72 UrhG* (Nomos 2020), p. 27.

[276] Stefan Ricke, *Entwicklung des rechtlichen Schutzes von Fotografien in Deutschland unter besonderer Berücksichtigung der preußischen Gesetzgebung* (Lit 1998), p. 44.

[277] Stefan Ricke, *Entwicklung des rechtlichen Schutzes von Fotografien in Deutschland unter besonderer Berücksichtigung der preußischen Gesetzgebung* (Lit 1998), p. 46.

[278] Axel Nordemann, *Die künstlerische Fotografie als urheberrechtlich geschütztes Werk* (Nomos 1992), p. 7.

[279] Sec. 12 of the Gesetz zum Schutze der Urheberrechte an literarischen Erzeugnissen und Werken der Kunst vom 28. Juni 1865.

[280] In English, *'Law concerning the Protection of Photographs against Unauthorized Reproduction'*.

[281] Axel Nordemann, *Die künstlerische Fotografie als urheberrechtlich geschütztes Werk* (Nomos 1992), p. 8.

[282] Artur-Axel Wandtke, Winfried Bullinger & Michael Bohne, *Praxiskommentar Urheberrecht: UrhG, UrhDaG, VGG, InsO, UKlaG, KUG, EVtr, InfoSoc-RL, Portabilitäts-VO* (C.H. Beck, 6th ed. 2022), p. 54.

Therefore, all photographic products were to be protected, regardless of their artistic or non-artistic character.[283] Using today's terminology, all photographic products were eligible for copyright protection, whether original or not.[284] The term of protection provided in its Section 6 was in a duration of five years and could be calculated in two ways, depending on the publication date of the photographic product. The first option was to calculate the five-year term from the end of the calendar year in which the reproduction of the photographic product was originally published.[285] Alternatively, if no reproductions were officially published, the calculation of the term would start at the end of the calendar year in which the negative of the photographic product was originally produced.[286] The peculiarity of the protection granted was in the fact that only the technical performance of the author carried out through the production process of the photographic product was to be recognized as protectable, whereas the protection of the artistic, personal intellectual, and creative components of the photographic product were still considered to be unprotectable.[287] The idea of granting protection to photographic products as works of art therefore still faced general rejection.[288]

The second piece of suprastate legislation applied exclusively and uniformly within the German Empire relevant to the protection of photographic products was the KUG,[289] which replaced the PG in 1907. The ongoing struggle to establish photographic products as works of fine art with sufficient artistic features materialized in the wording of the provisions of the KUG and the subsequent protection it offered.[290] Using slightly different terminology than the PG, (but with the identical meaning), the KUG only provided protection to *Werke der Photographie* (*works of photography*), a phrase with the identical meaning of *photographic works*.[291] The wording used in the PG and KUG, as well the lack of differentiation between the two types of photographic products could be viewed as conflicting.[292] Nonetheless, the consensus on the eligibility of photographic products for protection under the KUG was that it did not differentiate between types of photo-

283 Ilva Johanna Schiessel, *Reichweite und Rechtfertigung des einfachen Lichtbildschutzes gem. § 72 UrhG* (Nomos 2020), p. 28.

284 Yves Gaubiac. Brigitte Lindner & John N. Adams. 'Duration of Copyright'. In: Estelle Derclaye (ed.) *Research handbook on the future of EU copyright* (Edward Elgar Publishing 2009), p. 166.

285 Sec. 6 of the PG.

286 *Ibid.*

287 Ilva Johanna Schiessel, *Reichweite und Rechtfertigung des einfachen Lichtbildschutzes gem. § 72 UrhG* (Nomos 2020), p. 28.

288 Horst Heitland, *Der Schutz der Fotografie im Urheberrecht Deutschlands, Frankreichs und der Vereinigten Staaten von Amerika* (C.H. Beck 1995), p. 15.

289 In English: *'German Artistic Copyright Act'*.

290 Ilva Johanna Schiessel, *Reichweite und Rechtfertigung des einfachen Lichtbildschutzes gem. § 72 UrhG* (Nomos 2020), p. 29.

291 Sec. 3 of the KUG.

292 Axel Nordemann, 'Schutz der Lichtbilder'. In: Axel Nordemann et al., *Urheberrecht: Kommentar zum Urheberrechtsgesetz, Verlagsgesetz, Urheberrechtswahrnehmungsgesetz* (W. Kohlhammer, 11th ed. 2014), p. 1481.

graphic products or their character. Therefore, the product's result from individual creative activity or its having an artistic purpose were not criteria to be assessed for copyrightability.[293] Here too, in today's terms, both original and non-original photographic products were eligible for copyright protection.[294] Moreover, the KUG abolished *formalities* previously accepted as prerequisites for copyrightability.[295] Such prerequisites can be referred to as formalities, upon the completion of which the copyright protection depended.[296] Prior to the KUG, each published photographic product had to be accompanied by a written statement, including information about the photographer or publisher, the name of the company, its address, and the date of production.[297]

Also identical to the PG, the KUG continued to protect works produced by a *process* similar to photography.[298] Section 26 of the KUG granted a general term of protection of 10 years after publication to photographic products.[299] In the case of non-published photographic products, Section 29 of the KUG again provided protection of 10 years; however, the calculation of this started after the end of the calendar year in which the author of the particular photographic product died.[300] The existence of this relatively limited ten-year term of protection (which was shorter than those of other works of fine art that enjoyed protection in accordance to the KUG), was caused by a specific feature of the protection scheme introduced at that time[301]: the absence of the lower threshold for protection requirement, which meant that all photographic products were to be protected without any distinction regarding their character whatsoever. The shorter term of protection was to compensate for such wide, indeed nearly unlimited, eligibility of photographic products for copyright protection according to the KUG, as opposed to other works of fine art.

The terms of protection applicable to photographic products as well as other works of fine art were both extended to 25 years after an amendment of the KUG, which took place in 1940, but the overall protection scheme introduced by the KUG in 1907 was not fundamentally affected by this amendment. The reason for extending equal protection to all types of photographic products was of a purely practical

293 Axel Nordemann, *Die künstlerische Fotografie als urheberrechtlich geschütztes Werk* (Nomos 1992), p. 8.

294 Yves Gaubiac, Brigitte Lindner & John N. Adams. 'Duration of Copyright'. In: Estelle Derclaye (ed.) *Research handbook on the future of EU copyright* (Edward Elgar Publishing 2009), p. 166.

295 Thomas Platena, *Das Lichtbild im Urheberrecht: Gesetzliche Regelung und Technische Weiterentwicklung* (Peter Lang 1998), p. 44.

296 Stef van Gompel & Stef Johan van Gompel, *Formalities in Copyright Law: An Analysis of Their History, Rationales and Possible Future* (Wolters Kluwer 2011), p. 83.

297 Sec. 5 of the PG.

298 Sec. 3 of the KUG.

299 Sec. 26 of the KUG.

300 Sec. 29 of the KUG.

301 Ilva Johanna Schiessel, *Reichweite und Rechtfertigung des einfachen Lichtbildschutzes gem. § 72 UrhG* (Nomos 2020), p. 29.

nature—differentiating between what ultimately became *photographic works* and *photographs* had proven to be highly problematic in practice.[302] At the same time the KUG was being adopted, the advisory commission also stated that any attempt to distinguish between these types of photographic products would prove to be difficult in practice.[303] Moreover, the gradual strengthening of photography's position as an artistic medium within society further contributed to the extension of the term of protection.[304]

5.7 The Reform of 1965

The third, currently still effective piece of German legislation concerning photographic products came into force in January 1966.[305] The UrhG effectively replaced the KUG in its entirety, overriding the KUG's applicability throughout the whole German copyright framework. The UrhG also introduced several novelties related to photographic products and their protection. Its adoption was, to some extent, caused by the criticism concerning the undifferentiated eligibility of photographic products for copyright protection, especially in light of the constant expansion, availability, and accessibility of photographic equipment and its subsequent use by the general public.[306]

Enactment of the UrhG represented the first differentiation between photographic products adopted in German legislation.[307] The wording of the UrhG presented a new classification of protected works—a list, part of which included *Lichtbildwerke* (*photographic works* or *light picture works*), as well as works created similarly to photographic works.[308] *Lichtbildwerke* can be seen as an umbrella term for the previously used terms of *photographische Werk* and *Werke der Photographie*. Section 72 of the UrhG introduced another new expression—*Lichtbilder* (*light pictures*).[309] This notion encompassed photographic products, referred to as (simple) photographs, without the qualities of, or not reaching to the standards of *Lichtbildwerke*, (photographic works). By differentiating between *Lichtbildwerke* (*photographic works*)

302 *Entwurf eines Vierten Gesetzes zur Änderung des Urheberrechtsgesetzes. Deutscher Bundestag – 13. Wahlperiode. Drucksache 13/781* (1. Oct. 2024), https://dserver.bundestag.de/btd/13/007/1300781.pdf.

303 Report of the X. commission on the draft law on copyright in works of visual arts and photography – No. 30 of the printed matter. Reichstagprotokolle, 1905/06,11, Anlage Nr. 448.

304 Ilva Johanna Schiessel, *Reichweite und Rechtfertigung des einfachen Lichtbildschutzes gem. § 72 UrhG* (Nomos 2020), p. 29.

305 In English: *'Act on Copyright and Related Rights'*.

306 Ilva Johanna Schiessel, *Reichweite und Rechtfertigung des einfachen Lichtbildschutzes gem. § 72 UrhG* (Nomos 2020), p. 30.

307 Horst Heitland, *Der Schutz der Fotografie im Urheberrecht Deutschlands, Frankreichs und der Vereinigten Staaten von Amerika* (C.H. Beck 1995), p. 18.

308 Sec. 2 of the UrhG.

309 Sec. 72 of the UrhG.

and *Lichtbilder* (*photographs*), the legislation was able to separate or distinguish between photographic products. Therefore, since the beginning of 1966 onwards, the legal terminology used in connection with products of photographic origin in Germany is *Lichtbildwerke* (*photographic works*) and *Lichtbilder* (*photographs*).

The concept of a *photographic work* was to recognize the creative achievement contained therein,[310] while the concept of a *photograph* only recognized the purely technical achievement contained therein.[311] This distinction between the two types of photographic products did not make any apparent sense in practice, as provisions applicable to photographic works were to be applied to photographs *mutatis mutandis*, according to Section 72 of the UrhG.[312] The protection duration of both types of photographic products previously enacted by the amendment to the KUG in 1940 remained the same at 25 years. Since the term of protection was identical for both types of photographic products, and hence carried the same legal consequences and effects, the distinction was of a purely theoretical significance.

In other words, regardless of whether a photographic product was labelled as a *photographic work* or a *photograph* within the meaning of the UrhG, both would receive the same term of protection of 25 years from the date of its publication or production.[313] Nonetheless, by introducing this division, the German legislation admitted that products of the photographic craft, namely photographic works, could be eligible for the same type of protection as works of fine art, and other works falling under Section 2 of the UrhG, although for a shorter period of time.[314]

The predictable practical issues arising from clearly differentiating between the two types of photographic products (including in the different lengths of the term of protection) helped the German legislation rationalize its avoidance of the issue.[315] Critics predicted that assessing photographic products with the aim of classifying them as either photographic works or photographs would pose extraordinary[316] or even insurmountable[317] difficulties in practice. The shorter term

310 Ilva Johanna Schiessel, *Reichweite und Rechtfertigung des einfachen Lichtbildschutzes gem. § 72 UrhG* (Nomos 2020), p. 31.

311 *Entwurf eines Vierten Gesetzes zur Änderung des Urheberrechtsgesetzes. Deutscher Bundestag – 13. Wahlperiode. Drucksache 13/781* (1. Oct. 2024), https://dserver.bundestag.de/btd/13/007/1300781.pdf.

312 Gunda Dreyer et al., *Urheberrecht: Urheberrechtsgesetz, Verwertungsgesellschaftengesetz, Kunsturhebergesetz* (C. F. Müller, 4th ed. 2018), p. 1335.

313 Axel Nordemann, *Die künstlerische Fotografie als urheberrechtlich geschütztes Werk* (Nomos 1992), p. 11.

314 Philine Pohlhausen, *Das Original in der Fotografie im Lichte des Urheberrechts* (Nomos 2021), p. 194.

315 *Entwurf eines Vierten Gesetzes zur Änderung des Urheberrechtsgesetzes. Deutscher Bundestag – 13. Wahlperiode. Drucksache 13/781* (1. Oct. 2024), https://dserver.bundestag.de/btd/13/007/1300781.pdf.

316 *Entwurf eines Vierten Gesetzes zur Änderung des Urheberrechtsgesetzes. Deutscher Bundestag – 13. Wahlperiode. Drucksache 13/781* (1. Oct. 2024), https://dserver.bundestag.de/btd/13/007/1300781.pdf.

317 *Ibid.*

of protection, as opposed to those of other (more traditional) works of art became another target of widespread criticism in the years to come, as *Heitland* quoted *Gerstenberg*.[318]

Nonetheless, the German legislator presupposed that only a small number of photographic products would actually meet the requirements prescribed for works, and by doing so, become eligible for copyright protection as photographic works.[319] Clearly, the considerations by the German legislator suggest the requirements to classify photographic products as photographic works would be expected to be significantly higher than those for photographs, as *Overbeck* quoted *Schricker* and *Loewenheim*.[320] Also, if this differentiation were not introduced, one could be under the impression that no photographic products of creative nature existed.[321] In terms of photographic products, the reform introduced by the UrhG can therefore be viewed more of an dogmatic than a practical nature.[322]

5.8 The Reform of 1985

Prior to the amendment of the UrhG introduced on 1 July 1985, both photographic works and photographs were completely equal in the eyes of the law.[323] But given the numerous concerns raised regarding the de facto unequal treatment of photographic works vis-à-vis photographs, the German legislator drafted an amendment adjusting the legal status quo.[324] It was therefore only after this amendment of the UrhG that this seemingly theoretical dual protection system became unambiguous in practice. Since attitudes towards photography among the general public as well as among artists and publishers had changed, with a large consensus recognizing photography and its products as works of art, the continuing less favourable treatment of photographic works under the UrhG was becoming

318 Horst Heitland, *Der Schutz der Fotografie im Urheberrecht Deutschlands, Frankreichs und der Vereinigten Staaten von Amerika* (C.H. Beck 1995), p. 19.

319 *Entwurf eines Vierten Gesetzes zur Änderung des Urheberrechtsgesetzes. Deutscher Bundestag – 13. Wahlperiode. Drucksache 13/781* (1. Oct. 2024), https://dserver.bundestag.de/btd/13/007/1300781.pdf.

320 Melanie Overbeck, Der Lichtbildschutz gem. § 72 UrhG im Lichte der Digitalfotografie (Lit 2018), p. 105.

321 *Entwurf eines Vierten Gesetzes zur Änderung des Urheberrechtsgesetzes. Deutscher Bundestag – 13. Wahlperiode. Drucksache 13/781* (1. Oct. 2024), https://dserver.bundestag.de/btd/13/007/1300781.pdf.

322 Axel Nordemann, *Die künstlerische Fotografie als urheberrechtlich geschütztes Werk* (Nomos 1992), p. 11.

323 Wilhelm Nordemann et al., *Urheberrecht: Kommentar zum Urheberrechtsgesetz und zum Urheberrechtswahrnehmungsgesetz: Mit den Texten der Urheberrechtsgesetze der DDR, Österreichs und der Schweiz* (Kohlhammer, 7th ed. 1988), p. 72.

324 Wilhelm Nordemann et al., *Urheberrecht: Kommentar zum Urheberrechtsgesetz und zum Urheberrechtswahrnehmungsgesetz: Mit den Texten der Urheberrechtsgesetze der DDR, Österreichs und der Schweiz* (Kohlhammer, 7th ed. 1988), p. 323.

increasingly untenable.[325] The position of photographic works within the German copyright framework was seen as disadvantageous compared to other works of art as well as to photographs, based on the fact that photography had established itself as an artistic medium.[326]

The 1985 amendment created a subclassification of what had previously been simply *photographs*. Section 72 divided photographs into *Lichtbilder, die Dokumente der Zeitgeschichte sind* (photographs documenting contemporary history) and *anderen Lichtbilder* (other photographs). The terms of protection to be granted were to be 50 years for the former, and 25 years for the latter. Both terms of protection were to be calculated from the date of original publication or the date of their production, if they had not been published. This officially specified photographs from the joint protection with photographic works, and a separate form of legal protection by a related right was created for this specifically reclassified type of photographic products.

Explicitly recognizing *'photographs documenting contemporary history'* by excluding them from *photographs* as well as granting them a longer term of protection was justified by arguing that the image and information such photographs often bear play a significant role in society. The idea was that a long period of time after the actual documentation of the object or event would have to pass before such photographs could provide a benefit to society.[327] However, the UrhG did not specify what *photographs documenting contemporary history* meant.[328]

The protection period of *Lichtbildwerke* (photographic works) was extended to 70 years by Section 64 of the UrhG. Moreover, the calculation of this new term of protection started upon the death of the author—the photographer. By doing so, the German legislator finally made photographic works equal to other works of art within the meaning of Section 2 of the UrhG, including by granting a corresponding term of protection. In respect to this, the reform of 1985 also ended the equal status of all photographic products under the UrhG.[329]

The differentiation between the various types of photographic products certainly brought about concerns about properly distinguishing between the two types, in light of the effect this differentiation had in practice by different lengths of protection periods. Nonetheless, the previously emphasized concerns regarding this differentiation came to be seen as not so significant now.[330]

---

325 Ilva Johanna Schiessel, *Reichweite und Rechtfertigung des einfachen Lichtbildschutzes gem. § 72 UrhG* (Nomos 2020), p. 33.

326 Axel Nordemann, *Die künstlerische Fotografie als urheberrechtlich geschütztes Werk* (Nomos 1992), p. 18.

327 *Entwurf eines Gesetzes zur Änderung von Vorschriften auf dem Gebiet des Urheberrechts Drucksache 10/837, Drucksache 10/3360* (1. Nov. 2024), https://dserver.bundestag.de/btd/10/033/1003360.pdf.

328 Horst Heitland, *Der Schutz der Fotografie im Urheberrecht Deutschlands, Frankreichs und der Vereinigten Staaten von Amerika* (C.H. Beck 1995), p. 82.

329 Axel Nordemann, *Die künstlerische Fotografie als urheberrechtlich geschütztes Werk* (Nomos 1992), p. 13.

330 Horst Heitland, *Der Schutz der Fotografie im Urheberrecht Deutschlands, Frankreichs und der Vereinigten Staaten von Amerika* (C.H. Beck 1995), p. 19.

5.9 The Reform of 1995

The purpose of the third amendment of the UrhG, effective 1 July 1995, was the transposition of the Term Directive I, the aim of which was to fully harmonize the term of (copyright) protection of *photographic works*, while leaving the protection of *other photographs* within its meaning at the discretion of Member States.[331] As a result, the scope of the harmonization only affected photographic works within the meaning of Term Directive I.

The implementation of the Directive resulted in replacing the classification system separating *Lichtbilder, die Dokumente der Zeitgeschichte sind* (*photographs documenting contemporary history*) from *anderen Lichtbildern* (*other photographs*) with a single related right-type of protection applicable to all photographic products within the meaning of Section 72 of the UrhG. Without having to differentiate between what a photograph depicted, all *Lichtbildern* (*photographs*) were to be eligible for this related type of protection in a duration of 50 years. As with previous amendments, the German legislation justified the extended protection term on grounds that the growing economic value of *Lichtbildern* should be taken into account, rather than disregarded.[332]

The unification of the two types of photographic products under the joint term of *Lichtbild* (*photograph*) was also justified by the considerable legal uncertainty connected to the categorization presupposed by the UrhG.[333] The calculation of the unified term of protection was to have been made from the first publication of a photographic product, or if its first authorized communication to the public had taken place earlier, after such publication. If the photograph had never been lawfully communicated to the public or published within a period of 50 years, the protection period would be calculated starting from its production date.[334]

The amendment of 1 July 1995, laid down the final form of the currently effective division between the two types of photographic products; this has had clear legal consequences. The effect has been to create two different terms of protection, one for each type of these photographic products—*photographic works* and *photographs*. A crucial element of the shift from the equal legal treatment of photographic works and photographs to their reclassification is the corresponding shift of perception of photography and its products as an artistic medium.[335] In opposition to such

[331] Art. 6 of the Term Directive I.

[332] *Entwurf eines Vierten Gesetzes zur Änderung des Urheberrechtsgesetzes. Deutscher Bundestag – 13. Wahlperiode. Drucksache 13/781* (1. Oct. 2024), https://dserver.bundestag.de/btd/13/007/1300781.pdf; Ilva Johanna Schiessel, *Reichweite und Rechtfertigung des einfachen Lichtbildschutzes gem. § 72 UrhG* (Nomos 2020), p. 36.

[333] Ilva Johanna Schiessel, *Reichweite und Rechtfertigung des einfachen Lichtbildschutzes gem. § 72 UrhG* (Nomos 2020), p. 35.

[334] Sec. 72 (3) of the UrhG.

[335] Wilhelm Nordemann et al., *Urheberrecht: Kommentar zum Urheberrechtsgesetz und zum Urheberrechtswahrnehmungsgesetz: Mit den Texten der Urheberrechtsgesetze der DDR, Österreichs und der Schweiz* (Kohlhammer, 7th ed. 1988), p. 323.

division in term of protection, stood those who still saw *extraordinary difficulties* in distinguishing between these two types of photographic products.[336]

In practice, the division between photographic works and photographs might seem irrelevant, since both types are nonetheless protected.[337] However, before the corresponding term of protection expires, the question regarding the type of protection the photographic product is entitled to should nonetheless be resolved.[338] Amongst the various reasons for distinguishing between the two photographic products concerns legal certainty, and the corresponding possible economic interests and claims of any rightsholders. Nevertheless, distinguishing between these two types in individual cases might still prove difficult, as *Pohlhausen* quoted *Fleer*.[339] According to some, this state of affairs itself is capable of creating substantial legal uncertainty.[340]

Within this context, the steps that German legislator has taken to create this differentiation can also be seen as an effort to differentiate between creative and non-creative photographic products.[341] In cases of photographs, for example, the photographer is required to perform in such a perfect and technical manner that making any artistic statement on their own is simply ruled out.[342] In contrast, any photographic product which goes, in terms of its features, beyond pure technical imagery would be considered a photographic work.[343]

Providing protection even to photographic products that are intended to reproduce objects as realistically as possible is justified by the fact that even these photographic products require certain financial and technical effort incurred, for example, by the author.[344] Similarly to common-law copyright frameworks, such an approach seems to have a utilitarian nature, given that these photographs might have substantial economic implications. To provide one final concluding example regarding photographs, only products of photography of pure technical nature can be considered photographs—for example a photographic product, which any photographer with the same abilities would be able to reproduce at any given time.[345]

---

336 *Entwurf eines Vierten Gesetzes zur Änderung des Urheberrechtsgesetzes. Deutscher Bundestag – 13. Wahlperiode. Drucksache 13/781* (1. Oct. 2024), https://dserver.bundestag.de/btd/13/007/1300781.pdf.

337 BGH, I ZR 55/97, 3. Nov. 1999, 'Werbefotos' *GRUR*. 2000, p. 317.

338 Schulze, G. Schutz der Lichtbilder. In: Thomas Dreier & Gernot Schulze, *Urheberrechtsgesetz: Verwertungsgesellschaftengesetz, Kunsturhebergesetz: Kommentar* (C.H. Beck, 6th ed. 2018), p. 1354.

339 Philine Pohlhausen, *Das Original in der Fotografie im Lichte des Urheberrechts* (Nomos 2021), p. 196.

340 Hartwig Ahlberg, 'Geschützte Werke'. In: Philipp Möhring et al. (eds.), *Urheberrecht: UrhG, KUG, UrhWahrnG, VerlG; Kommentar* (C.H. Beck, 3rd ed. 2014), p. 56.

341 Ilva Johanna Schiessel, *Reichweite und Rechtfertigung des einfachen Lichtbildschutzes gem. § 72 UrhG* (Nomos 2020), p. 63.

342 Haimo Schack, *Kunst und Recht: bildende Kunst, Architektur, Design und Fotografie im deutschen und internationalen Recht* (Mohr Siebeck, 3rd ed. 2017), p. 454.

343 OLG Nürnberg, 3 U 3760/00, 27. Mar. 2001, 'Dienstanweisung'. *GRUR-RR*, 2001, p. 225 ff.

344 Endress Wanckel, *Foto- Und Bildrecht* (C.H. Beck, 5th ed. 2017).

345 Axel Nordemann & Friedrich Nicolaus Heise, 'Urheberrechtlicher Schutz für Designleistungen in Deutschland und auf europäischer Ebene'. *ZUM* 128 (2001), p. 128.

As already mentioned above, the revocation of the classification system recognizing certain photographic products as *photographs documenting contemporary history* and thus eligible for a related type of legal protection was also one of the outcomes of the Reform of 1995. This was caused by the recognition that the overall impact of conscious intellectual and creative choices affecting and altering the character of a photographic product is limited by the completion of the said product itself.[346] In light of this, the established emphasis on the conscious intellectual and creative involvement of the author was manifested in the impossibility of attributing any subsequent events after the final production of a photographic product to an ex-post discovery of the absent individuality. Although this principle is more applicable to photographic works, due to the decisive attributes of *conscious intellectual and creative involvement*, it was nonetheless also applied to the said subsection of photographs. Therefore, in 1995, the German legislator articulated this principle by discarding the explicit recognition of *photographs documenting contemporary history*. The reason for their extended period of protection was that this type of photographic product usually only became valuable after events outside of the author's scope of influence occurred within the society—what had been mere *photographs* for the author became something special, but not as a result of intervention by the author. However, the Reform of 1995 put an end to this distinction.

5.10 Requirements of Protection of Photographic Products

The purpose of the corresponding type and term of protection is to reward the author for their performance throughout the production process of a photographic product. With a photographic work, copyright itself rewards the author's own intellectual performance, whereas with a photograph, a related right type of protection rewards the author for the performance of another kind.[347] Such performance of another kind can be labelled as purely personal, technical, economic, and/or organizational, while nevertheless lacking a creative character, as *Schiessel* quoted *Dreier*.[348]

Both the protection of photographic works and photographs (along with *works produced by processes similar to photography* and *products manufactured in a similar manner to photographs*), require a protectable object—the photographic product. If one claims or grants one of these two forms of legal protection, it must first be determined whether a protectable photographic product even exists, i.e., whether

[346] Ilva Johanna Schiessel, *Reichweite und Rechtfertigung des einfachen Lichtbildschutzes gem. § 72 UrhG* (Nomos 2020), p. 53.

[347] Gesetzesbegründung vom 23. 03. 1962, BTDrucks, IV/270, p. 33f.

[348] Ilva Johanna Schiessel, *Reichweite und Rechtfertigung des einfachen Lichtbildschutzes gem. § 72 UrhG* (Nomos 2020), p. 42.

the prescribed technical requirements for its existence were met.[349] As mentioned above, once this is the case, any decision must be based on an objective assessment, as opposed to the subjective opinions of the author. Copyrightability, for example, does not solely depend on the assertions of authors, but rather on the creative activities they undertook in connection with the product in question.[350]

In general, the requirement of protection in the German copyright framework in relation to photographic products, whether by copyright or a related right, is that the product must be created through the use of radiant energy, most often light rays, as *Schack* quoted *Platena*.[351] Therefore, any kind of a photographic process that includes image creation based on the use of radiant energy may lead to the production of a photographic product. This can subsequently become eligible for a corresponding type of legal protection.[352]

In sum, radiant energy is an essential component of a photographic product, without which the technical requirements for its existence cannot be fulfilled.[353] Therefore, any photographic product, whether it is a photographic work, photograph, or a product similar to either, must be produced by a photographic (or similar) process that uses radiant energy.[354]

5.11 Irrelevant Requirements for Protection of Photographic Products

What becomes of importance in this context is also the protection of *products produced by processes similar to photography* in accordance with Section 2 (1) of the UrhG as well as of products *manufactured in a similar manner to photographs* in accordance with Section 72 (1) of the UrhG. Because the law focuses on the photographic nature of the creation process, it can encompass products with a similar photographic nature. What matters is how the photographic product is produced, rather than how it is further reproduced.[355] Extending protection to all products produced or manufactured by similar processes or in a similar manner serves to cover all produc-

349 Ilva Johanna Schiessel, *Reichweite und Rechtfertigung des einfachen Lichtbildschutzes gem. § 72 UrhG* (Nomos 2020), p. 43.

350 Haimo Schack, *Urheber- und Urhebervertragsrecht* (Mohr Siebeck, 10th ed. 2021), p. 108.

351 Haimo Schack, *Kunst und Recht: bildende Kunst, Architektur, Design und Fotografie im deutschen und internationalen Recht* (Mohr Siebeck, 3rd ed. 2017), p. 452.

352 Artur-Axel Wandtke, Winfried Bullinger & Michael Bohne, *Praxiskommentar Urheberrecht: UrhG, UrhDaG, VGG, InsO, UKlaG, KUG, EVtr, InfoSoc-RL, Portabilitäts-VO* (C.H. Beck, 6th ed. 2022), p. 1425.

353 Horst Heitland, *Der Schutz der Fotografie im Urheberrecht Deutschlands, Frankreichs und der Vereinigten Staaten von Amerika* (C.H. Beck 1995), p. 23.

354 Axel Nordemann, *Die künstlerische Fotografie als urheberrechtlich geschütztes Werk* (Nomos 1992), p. 66.

355 BGH, I ZR 118/60, 27. Feb. 1962, 'AKI' *GRUR*. 1962, p. 470.

tion techniques resembling photography.[356] By doing so, any kind of product similar to that of photographic can be covered by the corresponding type of protection. Such an open approach towards the definitions also limits the need to respond to the emergence of every new photographic technique by amending the legislation.

Therefore, the test related to granting protection to photographic products under the German copyright framework consists of two parts, connected to the production process. The first question concerns the existence and role of a radiation source. The second question concerns the mental involvement and creative freedom of the author in the production process. Based on the cumulative answers to both questions, it becomes possible to differentiate between the two main types of photographic products—*photographic works* and *photographs*.

However, it is again important to highlight the fact that eligibility for the relevant type of protection arises regardless of the content depicted in a photographic product.[357] The content may even be of an unlawful or immoral nature.[358] In sum, the nature of the content depicted in a photographic product is irrelevant for its eligibility for the corresponding type of protection. What is crucial is not the content itself, but rather how the content is brought into the photographic product in question and what choices the author—the photographer—made to form and shape the image's appearance. In other words, none of the two types of protection arise for photographic products that directly depict selected objects or processes without any form of human involvement.[359]

Also, any questions related to the education, experience, age, or social status of the photographer are irrelevant. In the eyes of the German copyright framework, even an amateur photographer is perfectly capable of producing a photographic work, meaning a photographic product fully eligible for copyright.[360] Only the photographic product alone and what it emanates may come under any assessment for protection.[361] In this sense, it is also worth noting that the cause, purpose, and motive behind the creation of a photo and its design is irrelevant for the purposes of their classification and protectability.[362]

[356] Ilva Johanna Schiessel, *Reichweite und Rechtfertigung des einfachen Lichtbildschutzes gem. § 72 UrhG* (Nomos 2020), p. 45.

[357] Artur-Axel Wandtke, Winfried Bullinger & Michael Bohne, *Praxiskommentar Urheberrecht: UrhG, UrhDaG, VGG, InsO, UKlaG, KUG, EVtr, InfoSoc-RL, Portabilitäts-VO* (C.H. Beck, 6th ed. 2022), p. 1424.

[358] BGH, I ZR 282/97, 13 Apr. 2000, 'Mattscheibe' *GRUR* 2000, p. 705 ff.

[359] Artur-Axel Wandtke, Winfried Bullinger & Michael Bohne, *Praxiskommentar Urheberrecht: UrhG, UrhDaG, VGG, InsO, UKlaG, KUG, EVtr, InfoSoc-RL, Portabilitäts-VO* (C.H. Beck, 6th ed. 2022), p. 1424.

[360] Artur-Axel Wandtke, Winfried Bullinger & Michael Bohne, *Praxiskommentar Urheberrecht: UrhG, UrhDaG, VGG, InsO, UKlaG, KUG, EVtr, InfoSoc-RL, Portabilitäts-VO* (C.H. Beck, 6th ed. 2022), p. 79.

[361] Ilva Johanna Schiessel, *Reichweite und Rechtfertigung des einfachen Lichtbildschutzes gem. § 72 UrhG* (Nomos 2020), p. 53.

[362] Philine Pohlhausen, *Das Original in der Fotografie im Lichte des Urheberrechts* (Nomos 2021), p. 197.

5.12 Types of Photographic Products

The constant development of technology, photography or otherwise, allowed massive proliferation of photographic equipment to the wider public, which in turn opened up the possibilities of its use in unique and different ways. These new uses would not have to be artistic or creative. However, the increase in the number and type of photographic products raised questions about whether all photographic products should be protected equally, regardless of their character, and if not, what the distinguishing criteria should be and where these borders should be drawn.[363]

The currently effective wording of the UrhG officially recognizes four types of protectable photographic products: photographic works, works produced by processes similar to photography, photographs, and products manufactured in a similar manner to photographs. Using the terminology based on their visual nature, photographic works can be described as *designed*, while photographs *depict*.[364] In other words, photographic works are designed and through such design contain a statement, whereas photographs merely depict without further conveying any additional statement regarding what they depict.[365] This *designed* and *depicting* nature is also applicable to *works produced* or respectively *products manufactured*. The following sections are dedicated to an individual overview of each of these types.

5.13 Photographic Works—Lichtbildwerke

According to the UrhG, photographic works, or *Lichtbildwerke*, designate a photographic product eligible for copyright protection. In the German copyright framework, copyright is a valuable designation, as it can only be conferred upon the most prominent and valuable photographic products.[366] A photographic product itself must meet certain conditions and bear specific characteristics for it to be recognized as a work worthy of copyright protection—i.e., a photographic work. The exact conditions and characteristics will be elaborated on below.

According to the wording of Section 2 of the UrhG, a photographic work is defined as a photographic product constituting the author's personal intellectual creation. To classify a photographic product as a photographic work, it must contain a *personal intellectual creation* demonstrated by the author's activity embodied

[363] Ekkehard Gerstenberg, 'Fototechnik und Urheberrecht' In: Georg Herbst (ed.) *Festschrift für Rainer Klaka*. (J. Schweitzer Verlag 1987), p. 120.

[364] Ulrich Loewenheim et al., *Urheberrecht: UrhG, KUG, VGG: Kommentar* (C.H. Beck, 6th ed. 2020), p. 1559.

[365] Axel Nordemann, *Die künstlerische Fotografie als urheberrechtlich geschütztes Werk* (Nomos 1992), p. 106.

[366] Haimo Schack, *Kunst und Recht: bildende Kunst, Architektur, Design und Fotografie im deutschen und internationalen Recht* (Mohr Siebeck, 3rd ed. 2017), p. 6.

therein.[367] A crucial element of this definition is the creative leeway[368] or creative parameters[369] available to the author during the production process of the photographic work. This presence of a characteristic of a *personal intellectual creation within the photographic product itself* not only determines its copyrightability, but also at the same time determines the threshold under which a Section 72 related right reserved for *photographs* resides.[370] The concept of a *photographic work* under Section 2 of the UrhG therefore presupposes the conscious intellectual involvement of the author in the production process at the time of production of the said photographic work, particularly an awareness regarding the creative circumstances and opportunities the production process entails and its final outcome features.[371] If the intellectual involvement of the author is not invested in and manifested in the final photographic product, one cannot speak of a photographic work within the meaning of Section 2 of the UrhG. Therefore, the author must be fully aware of the fact that they are conducting their production activities with the purpose of producing a photographic work.

Even when it comes to photographic products, the requirement of individuality plays a major role as a tool for distinguishing between photographic works and photographs.[372] Only photographic products distinguishable through their individuality can be considered photographic works.[373] In other words, photographic works have a peculiar character.[374] Verbally analysing the concept of a *photographic work*, makes it clear that photographic works are simply photographs with a character of a *work*.[375] Apart from requirements prescribed for a photographic product, a photographic work must also meet the requirements prescribed for a work. If individuality is present in a photographic product, it expresses a statement based on

[367] Ilva Johanna Schiessel, *Reichweite und Rechtfertigung des einfachen Lichtbildschutzes gem. § 72 UrhG* (Nomos 2020), p. 53.

[368] Artur-Axel Wandtke, Winfried Bullinger & Michael Bohne. *Praxiskommentar Urheberrecht: UrhG, UrhDaG, VGG, InsO, UKlaG, KUG, EVtr, InfoSoc-RL, Portabilitäts-VO* (C.H. Beck, 6th ed. 2022), p. 77.

[369] Artur-Axel Wandtke, Winfried Bullinger & Michael Bohne. *Praxiskommentar Urheberrecht: UrhG, UrhDaG, VGG, InsO, UKlaG, KUG, EVtr, InfoSoc-RL, Portabilitäts-VO* (C.H. Beck, 6th ed. 2022), p. 78.

[370] Ilva Johanna Schiessel, *Reichweite und Rechtfertigung des einfachen Lichtbildschutzes gem. § 72 UrhG* (Nomos 2020), p. 46.

[371] Ilva Johanna Schiessel, *Reichweite und Rechtfertigung des einfachen Lichtbildschutzes gem. § 72 UrhG* (Nomos 2020), p. 58.

[372] Axel Nordemann, 'Das Werk'. In: Axel Nordemann et al., *Urheberrecht: Kommentar zum Urheberrechtsgesetz, Verlagsgesetz, Urheberrechtswahrnehmungsgesetz* (W. Kohlhammer, 11th ed. 2014), p. 190.

[373] Gernot Schulze, 'Geschützte Werke'. In: Thomas Dreier & Gernot Schulze. *Urheberrechtsgesetz: Verwertungsgesellschaftengesetz, Kunsturhebergesetz: Kommentar* (C.H. Beck, 6th ed. 2018), p. 143.

[374] BGH, Ib ZR 77/65, 4. Nov. 1966, 'Skai-cubana'. *GRUR*. 1967, 315.

[375] Thomas Platena, *Das Lichtbild im Urheberrecht: Gesetzliche Regelung und Technische Weiterentwicklung* (Peter Lang 1998), p. 243.

the product's design.[376] Such a statement can only be created through author's will to creatively design, thus making the author's will one of the constituents of individuality, as *Nordemann* quoted *Riedel* and *Schuhmann*.[377]

Without the author's will, especially their will to act and create, we cannot speak of a protectable photographic product to begin with.[378] The existence of a will of the author precludes all unprotectable photographic products, such as those created by chance or coincidence. However, as *Kai Vinck* has pointed out, if chance itself is wilfully employed as a creative design by the author, this very decision to allow chance constitutes an expression of individuality.[379] Here, the requirement of individuality will be fulfilled by the photographer's wilful adjustments in connection with the employment of chance, thus making its exploitation possible.[380] It is therefore the creative nature of the author's individuality displayed in a photographic work that serves as the main criterion distinguishing it from (mere) photographs.[381] In practice, however, the determination between photographic products produced by chance and wilfully would prove to be almost impossible if the photographer did not choose to disclose the true circumstances of their production.[382]

Having established the key role of manifested individuality in the potential design of a photographic product, I now turn to the role of its presence in a photographic product and the subsequent effects on such a product's protectability. According to the established judicial position, no special (i.e., high) degree of creative design is required.[383] Therefore, even photographic products having average or below-average designs will suffice and are eligible for copyright protection. However, even these designs must still be distinguishable.[384] This means that even a minimum effort related to designing the final appearance of a photographic product will result

376 Axel Nordemann, 'Das Werk'. In: Axel Nordemann et al., *Urheberrecht: Kommentar zum Urheberrechtsgesetz, Verlagsgesetz, Urheberrechtswahrnehmungsgesetz* (W. Kohlhammer, 11th ed. 2014), p. 191.

377 Axel Nordemann, *Die künstlerische Fotografie als urheberrechtlich geschütztes Werk* (Nomos 1992), p. 107.

378 Thomas Platena, *Das Lichtbild im Urheberrecht: Gesetzliche Regelung und Technische Weiterentwicklung* (Peter Lang 1998), p. 197.

379 Wilhelm Nordemann et al. *Urheberrecht: Kommentar zum Urheberrechtsgesetz und zum Urheberrechtswahrnehmungsgesetz: Mit den Texten der Urheberrechtsgesetze Österreichs und der Schweiz* (W. Kohlhammer, 9th ed. 1998), § 2 Rn. 12.

380 Melanie Overbeck, *Der Lichtbildschutz gem. § 72 UrhG im Lichte der Digitalfotografie* (Lit 2018), p. 52.

381 Philine Pohlhausen, *Das Original in der Fotografie im Lichte des Urheberrechts* (Nomos 2021), p. 198.

382 Ekkehard Gerstenberg, 'Fototechnik und Urheberrecht' In: Georg Herbst (ed.) *Festschrift für Rainer Klaka*. (J. Schweitzer Verlag 1987), p. 124.

383 BGH, I ZR 55/97, 3. Nov. 1999, 'Werbefotos' *GRUR*. 2000, p. 317.

384 Axel Nordemann, 'Das Werk'. In: Axel Nordemann et al., *Urheberrecht: Kommentar zum Urheberrechtsgesetz, Verlagsgesetz, Urheberrechtswahrnehmungsgesetz* (W. Kohlhammer, 11th ed. 2014), p. 192.

in its transformation into a photographic work. The photographic work must therefore be created specifically for a relevant shot and not taken mindlessly.[385]

What becomes important when assessing a photographic product's legal status, is whether it is capable of depicting reality only objectively or also subjectively, and therefore according to the photographer's personal preferences.[386] If such a subjective transformation were not possible, one could not speak of a photographic work. Such situations would include the absence of the author's creative will, without which a designed photographic work cannot be created.[387] Nonetheless, it is settled that the *reality* that photographic works depict is not simply photographed, but rather individually adjusted and accentuated through deliberate manipulation performed by the photographer.[388] The communication conducted through the photographic product by its author must go beyond what is depicted in it, if the photographic product is to be considered a photographic work.[389] The activities of the photographer that reveal the design inherent in a photographic work, include various deliberate choices related to adjustment and selection of composition, lighting, exposure time, retouching, etc., *Pohlhausen* quoted criteria summed up by *Fleer*.[390]

In contrast to the traditional understanding of the pure, objective duplication of reality, the depiction of reality described in a *work* must be seen as a reproduction of the photographer's subjective perception.[391] However, the correct perception and identification of the photographer's subjectively highlighted parts of reality in a photographic work always depends on the skills and experience of the audience perceiving the respective photographic product.[392] It is worth noting that the subjective perception can only be applied towards the design and form of reality, not to the actual existence of the reality itself.[393] Therefore, the photographer's individual view manifested in the product must be based on existing and verifiable subjects or objects.[394]

385 Gernot Schulze. 'Geschützte Werke'. In: Thomas Dreier & Gernot Schulze, *Urheberrechtsgesetz: Verwertungsgesellschaftengesetz, Kunsturhebergesetz: Kommentar* (C.H. Beck, 6th ed. 2018), p. 144.

386 Axel Nordemann, *Die künstlerische Fotografie als urheberrechtlich geschütztes Werk* (Nomos 1992), p. 90.

387 Axel Nordemann, *Die künstlerische Fotografie als urheberrechtlich geschütztes Werk* (Nomos 1992), p. 108.

388 Schweizerisches Bundesgericht, 4 C.117/2003, 5. Sep. 2003, 'Bob Marley-Foto'. *GRUR Int* 2004, p. 1044 ff.

389 Astrid Meckel, 'Lichtbilder'. In: Gunda Dreyer et al., *Urheberrecht: Urheberrechtsgesetz, Verwertungsgesellschaftengesetz, Kunsturhebergesetz* (C.F. Müller, 4th ed. 2018), p. 1338.

390 Philine Pohlhausen, *Das Original in der Fotografie im Lichte des Urheberrechts* (Nomos 2021), p. 196.

391 Melanie Overbeck, *Der Lichtbildschutz gem. § 72 UrhG im Lichte der Digitalfotografie* (Lit 2018), p. 43.

392 Thomas Hoeren, Urheberrechtliche Probleme des Dokumentarfilms. *GRUR.* 1992, p. 145.

393 Melanie Overbeck, *Der Lichtbildschutz gem. § 72 UrhG im Lichte der Digitalfotografie* (Lit 2018), p. 43.

394 Jan Franzen & Albrecht Götz von Olenhusen, 'Lichtbildwerke, Lichtbilder und Fotoimitate: Abhängige Bearbeitung oder freier Benutzung?' *UFITA* 435 (2007), p. 435.

According to *Nordemann*, the criteria that should qualify a photographic product as a photographic work can be divided into categories, such as pictorial statement, general image organization, viewpoint, light and lighting, colour and colour contrast, other contrasts, choice of recording time, experimental design means, other design resources, and the person of the author, as he summed up various criteria from German case law and experts.[395] It is through the creative choices that the author (photographer) makes with respect to these categories that allows them to individually (subjectively) alter the objective photographed reality and accentuate whatever component or components they find relevant or important to their artistic statement.[396]

5.14 Photographs—Lichtbilder

In the simplest of terms, photographs have been described as photographic works lacking the character of a work.[397] The content of the previous definition was later modified in such a way that the term *photograph* described *photographs without the character of a work*, thus omitting the reference to photographic works altogether.[398] Others have proposed the reverse, stating a photograph with the character of a work is therefore a photographic work, as *Platena* quoted *Hertin*.[399] This makes explicit that every photographic work is also a photograph, while also demonstrating superiority of photographic works in terms of design (which in turn entails eligibility for a longer term of copyright protection).

In any case, the lack of individuality is what demonstrates that it does not qualify as a photographic work. As a result, if a photographic work lacks the presence of individuality, it can be considered for categorization as a photograph within the meaning of Section 72 of the UrhG.[400] Nonetheless, a minimum level of personal intellectual achievement is still expected to be present in a photograph.[401] However, the expected presence of a *minimum* level serves as a tool to differentiate between

395 Axel Nordemann, *Die künstlerische Fotografie als urheberrechtlich geschütztes Werk* (Nomos 1992), p. 34.

396 Haimo Schack, *Kunst und Recht: bildende Kunst, Architektur, Design und Fotografie im deutschen und internationalen Recht* (Mohr Siebeck, 3rd ed. 2017), p. 451.

397 Wilhelm Nordemann et al., *Urheberrecht: Kommentar zum Urheberrechtsgesetz und zum Urheberrechtswahrnehmungsgesetz: Mit den Texten der Urheberrechtsgesetze der DDR, Österreichs und der Schweiz* (Kohlhammer, 7th ed. 1988), p. 324.

398 Wilhelm Nordemann et al. *Urheberrecht: Kommentar zum Urheberrechtsgesetz und zum Urheberrechtswahrnehmungsgesetz: Mit den texten der Urheberrechtsgesetze der Früheren DDR, Österreichs und der Schweiz* (W. Kohlhammer, 8th ed. 1994), p. 461.

399 Thomas Platena, *Das Lichtbild im Urheberrecht: Gesetzliche Regelung und Technische Weiterentwicklung* (Peter Lang 1998), p. 84.

400 Ilva Johanna Schiessel, *Reichweite und Rechtfertigung des einfachen Lichtbildschutzes gem. § 72 UrhG* (Nomos 2020), p. 52.

401 BGH, I ZR 55/97, 3. Nov. 1999, 'Werbefotos' *GRUR*. 2000, p. 317.

protected and unprotected photographic products.[402] The former includes photographic works and photographs, while the latter includes the outcomes of purely mechanical and automatic creation processes. Therefore, this *minimum* level of personal intellectual achievement will always be present in a photographic work or a photograph if a natural person was involved in its creation, albeit to a minimum extent, while assuming the role of the author.

The importance of technical performance primarily lies in its function—it serves as a starting point, a prerequisite, for the protection of any photographic product. As mentioned above, any technical performance must be paired with expenditure of, (at least) minimal intellectual performance. It must be human work.[403] Such performance of an intellectual nature can naturally only be attributed to human beings. This said attributability therefore serves as a tool to demonstrate the existence of a link between a photograph and its author, the person, but at the same time the prescribed minimum extent demonstrates that the threshold for the production of a photographic work is not exceeded.[404] Successful demonstration of the two levels is precluded in situations where the conditions under which a photographic product is produced are virtually predetermined.[405] Among other things, this excludes any photographic product created in circumstances in which the author did not exercise or waived their influence on the final appearance of the such a product.[406]

The existence of a related right type of protection, through which photographs can be protected, is justified by the fact, that according to some, most photographic products (out of the vast amount produced) do not meet the criteria prescribed by law for personal intellectual creations—photographic works.[407] Since they do not possess the qualities of photographic works within the meaning of Section 2 of the UrhG, this subsequently results in the impossibility of granting such photographic products copyright protection. Nevertheless, a separate (related) type of protection, different from that of copyright, was devised. Some have referred to this related right as ancillary copyright substructure.[408] Another rationale behind enabling the protection of photographs by a separate (related) right distinguishable from copyright is that photographs, as a subject-matter, are not of a creative nature and can

[402] Anne Lauber-Rönsberg. 'Lichtbilder'. In: Philipp Möhring et al. (eds.), *Urheberrecht: UrhG, KUG, UrhWahrnG, VerlG; Kommentar* (C.H. Beck, 3rd ed. 2014), p. 811.

[403] Thomas Platena, *Das Lichtbild im Urheberrecht: Gesetzliche Regelung und Technische Weiterentwicklung* (Peter Lang 1998), p. 94.

[404] Ilva Johanna Schiessel, *Reichweite und Rechtfertigung des einfachen Lichtbildschutzes gem. § 72 UrhG* (Nomos 2020), p. 68.

[405] Artur-Axel Wandtke, Winfried Bullinger & Michael Bohne, *Praxiskommentar Urheberrecht: UrhG, UrhDaG, VGG, InsO, UKlaG, KUG, EVtr, InfoSoc-RL, Portabilitäts-VO* (C.H. Beck, 6th ed. 2022), p. 1426.

[406] Gunda Dreyer, 'Geschützte Werke'. In: Gunda Dreyer et al., *Urheberrecht: Urheberrechtsgesetz, Verwertungsgesellschaftengesetz, Kunsturhebergesetz* (C.F. Müller, 4th ed. 2018), p. 171.

[407] Haimo Schack, *Urheber- und Urhebervertragsrecht* (Mohr Siebeck, 9th ed. 2019), p. 380.

[408] Schulze, G. Schutz der Lichbilder. In: Thomas Dreier & Gernot Schulze, *Urheberrechtsgesetz: Verwertungsgesellschaftengesetz, Kunsturhebergesetz: Kommentar* (C.H. Beck, 6th ed. 2018), p. 1354

be considered more *re-creative*.[409] According to this view, photographs therefore cannot be eligible for protection on the same grounds as photographic works, since photographs do not possess the qualities of photographic works.

As already mentioned, the protection of photographs via the related right type of protection is mostly justified by technical, financial, or other forms of effort spent in the course of their production, as *Nordemann* quoted *Loewenheim* and *Vogel*.[410] Without such eligibility, a photographer could face a lack of protection of their efforts (i.e., their *investment*) in the production of such photographs, whatever those efforts may have been, or lose it altogether. In accordance to the wording of Section 72 (3) of the UrhG, the term of protection applicable to photographs is 50 years after the publication of a photograph.[411] Although limited and shorter than copyright, the protection by a related right has led to a significant expansion of the realm of protectable photographic products within the German legal framework.[412]

Whether a photographic product can be protected by a related right type of protection in accordance with Section 72 of the UrhG depends on two cumulative conditions being met. Such a photographic product must bear objective characteristics of a photographic product and at the same time be attributable to a person from whom it originated.[413] However, the underlying and most distinguishable condition upon which the protection of a photographic product by the related right type of protection depends is a sufficient demonstration of technical performance, as opposed to the personal intellectual performance required by the copyright protection.[414] Therefore, no creative achievement is required, but rather technical effort is.[415] By introducing this requirement, the German legislator ensured that the protection of any product of human origin belonging to the realm of photography would be considered on the basis of the demonstrated technical performance in the course of its creation.[416]

---

409 Thomas Dreier & Louisa Specht, 'Germany'. In: Reto M. Hilty, (ed.). *Balancing copyright: a survey of national approaches* (Springer, 2012), p. 431.

410 Axel Nordemann, 'Schutz der Lichtbilder'. In: Axel Nordemann et al., *Urheberrecht: Kommentar zum Urheberrechtsgesetz, Verlagsgesetz, Urheberrechtswahrnehmungsgesetz* (W. Kohlhammer, 11th ed. 2014), p. 1480.

411 Sec. 72 (3) of the UrhG.

412 Thomas Platena, *Das Lichtbild im Urheberrecht: Gesetzliche Regelung und Technische Weiterentwicklung* (Peter Lang 1998), p. 89.

413 Wilhelm Nordemann, 'Lichtbildschutz für fotografisch hergestellte Vervielfältigungen'. *GRUR* 15 (1987), p. 15.

414 Axel Nordemann, 'Schutz der Lichtbilder'. In: Axel Nordemann et al., *Urheberrecht: Kommentar zum Urheberrechtsgesetz, Verlagsgesetz, Urheberrechtswahrnehmungsgesetz* (W. Kohlhammer, 11th ed. 2014), p. 1484.

415 Anne Lauber-Rönsberg, 'Lichtbilder'. In: Philipp Möhring et al. (eds.), *Urheberrecht: UrhG, KUG, UrhWahrnG, VerlG; Kommentar* (C.H. Beck, 3rd ed. 2014), p. 807.

416 Artur-Axel Wandtke, Winfried Bullinger & Michael Bohne. *Praxiskommentar Urheberrecht: UrhG, UrhDaG, VGG, InsO, UKlaG, KUG, EVtr, InfoSoc-RL, Portabilitäts-VO* (C.H. Beck, 6th ed. 2022), p. 1422.

5.15 The Relationship Between Photographic Works and Photographs

The wording of Section 72 (1) of the UrhG explicitly states that the provisions of the UrhG applicable to photographic works shall be applicable *mutatis mutandis* to photographs. The exception from this *mutatis mutandis* regime is the different (shorter) term of protection applicable to photographs, since photographic works enjoy the standard term of protection applicable to other *works*. Such cumulative granting of a related right type of protection within the meaning of Section 72 of the UrhG to photographic works eligible for copyright protection signifies the intention of the German legislator to align both types of photographic products, and by doing so, eliminate the need to distinguish between the two.[417] However, the need to distinguish these might just be postponed and arise in the future nonetheless, as the chapters below demonstrate.

Copyright applicable to photographic works and related right applicable to photographs are therefore not mutually exclusive; they complement each other.[418] As such, all photographic works also enjoy protections applicable to photographs. This is due to the fact that all photographic works also possess the minimum features required by the UrhG for protection by a related right type of protection, upon which the additional requirements of *higher* protection by copyright are built. Providing a different perspective, every photographic product surpassing above the threshold for photographs is considered a photographic work, because all photographic works possess the necessary minimum requirement for their classification as photographs. To conclude, every photographic work also represents a photograph, but not every photograph constitutes a photographic work.[419]

The so-called *dual protection* described in the previous paragraph allows protection by a related right in any case and leaves the considerations regarding the character of a photographic product in question to be open.[420] The evident positive outcome of such an approach is the securing of at least a minimum level of protection every time the minimum requirements prescribed for photographs are met. However, the negative outcome would then be the omission or postponement of a full assessment of the photographic product in question, thus leaving the question

417 Dorothee Thum, 'Germany'. In. Silke von Lewinski, *Copyright throughout the World* (Thomson/West 2022), p. 16–32.

418 Axel Nordemann, 'Schutz der Lichtbilder'. In: Axel Nordemann et al., Urheberrecht: Kommentar zum Urheberrechtsgesetz, Verlagsgesetz, Urheberrechtswahrnehmungsgesetz, (W. Kohlhammer, 11th ed. 2014), p. 1480.

419 Ilva Johanna Schiessel, *Reichweite und Rechtfertigung des einfachen Lichtbildschutzes gem. § 72 UrhG* (Nomos 2020), p. 62.

420 Artur-Axel Wandtke, Winfried Bullinger & Michael Bohne. *Praxiskommentar Urheberrecht: UrhG, UrhDaG, VGG, InsO, UKlaG, KUG, EVtr, InfoSoc-RL, Portabilitäts-VO* (C.H. Beck, 6th ed. 2022), p. 1422.

whether a photographic product has the character of a photograph or a photographic work unanswered.

5.16 Minimum Personal Intellectual Performance

Photographic products that fail to reach the threshold set for (photographic) works on account of being a purely technical outcome of photographic production are considered photographs within the meaning of Section 72 of the UrhG. Based on this, one could reach a conclusion that a photograph does not have to bear, at least certain minimal, intellectual characteristics of its author. However, as already mentioned above, the requirement of a demonstration of technical performance must still be linked to a natural person.[421] Therefore, in addition to the visible presence of the technical performance, a minimum personal intellectual performance[422] or personal achievement[423] of the person producing the photograph is still required.[424] However, the effects of such intellectual performance must not exceed the threshold reserved for a photographic work.

The concept of minimum personal intellectual performance can be introduced in more comprehensive detail by using a photographic work within the meaning of Section 2 of the UrhG as an example. If the effects of the creative steps taken by the photographer required for the creation of a photographic work are detached from the said photographic work, what is one left with is the core minimum content of each photographic work—and also a photograph. The said core content is the personal design, the origin of which is the minimum intellectual achievement of the photographer necessary for the production of a photograph.[425] If the author wishes to produce a photographic work, they must build, hypothetically speaking, a superstructure on top of this core content of the minimum intellectual performance. The superstructure itself would then represent the creative effects, in other words the results of the creative activity of the photographer.

Moreover, the reason this additional requirement of minimum personal intellectual performance on top of the technical performance exists to exclude mere realistically duplicating or reproducing photocopies of photographic works or photographs without any mental (intellectual) involvement.[426] For a protection to arise,

---

421 Heinrich Hubmann, Alexander Peukert & Manfred Rehbinder, *Urheberrecht und verwandte Schutzrechte: ein Studienbuch* (C.H. Beck, 19th ed. 2023), p. 231.

422 Martin Vogel, 'Lichtbilder'. In: Ulrich Loewenheim et al., *Urheberrecht: UrhG, KUG, VGG: Kommentar* (C.H. Beck, 6th ed. 2020), p. 1569.

423 BGH, I ZR 147/89, 10. Oct. 1991. 'Bedienungsanweisung' *NJW*. 1992, p. 689.

424 Ilva Johanna Schiessel, *Reichweite und Rechtfertigung des einfachen Lichtbildschutzes gem. § 72 UrhG* (Nomos 2020), p. 69.

425 Wilhelm Nordemann, 'Lichtbildschutz für fotografisch hergestellte Vervielfältigungen'. *GRUR* 15 (1987), p. 15.

426 Thomas Dreier & Gernot Schulze, *Urheberrechtsgesetz: Urheberrechts-Diensteanbieter-Gesetz, Verwertungsgesellschaftengesetz, Nebenurheberrecht, Kunsturhebergesetz: Kommentar* (C.H. Beck, 7th ed. 2022), p. 1479.

an *original* photographic product must be produced, as opposed to a mere reproduction.[427] Within this context, the adjective *original* is used as the first initial or master image.[428] It is this master image into which the author has placed, for the first time, their minimum personal intellectual performance.[429] In practice, the non-exclusion of such reproduction activities from their eligibility for protection by a related right could lead to, for example, a virtually perpetual duration of rights, if every new reproduction could be considered a new protected photographic product.[430] Any copies of a purely technical nature, even if produced through the employment of radiant energy, are excluded from protection within the meaning of the UrhG.[431] What is therefore decisive for the purposes of the assessment of existence of the original is the nature of the reproduction process and photographer's level of intellectual involvement therein.[432]

The different degree of the author's intellectual involvement defined for the purposes of assessment of the *original* and its copy, as well as subsequently distinguishing between the two, can be also illustrated by the constraints a person is bound by during the production process. The production of an original is characterized by the relative creative freedom when selecting its features, whereas the production of its copy must be conducted within the boundaries previously defined by the author of the original.[433] Being bound to these restrictions precludes the production of another original and only provides room for mere technical performance.

There are varying opinions on what the requirement of minimum personal intellectual performance means in practice and how it materializes in the actions of the author. According to *Nordemann*, this requirement must be viewed in light of characteristics of a photographic work. Based on this, it can be seen as a minimal mental activity of the author performed during the production of a photographic product, and excluding the creative achievement required and reserved solely for the production of a photographic work.[434] Some see the requirement, inter alia, in the skill of operating the technical apparatus used throughout the production process of a photographic product, again excluding the presence of individuality of a photographic work.[435] Still, what is evident from both opinions above is the condition of not ex-

427 Paul Abel, *Urhebervertragsrecht: Handbuch* (Nomos 2022), p. 1053.

428 Ilva Johanna Schiessel, *Reichweite und Rechtfertigung des einfachen Lichtbildschutzes gem. § 72 UrhG* (Nomos 2020), p. 69.

429 Thomas Platena, *Das Lichtbild im Urheberrecht: Gesetzliche Regelung und Technische Weiterentwicklung* (Peter Lang 1998), p. 247.

430 Ekkehard Gerstenberg, 'Fototechnik und Urheberrecht'. In: Herbst, G. *Festschrift für Rainer Klaka.* (J. Schweitzer Verlag 1987), p. 126.

431 For example Sec. 68 of the UrhG.

432 Ilva Johanna Schiessel, *Reichweite und Rechtfertigung des einfachen Lichtbildschutzes gem. § 72 UrhG* (Nomos 2020), p. 71.

433 BGH, I ZR 104/17, 20. Dec. 2018, 'Museumsfotos' *GRUR* 2019, p. 284.

434 Wilhelm Nordemann, 'Lichtbildschutz für fotografisch hergestellte Vervielfältigungen'. *GRUR* 15 (1987), p. 15.

435 Ulrich Loewenheim et al., *Urheberrecht: Kommentar* (C.H. Beck, 5th ed. 2017), p. 1655.

ceeding the threshold reserved solely for photographic works. Otherwise, it would no longer be possible to speak of a *minimum amount* of performance anymore. On the other hand, some have found the circumstances of production conditions, along with attributability of a photographic product to a natural person, as decisive for the purposes of *minimum* intellectual performance.[436]

However different the decisive criteria for the existence and assessment of the minimum intellectual performance might be, the purpose of its presence in a photograph remains unchanged. It represents the lower threshold for photographs' protection by a related right. This contrasts with the higher threshold for photographic works eligible for copyright protection, but also demonstrates the existence of a link between photographs and photographic works for distinguishing between the two.[437] The lower requirement, in the form of *minimum intellectual effort* by the author, serves to justify the use of related rights and therefore also the shorter protection period.[438] In other words, the different level of intellectual involvement of the author is reflected in the different status of photographic works and photographs. Nevertheless, if the photographer decides to demonstrate even a minimal amount of motivation and will in the expenditure of intellectual performance, the requirement for protection provision in accordance with the Section 72 of the UrhG is fulfilled, as *Werner* quoted *Overbeck*.[439]

If the eligibility of photographic products possessing the minimum intellectual performance was not so easily accessible, or if such type of protection were abolished altogether, it could prove to be detrimental to photographers.[440] In such cases, most probably a significant number of photographic products could not be recognized as eligible for the corresponding type of protection and treated as such. Naturally, in such a state of affairs, rightly justified protection based on the *minimum intellectual performance* requirement would be denied.

5.17 Differences in the Protection of 'Photographic Works' and 'Photographs'

The most apparent difference between these two types of protection is the different duration of protection associated with each type of photographic product.

[436] Artur-Axel Wandtke et al., *Praxiskommentar Urheberrecht: UrhG, VGG, InsO, UKlaG, KUG, EVtr, InfoSoc-RL* (C.H. Beck, 5th ed. 2019), § 72, Rn. 27.

[437] Ilva Johanna Schiessel, *Reichweite und Rechtfertigung des einfachen Lichtbildschutzes gem. § 72 UrhG* (Nomos 2020), p. 68.

[438] Thomas Platena, *Das Lichtbild im Urheberrecht: Gesetzliche Regelung und Technische Weiterentwicklung* (Peter Lang 1998), p. 171.

[439] Julia Werner, *Die Reformbedürftigkeit des Lichtbildschutzes nach Paragraph 72 UrhG aus Rechtsökonomischer Perspektive* (Peter Lang 2023), p. 74.

[440] Julia Werner, *Die Reformbedürftigkeit des Lichtbildschutzes nach Paragraph 72 UrhG aus Rechtsökonomischer Perspektive* (Peter Lang 2023), p. 74.

Photographic works, as eligible for copyright protection, may be protected for 70 years *post mortem auctoris*, whereas photographs, falling under a related right type of protection, may be protected for 50 years from the moment of their *release*.

Another significant difference is laid down in Section 23 of the UrhG, which provides protection against adaptations and transformations of works. From the wording of Section 23, it is evident that protection only extends to *works*. Such circumstances exclude photographs from this protection, since these do not meet the criteria prescribed for works. The basis for this protection is the individuality of the design, which only a photographic work can possess.[441] Therefore, recreations of motifs depicted in photographs are not covered by Section 23 of the UrhG.

In practice, the distinction between photographic works and photographs is also evident in the context of protection provided to their parts through each respective type of protection. In case of a photograph, the corresponding related right type of protection protects the performance of the photographer materialized therein, which can be clearly distinguished and separated from the environment.[442] From this definition, it can be deduced that a photograph is to be seen as a holistic whole. Therefore, in principle, the related right protects photographs as whole, including all individual parts, irrespective of their size. In contrast, copyright protection of a photographic work protects the performance of the photographer materialized therein, which cannot be separated from the environment.[443] This definition thus makes it clear that a photographic work is to be seen as modular—consisting of various parts. Therefore, while copyright also protects photographic works as a whole, its individual parts are only protected to the extent that these are personal intellectual creations in themselves. If a single part did not bear the characteristics of a photographic work, it would not be eligible for copyright protection. Within this context, protection by a related right might seem more suitable for elements of a photograph in case of an infringement than the one provided by copyright. Moreover, protection of individual parts might seem less favourable in the case of a photographic work, since the higher requirement for protection also transferred onto the individual parts.

---

441 Jan Franzen & Albrecht Götz von Olenhusen, 'Lichtbildwerke, Lichtbilder und Fotoimitate: Abhängige Bearbeitung oder freier Benutzung?' *UFITA* 435 (2007), p. 435.

442 Simon Apel, 'Überlegungen zu einer Reform des Lichtbildschutzgesetzes (§ 72 UrhG)'. In: Martin Vogel, Albrecht Götz von Olenhusen, & Thomas Gergen (eds.) *Kreativität und Charakter: Recht, Geschichte und Kultur in schöpferischen Prozessen: Festschrift für Martin Vogel zum siebzigsten Geburtstag* (Verlag Dr. Kovač 2017), p. 212.

443 *Ibid.*

5.18 Products Similar to Photographic Works and Photographs

Some consider the distinguishing of *Werke, die ähnlich wie Lichtbildwerke geschaffen werden* (works produced by processes similar to photography) from *Erzeugnisse, die ähnlich wie Lichtbilder hergestellt werden* (products manufactured in a similar manner to photographs) from their traditional equivalents as unfortunate, since the already broad definition of the terms *Lichtbildwerke* and *Lichtbilder* could conceivably and conveniently include every possible photographic product.[444] Nonetheless, by using such a wide and open approach, the German legislator accounts for the complexity, varieties, and constant developments and innovations of the production processes of photographic products.[445] The UrhG took the same approach towards separating *similar works* in reference to cinematographic works.[446] Therefore, however redundant such separation might seem, specifically referring to *works produced* and *products manufactured*, it allows the respective provisions of the UrhG to conceivably cover any photographic products that may originate via photographic production processes yet to be introduced and exploited in the future, as *Werner* quoted *Schricker*, *Loewenheim* and *Vogel*.[447] In this respect, the purpose of both clauses is to create open possibilities for protection of products that equivalent to photographic works or photographs due to their similar production or manufacturing processes.[448] The approach allows any doubts regarding the categorization of these products to be avoided.

When referring to *works produced and products manufactured*, *photographic works* are equivalent to *works produced by processes similar to photography*,[449] whereas *photographs* are *products manufactured in a similar manner to photographs*.[450] By making this linguistic distinction between these types of photographic products, the legislation is also to distinguish between the processes leading to the creation of these photographic products. Within this context, the term *produced* refers to a production process that includes the full intellectual involvement of the author, the consequence of which can only be an intellectual creation, the work similar to a photographic work. In contrast, the term *manufactured* merely refers to manufacturing process, the outcome of which is a product of minimal intellectual

---

[444] Axel Nordemann, *Die künstlerische Fotografie als urheberrechtlich geschütztes Werk* (Nomos 1992), p. 63.

[445] Thomas Platena, *Das Lichtbild im Urheberrecht: Gesetzliche Regelung und Technische Weiterentwicklung* (Peter Lang 1998), p. 121.

[446] Sec. 2 of the UrhG.

[447] Julia Werner, *Die Reformbedürftigkeit des Lichtbildschutzes Nach Paragraph 72 UrhG aus Rechtsökonomischer Perspektive* (Peter Lang 2023), p. 30.

[448] Thomas Platena, *Das Lichtbild im Urheberrecht: Gesetzliche Regelung und Technische Weiterentwicklung* (Peter Lang 1998), p. 120.

[449] Sec. 2 of the UrhG.

[450] Sec. 72 of the UrhG.

content, i.e., similar to a photograph. Nonetheless, even with their assignment to photographic works and photographs based on their similarities with the two, both types of similar products are conceptually independent.[451]

Regardless of how different or similar the production or manufacturing processes and their results may be in comparison to those of photographic works and photographs, the criteria for protection of *works produced* and *products manufactured* under the corresponding type of protection must align with those stipulated for the two *regular* photographic products. Within the context of copyright protection, a *work produced* must exhibit the characteristics of a *work*, with its *personal intellectual creation* requirement. On the other hand, to be granted the related right type of protection, a *product manufactured* must demonstrate the *minimal intellectual involvement* of its author.

Also, the result of the production or manufacturing process must still be comparable to a photographic work or a photograph; otherwise, one could not speak of *works produced and products manufactured*.[452] Therefore, the similarity of the production or manufacturing process to that of photographic one lies in its effects and results.[453] The *effect* is a change in the nature of a product due to a similar photographic production or manufacturing process, while the *result* is a final work or product similar to a photographic work or photograph. The result of this process must, however, still retain its depicting function.[454] If a product does not depict reality in a certain way, it cannot be considered a *work produced or product manufactured* within the meaning of the UrhG, since it would not fulfil one of the basic functions of photography.

Nonetheless, it must be noted that the distinction to be made between a work produced by a process similar to photography, or a product manufactured in a similar manner to a photograph, and a photographic work or photograph, is of a purely dogmatic nature, since the scope of protection is identical to the two types of photographic products that such products of similar nature would primarily be assigned to, as *Werner* quoted *Nordemann*.[455]

451 Thomas Platena, *Das Lichtbild im Urheberrecht: Gesetzliche Regelung und Technische Weiterentwicklung* (Peter Lang 1998), p. 119.

452 Melanie Overbeck, *Der Lichtbildschutz gem. § 72 UrhG im Lichte der Digitalfotografie* (Lit 2018), p. 64.

453 Axel Nordemann, *Die künstlerische Fotografie als urheberrechtlich geschütztes Werk* (Nomos 1992), p. 66.

454 Melanie Overbeck, *Der Lichtbildschutz gem. § 72 UrhG im Lichte der Digitalfotografie* (Lit 2018), p. 59.

455 Julia Werner, *Die Reformbedürftigkeit des Lichtbildschutzes Nach Paragraph 72 UrhG aus Rechtsökonomischer Perspektive* (Peter Lang 2023), p. 31.

5.19 The Transition from a Photograph to a Photographic Work

Given the previously mentioned eternal issues related to differentiation between photographic works and photographs, the purpose of Section 72 of the UrhG might also lie in some, to a certain extent, postponement of distinguishing between the two. This is accomplished by setting a minimum requirement for the protectability of a photographic product by a related right, thus satisfying rightsholders with a degree of protection and leaving a final assessment to be made, if at all, in the future. Such approach entailing no upper limit for protection as a photographic work, with a focus on the lower limit for protection as a photograph, might prove satisfactory until the author claims protection as a photographic work.[456] However, according to some, in the vast majority of cases, the courts are spared from having to deal with such questions due to the already mentioned *double protection*.[457] Therefore, if the question of distinction between the two types of photographic products is not determinative or decisive for the legal dispute, it can be waived on the grounds of guaranteed protection by the related right in Section 72 of the UrhG.[458]

Distinguishing between a photographic work and a photograph cannot be based on a technical point of view, since both products share this. One must rather focus on the missing or present property as a *work*, as *Heitland* quoted *Hertin*.[459] Nonetheless, precisely distinguishing between a photographic work and a photograph must be done on a case-by-case basis and supported by a thorough and unbiased assessment of the creation process of the photographic product and its background, not excluding the ideas of its author.[460] No universal rule applicable to all photographic products in this sense exists. In general, however, the upper limit of eligibility of photographs for protection by a related right can be defined by the help of the lower limit at which a photographic work becomes ineligible for copyright. One can speak of a photograph within the meaning of Section 72 of the UrhG when, due to the absence of individuality, one can no longer refer to a creative content in connection with a photographic work, or the photographer's *handwriting* is no longer

[456] Thomas Dreier & Gernot Schulze, *Urheberrechtsgesetz: Urheberrechts-Diensteanbieter-Gesetz, Verwertungsgesellschaftengesetz, Nebenurheberrecht, Kunsturhebergesetz: Kommentar* (C.H. Beck, 7th ed. 2022), p. 1477.

[457] Artur-Axel Wandtke, Winfried Bullinger & Michael Bohne. *Praxiskommentar Urheberrecht: UrhG, UrhDaG, VGG, InsO, UKlaG, KUG, EVtr, InfoSoc-RL, Portabilitäts-VO* (C.H. Beck, 6th ed. 2022), p. 1423.

[458] Ilva Johanna Schiessel, *Reichweite und Rechtfertigung des einfachen Lichtbildschutzes gem. § 72 UrhG* (Nomos 2020), p. 46.

[459] Horst Heitland, *Der Schutz der Fotografie im Urheberrecht Deutschlands, Frankreichs und der Vereinigten Staaten von Amerika* (C.H. Beck 1995), p. 21.

[460] Ilva Johanna Schiessel, *Reichweite und Rechtfertigung des einfachen Lichtbildschutzes gem. § 72 UrhG* (Nomos 2020), p. 60.

recognizable.[461] In other words, if a photographer gives up on the personalization of a photographic product through the choices available, such photographic product cannot be considered a photographic work, but only rather a photograph. As a result, the photographic work hypothetically descends to the *lower* realm of photographs.

The absence of the existence of a blanket approach towards the assessment of photographic products and their possible subsequent protection by a corresponding type of protection is caused by hypothetically endless array of creative approaches to the production process of such products.[462] The impossibility of demarcating the borders of these approaches therefore results in this case-by-case individual assessment approach. Only such an individual approach can identify the individuality exhibited by the author in a photographic work that gives rise to copyright protection. This practically borderless array thus provides the author with an environment suitable for implementing their creative ideas and allowing their individuality to be manifested in a photographic work.

However, in light of the fluid and unclear border between photographic works and photographs in the German copyright framework, the German legislator has gradually been shifting their attention to the lower limit of protection, which, hypothetically speaking, divides photographs and (unprotectable) photographic products. As already mentioned, since the actual distinguishing between photographic works and photographs often loses importance in practice, the question that arises is not about what kind of protection will be provided, but rather if any protection will be provided at all.[463]

5.20 Unprotectable Photographic Products

Taking all this into account, it becomes evident that not all technical processes, even if they are related to photography, qualify a product as a (protectable) photographic work or a photograph under the UrhG. Therefore, in addition to these positive definitions of protectable photographic products, photographic works, and photographs, it is also important to provide a negative definition to provide the reader with the greatest possible insight into the topic.

By setting a limit between (protectable) photographic works and photographs, German legislator seemingly resolved the difficulties of distinguishing between the two. However, since the UrhG does not provide protection *en bloc* to all photographic products, the need to further distinguish between photographs and (unprotectable)

[461] Jan Franzen & Albrecht Götz von Olenhusen, 'Lichtbildwerke, Lichtbilder und Fotoimitate: Abhängige Bearbeitung oder freier Benutzung?' *UFITA* 435 (2007), p. 435.

[462] Axel Nordemann, *Die künstlerische Fotografie als urheberrechtlich geschütztes Werk* (Nomos 1992), p. 111.

[463] Ilva Johanna Schiessel, *Reichweite und Rechtfertigung des einfachen Lichtbildschutzes gem. § 72 UrhG* (Nomos 2020), p. 61.

photographic products only shifted to the lower levels of the German copyright framework; but was not fully resolved. This situation thus requires formulating additional delimitation requirements within this lower level, thus creating a scheme of three types of photographic products—photographic works, photographs, and unprotectable photographic products below the threshold of protection by a related right used for photographs. This does not achieve the purpose of the law, which was to eliminate such delimitation issues.[464] The need for delimitation criteria in the lower level of protection is especially important, since the UrhG does not specify any kind of lower limit for protection.[465]

Previous chapters established that the distinguishing criterion between photographic works and photographs is the existence of the author's personal intellectual creation, or the individuality manifested by the author's personal intellectual and creative involvement. The criterion of creativeness excludes photographic products from their classifications as photographic works along with their copyrightability, and figuratively moves them lower into the realm of a related right type of protection eligibility reserved for photographs within the meaning of Section 72 of the UrhG.

Once a photographic product reaches this lower level, it must be assessed to determine if it falls under protection by a related right within the meaning of Section 72 of the UrhG, or if it should be excluded from the protection offered by the UrhG altogether. Examples of such situations would be photographic products that fulfil the criterion of being photographic in nature, but no other feature required for their protection within the meaning of the UrhG exists.[466]

As elaborated on in the previous section, here too, the lower limit of eligibility for protection of photographs can be employed in order to determine the figurative upper level at which photographic products become unprotectable by the related right type of protection within the meaning of Section 72 of the UrhG. Due to the already low limit for the eligibility for protection of photographs, for a photographic product to be wholly unprotectable means setting the limit for a *photographic product* to be of purely technical reproduction nature.[467] Therefore, for the purposes of distinguishing between photographs and unprotectable photographic products, minimum personal intellectual performance is the key requirement. It functions as a tool to distinguish between similar categories of photographic products, between

[464] Ilva Johanna Schiessel, *Reichweite und Rechtfertigung des einfachen Lichtbildschutzes gem. § 72 UrhG* (Nomos 2020), p. 77.

[465] Simon Apel, 'Überlegungen zu einer Reform des Lichtbildschutzgesetzes (§ 72 UrhG)' In: Martin Vogel, Albrecht Götz von Olenhusen, & Thomas Gergen (eds.) *Kreativität und Charakter: Recht, Geschichte und Kultur in schöpferischen Prozessen: Festschrift für Martin Vogel zum siebzigsten Geburtstag* (Verlag Dr. Kovač 2017), p. 209.

[466] Ilva Johanna Schiessel, *Reichweite und Rechtfertigung des einfachen Lichtbildschutzes gem. § 72 UrhG* (Nomos 2020), p. 64.

[467] Jan Franzen & Albrecht Götz von Olenhusen. Lichtbildwerke, Lichtbilder und Fotoimitate: Abhängige Bearbeitung oder freier Benutzung? *UFITA*. 2007, p. 435.

which a certain degree of factual comparability exists.[468] The existence of such factual comparability therefore presupposes a need for distinguishing based on certain criteria.

As *Ilva Johanna Schiessel* has noted, traditionally, the BGH has recognized and affirmed this requirement on numerous occasions as a delimitation criterion between photographic works and photographs, in other words for the eligibility of a photographic product for a corresponding type of protection within the meaning of the UrhG.[469] If no sufficient comparability can be recognized between photographic products, it is then characterized by a minimal amount or total lack personal intellectual performance.[470] Photographic products without the presence of a minimum level of personal intellectual performance cannot be considered for any kind of type of legal protection available to photographic products within the meaning of the UrhG. Such examples of photographic products not eligible for any kind of protection within the meaning of the UrhG might include photographic products from *speed trap* cameras or computer-generated images, for example.[471]

5.21 The Relationship between Photographic Works and the Concept of Kleine Münze

The concept of *kleine Münze* is also applicable to photographic products—or photographic works, to be more precise. In photographic works, it is the statement based on creativity, through which the individuality of a photographic product is manifested.[472] In respect to this, the minimum prescribed extent of creativity height is achieved whenever a photographic product is *individual*.[473] This definition of the lower limit for copyrightability is defined in practice by works referred to as *kleine Münze*.[474] The low setting of this level ensures the copyrightability of most photographic products as photographic works. If a photographic product is assessed to determine its protectability, one must look at the *quantitatives Element der Individualität* (*quantitative element of individuality*). It is in this way devised by *Schricker*

468 Ilva Johanna Schiessel, *Reichweite und Rechtfertigung des einfachen Lichtbildschutzes gem. § 72 UrhG* (Nomos 2020), p. 63.

469 Ilva Johanna Schiessel, *Reichweite und Rechtfertigung des einfachen Lichtbildschutzes gem. § 72 UrhG* (Nomos 2020), p. 65.

470 *Ibid.*

471 Gunda Dreyer et al., *Urheberrecht: Urheberrechtsgesetz, Verwertungsgesellschaftengesetz, Kunsturhebergesetz* (C.F. Müller, 4th ed. 2018), p. 1339.

472 Axel Nordemann, *Die künstlerische Fotografie als urheberrechtlich geschütztes Werk* (Nomos 1992), p. 106.

473 Axel Nordemann, 'Germany'. In: Ysolde Gendreau, Axel Nordemann, & Rainer Oesch (eds.). *Copyright and photographs: an international survey* (Kluwer Law International 1999), p. 139.

474 Axel Nordemann et al., *Urheberrecht: Kommentar zum Urheberrechtsgesetz, Verlagsgesetz, Urheberrechtswahrnehmungsgesetz* (W. Kohlhammer, 11th ed. 2014), p. 140.

that the German copyright framework recognizes the level of creativity, as *Nordemann* quoted him.[475] However, it is still not sufficiently settled whether the level of requirement of protection for works known as *kleine Münze* is identical with the level for creativity or above it.[476] Nonetheless, such questions might not be of relevance since it is generally agreed that *kleine Münze* works indeed possess an adequate level of creativity to be successfully protectable by copyright.

However, the *kleine Münze* doctrine is not to be interchanged with the two-tier system of protection of photographic products within the German copyright framework. The purpose of this two-tier system of protection applied in Germany is to differentiate between photographic works and photographs. This is done via separate types of available protection. The higher tier of protection by copyright is reserved for photographic works, while the other, the lower tier of protection by a related right, is reserved for photographs. Therefore, the core concept of the two-tier system is of the granting of two separate types of protection to separate types of photographic products. On the other hand, the concept of *kleine Münze* only assures the protection of photographic works which found themselves at the lower levels of copyright due to the minor creativity and individuality they display. It is therefore a differentiation within copyright protection itself, but with no apparent effects for such less creative photographic products in practice. In other words, if a photographic work is labelled as *kleine Münze*, it is protected in the lower spectrum of copyright, but still by full copyright protection, nonetheless. Therefore, for the purposes of copyright protection, it is only possible to distinguish between two groups of photographic products—eligible and ineligible. No third group exists, as the *kleine Münze* are a subgroup of copyright-eligible photographic products. The *kleine Münze* photographic works do not form a separate category and are always eligible for copyright protection.[477]

Therefore, even the *kleine Münze* photographic works are still considered personal intellectual creations.[478] This can be derived from the already elaborated requirement of personal intellectual performance, albeit minimal, and also by their recognized copyrightability. The application of the *kleine Münze* concept to photographic products therefore has resulted in extending protection by copyright even to photographic products containing average or below-average designs.[479]

---

[475] *Ibid.*

[476] Horst Heitland, *Der Schutz der Fotografie im Urheberrecht Deutschlands, Frankreichs und der Vereinigten Staaten von Amerika* (C.H. Beck 1995), p. 51.

[477] Axel Nordemann, *Die künstlerische Fotografie als urheberrechtlich geschütztes Werk* (Nomos 1992), p. 117.

[478] Axel Nordemann, *Die künstlerische Fotografie als urheberrechtlich geschütztes Werk* (Nomos 1992), p. 116.

[479] Axel Nordemann & Friedrich Nicolaus Heise, 'Urheberrechtlicher Schutz für Designleistungen in Deutschland und auf europäischer Ebene'. *ZUM* 128 (2001), p. 128.

5.22 Concluding Remarks on the German Copyright Framework

In general terms, the German copyright framework only allows copyrightability of products (works) that possess the qualities of an *author's own intellectual creation*. Such works must possess individuality in order for these to surpass the threshold set via the German concept of *Schöpfungshöhe*. After surpassing this threshold, such works become eligible for copyright protection under German copyright law—in other words original.

The German legal framework differentiates between two categories of photographic products: photographic works and photographs. For the former to enjoy copyright protection, they must follow the requirements prescribed for works, therefore the *author's own intellectual creation*. For the latter, to fall under a related right type of protection, meeting the requirement of displaying a minimal amount of personal intellectual achievement suffices.

Apart from the twofold treatment of photographic products, another significant peculiarity of the German copyright framework is the concept of the *kleine Münze*, which allows for the eligibility for copyright protection of works with even a minimal display of individuality.

To conclude, the German copyright framework seems to be favourable to the protection of photographic products. This is manifested in two ways. First, photographic works have been included into the realm of copyright protection even when displaying a minimal amount of individuality. Such copyrightability is based on the *kleine Münze* concept. Second, a related right has allowed the inclusion of photographs into the realm of legal protection even when displaying, only a minimal amount of personal intellectual achievement. As a result, the vast majority of photographic products are considered to be eligible for protection under the UrhG, with the most evident difference only being the duration of protection.

6 THE DEVELOPMENT OF THE ORIGINALITY STANDARD IN THE COPYRIGHT FRAMEWORK OF FRANCE

The second national framework of a Member State to be assessed is France. As stated in the introduction, I chose the French copyright framework due to its assumed similarities with outcomes of EU harmonization, particularly in the use of the requirement of originality. Moreover, the treatment of photographic products within the French national copyright framework is characterized by the recognition of only *original* and *non-original* photographic products. Only the former is eligible for copyright protection; the latter remains outside of any eligibility for protection whatsoever, either within the meaning of copyright or related rights type of protection. This profoundly contrasts with Germany's two-step treatment and the corresponding eligibility of photographic products for protection by either copyright or a related right type of protection. This offers yet another reason to analyse France's copyright framework.

However, before turning to the assessment of the development, position, and treatment of photographic products in France, I first present some general characteristics of the French copyright framework. To do so, I again first turn to the concept of a *work*. After assessing and defining the general attributes of this concept, other related concepts inherent to the French copyright framework will be subsequently assessed and defined. After laying down this general foundation, I then turn to a more specific assessment related to photographic products. In sum, this chapter follows the same structure as that of the previous chapter on the German national copyright framework.

6.1 The Chapter's Relationship to the Selected Hypotheses and Research Questions

The purpose of this chapter is to prepare an overview of theoretical knowledge presenting the development of the national copyright framework of France and its traditional approach to providing copyright protection to photographic products. This overview will then serve as the basis for confirming or rejecting Research

Questions B and C in Chapter 12, which is dedicated to the effects of EU harmonization on the French copyright framework.

6.2 The Concept of a Work

In terms of legislation, the French copyright framework is primarily governed by the CPI.[480] Article L111-1 of the CPI states that the author of an *œuvre de l'esprit* (work of the mind) shall *'enjoy in that work, by the mere fact of its creation, an exclusive intangible property right which shall be enforceable against all other persons'*.[481] Article L112-1 of the CPI provides protection to all *œuvres de l'esprit*, regardless of their kind, form of expression, merit, or purpose.[482] This concept of a *work of the mind* was first introduced in 1793 and it gradually developed into a central concept of French copyright law.[483]

Nonetheless, the wording of the CPI does not provide for any definition of the term *œuvre*, neither does it provide any details about potential qualities or characteristics of this term.[484] On the other hand, this lack of any legislative definition of a *work* allows the law to adapt and remain open to new types of subject-matter, and in doing so, it has at the same time proved the resilience of the French copyright framework for any new trends related to potentially copyrightable subject-matter.[485] Given the issues arising from the material meaning of a *work* and the absence of a legislative definition for it, jurisprudence has been the only source to provide sufficient clarification.[486] This approach is different than the one chosen by the German legislator via the UrhG, which explicitly refers to subject-matter eligible for copyright protection as *persönliche geistige Schöpfungen* (*personal intellectual creations*). As detailed below, the French approach is very similar to that of the EU's harmonized approach, since the EU legislator does not provide any positive definition of copyright-eligible subject-matter either. Instead, characteristics decisive for the eligibility of a product for copyright protection have been determined by case law.

Based on the absence of any official legislative definition, the CPI's Article L112-2 tries to remedy the legislative deficiency and provides at least an indicative

480 *Intellectual Property Code* (10. Sep. 2024), https://wipolex-res.wipo.int/edocs/lexdocs/laws/en/fr/fr467en.html.

481 Art. L111-1 of the CPI.

482 Art. L112-1 of the CPI.

483 Horst Heitland, *Der Schutz der Fotografie im Urheberrecht Deutschlands, Frankreichs und der Vereinigten Staaten von Amerika* (C.H. Beck 1995), p. 136.

484 Christophe Caron, *Droit d'auteur et droits voisins* (LexisNexis, 6th ed. 2020), p. 59.

485 Pierre Sirinelli & Alexandra Bensamoun, 'France'. In: Silke von Lewinski, *Copyright throughout the World* (Thomson/West 2022), pp. 15–16.

486 Pierre-Yves Gautier, *Propriété littéraire et artistique* (Presses universitaires de France 2019), p. 49.

list of 14 examples of types of products regarded as *works of the mind*.[487] It is possible to use this list to determine the factors contributing to classification: a product and the ideas on which that product is based.[488] This list is non-exhaustive and fulfils a supplementary role to Article L112-1 and the vague definition, (or more precisely the lack of) of a *work of the mind* by enumerating the approximate areas where products should originate from.[489] The only hint that the CPI provides regarding the definition of the concept itself is in the wording of Article L112-1, which outlines the elements that may *not* to be taken into consideration during the assessment process of a potential *work of the mind*. In other words, this Article indicates elements indifferent to the definition of the concept itself.[490] Some of these elements include the kind, form of expression, merit, or purpose of the assessed potential work.

As already stated, apart from the mention in Article L112-1 and the list of works provided in the Article L112-2 of the CPI, no clear legislative definition of the term *work of the mind* exists in French legislation.[491] The notion itself might seem so broad as to practically entail all creations of conscious human activity. The advantage of such a broad and open definition lies in its flexibility to cover the largest possible number of potential works.[492] However, the concept must be interpreted in a narrower way to exclude products ineligible for copyright protection, as *Lucas* quoted *Dietz*.[493] Nonetheless, a concept open to interpretation is a concept open to evolution.[494]

Nevertheless, Article L112-2 of the CPI at least defines in a positive manner which (types of) products may be considered *works of the mind*. In respect to this, the non-exhaustive nature of the list and the examples of work categories allow any product qualifying as a work to be eligible for copyright protection, and need not be constrained by the particular categories of works listed in Article L112-2 of the CPI.[495] Moreover, the inclusion of products on the list and their subsequent

[487] Stéphanie Carre, 'France'. In: Reto, M. Hilty (ed). *Balancing copyright: a survey of national approaches*, (Springer 2012), p. 387.

[488] Valérie-Laure Benabou. 'Der Schutzumfang des Urheberrechts in Frankreich'. In: Reto M. Hilty, Christophe Geiger, & Valérie-Laure Benabou (eds.), *Impulse für eine europäische Harmonisierung des Urheberrechts: Urheberrecht im deutsch-französischen Dialog* (Springer 2007), p. 148.

[489] Michel Vivant, Jean-Louis Navarro & Jean-Louis Bilon, *Code de la propriété intellectuelle* (LexisNexis, 13th ed. 2012), p. 160.

[490] Christophe Caron, *Droit d'auteur et droits voisins* (LexisNexis, 6th ed. 2020), p. 59

[491] Valérie-Laure Benabou, 'Der Schutzumfang des Urheberrechts in Frankreich'. In: Reto M. Hilty, Christophe Geiger, & Valérie-Laure Benabou (eds.), *Impulse für eine europäische Harmonisierung des Urheberrechts: Urheberrecht im deutsch-französischen Dialog* (Springer 2007), p. 144.

[492] Pierre Sirinelli, *Propriété littéraire et artistique* (Dalloz, 2nd 2004), p. 12.

[493] André Lucas et al., *Traité de la propriété littéraire et artistique* (LexisNexis, 5th ed. 2017), p. 67.

[494] Michel Vivant & Jean-Michel Bruguière, *Droit d'auteur et droits voisins* (Dalloz, 4th ed. 2019), p. 157.

[495] Frédéric Pollaud-Dulian, *Le droit d'auteur: propriété intellectuelle* (Economica, 2nd ed. 2014), p. 196.

classification is based on their content, not their form.[496] Moreover, falling into one of the categories of works within the meaning of Article L112-2 of the CPI does not automatically ensure eligibility of a product by copyright protection.[497] On the other hand, not falling into one of the categories of works does not necessarily mean such product is not eligible for copyright protection. Such a state of affairs affirms the independent position of *originality* as the sole criterion for eligibility of a product by copyright protection within the French copyright framework. It can be concluded that the decisive factor upon which lies the classification of a product into the realm of *works* within the meaning of Article L112-2 of the CPI is its information content (statement), thus contributing to its clear identification as a *work of the mind*.[498]

Analysing the concept of what a *work* is with the aim of providing a definition for the term can be conducted from either an objective or a subjective perspective. The idea behind the objective approach is to focus only on the outcome, while ignoring the process that led to it as irrelevant.[499] In contrast, the subjective approach focuses on the causal link between the creation itself and its creator—the author.[500] However, the goal to understand the concept itself in its complexity requires incorporating both approaches.

For a product to reach a state in which it would be eligible for copyright protection, it must consist of two elements recognized by the French copyright law. To clarify the two elements, *Pierre-Yves Gautier* proposed a metaphor comparing a work to a human being, in that both consist of a body and a soul. The element of originality serves as the soul of the work, whereas the body consists of a form.[501] Therefore, a work must be a work of the mind in the sense that it bears an imprint of the author's personality, and at the same time this work must be expressed in a particular form. Therefore, the work itself in practice consists of two parts: the physical (the bearer) and the mind (intellectual) component.[502] To understand this dualism better, figuratively speaking, both elements exist parallel to each other in a work, but do not mix.[503] One must distinguish between the physical *body* and the *soul*—the mental contribution of the author imprinted on it.

---

[496] Valérie-Laure Benabou, 'Der Schutzumfang des Urheberrechts in Frankreich'. In: Reto M. Hilty, Christophe Geiger, & Valérie-Laure Benabou (eds.), *Impulse für eine europäische Harmonisierung des Urheberrechts: Urheberrecht im deutsch-französischen Dialog* (Springer 2007), p. 148.

[497] Frédéric Pollaud-Dulian, *Le droit d'auteur: propriété intellectuelle* (Economica, 2nd ed. 2014), p. 202.

[498] Valérie-Laure Benabou, 'Der Schutzumfang des Urheberrechts in Frankreich' In: Reto M. Hilty, Christophe Geiger, & Valérie-Laure Benabou (eds.), *Impulse für eine europäische Harmonisierung des Urheberrechts: Urheberrecht im deutsch-französischen Dialog* (Springer 2007), p. 148.

[499] André Lucas et al., *Traité de la propriété littéraire et artistique* (LexisNexis, 5th ed. 2017), p. 67.

[500] André Lucas et al., *Traité de la propriété littéraire et artistique* (LexisNexis, 5th ed. 2017), p. 67.

[501] Pierre-Yves Gautier, *Propriété littéraire et artistique* (Presses universitaires de France 2019), p. 50.

[502] Valérie-Laure Benabou, 'Der Schutzumfang des Urheberrechts in Frankreich' In: Reto M. Hilty, Christophe Geiger, & Valérie-Laure Benabou (eds.), *Impulse für eine europäische Harmonisierung des Urheberrechts: Urheberrecht im deutsch-französischen Dialog* (Springer 2007), p. 146.

[503] *Ibid.*

Therefore, even in the realm of works of the mind, it is necessary to distinguish between the two for the purposes of copyright law, since not every *work of the mind* can be also considered a work within the meaning of the CPI.[504] Such works would entail those fulfilling all criteria but one, that of the imprint of their author's personality. Without the presence of this imprint, such works would not be able to surpass the threshold for copyrightability within the French copyright framework.

6.3 The Creation Process of a Work

The creation process of a work can be divided into three stages—idea, composition, and personal expression.[505] Although initially devised in connection with the creation process of literary works, it can be nonetheless universally applied to the creation process of any work, photographic or otherwise. It can be stated, that the degree of the involvement of the photographer during these three stages is determinative for possible recognition of a photographic product as a work within the meaning of the CPI.[506]

First, during the *idea* stage, an idea is formed within the mind of the author. Such an idea must comprise an intention to create a certain work through wilful steps of a creative nature. The idea must also include, at least to an approximate extent, details regarding the intended looks and characteristics of the work-to-be. It must be noted, however, that according to the idea/expression dichotomy concept, ideas themselves are precluded from eligibility for copyright protection. In other words, *les idées sont de libre parcours* (*ideas are free to roam*).[507] Within the French copyright framework, the ideas are referred to as having *de libre parcours* (*free range*), since no person is capable of owning them due to their exclusively mental form.[508] It is only through their materialization into a form perceptible by human senses that protection can be considered. In other words, the law only protects the work as a form, but not the idea it was created from.[509] In photography, for example, a certain style of production of photographic products corresponds to an idea and is therefore unprotectable. However, if a style is of such a distinctive nature that the personality of the photographer can be identified in it, it can be protectable.[510]

504 Michel Vivant & Jean-Michel Bruguière, *Droit d'auteur et droits voisins* (Dalloz, 4th ed. 2019), p. 191.

505 Henri Desbois, *Le droit d'auteur en France* (Dalloz, 3rd ed. 1978), p. 12.

506 Antoine Latreille, 'L'appropriation des photographies d'œuvres d'art: éléments d'une réflexion sur un objet de droit d'auteur,' *Recueil Dalloz* 299 (2002), p. 299.

507 Michel Vivant & Jean-Michel Bruguière, *Droit d'auteur et droits voisins* (Dalloz, 4th ed. 2019), p. 177.

508 Antoine Latreille, 'From Idea to Fixation: A View of Protected Works' In: Estelle Derclaye, *Research Handbook on the Future of EU Copyright* (Edward Elgar Publishing 2009), p. 134.

509 *Code de la propriété intellectuelle 2022* (LexisNexis 2021), p. 195.

510 Pierre-Yves Gautier & Nathalie Blanc, *Droit de la propriété littéraire et artistique* (LGDJ 2021), p. 45.

Second, during the *composition* stage, the work itself is prepared to be *assembled* according to the initial idea formed during the previous stage. This stage therefore consists of devising a plan to implement the idea itself in the form of a work, in a certain designed order. The *composition* stage entails creative steps of the author leading towards the materialization of their work-to-be. The second stage can also be referred to as transition stage between the author's idea and their personal expression.[511] It is the active involvement of the photographer in the composition of a photographic work-to-be; their intervention is what contributes significantly to the work's creation.[512]

Third, during the *personal expression* stage, the work is manifested in a form perceptible by human senses. Also, the manifestation itself must be done via author's creative steps, which emanate their personal style and preferences. The creation process, which is concluded by personal expression, has been described by some as *the art of capturing a mentally anticipated form.*[513] Therefore, to even consider whether a product is eligible for copyright protection, the product must first be a creation with a form.[514]

The outcome of all three stages combined should be an original work bearing an imprint of the author's personality. The form that this imprint of the author's personality takes depends on the type and nature of the steps taken during the composition stage, and on the final form of the expression itself.[515] Nonetheless, the imprint of the author's personality may manifest itself either in the composition or expression, or during both stages simultaneously. Simply put, the idea is unprotectable in any case; however, the material manifestation of the composition or the expression may fall under copyright protection.[516]

6.4 The Concept of 'l'Unité des Arts'—the Unity of the Arts

Granting copyright protection to all works of the mind, regardless of their genre, form of expression, merit, or purpose was adopted by passing an amendment to the

511 Ysolde Gendreau, *La protection des photographies en droit d'auteur français, américain, britannique et canadien* (LGDJ 1994), p. 23.

512 Antoine Latreille, 'L'appropriation des photographies d'œuvres d'art: éléments d'une réflexion sur un objet de droit d'auteur,' *Recueil Dalloz* 299 (2002), p. 299.

513 Antoine Latreille, 'La création photographique face au juge : entre confusion et raison,' 31 *LÉGIPRESSE* 139 (2010), p. 139.

514 Christophe Geiger, 'Liberté de l'image et droit d'auteur,' 26 *LÉGIPRESSE* 84 (2005), p. 84.

515 Frédéric Pollaud-Dulian, *Le droit d'auteur: propriété intellectuelle* (Economica, 2nd ed. 2014), p. 203.

516 Ysolde Gendreau, *La protection des photographies en droit d'auteur français, américain, britannique et canadien* (LGDJ 1994), p. 44.

CPI in 1957. However, the theory was known and applied in French jurisprudence as early as 1839. According to *Eugène Pouillet*:

'L'art, il faut le dire, n'a pas de limite; il n'a ni commencement ni fin; il n'est que l'expression de la création l'esprit, l'art manifeste. ('Art, it must be said, has no limits; it has neither beginning nor end; it is only the expression of the creation conceived by the human mind.')'.[517]

Rephrased for the purposes of French copyright law, this has been interpreted as *there is only one art.*[518] The granting of protection to all works of the mind in the French copyright framework is based on and advocated in the concept of the concept of *l'unité de l'art (the unity of art)*[519] or *il n'existe qu'un art* (*there is only one art*).[520]

In practice, abolishing the assessment of the four aforementioned elements (genre, form of expression, merit, and purpose) resulted in granting copyright protection to all works regardless of their artistic features and purpose of creation.[521] Therefore, the same criteria for protection are applied to all forms of artistic expressions. A work cannot be denied copyright protection based, for example, on its utilitarian or any other form.[522]

In other words, this approach prevents discrimination between types of works or an application of a hierarchy between these,[523] as any work may be protected, regardless of its purpose.[524] Within this context, the theory of the unity of the arts became in practice an instrument of great effectiveness for the purposes of protecting investments made in connection with the creation of a product.[525]

The effects of applying the unity of the arts concept in practice has created a very wide scope for copyrightability.[526] Apart from products of utilitarian nature, such a wide understanding made it possible for even products of modest nature to become eligible for copyright protection. Thus, the concept of the unity of the arts has also overlapped with another concept applied within the French copyright framework: that of protection of *la petit monnaie*, the French variant of German *small coin.*

---

517 Eugène Pouillet, *Traité des dessins et modèles de fabrique* (Imprimerie et libraire générale de jurisprudence, 1884), p. X.

518 Frédéric Pollaud-Dulian, *Le droit d'auteur: propriété intellectuelle* (Economica, 2nd ed. 2014), p. 191.

519 Lucie Tréguier & William van Caenegem, 'Copyright, Art and Originality: Comparative and Policy Issues,' 8 *Global Journal of Comparative Law* 95 (2019), p. 95.

520 *Ibid.*

521 Frédéric Pollaud-Dulian, *Le droit d'auteur: propriété intellectuelle* (Economica, 2nd ed. 2014), p. 190.

522 Lucie Tréguier & William van Caenegem, 'Copyright, Art and Originality: Comparative and Policy Issues,' 8 *Global Journal of Comparative Law* 95 (2019), p. 95.

523 Frédéric Pollaud-Dulian, *Le droit d'auteur: propriété intellectuelle* (Economica, 2nd ed. 2014), p. 177.

524 Nicolas Bouche, *Intellectual Property Law in France* (Wolters Kluwer, 3rd ed. 2017), p. 52.

525 Christophe Caron, *Droit d'auteur et droits voisins* (LexisNexis, 6th ed. 2020), p. 105.

526 Christophe Caron, *Droit d'auteur et droits voisins* (LexisNexis, 6th ed. 2020), p. 107.

6.5 The Concept of la petite monnaie—'Small Change'

Since the 19th century, French jurisprudence gradually began to recognize products of a utilitarian nature and function as being eligible for copyright protection. Such recognition signified a departure from the traditional approach to originality. However, some have asserted that the creation of products of this nature still entail choices, even though these are not of a sufficiently arbitrary character to be decisive for a finding of originality.[527] Therefore, the imprint of the author's personality cannot be made manifest through such choices—only a generic and objectively measurable know-how indistinguishable from those of other creators is manifested. Nonetheless, some maintained that the *la petite monnaie*[528] should remain protected, as these works represent the lowest step on the hypothetical ladder of originality, as *Lucas* put it, quoting *Pouillet.*[529]

The eligibility of the *la petite monnaie* for copyright protection is based on the traditional presumption that originality cannot be measured, and its existence—to any extent—is sufficient for a finding of originality.[530] The extent to which originality, in the form of the imprint of its author's personality is detectable in a product is irrelevant for the purposes of copyrightability—it simply needs to exist.[531] Following this, the eligibility of products for copyright protection that display a minimal degree of originality is provided in a *stricto sensu* manner.[532] The outcome of such a generous approach of the French copyright framework is that all original works are protected by copyright, regardless of their banality, ordinariness, horribleness, shockingness, meaninglessness, or incomprehensibility.[533]

---

527 André Lucas et al., *Traité de la propriété littéraire et artistique* (LexisNexis, 5th ed. 2017), p. 131.

528 The author considers it necessary to provide the reader with a brief comparison of the French concept of *'la petite monnaie'* and the German concept of *'kleine Münze'*. Both national concepts are not fundamentally different, as their purpose is to protect by copyright products possessing original or individual features, albeit minimum, which nonetheless still enable such protection. Whether it is within the French or German copyright framework, the protectability of such products is ensured.

529 André Lucas et al., *Traité de la propriété littéraire et artistique* (LexisNexis, 5th ed. 2017), p. 132.

530 André Lucas et al., *Traité de la propriété littéraire et artistique* (LexisNexis, 5th ed. 2017), p. 159.

531 André Lucas, *Propriété littéraire et artistique* (Dalloz, 5th ed. 2015), p. 20.

532 Tribunal de Commerce de Bruxelles, St Gobain v. SVPC, 1924, p. 217.

533 Pierre Frémond, *Le droit de la photographie, le droit sur l'image* (Publicness, 3rd ed. 1985), p. 26.

6.6 The Development of the Concept of Originality in the French Copyright Framework

The ultimate factor that determines whether a product is granted protection within the copyright framework of the France is *originalité* (originality).[534] The requirement of originality serves as a convenient tool to classify the subject-matter for protection within the French copyright framework, thus setting a certain specific condition and narrowing down the scope of copyright and the range of potential subject-matter accordingly.[535] In respect to this, protection cannot be conferred upon a product without it first being declared as original. In other words, the product must have an original character.[536] It is through this originality that a product is granted copyrightability as a work of mind.[537] Establishing originality is based on the link between the author and their work, in which the work serves as an extension of author themselves.[538] The presence of originality itself in a work can be defined as having the imprint of the author's personality manifested by *personalized effort* or the *intellectual contribution* of the author.[539] Originality occurs in a product when its creator (author) has made their arbitrary choices throughout the production process.[540]

As a concept, the requirement of originality in French jurisprudence began to emerge at the beginning of the 19th century. This origin, however, displays a complete lack of any conceptual legal approach towards the establishment and application to originality as a concept.[541] In the beginning, the meaning of the concept had various connotations, including *novelty* or *'not being a reproduction of any previous work'*.[542] However, by the end of the 19th century, the concept was applied according to its current meaning, first as *une touche profondément personnelle* (a *deeply personal touch*), then gradually established as *un véritable travail intellectuel* (*true*

534 Michel Vivant & Jean-Michel Bruguière, *Droit d'auteur et droits voisins* (Dalloz, 2nd ed. 2012), p. 232.

535 Stéphanie Carre, 'France'. In: Reto, M. Hilty (ed). *Balancing copyright: a survey of national approaches* (Springer 2012), p. 392.

536 Cour de Cassation (Ch. Crim.), 97-83.243, 7 Oct. 1998, *RIDA* 1999, No. 180, p. 327.

537 Cour de Cassation (Ch. Crim.), 97-83.243, 7 Oct. 1998, *RIDA* 1999, No. 180, p. 327.

538 André Lucas et al., *Traité de la propriété littéraire et artistique* (LexisNexis, 5th ed. 2017), p. 145.

539 Stéphanie Carre, 'France'. In: Reto, M. Hilty (ed). *Balancing copyright: a survey of national approaches* (Springer 2012), p. 392.

540 Brad Spitz, *Guide to Copyright in France: Business, Internet and Litigation* (Kluwer Law International 2015), p. 13.

541 André Lucas et al., *Traité de la propriété littéraire et artistique* (LexisNexis, 5th ed. 2017), p. 126.

542 Michel Vivant & Jean-Michel Bruguière, *Droit d'auteur et droits voisins* (Dalloz, 2nd ed. 2012), p. 234.

intellectual work), and eventually a *pensée originale et personnelle de l'auteur (original and personal thought of the author)*.[543]

However, the term itself and the concept it represents still lacks any legislative definition and remains very abstract.[544] The language of the CPI itself never uses the term *originality* in connection with works eligible for copyright protection. Only Article L112-4 uses the term of an *original character* regarding the title of a work of the mind. This Article states that if the title of a work of the mind is original in character, it is protected in the same way as the work itself.[545] In light of this state of affairs, the definition of *originality* and its application in jurisprudence seems to be necessary.

6.7 The Relationship Between 'Novelty', 'Being New' and 'Originality'

The term originality itself is clearly therefore not used as a synonym for 'new', but rather as *spécifique en soi* (specific in itself)[546] or *spécifique à son auteur* (specific to its author).[547] Therefore, a product can be original, even if it is not objectively (absolutely) new.[548] Such situations would encompass products based on previously existent ones, but which still bear an imprint of their author's personality. Nonetheless, the presence of this imprint of an author's unique personality suggests that an achievement was accomplished in a form and way not accomplished before, or which others had not been able to accomplish previously.[549] However, the presence of originality also implies a certain novelty of a product,[550] and the presence of originality strengthens this implied novelty, as *Caron* quoted *Le Tarnec*. Therefore, hypothetically speaking, each product can be considered to be new in its own way, regardless of its originality. It logically follows that while each original product is new, not every new product is necessarily original. Nonetheless, France's *Cour de Cassation* stated that the idea of novelty is irrelevant for a finding of originality in a product.[551] For example, in relation to prior art, the manifestation of the author's creative personality resulting in originality will serve as proof of sufficient

543 Michel Vivant & Jean-Michel Bruguière, *Droit d'auteur et droits voisins* (Dalloz, 2nd ed. 2012), p. 235.

544 Pierre-Yves Gautier, *Propriété littéraire et artistique* (Presses universitaires de France 2019), p. 50.

545 Art. L112-4 of the CPI.

546 Basile Ader, 'L'évolution de la notion d'originalité dans la jurisprudence,' 34 *LEGICOM* 43 (2005), p. 43.

547 Pierre-Yves Gautier, *Propriété littéraire et artistique* (Presses universitaires de France 2019), p. 50.

548 Nicolas Bouche, *Intellectual Property Law in France* (Wolters Kluwer, 3rd ed. 2017), p. 51.

549 Christophe Caron, *Droit d'auteur et droits voisins* (LexisNexis, 6th ed. 2020), p. 87.

550 *Ibid.*

551 Nicolas Binctin, *Droit de la propriété intellectuelle: droit d'auteur, brevet, droits voisins, marque, dessins et modèles* (LGDJ, 7th ed. 2022), p. 75.

difference—i.e., the novelty.[552] More specifically, the presence of the imprint of an author's personality serves as proof of a product's difference from other prior products. This can be referred to as novelty. Therefore, in practice, novelty and originality often merge.

Originality is moreover a subjective criterion, while novelty is an objective one.[553] In terms of photography, two or more photographers can depict the same object or subject differently, even if the photographic products were produced at the same time and place. For the purposes of the existence of originality, it is presumed that each photographic product will depict the selected object or subject in a way unique to the photographer, in their personal style.[554] For example, photographic products depicting a well-known tourist attraction would not be objectively novel, but each such depiction could in theory be original. Novelty and originality are therefore not mutually exclusive; a lack of novelty does not preclude the existence of originality.[555] From this perspective, the French approach to determining originality is subjective, rather than objective.[556] The latter, *objective* approach could be employed, for example, in patent law, where novelty serves as a determining criterion for registrability.[557]

The debate on the relationship between novelty and originality can be concluded by adjusting the definition of originality in relation to novelty. In order to sufficiently distinguish the two, originality in a product can be described as the novelty specific to its author.[558] The author must still employ creative choices originating from their unique personality in order to be able to create an original product, novel to them.

6.8 The Traditional French Approach to Originality

Within the French copyright framework, the application of the originality criterion did not pose any significant issues (for example, in terms of its ambiguity) until the 1950s.[559] This unproblematic and unambiguous application could be linked to the limited types of existent and legally recognized—and therefore copyrightable—products. In fact, this official legal recognition was initially limited to sculptures, literary works, and works of fine art. Viewed in this way, the traditional approach to

[552] Pierre-Yves Gautier & Nathalie Blanc, *Droit de la propriété littéraire et artistique* (LGDJ 2021), p. 43.

[553] Patrick Tafforeau & Cédric Monnerie, *Droit de la propriété intellectuelle: propriété littéraire et artistique, propriété industrielle, droit international* (Gualino-Lextenso, 4th ed. 2015), p. 71.

[554] Pierre Frémond, *Le droit de la photographie, le droit sur l'image* (Publicness, 3rd ed. 1985), p. 26.

[555] Henri Desbois, *Le droit d'auteur en France* (Dalloz, 3rd ed. 1978), p. 5.

[556] *Code de la propriété intellectuelle: annoté et commenté* (Dalloz, 23e édition ed. 2023), p. 36.

[557] Henri Desbois, *Le droit d'auteur en France* (Dalloz, 3rd ed. 1978), p. 6.

[558] Christophe Caron, *Droit d'auteur et droits voisins* (LexisNexis, 6th ed. 2020), p. 88.

[559] Christophe Caron, *Droit d'auteur et droits voisins* (LexisNexis, 6th ed. 2020), p. 84.

originality within the French copyright framework can be also seen as very limited in terms of its applicability. It was only with the emergence of new technologies, which gave rise to new potentially copyrightable matter, that the application of *originality* became more challenging.

The traditional French definition of originality is understood to describe an expression of the author's personality.[560] Through the expression of this personality of the author, the product which bears it becomes a work according to the French copyright law. The transition from an unprotected product to a protected work is therefore based on the unique character given to it through its author's personality.

As a result, this traditional approach to originality, especially its emphasis on personality, reflects the French personalist approach to copyright law.[561] This approach also justifies the existence and application of moral rights.[562] If the whole system of traditional originality is based on the presence of the personality of the author in a product through its imprint, then by extension, its presence in the product remains there even after the death of the author and until the destruction of the product. Therefore, within this context, the protection of the author's moral (personal) rights seems natural even after their death.

6.9 The Modern French Approach to Originality

Findings of originality gradually began to be made in more and more products of common and utilitarian nature.[563] The salad basket, for example, was found to be original due to its presentation in an original manner and in a way pleasing to the eye, as *Gautier* quoted a 1961 decision of the *Cour de cassation*.[564] The shift towards a broader understanding of originality itself (as manifested by its extension to products outside of traditional realm of Article L112-2 of the CPI) can be seen as a hidden securing of the investment made in connection with the production of a product in question.[565] The attraction of copyright protection for a product stems from the very nature of copyright itself: the emergence of copyright protection is not bound to any formalities or subject to any fees. Last but not least, copyright offers a convenient term of protection.

The modern French approach to originality also lies in its expansion to areas containing subject-matter that was not originally and traditionally intended to be eligible for copyright protection. In other words, products of nature thought to be

560 Christophe Caron, *Droit d'auteur et droits voisins* (LexisNexis, 6th ed. 2020), p. 84.

561 Christophe Caron, *Droit d'auteur et droits voisins* (LexisNexis, 6th ed. 2020, p. 85.

562 *Ibid.*

563 Michel Vivant & Jean-Michel Bruguière, *Droit d'auteur et droits voisins* (Dalloz, 4th ed. 2019), p. 281.

564 Pierre-Yves Gautier & Nathalie Blanc, *Droit de la propriété littéraire et artistique* (LGDJ 2021), p. 54.

565 Christophe Caron, *Droit d'auteur et droits voisins* (LexisNexis, 6th ed. 2020), p. 86.

unsuitable for this purpose before have now been found to be capable of carrying the imprint of personality of their author.

According to *Sirinelli* and *Lucas*, the general premise of the modern French approach to originality involves seeing it as a concept with *variable geometry*, taking on different meanings depending on the product in question, as *Varnerot* quoted them.[566] This means that the modern French approach must be seen as being more objective. The main difference lies in the accepted manifestation of originality itself within a product. The modern French approach focuses more on the *marque de la contribution intellectuelle de l'auteur (mark of the author's intellectual contribution),* whereas the classical approach on the *empreinte de la personnalité de l'auteur (imprint of the author's personality).*[567] It is evident that the *mark of the author's intellectual contribution* and the *imprint of the author's personality* vary in the extent to which the author personally contributes to the manifestation of originality in a product. In the case of the former, this is more objective; in the case of the latter, it is more subjective. The modern French approach has been applied in cases involving databases and *small change* products, such as catalogues, guides, etc.[568]

As a result, copyright itself is threatened with fragmentation due to competing perspectives of its understanding—the traditional and the economic. [569] If a product is found to be original as a result of a *mark of the author's intellectual creation*, it may be difficult to justify moral rights traditionally affiliated with an *imprint of the author's personality.*[570]

6.10 Negative Elements of Originality

The first element which precludes any emergence of originality in a product is accuracy or exactness.[571] If a person, willing to assume the role and position of an author, does not employ their personality in a creative way in the steps they take throughout the production process of a product, the product cannot be declared to be original. In practice, two main scenarios may lead to an accurate or exact product to be produced. The first one entails faithful and slavish copying of a protected work of another author or of an unprotected product. The second one entails products produced by strictly following well-known know-how. In either case the outcome of these scenarios would be a product that would be ineligible for copyright protection.

The second element that precludes the emergence of originality in a product is *constraints*.[572] Such constraint can affect the author, the production process, or both

[566] Valérie Varnerot, *Leçons de droit de la propriété littéraire et artistique* (Ellipses 2012), p. 55.
[567] *Ibid.*
[568] Valérie Varnerot, *Leçons de droit de la propriété littéraire et artistique* (Ellipses 2012), p. 56.
[569] Valérie Varnerot, *Leçons de droit de la propriété littéraire et artistique* (Ellipses 2012), p. 55.
[570] *Ibid.*
[571] Christophe Caron, *Droit d'auteur et droits voisins* (LexisNexis, 6th ed. 2020), p. 91.
[572] Christophe Caron, *Droit d'auteur et droits voisins* (LexisNexis, 6th ed. 2020), p. 92.

at the same time. It can take many forms—it may be the instructions one must follow, or the standardization requirements, specifications, orders, or technical considerations. In practice, all these examples affect the production process of a product to such an extent that any conduct falling outside of the set boundaries would be undesirable. In other words, the room governed by constraints within which the production process takes place is so narrow and limited that the author is unable to behave according to their personal preferences. This ultimately results in the impossibility of manifestation of their personality, due to these external limitations.

The third element that precludes the emergence of originality in a product is banality.[573] If a product cannot be differentiated from others, if the product does not stand out from the mass of the currently available, then the law does not consider the personality of the author to have been manifested in a manner and to such an extent to be recognizable as being eligible for copyright protection.

The fourth element that precludes the emergence of originality in a product is anteriority.[574] This element can also be exchanged for posteriority in practice, depending on the perspective of the assessment. Simply put, if an author borrows protected elements from an anterior (prior) work, the posterior (later) product cannot be original. This assumption operates on the basis of novelty, which implies the existence of an original work.

6.11 Positive Elements of Originality

The first positive element of originality relates to the clarification of the degree of originality in a product. In other words, there is a question of any presence of originality itself in a product, and the extent to which it may reside in a product. Quite simply, it does not matter whether a product displays originality only in one, some, or all of its constituting elements, it is fully eligible for copyright protection in all such scenarios.[575] In other words, copyrightability does not depend on the extent or amount of originality a certain product possesses.

The second positive element of originality relates to the possible exploitation of arbitrary choices by the author.[576] First, such opportunity for arbitrary choice must exist and must also be available to the author for the intended production process. Secondly, the author must subsequently take advantage of and employ these existent and available choices throughout the production process of a product. It is by doing so that the author can freely and creatively employ their personality, with the outcome of its imprint in a product. The arbitrary nature of the author's choices can

573 *Ibid.*
574 Christophe Caron, *Droit d'auteur et droits voisins* (LexisNexis, 6th ed. 2020), p. 93.
575 Christophe Caron, *Droit d'auteur et droits voisins* (LexisNexis, 6th ed. 2020), p. 94.
576 *Ibid.*

be considered the inverse counterpart to the aforementioned negative element of constraints.

6.12 The Presence of Originality in a Product and its Elements

In a product, the imprint of its author's personality does not manifest itself in the entirety of the product, but rather through its individual elements.[577] However, not all elements that a product consists of are suitable to bear the imprint of the author's personality. Some elements, due to their nature, simply do not allow to be creatively processed and shaped according to the author's intentions. Therefore, it is only those individual elements that can be creatively altered and from which the product consists, that can be the bearers of originality in a product. This presence of originality is significant not only for the protection of the whole product, but also its individual parts. If one was to excerpt an individual element from a product that did not benefit from copyright protection due to the lack of presence of an imprint of the author's personality, the excerption and subsequent use of this particular element would not constitute an infringement of copyright. The more individual elements bear the imprint of author's personality, the more complexly the work itself is protected. It can be therefore said that the product is more comprehensively protected by copyright if it consists of multiple elements capable of bearing the imprint of the author's personality, and at the same time, the author took advantage of this capability. Nonetheless, for the finding of originality in a product (in other words, for a product to be eligible for copyright protection as a work) the presence of originality in only one of its constituting elements would suffice.[578] Such element must, however, distinguish the whole product from other products of a banal or generic nature, and thus make it original.

Distinguishing between elements carrying originality and those which do not is especially important in cases of infringement. Only elements that themselves constitute bearers of originality through the imprint of their author's personality can establish an infringement.[579] Therefore, a product would be eligible for copyright protection in its entirety, even if only one of its elements carried an imprint of the personality of its author, but it would be only this element that would be protectable from its excerption from the product, in the structure of which it participates, and from subsequent unauthorized use. Therefore, the use of non-original elements of an otherwise wholly copyright protected work cannot be identified as infringing on

[577] André Bertrand, *Droit d'auteur* (Dalloz, 3rd ed. 2010), p. 135.

[578] Xavier Linant de Bellefonds & Célia Zolynski, *Droits d'auteur et droits voisins* (Dalloz 2002), p. 48.

[579] *Ibid.*

copyright.[580] Elements that do not carry the imprint of the personality of their author are looked on as unprotected for the purposes of copyright law.

6.13 The Degree of Originality

The French tradition of copyright also differentiates between *absolute* and *relative* originality. According to *Colombet*, the former is based on the premise that a work was created independently of pre-existing works, as *Heitland* quoted him, while the creation of the latter was in fact based on previously known and already existent works.[581] This means that works can be divided into two categories when assessing originality. The first category consists of absolutely original works, while the second of relatively original works.[582] The former category includes works which do not borrow from previously existent works and are therefore novel and original. Absolutely original works are therefore not legally dependent on other works.[583] The latter category includes works that borrow from previously existent works and are therefore original, but not novel. These relatively original works are therefore legally dependent on protected elements of other pre-existent works.[584] In other words, absolutely original works are original (genuine), while relatively original works are derivative. Regardless of the degree of originality present therein, both subcategories of original works are equally eligible for copyright protection.

Absolutely original works are listed in Article L112-2 of the CPI. The list includes 14 types of works which are considered capable of originating directly—originally—from their author and at the same time independently of any other existent works. It can be said that an absolutely original work does not *owe* anything to any pre-existing work(s).[585] However, the said list in Article L112-2 is not exhaustive. Certain doubts can be raised about the fact that some products are referred to as *absolutely original*, which somehow suggests their superiority in comparison to other products. Given all known types of creations, in addition to already known and employable practices and procedures, the creation of a work lacking reference to *any* previously existent works is most likely impossible.[586]

---

580 Christophe Caron, *Droit d'auteur et droits voisins* (LexisNexis, 6th ed. 2020), p. 86.

581 Horst Heitland, *Der Schutz der Fotografie im Urheberrecht Deutschlands, Frankreichs und der Vereinigten Staaten von Amerika* (C.H. Beck 1995), p. 138.

582 Patrick Tafforeau & Cédric Monnerie, *Droit de la propriété intellectuelle: propriété littéraire et artistique, propriété industrielle, droit international* (Gualino-Lextenso, 4th ed. 2015), p. 73.

583 Henri Desbois, *Le droit d'auteur en France* (Dalloz, 3rd ed. 1978), p. 9.

584 *Ibid.*

585 Pierre Sirinelli, *Propriété littéraire et artistique* (Dalloz, 2nd 2004), p. 17.

586 Eva-Marie König, *Der Werkbegriff in Europa: eine rechtsvergleichende Untersuchung des britischen, französischen und deutschen Urheberrechts* (Mohr Siebeck 2015), p. 185.

This approach to originality can be seen in Article L112-3 of the CPI, which allows for copyright protection of translations, adaptations, etc.[587] The list of works contained therein is exhaustive. It is precisely these types of works that are not excluded as *unoriginal* as a result of any connection to, or existence based on pre-existing works. These works can be also referred to as *derivative*.[588] What is of importance for the categorization of a work as relatively original is that it borrows certain formal elements from other pre-existing works, but still includes an additional personal treatment included by the author.[589] Therefore, the existence of a category of *relativement original* (relatively original) works can simply be seen as a necessary counterpart to those that are *absolument original* (absolutely original).[590] Nonetheless, a product is either original or not.[591] The degree of originality only allows the assessing individual to come to a conclusion more easily, and more quickly, while also giving the decision a less ambiguous rationale.[592]

6.14 Criteria Excluded from the Assessment of Originality

The reason the French legislator excludes the criteria below was to reduce the possibility of arbitrary or erroneous court decisions. By doing so, the courts were given narrower room for manoeuvre as well as a greater clarity while assessing a product for the presence of originality. The purpose of exclusion of these elements is to signify that they are meaningless when determining the eligibility of a product for copyright protection, as the sole condition is its originality.[593]

The exclusion of the following criteria from the originality assessment proves that the concept of originality is independent of the intended result sought by the author in their product.[594] The excluded criteria are sometimes referred to as *conditions négatives* (negative conditions).[595] The sole purpose of these criteria is to prevent products otherwise eligible for copyright from being excluded arbitrarily or maliciously.[596] In addition, the exclusion of these elements from the assessment

587 Art. L112-3 of the CPI.

588 André Bertrand, *Droit d'auteur* (Dalloz, 3rd ed. 2010), p. 156.

589 Pierre Sirinelli, *Propriété littéraire et artistique* (Dalloz, 2nd 2004), p. 17.

590 Eva-Marie König, *Der Werkbegriff in Europa: eine rechtsvergleichende Untersuchung des britischen, französischen und deutschen Urheberrechts* (Mohr Siebeck 2015), p. 185.

591 Xavier Linant de Bellefonds & Célia Zolynski, *Droits d'auteur et droits voisins* (Dalloz 2002), p. 46.

592 Xavier Linant de Bellefonds & Christophe Caron, *Droits d'auteur et droits voisins: propriété littéraire et artistique* (Delmas, 2nd ed. 1997), p. 34.

593 *Code de la propriété intellectuelle 2022* (LexisNexis 2021), p. 196.

594 André Bertrand, *Droit d'auteur* (Dalloz, 3rd ed. 2010), p. 127.

595 Pierre Sirinelli, *Propriété littéraire et artistique* (Dalloz, 2nd 2004), p. 11.

596 Christophe Caron, *Droit d'auteur et droits voisins* (LexisNexis, 6th ed. 2020), p. 104.

process is designed to present the judge with a *cleansed* production process to focus solely on the product's creative nature.[597] Nonetheless, a similar statement was also made by the *Cour de Cassation*. The Court noted that the judge cannot base their assessment of originality on the artistic value or commercial purpose of a product, unless they want the decision to be annulled.[598]

6.14.1 Genre

The genre of the work is represented by its categorization into one of the 14 listed in Article L112-2 of the CPI. The genre here can be seen as a family consisting of related members: works.[599] The form of expression is represented by the process that was employed during its production process and the form in which it was presented to the public.[600] It therefore refers to the distinction between various works, classically categorized as literary, artistic, and musical. The general premise upon which the exclusion of *genre* is built is that no product should be excluded from copyrightability by principle or due to its affiliation or non-affiliation with a certain category of products.[601] However, the form of representation must make it possible for the audience to perceive it by senses. Article L112-1, however, does not specify how the term *genre* is defined, and how any prohibition of taking *genre* into consideration should be applied in practice.

Moreover, basing a decision regarding originality solely on a product's affiliation to a certain genre goes directly against the requirement of the case-by-case assessment required by the nature of originality. Therefore, regardless of its genre, a product must be assessed individually. However, it may be true that products belonging to a certain genre may seem to be pre-excluded from a finding of originality due to their affiliation to that very genre.[602] This is currently especially true for fragrances, perfumes, or olfactory products in general. Nonetheless, such products are not excluded from copyrightability due to their affiliation with the olfactory genre, but due to the impossibility of humans perceiving and experiencing them with sufficient precision and objectivity.[603] The same is also true for gustatory products, their taste in particular.

[597] Michel Vivant & Jean-Michel Bruguière, *Droit d'auteur et droits voisins* (Dalloz, 4th ed. 2019), p. 278.
[598] Cour de Cassation (Ch. Crim.), 68-90.076, 13 Feb. 1969.
[599] Michel Vivant & Jean-Michel Bruguière, *Droit d'auteur et droits voisins* (Dalloz, 4th ed. 2019), p. 279.
[600] Frédéric Pollaud-Dulian, *Le droit d'auteur: propriété intellectuelle* (Economica, 2nd ed. 2014), p. 178.
[601] André Lucas, *Propriété littéraire et artistique* (Dalloz, 5th ed. 2015), p. 26.
[602] Christophe Caron, *Droit d'auteur et droits voisins* (LexisNexis, 6th ed. 2020), p. 101.
[603] Michel Vivant & Jean-Michel Bruguière, *Droit d'auteur et droits voisins* (Dalloz, 4th ed. 2019), p. 280.

6.14.2 Form of Expression

Each separate genre of works may also allow for different modes and types of expression.[604] It is therefore important this diversity remains irrelevant for the purposes of copyright law. Through it, the form of expression allows the product to be communicated to the public—its potential consumers. In practice, this requirement ensures that the eligibility of a product for copyright protection is not automatic and based solely on its form of expression.[605] In other words, the form of the said communication of a product to the public is irrelevant for its possible copyrightability and any form of discrimination based on it is prohibited.[606] Therefore, copyrightability, or its refusal, cannot rely merely on a product's form.

Closely connected to the form and mode of expression, is the nature of the possible carrier of the work. It is settled law in French jurisprudence that the intangibility or durability of a carrier, and therefore of the product as such, is irrelevant for the purposes of its copyrightability.[607] Therefore, if a work of the mind is fixed, it must be assessed independently of the nature of the carrier.[608]

6.14.3 Merit

The insignificance of merit of a product for the purposes of copyright protection is especially important for the objectivity of its originality assessment process. In respect to this, any value judgement based on the artistic value of a product is prohibited outright.[609] In other words, the judge cannot assume the position of an art critic to evaluate the qualities of a product they are assessing.[610] Cultural worth may also not be taken into account.

This prohibition applies to both the qualitative and quantitative merit of a product.[611] The courts therefore cannot base their decisions on the qualitative features of a product, most frequently the artistic value, but also on quantitative aspects such as size, length, or number. Therefore, any efforts the creator made, and any difficulties encountered during the production process of a product are irrelevant.[612]

604 *Ibid.*
605 André Lucas et al., *Traité de la propriété littéraire et artistique* (LexisNexis, 5th ed. 2017), p. 110.
606 André Françon, *Cours de propriété littéraire, artistique et industrielle* (Les Cours de droit 1999), p. 163.
607 Pierre Sirinelli, *Propriété littéraire et artistique* (Dalloz, 2nd 2004), p. 13.
608 André Bertrand, *Droit d'auteur* (Dalloz, 3rd ed. 2010), p. 151
609 André Lucas et al., *Traité de la propriété littéraire et artistique* (LexisNexis, 5th ed. 2017), p. 111.
610 Christophe Caron, *Droit d'auteur et droits voisins* (LexisNexis, 6th ed. 2020), p. 103.
611 André Bertrand, *Droit d'auteur* (Dalloz, 3rd ed. 2010), p. 149.
612 Christophe Caron, *Droit d'auteur et droits voisins* (LexisNexis, 6th ed. 2020), p. 103.

Nonetheless, in practice, the criterion of merit is often indirectly taken into consideration.[613] Judges, out of fear of basing their decision on prohibited features of a product, tend to be more lenient in their assessment. As a result, originality might be credited to a product based on features that would normally be non-decisive or prohibited for it, or originality might be denied simply due to the absence of merit.[614] In the case of photographic products, a judge may very often take merit into account, for example in the form of the talent of the photographer, and subsequently base their finding of originality on such disguised grounds.[615]

6.14.4 Purpose

The prohibition on considering the purpose of a product's existence, (in other words, the role it fulfils in society, the reason behind its creation, or the use it was assigned to) is closely connected to the concept known as the *'unity of the arts'*, and is a key part of the French copyright framework, as discussed at the beginning of this chapter.[616] The core of this concept lies in understanding the impossibility of precisely distinguishing between various types of manifestations that art takes, and thus proceeding to protect all of them in order to prevent discrimination.[617] Again, the sole purpose of such an approach is to eliminate discrimination against products with respect to their access to copyright protection based solely on their given purpose, which can very well be artistic or utilitarian.[618] Here, the form of a product must be separable from its function to be eligible for copyright.[619] Therefore, the existence of a function in a product does not automatically exclude the eligibility of the product itself by copyright protection, if this function can be separated.[620] This approach of separability is manifested within the French copyright framework through the *théorie de la séparabilité* (separability theory).[621]

The exclusion of the product's purpose from the originality assessment process was also necessitated from practice. It proved to be very difficult in practice to distinguish between traditional and applied arts and implementing such a distinction

613 André Lucas et al., *Traité de la propriété littéraire et artistique* (LexisNexis, 5th ed. 2017), p. 111.

614 Pierre Sirinelli, *Propriété littéraire et artistique* (Dalloz, 2nd 2004), p. 14.

615 Michel Vivant & Jean-Michel Bruguière, *Droit d'auteur et droits voisins* (Dalloz, 4th ed. 2019), p. 288.

616 Pierre Sirinelli & Alexandra Bensamoun, 'France'. In: Silke von Lewinski, *Copyright throughout the World* (Thomson/West 2022), p. 15–29.

617 Christophe Caron, *Droit d'auteur et droits voisins* (LexisNexis, 6th ed. 2020), p. 105.

618 André Françon, *Cours de propriété littéraire, artistique et industrielle* (Les Cours de droit 1999), p. 163.

619 André Bertrand, *Droit d'auteur* (Dalloz, 3rd ed. 2010), p. 154.

620 André Lucas, *Propriété littéraire et artistique* (Dalloz, 5th ed. 2015), p. 21.

621 Christophe Caron, *Droit d'auteur et droits voisins* (LexisNexis, 6th ed. 2020), p. 74.

would run contrary to the efforts of trying to integrate products of art into daily life.[622]

6.14.5 Know-How

The French copyright framework traditionally does not recognize the pure implementation of know-how as a constituent of originality in a product.[623] Know-how according to French copyright law is seen as routine, uncreative, and banal activity, through which the imprint of one's personality cannot be displayed in a product. The exclusion of know-how from conditions relevant for copyrightability stems from the presumed standardized nature of procedures and steps it entails, in addition to the preclusion of any steps beyond those set by know-how. For the purposes of the French copyright framework, the person involved in a production process governed by know-how is seen as a mere executor or operator of a particular production technique.[624]

However, the total exclusion of know-how cannot be applied too extensively in practice. This is because every creative activity entails, a certain extent of necessary know-how.[625] In other words, the employment of know-how into the production process of a product, (which is sometimes necessary for production), cannot outright disqualify a product from copyrightability.[626] Traditionally, this has been especially true for the production process of photographic products.[627] Photographic production processes demonstrate how know-how is crucial for the result: a photographic product. What is necessary is that the employed know-how does not exceed the amount of creative activity. It is through the primacy of creative activity over know-how that the product becomes recognizable as a work eligible for copyright protection. In other words, know-how must not govern the creation process entirely.

[622] Michel Vivant & Jean-Michel Bruguière, *Droit d'auteur et droits voisins* (Dalloz, 4th ed. 2019), p. 290.

[623] André Bertrand, *Droit d'auteur* (Dalloz, 3rd ed. 2010), p. 123.

[624] Michel Vivant & Jean-Michel Bruguière, *Droit d'auteur et droits voisins* (Dalloz, 4th ed. 2019), p. 172.

[625] André Lucas, *Propriété littéraire et artistique* (Dalloz, 5th ed. 2015), p. 13.

[626] Michel Vivant & Jean-Michel Bruguière, *Droit d'auteur et droits voisins* (Dalloz, 4th ed. 2019), p. 172.

[627] Pierre Sirinelli, *Propriété littéraire et artistique* (Dalloz, 2nd 2004), p. 32.

6.15 The Completion of Certain Formalities

The point of the principle is that for a copyright protection to arise in a product, no prior formalities, such as administrative procedures or legal deposits are required.[628] Also, any types of prior registrations, such as those required within the realm of industrial property, are not required.[629] As repeated on numerous occasions, only originality is decisive. Copyright law within the French copyright framework protects works simply by virtue of their creation, presupposing they are original.[630] The said principle is also confirmed by two provisions of the CPI, namely Articles L111-1 and L111-2.

6.16 Fixation

In general, the CPI does not condition copyrightability by the fixation of a product in a certain way. According to Article L111-1, only the *sole act of creation* is required, without further specifications implying possible fixation.[631] The only exception are choreographic works, circus acts, and tricks and pantomimes, within the meaning of Article L112-2 of the CPI.[632] However, without the actual fixation of a product, the exercise of copyright by its holder(s) might prove to be problematic.[633] Nonetheless, on two occasions, French courts found that the publication of oral speeches in a written form without the consent of the authors infringed on their (copy)rights.[634]

Given their nature, photographic products (as well as products produced using techniques similar to photography), must be fixed on some kind of carrier, whether it be analogue or digital. It is not a requirement prescribed by the law, but a mere technical necessity originating from the very nature of the subject-matter itself and technical necessities associated with it. The only exception might be, a *'camera obscura'*, which is a technical device capable of projecting an image onto a wall, paper, or other chosen area, through a hole or lens. The projected image is perfectly capable of being perceivable by human senses; however, it is not fixed, but only ephemeral or fleeting.[635]

---

628 Pierre Sirinelli, *Propriété littéraire et artistique* (Dalloz, 2nd 2004), p. 11.

629 Valérie Varnerot, *Leçons de droit de la propriété littéraire et artistique* (Ellipses 2012), p. 61.

630 Xavier Linant de Bellefonds & Christophe Caron, *Droits d'auteur et droits voisins: propriété littéraire et artistique* (Delmas, 2nd ed. 1997), p. 41.

631 Art. L111-1 of the CPI.

632 Art. L112-2 of the CPI.

633 Christophe Caron, *Droit d'auteur et droits voisins* (LexisNexis, 6th ed. 2020), p. 71.

634 Tribunal de grande instance de Paris (1ère Ch.), 20 Nov. 1991 ; Commented by André Kéréver. *RIDA*. 1992, p. 340.

635 Susan Sontag, *On Photography* (Penguin Books 2008), p. 88.

6.17 A Form of an Exclusively Functional Nature

The positive definition of a form of a product will be discussed in more detail in a separate section. Here, this subsection will only outline a negative definition of *form* along with features that are irrelevant for copyrightability. If the form of a certain product does not, hypothetically speaking, serve its creative aesthetic, and is solely and in its entirety dedicated to the technical functioning of the said product, the form cannot be eligible for copyright protection.[636] Nonetheless, a product can have a mixed nature, with some of its parts eligible for copyright protection due to its creative processing, while other parts would be ineligible for copyright due to their functional nature. The significance of excluding forms of a functional nature is to prevent access to copyright by subject-matter traditionally protected by different forms of protection, such as patent law.[637]

6.18 Content

Copyright only protects the form, and not the content of a product. The content of a product is therefore irrelevant for its copyrightability. The same criterion also applies to photographic products. Therefore, whatever a photographic product might depict (i.e., whatever its content might be), the only decisive criterion for the copyrightability of the photographic product is its original form, bearing the imprint of personality of its author. In other words, the way the content is depicted is decisive for the copyrightability, rather than the nature of the content itself.

6.19 Immoral or Illicit Nature

Closely connected to the content of a product is the moral or legal standing of a product. The immoral or illicit nature of a product does not and cannot preclude its eligibility for copyright protection.[638] Therefore, pornographic or illegal products can still be *original*.

The assessment of a product for elements of immorality or illegality is not the role of copyright. If copyright law were forced to include this aspect of a product in assessments of originality, the assessment could become a tool for censorship or law enforcement, at the hands of a legislator.[639] Also, it must be noted that the immoral,

636 Christophe Caron, *Droit d'auteur et droits voisins* (LexisNexis, 6th ed. 2020), p. 72.

637 Christophe Caron, *Droit d'auteur et droits voisins* (LexisNexis, 6th ed. 2020), p. 73.

638 Christophe Caron, *Droit d'auteur et droits voisins* (LexisNexis, 6th ed. 2020), p. 102.

639 *Ibid.*

or illegal status of a product can change over the course of time. Originally immoral or illegal products may become moral or legal and vice versa.

6.20 Constituents of Originality in a Product

Having enumerated and defined which criteria must be excluded from the originality assessment process of a product, only the *cleansed* production process should be left for any assessment. However, judges still require guidance in identifying the constituents that can serve to demonstrate originality in a product. In other words, after providing a negative definition by excluding various criteria, I then develop a positive definition based on criteria decisively constituting originality.

6.21 Creative Activity

Only a product that is the result of a creative activity can be considered a work of the mind within the meaning of the CPI, and therefore eligible for copyright protection.[640] This creative activity must consist of choices by the author leading towards the creation of the desired and planned product. However, the choices of the author must be of a certain nature. For a choice be relevant for the purposes of copyright law, it must first and foremost be free. In other words, the choice must be made with the full discretion of the author. Secondly, the choice must have a creative nature.

6.22 Creation

For the creative activity to be of relevance for copyright law, it must result in a creation. The creation itself is considered to be the cornerstone upon which any copyright protection can be built.[641] The creation itself arises as the realization of author's conception devised in connection with the intended outcome, as *Lucas* quoted the decision of the *Cour de cassation*.[642] It can be defined as consisting of two constituents—the intellectual investment and the physical act of shaping.[643] Both constituents must originate from the author. The existence of a creation serves as a prerequisite for any considerations regarding copyrightability. Inversely, the

640 André Lucas et al., *Traité de la propriété littéraire et artistique* (LexisNexis, 5th ed. 2017), p. 68.

641 André Bertrand, *Droit d'auteur* (Dalloz, 3rd ed. 2010), p. 121.

642 André Lucas, *Propriété littéraire et artistique* (Dalloz, 5th ed. 2015), p. 14; Cour de Cassation (Ch. Civ. No. 1), 97-20820, 17 Oct. 2000.

643 Xavier Linant de Bellefonds & Christophe Caron, *Droits d'auteur et droits voisins: propriété littéraire et artistique* (Delmas, 2nd ed. 1997), p. 25.

absence of a creation precludes the initiation of any such consideration about copyright eligibility.

Since only the act of creation of a product is of relevance for its originality assessment, it is first necessary to establish at which point in time one can speak of a creation.[644] In addition to other legislation, Article L111-1 of the CPI states that the author enjoys the exclusive property rights vested in the work by the sole fact of its creation.[645] This wording therefore suggests that for copyright to arise in a work, the work must first take the form of a creation.

Therefore, creation itself can be defined as a legal fact which is a result of a conscious human activity, and which must then result in a modification of reality.[646] The legal fact must be recognized by law as capable of causing effects recognized by law, in this case the creation recognizable as a work within the meaning of the copyright law. The activity leading up to the creation must be performed by a human being who is aware of the consequences. Reality must be also modified in a creative and unique way so as to reflect the author's personality.

Differentiating between types of creations may be based on their differing creation processes. The first group of creations differentiated via this criterion encompasses *créations réalisées* (*created creations*), while the second one includes *créations fixées* (*fixed creations*).[647] The former group includes creations, the creation process of which consisted of putting together elements, combining elements, or transforming elements. The latter group includes creations whose creation process constituted the fixation of ephemeral elements into or onto a tangible or physical carrier. *Created creations* include literary works and works of art, while the *fixed creations* include photographic products.

It can be therefore deduced that a prerequisite for a work within the meaning of the CPI is the creation itself. Moreover, only creations may be considered *works* within the meaning of the CPI; however, not all creations are automatically works.[648] It is for this reason that it is necessary to distinguish between creations to separate those that possess protectable characteristics from those that do not.

6.23 Awareness of the Result/Creation

The very nature of the notion of the *œuvre de l'esprit* (work of the mind) in connection with a product eligible for copyright protection suggests that such a product would be created by a person who, to a certain extent, was aware of the possible

644 Frédéric Pollaud-Dulian, *Le droit d'auteur: propriété intellectuelle* (Economica, 2nd ed. 2014), p. 177.
645 Art. L111-1 of the CPI.
646 Christophe Caron, *Droit d'auteur et droits voisins* (LexisNexis, 6th ed. 2020), p. 60.
647 André Bertrand, *Droit d'auteur* (Dalloz, 3rd ed. 2010), p. 122.
648 Christophe Caron, *Droit d'auteur et droits voisins* (LexisNexis, 6th ed. 2020), p. 60.

result of their conduct.[649] From this it can be therefore presumed that the author is conscious of the consequences of their creative actions to the extent that they may be creating a product with the potential to be a work. This requirement thus excludes products created by chance from copyrightability due to the lack of any creative and mental involvement of a person.[650] In other words, a lack of a mental link between the creator and their created product automatically disqualifies the product from copyrightability. However, this does not disqualify products created by a wilful and deliberate incorporation of chance or by setting up conditions for the use of chance.[651] The very same is applicable to the incorporation of spontaneity into the creation process.[652] Therefore, if chance or spontaneity is found to be a desired component and at the same time willingly incorporated by the author into the production process as such, the created product cannot be excluded from copyrightability on grounds of its creation by chance or spontaneity.

Closely connected to the requirement of being aware of the result/creation is the legal standing of minors, infants, and mentally ill subjects devoid of any will. Creations created by such individuals may lack this crucial component establishing copyrightability. What must be established within this context is whether the creator possesses the capacity to wilfully create to such an extent that the result would be recognizable for the purposes of copyright law.[653] Therefore, if the mind of such an individual were not capable of realizing the potential outcome of their actions, or if such actions were not wilful, the creations would not qualify to benefit from the status of a work within the meaning of the CPI.[654] Nonetheless, the absence or presence of this component would have to be assessed on an individual basis.

6.24 Human Intervention

Originality, regardless of which conception one may apply in practice, still implies the presence of an author's personality.[655] In this respect, and in accordance with current law and practice, only a human being can give rise to a work within the meaning of the CPI.

---

649 André Lucas et al., *Traité de la propriété littéraire et artistique* (LexisNexis, 5th ed. 2017), p. 77.

650 André Lucas, *Propriété littéraire et artistique* (Dalloz, 5th ed. 2015), p. 13.

651 André Lucas et al., *Traité de la propriété littéraire et artistique* (LexisNexis, 5th ed. 2017), p. 79.

652 Christophe Caron, *Droit d'auteur et droits voisins* (LexisNexis, 6th ed. 2020), p. 65.

653 Michel Vivant & Jean-Michel Bruguière, *Droit d'auteur et droits voisins* (Dalloz, 4th ed. 2019), p. 169.

654 Christophe Caron, *Droit d'auteur et droits voisins* (LexisNexis, 6th ed. 2020), p. 64.

655 Michel Vivant & Jean-Michel Bruguière, *Droit d'auteur et droits voisins* (Dalloz, 4th ed. 2019), p. 159

6.25 Modification of Reality

As mentioned above, the modification of reality is one of the constituents of a creation that entitles it to qualify as a work within the meaning of the CPI. Reality consisting of pre-existing elements should be modified by the author.[656] As already stated, this modification must be carried out in a creative way by the author personally, such that the new modified reality bears an imprint of their personality. Cases, in which reality prevents creativity to be employed and subsequently hides it or engulfs it entirely, rule out any finding of originality.[657]

The act modifying reality can be also referred to as the intellectual *re-appropriation* of reality by the author.[658] According to the premise that an author must make reality their own, the photographer must be able to claim ownership of a *reflet de la réalité* (reflection of reality) and also make the *fiction de la réalité* (fiction of reality) their own.[659] This *fiction of reality*, which is then produced by the photographic equipment, must be made their own (i.e., made personal) by the photographer through their personalised vision and creative steps, whereas the *reflection of reality* is materialized in the form of an actual photographic product.

For photography, the conditions of *engulfment by reality* would not be met in case of paparazzi photographic products. The paparazzi photographer only adheres to the conditions presented by reality, without creatively altering it.[660] The same can be said of a photographer producing a reproduction of a painting so faithfully that no subjectivity or personal interpretation and creative modification required for a finding of originality exists.[661]

6.26 Perceptibility by Human Senses

The requirement of perceptibility of a product by human senses is the practical materialization of the idea/expression dichotomy. It is only when the author's idea exits the realm of the mind and becomes perceptible to others that it becomes possible to consider copyrightability.[662] In other words, any protection of the initial idea as a work of the mind must be preceded by materialization of the idea.[663] According to *Cherpillod*, the idea *itself* has no relevance for copyright, due to it being

656 Christophe Caron, *Droit d'auteur et droits voisins* (LexisNexis, 6th ed. 2020), p. 65.

657 Michel Vivant & Jean-Michel Bruguière, *Droit d'auteur et droits voisins* (Dalloz, 4th ed. 2019), p. 170.

658 Bernard Edelman, *Le droit saisi par la photographie suivi de Le personnage et son double La rue et le droit d'auteur L'oeil du droit, nature et droit d'auteur* (Flammarion 2001), p. 35.

659 *Ibid.*

660 Cour d'appel de Paris, 5 Dec. 2007, *RTDCom*, 2008, p. 300.

661 Valérie Varnerot, *Leçons de droit de la propriété littéraire et artistique* (Ellipses 2012), p. 44.

662 André Lucas, *Propriété littéraire et artistique* (Dalloz, 5th ed. 2015), p. 14.

663 Cour de Cassation (Ch. Civ. No. 1), 97-20820, 17 Oct. 2000.

a preconception in the mind, incapable of actual representation due to the lack of its concretisation, as *Lucas* quoted him.[664] The product must simply become material in such a way that enables the idea to be (further) communicated, as *Lucas* continued to quote *Cherpillod*.[665] For a product to be eligible for copyright protection, perceptibility by only a certain intended fraction of public suffices.[666] Therefore, it is important to note that the way a product materializes does not have to be perceived universally, in other words by every possible spectator who exists.

The most common senses that are employed in the perception of a product are sight and hearing.[667] This ubiquity can be noted in the products that are produced most often. The former group entails traditional and contemporary works of visual art and literary works, while the latter group encompasses musical works. Naturally, audiovisual works represent a combination that can be perceived by both senses at once. A 1975 decision by the Paris Court of Appeal (*Cour d'appel de Paris*) ruled that it was, however, incorrect to exclude products perceptible by senses other than those of sight or hearing from copyright protection.[668] This ruling was later overturned, particularly in connection with products perceptible by smell.

The copyright protection of an olfactory product (a perfume) was denied by the *Cour de Cassation* in a 2013 decision due to the lack of form eligible for copyright.[669] Before the 2013 decision by the *Cour de Cassation*, the copyrightability of fragrances was seen as unproblematic.[670] By analogy, protection of gustatory products was denied as well. Nonetheless, this had already been done at the EU level by the CJEU in its *Levola Hengelo* decision.[671] Although these two cases both illustrate a form perceptible by senses, they are nonetheless not eligible for copyright protection.

Despite the rejection of the copyrightability of perfumes by the *Cour de Cassation*, the courts of lower instances continued to provide protection.[672] The *Cour de Cassation* rejected the possibility to copyright protect perfumes, but used a different reasoning than the CJEU. The *Cour de Cassation* rejected the claim on the basis of a simple implementation of know-how, rather than the use of activity that French law would connect with copyrightability.[673]

---

664 André Lucas et al., *Traité de la propriété littéraire et artistique* (LexisNexis, 5th ed. 2017), p. 81.

665 André Lucas et al., *Traité de la propriété littéraire et artistique* (LexisNexis, 5th ed. 2017), p. 91.

666 Christophe Caron, *Droit d'auteur et droits voisins* (LexisNexis, 6th ed. 2020), p. 69.

667 Christophe Caron, *Droit d'auteur et droits voisins* (LexisNexis, 6th ed. 2020), p. 68.

668 Cour d'appel de Paris (4é Ch.), 3 Jul. 1975, *RIDA* 1977, p. 108.

669 Cour de Cassation (Ch. Civ., Com.), 11-19872, 10 Dec. 2013.

670 Michel Vivant & Jean-Michel Bruguière, *Droit d'auteur et droits voisins* (Dalloz, 4th ed. 2019), p. 272.

671 CJEU, Case C-310/17, *Levola Hengelo BV v Smilde Foods BV*, 13 Nov. 2018, ECLI:EU:C:2018:899 (the said case will be elaborated on in more detail in the Chapter No. 10.4.1.8).

672 Antoine Latreille, 'From Idea to Fixation: A View of Protected Works' In: Estelle Derclaye, *Research Handbook on the Future of EU Copyright* (Edward Elgar Publishing 2009), p. 142.

673 Rodrigo Bercovitz & Rodríguez-Cano, *La unificación del derecho de propiedad intelectual en la Unión Europea* (Tirant lo Blanch, 2019), p. 52.

6.27 Form

In order for a creation to be considered a work of the mind within the meaning of the CPI, it must have a certain form, and that form must have an original nature.[674] The form represents a way in which a creation is expressed.[675] It is the form of the creation itself that provides us with hypothetical borders within which a certain creation is to *exist*, in order for it to be eligible for copyright protection. Outside of this realm that positively defines which creations are eligible for copyright protection, are creations that can be defined negatively—i.e., those that are ineligible for copyright protection. It can be said that the form can also be seen as a body to a work.[676] Figuratively speaking, what a body is for a human being, along with the functions it performs, the form is to a work. In this metaphor, the requirement of a certain form in fact evokes the outward expression of one's idea based on the idea/expression dichotomy.[677] The importance of the form and nature of a product was also highlighted by the *Cour de Cassation* in its 2013 decision. In it, the Court held that only creations expressed in a form perceptible by human senses could be eligible for copyright protection.[678]

However, when it comes to photographic products, the requirement of focusing solely on their form clashes with reality. To sufficiently and thoroughly assess a photographic product, judges resort to assessing its composition, the choice of lens, film, lighting, framing, exposure time or shooting angle, as *Vivant* and *Bruguière* quoted from French case law on the subject.[679] This requirement is somehow misleading, since often not only the expression, but also the composition is assessed. In respect to this, judges seem to have adapted to the diversity of the medium of photography and the possible ways of its expression.

6.28 The Originality Assessment Process

If one is to conduct a product assessment to determine its possible inclusion into the realm of copyright within the meaning of the CPI, the decision should not be solely based on the form of expression of the product, but rather on the information contained in the product. This can only occur for photographic products if they are

[674] Christophe Caron, *Droit d'auteur et droits voisins* (LexisNexis, 6th ed. 2020), p. 67.

[675] Nicolas Binctin, *Droit de la propriété intellectuelle: droit d'auteur, brevet, droits voisins, marque, dessins et modèles* (LGDJ, 7th ed. 2022), p. 52.

[676] Michel Vivant & Jean-Michel Bruguière, *Droit d'auteur et droits voisins* (Dalloz, 4th ed. 2019), p. 176.

[677] Pierre Sirinelli & Alexandra Bensamoun, 'France'. In: Silke von Lewinski, *Copyright throughout the World* (Thomson/West 2022), p. 15–30.

[678] Cour de Cassation (Ch. Civ., Com.), 11-19872, 10 Dec. 2013. *RTDCom.* 2014, p. 10.

[679] Michel Vivant & Jean-Michel Bruguière, *Droit d'auteur et droits voisins* (Dalloz, 4th ed. 2019), p. 325 ; Cour d'appel de Paris (4e Ch.), 24 May 2000, *Légipresse* 2000, p. 88.

an original expression creation achieved through the intellectual activity of their author.[680]

In most cases involving traditional creations, the presence of originality is considered natural and undisputed.[681] In the simplest of terms, whenever there is a traditional creation, there is almost always originality present.[682] However, products on the borderline raise questions regarding their copyrightability, thus necessitating an assessment of originality. This is especially true for photographic products.[683] Nevertheless, originality in a creation is generally presumed to be present, unless disputed.

It is exclusively up to the judge to assess the originality of a product in dispute. Moreover, this assessment must be made in the context of the moment and time of the product's creation,[684] and not the time of the assessment.[685] This is the only approach that can ensure that the originality of a product is, hypothetically speaking, embedded in the context of the corresponding period and its potential peculiarities. Therefore, the decision of a judge reached at the time of the dispute should reflect originality potentially acquired in the past.[686] Such an approach also must ensure that the assessment process takes into account circumstances relevant to the time of production of a product, which may have changed significantly during the time leading up to the instigation of the assessment process itself. In other words, this approach is designed to ensure that the product will be placed in the temporal context of its creation for the purposes of assessment.

The court assessment is especially important for products of unclear or ambiguous position in regard to the presence of originality.[687] As already mentioned, this is particularly applicable to photographic products, a subject-matter, where only a decision by the court can confirm or reject the presence of originality. Until the final decision of the court is reached, any such claims, whether in favour or against the presence of originality, are considered assumptions. This state of affairs, especially the need for a decision of the court on the matter, directly follows from the elusive nature of photography as a medium and the constant development of technologies and production processes connected with it.

[680] Horst Heitland, *Der Schutz der Fotografie im Urheberrecht Deutschlands, Frankreichs und der Vereinigten Staaten von Amerika* (C.H. Beck 1995), p. 138.

[681] André Lucas et al., *Traité de la propriété littéraire et artistique* (LexisNexis, 5th ed. 2017), p. 164.

[682] Patrick Tafforeau & Cédric Monnerie, *Droit de la propriété intellectuelle: propriété littéraire et artistique, propriété industrielle, droit international* (Gualino-Lextenso, 4th ed. 2015), p. 70.

[683] André Lucas, *Propriété littéraire et artistique* (Dalloz, 5th ed. 2015), p. 25.

[684] Cour d'appel de Paris, 25 avril 2000, *Annonces de la Seine*, Jun. 19, 2000.

[685] Pierre-Yves Gautier, *Propriété littéraire et artistique* (Presses universitaires de France 2019), p. 52.

[686] Pierre-Yves Gautier & Nathalie Blanc, *Droit de la propriété littéraire et artistique* (LGDJ 2021), p. 43.

[687] Christophe Caron, *Droit d'auteur et droits voisins* (LexisNexis, 6th ed. 2020), p. 99.

6.29 The 'Absence of Creativity' Threshold

It is worth noting that the French copyright framework traditionally does not recognize a creativity threshold of a product as a criterion upon which its copyrightability would be based.[688] The difference, in comparison to the traditional approach to such a threshold in the copyright framework of Germany, is evident.[689] As a result, every product bearing an imprint of its author's personality, albeit minimal, is considered original and therefore eligible for copyright protection.

6.30 The Development of Protection of Photographic Products in France and its Specific Features

The development of protection of photographic products within the French copyright framework can be chronologically divided into three time periods, based on major amendments to legislation by the French legislator. Each of these three periods are given a dedicated section below: the period prior to the year 1957; the period from 1957 to 1985; and the period since 1985. Each section presents the specific legal position and perception of photographic products at that time. The intention is to present the legal evolution of the requirements for the copyrightability of photographic products within the French copyright framework, thus demonstrating the changes in perception of the medium of photography over time and possibly identifying the potential origins and patterns of the current developments on the EU level.

According to *Schorn* and *Koloff*, initially, photography was welcomed as a new medium without major reservations in France, as *Heitland* quoted from their essay.[690] However, soon the course of the debate concerning the legal protection of photographic products headed in the direction of whether a photographic product could be considered art or not.[691] Initially, the categorization of photographic products as works of art was not considered appropriate in France. Traditionally for that time period, photography came to be seen as a mechanical and chemical process, and photographers were merely *operators*. In 1911, a French court in Toulouse

---

688 Frédéric Pollaud-Dulian, *Le droit d'auteur: propriété intellectuelle* (Economica, 2nd ed. 2014), p. 186.

689 French copyright law does not require a minimum level of creativity or artistic merit, upon the surpassing of which, the product would become eligible for copyright protection. Copyrightability is available to all products recognizable as *works of the mind* based solely on their originality, and irrespective of their classification in a specific type of works. For more, see Chapters 6.2 and 6.6.

690 Horst Heitland, *Der Schutz der Fotografie im Urheberrecht Deutschlands, Frankreichs und der Vereinigten Staaten von Amerika* (C.H. Beck 1995), p. 5.

691 Horst Heitland, *Der Schutz der Fotografie im Urheberrecht Deutschlands, Frankreichs und der Vereinigten Staaten von Amerika* (C.H. Beck 1995), p. 132.

(*Cour de Toulouse*) stated, that if, by any chance, a product of such a process were to evoke an artistic feeling, it still would not qualify as a work of art, because it was a purely industrial work.[692] In this initial period of copyright protection of photographic products, French legislator and jurisprudence failed to define requirements for protection of photographic products in a clear and uniform manner.[693]

To begin with, French copyright framework only provided (and still only provides) protection to photographic works, rather than to photographs (as in Germany)—the products of a purely mechanical performance.[694] No distinction in regard to the types of photographic products has ever been made in the CPI. It is therefore evident that a photographic product in the French copyright framework can only be eligible for copyright protection if it is a photographic work. No related right type of protection simply exists for photographic products. The position of the CPI that not all photographic products are regarded as works is natural, since no special protection for all photographic products was ever introduced in France.[695]

6.30.1 The Period Prior to 1957

Copyright protection of photographic products was initially based on the Decree of 19–24 July 1793. The eligibility of photographic products for copyright protection in accordance with this decree was based on an analogous application to paintings, as *Pollaud-Dulian* demonstrates by selected French case law.[696] The analogy was necessitated by the fact the medium of photography had not yet been invented at the time of adoption.[697] In the absence of clear legislative guidance, it was up to the courts to stipulate the conditions under which a photographic product was to be eligible for copyright protection.[698]

The French courts at first only considered artistic photographic products to be eligible for copyright protection. According to the courts, artistic photographic products were to be assessed in connection with the steps the photographer took in connection with two decisive criteria: the choice of the subject/object, and the choices made in connection with the arrangement of the subject, the framing, the

692 Cour de Toulouse, 17 Jul. 1911 (DP, 1912).

693 Horst Heitland, *Der Schutz der Fotografie im Urheberrecht Deutschlands, Frankreichs und der Vereinigten Staaten von Amerika* (C.H. Beck 1995), p. 152.

694 Ysolde Gendreau, Axel Nordemann, & Rainer Oesch (eds.), *Copyright and photographs: an international survey* (Kluwer Law International 1999), p. 117.

695 Horst Heitland, *Der Schutz der Fotografie im Urheberrecht Deutschlands, Frankreichs und der Vereinigten Staaten von Amerika* (C.H. Beck 1995), p. 143.

696 Frédéric Pollaud-Dulian, *Le droit d'auteur : propriété intellectuelle* (Economica, 2nd ed. 2014), p. 218.

697 Ysolde Gendreau, *La protection des photographies en droit d'auteur français, américain, britannique et canadien* (LGDJ 1994), p. 50.

698 Jean-Paul Oberthür, *Nouveau guide du droit d'auteur en photographie* (Annuaire de la photographie 1988).

shooting angle, lighting, etc.[699] However, assessments based on the choice of the subject or object would suppose to focus on the process, rather than the outcome. It was for this reason that the first criterion was gradually set aside and only the second criterion was relevant for findings of originality.

During this period, opinions regarding legal protection of photographic products were far from unanimous, ranging from refusing protection in general, to granting protection without any reservations whatsoever.[700] Both sides of the spectrum of opinions were based on stereotypes about photographic products and paintings, which will be further elaborated below.[701] With these two absolutist opinions on the protection of photographic products, a third approach prevailed that aimed to reconcile certain criteria upon which the protection could be established.[702] In sum, three main positions were held within the French copyright framework: no protection at all should be granted to photographic products; all photographic products should be granted copyright protection; and finally, only certain photographic products should be granted copyright protection.[703]

The first approach, which advocated total rejection of copyright protection, was based on the premise of a comparison between the author of a photographic product (the photographer) to the author of a painting (the painter).[704] According to *Thomas*, in this view, a photographic product was seen only as a product created through the combination of light radiation and the reaction of chemical substances, without any kind of mental intervention from authors themselves, as *Vivant* and *Bruguière* quoted him.[705] The room available for the intellectual involvement of the photographer was only perceived to be in the preparatory phase, therefore prior to the execution, or fixation, of the image itself.[706] The result of this approach was the total denial of any presence of personality of the author—the only basis upon which protection could have been granted. In sum the author of the photographic product was seen as a mere *operator* of a technical device. Figuratively speaking, the light itself was considered the author of any photographic product—and therefore no photographic product could ever be considered a work of the mind.[707]

---

699 *Ibid.*

700 Michel Vivant & Jean-Michel Bruguière, *Droit d'auteur et droits voisins* (Dalloz, 4th ed. 2019), p. 232.

701 Henri Desbois, *Le droit d'auteur en France* (Dalloz, 3rd ed. 1978), p. 80.

702 Michel Vivant & Jean-Michel Bruguière, *Droit d'auteur et droits voisins* (Dalloz, 2nd ed. 2012), p. 177.

703 Pierre Frémond, *Le droit de la photographie, le droit sur l'image* (Publicness, 3rd ed. 1985), p. 28.

704 Michel Vivant & Jean-Michel Bruguière, *Droit d'auteur et droits voisins* (Dalloz, 2nd ed. 2012), p. 177.

705 *Ibid.*

706 Michel Vivant & Jean-Michel Bruguière, *Droit d'auteur et droits voisins* (Dalloz, 2nd ed. 2012), p. 232.

707 Frédéric Pollaud-Dulian, *Le droit d'auteur : propriété intellectuelle* (Economica, 2nd ed. 2014), p. 218.

The stance of the advocates of this approach was based on the claim that no similarities existed between the photographer and the painter during the decisive moments of creation of a photographic product or a painting. According to *Thomas*, the decisive moment at which the personality of the author could have been imprinted into the photographic product, the moment of execution, was seen as being performed solely by the light, as *Vivant* and *Bruguière* quoted him.[708] The next logical step was that the difference between the painter and the photographer was in the choices available to both during the execution of the work itself.[709]

In this setting, the painter has the option to alter their vision of the composition in a creative way, while the photographer, on the other hand, can only faithfully and mechanically depict it.[710] In other words, the core of this claim lay in the fact that the moment of the recording process of an image onto the light-sensitive surface or a sensor could not be affected by the photographer. Therefore, the process of taking of a photographic product was considered to be impersonal and mechanical, without the capability of a notable personal—artistic—approach and a manifestation of photographer's personality, as *Heitland* quoted *Thomas*.[711]

Another reason given for the impossibility of copyright protection a photographic product was the photographer's inability to produce an imaginary image residing within their own mind in a form perceptible by human senses, since any such perceptible form would have to be created with the use of a technical apparatus: the camera, as *Nordemann* presented understanding of photography by *Desbois*.[712] In comparison to painting, the photographic camera was designated as playing the main role in the production of the photographic product, as opposed to the main role of a person, the painter, in the production process of a painting.

It can be said that the decisive activity for granting or rejecting copyright protection is the act of *taking* the photographic product.[713] The presence of the photographer's personality in a photographic product was admitted to a certain extent—it could manifest itself through steps taken in the preparatory and post-processing stages of production process.[714] However, the primacy given to the actual act of *taking* of a photographic product and the emphasis given to this moment as the originality constituent, meant that the limited (but begrudgingly admitted) presence of author's personality was irrelevant. In sum, photographic products were still not eligible for copyright protection.

---

[708] Michel Vivant & Jean-Michel Bruguière, *Droit d'auteur et droits voisins* (Dalloz, 4th ed. 2019), p. 232.

[709] Henri Desbois, *Le droit d'auteur en France* (Dalloz, 3rd ed. 1978), p. 81.

[710] *Ibid.*

[711] Horst Heitland, *Der Schutz der Fotografie im Urheberrecht Deutschlands, Frankreichs und der Vereinigten Staaten von Amerika* (C.H. Beck 1995), p. 132.

[712] Axel Nordemann, *Die künstlerische Fotografie als urheberrechtlich geschütztes Werk* (Nomos 1992), p. 54.

[713] Henri Desbois, *Le droit d'auteur en France* (Dalloz, 3rd ed. 1978), p. 84.

[714] *Ibid.*

The second approach utilized the same comparative heuristic as its counterpart—the comparison to painters and their products.[715] Advocates of this approach saw all photographic products comparable to paintings or drawings. Based on the indisputably established protection of the latter, the basis for protection of the former was clear.[716] According to *Bachelier*, the exercise of the photographer's mental activities during the preparatory phase of the photographic product's production process was an at least sufficient factor justifying the protection of photographic products, as *Heitland* quoted him.[717] According to this line of reasoning by *Pouillet*, all photographic products could be considered works of the mind, as *Pollaud-Dulian* quoted him.[718]

The third approach considered it appropriate undertake an assessment of a photographic product in order to identify criteria on which its protection could be justified and subsequently granted, rather than denying or granting protection *en bloc*.[719] *Desbois* referred to this third approach *eclectic*, given the inspiration it drew from the two absolutist perspectives.[720] Amongst the most commonly sought criteria in a photographic product was originality, which was manifested by the imprint of the author's personality through the various choices made throughout its production process.[721] According to proponents of this approach, the final decision regarding the presence of this imprint should be left to the judge to make.[722]

The granting of copyright protection to photographic products prior to 1957, can be characterized as random and prone to arbitrariness.[723] This was caused by the inconsistency of criteria applied by judges throughout the assessment process. Apart from resorting to the aforementioned criterion of originality, some judges focused on artistic qualities or tried to distinguish between photographic products taken by professional or amateur photographers.[724] This led to a rather uncertain legal situation, for both photographers and their creations.[725]

[715] Michel Vivant & Jean-Michel Bruguière, *Droit d'auteur et droits voisins* (Dalloz, 2nd ed. 2012), p. 177.

[716] Michel Vivant & Jean-Michel Bruguière, *Droit d'auteur et droits voisins* (Dalloz, 2nd ed. 2012), p. 232.

[717] Horst Heitland, *Der Schutz der Fotografie im Urheberrecht Deutschlands, Frankreichs und der Vereinigten Staaten von Amerika* (C.H. Beck 1995), p. 132.

[718] Frédéric Pollaud-Dulian, *Le droit d'auteur : propriété intellectuelle* (Economica, 2nd ed. 2014), p. 219.

[719] Michel Vivant & Jean-Michel Bruguière, *Droit d'auteur et droits voisins* (Dalloz, 2nd ed. 2012), p. 177.

[720] Henri Desbois, *Le droit d'auteur en France* (Dalloz, 3rd ed. 1978), p. 84.

[721] Michel Vivant & Jean-Michel Bruguière, *Droit d'auteur et droits voisins* (Dalloz, 2nd ed. 2012), p. 177.

[722] Frédéric Pollaud-Dulian, *Le droit d'auteur : propriété intellectuelle* (Economica, 2nd ed. 2014), p. 219.

[723] Jean-Paul Oberthür, *Nouveau guide du droit d'auteur en photographie* (Annuaire de la photographie 1988), p. 9.

[724] Michel Vivant & Jean-Michel Bruguière, *Droit d'auteur et droits voisins* (Dalloz, 4th ed. 2019), p. 232.

[725] Horst Heitland, *Der Schutz der Fotografie im Urheberrecht Deutschlands, Frankreichs und der Vereinigten Staaten von Amerika* (C.H. Beck 1995), p. 133.

6.30.2 The Period from 1957 to 1985

The Act of 11 March 1957 served as the modern predecessor to the CPI. The said Act was an attempt to remedy the legal uncertainty caused by the aforementioned lack of a uniform approach to judicial assessments of the protectability of photographic products. In essence, the said Act initiated official recognition of photographic products as works within the meaning of Article 3 as *les œuvres photographiques de caractère artistique ou documentaire et celles de même caractère obtenues par un procédé analogue à la photographie*[726] (photographic works of an artistic or documentary nature and those of the same nature obtained by a process similar to photography). By explicitly including photographic works into the wording of the Act, the French legislator made them objects of copyright protection. However, photographic products were then also subject to a separate specific requirement—the demonstration of the existence of artistic or documentary character.[727] For some, the requirement of *artistic and documentary character* was seen as two separate branches of an alternative protection scheme applicable to photographic products.[728] According to this perspective, any photographic product whose author would seek copyright protection would therefore fall outside of the requirement of being a *work of the mind* stipulated by the general clause of Article 3 of the Act of 11 March 1957, and would only be subject to meeting the requirement of having an artistic or documentary character.

What speaks against this perspective is a judgment by the Appellate Court of Paris (*Cour d'appel de Paris*) from 1970, in which it stated that photographic products were considered works (of the mind) if they possessed artistic or documentary character.[729] The same court also noted that the photographic products in question did not possess documentary character, and thus were not considered original and protected as works of the mind.[730] This would suggest it was the presence of an artistic or documentary character that replaced the required presence of author's personality and originality as a decisive criterion for copyrightability.

Thus, photographic products were subject to a particular and separate originality criterion.[731] By doing so, the French legislator excluded photographic products from the generally and solely applicable criterion for other types of works of the mind: the imprint of personality of the author.[732] The result in practice was that photo-

---

[726] Art. 3 of the Act of 11 March 1957.

[727] Michel Vivant & Jean-Michel Bruguière, *Droit d'auteur et droits voisins* (Dalloz, 2nd ed. 2012), p. 178.

[728] Caroline Carreau, *Mérite et droit d'auteur* (Librairie générale de droit et de jurisprudence 1981), p. 385.

[729] Cour d'appel de Paris, 30 Jun. 1970 (D, 1970).

[730] Cour d'appel de Paris, 30 Jun. 1970 (D, 1970).

[731] Ysolde Gendreau, Axel Nordemann, & Rainer Oesch (eds.), *Copyright and photographs: an international survey* (Kluwer Law International 1999), p. 117.

[732] Basile Ader, 'L'évolution de la notion d'originalité dans la jurisprudence,' 34 *LEGICOM* 43 (2005), p. 43.

graphic products had to fulfil the requirement of originality and at the same time also have an artistic or documentary character. However, subsequent jurisprudence as well as scholarly literature remained divided on this additional requirement, and their findings of both regarding the matter remained ambiguous. However, it was evident that the eligibility of photographic products for copyright protection was no longer solely dependent on the presence of the author's personality. If this were not true, the two newly introduced criteria would not make any sense, since the requirement for their copyrightability would remain unmodified.[733]

The intentions of French legislator for introducing this additional requirement are not clear, though one of the most likely reasons was to prevent the general eligibility of all photographic products for copyright protection.[734] Evidence for this assumption can be found in a 1973 decision by the *Court de Cassation*, in which it noted that the status of works of the mind (photographic works) with an artistic or documentary character was not to be recognised for all photographic products.[735] In other words, not every photographic product would simply be given the status of artistic or documentary character; at least one of the two prescribed characters were necessary for copyright protection.

Nonetheless, the distinction made between the protectable types of photographic products followed previous application practice devised by the French courts.[736] In their jurisprudence, the French courts gradually began to base their decisions less on the presence of imprint of author's personality, and more on the aesthetic value of the photographic product in question.[737] Unsurprisingly, only photographic products possessing artistic effects, or those depicting events interesting to the public, were found to be traditionally eligible for copyright protection.

The actual existence of an additional requirement, on top of the requirement of being a work, could be also deduced by the fact the wording of Article 3 of the Act of 11 March 1957 clearly refers to *les œuvres photographiques* (photographic works). However, in a 1961 decision, the *Cour de Cassation* stated that a photographic work of documentary nature does not have to bear the imprint of the personality of its author in order for it to be eligible for copyright protection.[738] In another decision, the *Cour de Paris* decided that the presence of originality suffices in order for photographic products used in advertising to be eligible for copyright protection.[739]

---

[733] Caroline Carreau, *Mérite et droit d'auteur* (Librairie générale de droit et de jurisprudence 1981), p. 371.

[734] Ysolde Gendreau, *La protection des photographies en droit d'auteur français, américain, britannique et canadien* (LGDJ 1994), p. 61.

[735] Cour de Cassation (Ch. Civ., No. 1), 71-13.028, 28 Feb. 1973

[736] Pierre-Yves Gautier & Nathalie Blanc, *Droit de la propriété littéraire et artistique* (LGDJ 2021), p. 100.

[737] Caroline Carreau, *Mérite et droit d'auteur* (Librairie générale de droit et de jurisprudence 1981), p. 359.

[738] Cour de Cassation (Ch. Crim.), 7 Dec. 1961, *Recueil Dalloz* 1962, p. 550.

[739] Cour d'appel de Paris, 21 Dec. 1988 (D, 1988).

The originality of the photographic product in the latter case was found in the many necessary steps the photographer had taken throughout the production process. For a product to be recognised as an original work within the meaning of the Act of 11 March 1957, and as such protected by copyright, an imprint of its author's personality must be present in it. The irrelevance of the existence of the said imprint for copyright protection is somewhat contradictory to the statements on the additionality of the artistic and documentary character to that of the work requirement.

Another contradiction lay in the requirement of the documentary and artistic character itself. How is a judge to assesses and make a possible finding of such a character without making a (prohibited) value judgement?[740] The necessity of determining the character of a photographic product invited judges to base their decisions on the aesthetic value of photographic products or the rarity of the subject-matter or object depicted. Moreover, by making copyright eligibility subject to a demonstration of the existence of one of the two aforementioned characteristics, any final decision was necessarily dependent on an assessment of merit; however, this was explicitly prohibited by French law.[741]

Since the French legislator did not provide any further guidance regarding the requirements or their nature, it was up to the courts to devise its application in practice, especially distinguishing among photographic products.[742] It must be noted, however, that the jurisprudence on the subject of distinguishing between the two types of characters recognized for the purposes of copyrightability did not help to sufficiently clarify the matter. In the simplest of terms, the *artistic* characteristic of a photographic work was to be incorporated into the traditional requirement of originality, while the *documentary* character of a photographic work did not require the presence of originality as such.[743]

By making photographic products subject to this additional requirement of having an artistic or documentary character, the French legislator eliminated the recognition of photographic products as potential works within the meaning of the Act of 11 March 1957. The additional requirement effectively eliminated the legislatively recognized potential value of a work and with it the associated equal protection.[744]

The classification between types of photographic products was to be carried out with a view to the intentions of the photographer and the content depicted. There were two options: the photographer intended to achieve an artistic effect, or the

740 Michel Vivant & Jean-Michel Bruguière, *Droit d'auteur et droits voisins* (Dalloz, 4th ed. 2019), p. 233.

741 Michel Vivant & Jean-Michel Bruguière, *Droit d'auteur et droits voisins* (Dalloz, 4th ed. 2019), p. 178.

742 René Gouriou, *La photographie et le droit d'auteur* (Pichon et Durand-Auzias 1959), p. 9.

743 Horst Heitland, *Der Schutz der Fotografie im Urheberrecht Deutschlands, Frankreichs und der Vereinigten Staaten von Amerika* (C.H. Beck 1995), p. 158.

744 Ysolde Gendreau, *La protection des photographies en droit d'auteur français, américain, britannique et canadien* (LGDJ 1994), p. 56.

photographer intended to neutrally document a certain event or object. However, such intentions (or the lack of them) might be difficult to prove in practice if they were contested. This was not made simple by the fact that the intentions of the photographer in regard to their future creation—the photographic product—might not necessarily correspond with the product's final features and character.[745]

Both criteria were complementary to each other.[746] Therefore, a photographic work could either bear an artistic or a documentary character, but not both at the same time. However, in some cases, the existence of signs of both a documentary and an artistic character could be found in a single photographic product.[747] A photographic product depicting an airplane may reveal an artistic character in the *personal imprint*, resulting from *technical skill*, while the documentary character may be represented by its information value.[748] According to *Gendreau*, such conduct of French courts was not correct, since as mentioned, a photographic product could either possess an artistic or documentary character, but not both at the same time.[749]

6.30.2.1 Documentary Character

The question of whether a photographic product could fulfil the requirement of originality and at the same time retain its documentary character became a dogmatic problem.[750] In a 1961 decision by the *Cour de Cassation*, a photographic product depicting a politician casting a vote during a referendum was found to be eligible for copyright protection, based solely on its documentary character.[751] Therefore, the presence of originality in the said photographic product was not found to be relevant for the purposes of copyright protection.

If the intentions of the author were not to create a photographic product of a documentary nature, the content of the photographic product could not be protected on such grounds, even if it became particularly valuable or interesting in the period of time following its production.[752] However, as already described, the intentions of the photographer might prove to be problematic. The requirement for the documentary character of a photographic product is opposed to the approach developed within the German copyright framework. The justification of the German legislation to extend protection to photographic products documenting historical events was

[745] Pierre Frémond, *Le droit de la photographie, le droit sur l'image* (Publicness, 3rd ed. 1985), p. 58.

[746] Frédéric Pollaud-Dulian, *Le droit d'auteur : propriété intellectuelle* (Economica, 2nd ed. 2014), p. 220.

[747] Henri Desbois, *Le droit d'auteur en France* (Dalloz, 3rd ed. 1978), p. 93.

[748] *Ibid.*

[749] Ysolde Gendreau, *La protection des photographies en droit d'auteur français, américain, britannique et canadien* (LGDJ 1994), p. 60.

[750] Horst Heitland, *Der Schutz der Fotografie im Urheberrecht Deutschlands, Frankreichs und der Vereinigten Staaten von Amerika* (C.H. Beck 1995), p. 164.

[751] Cour de Cassation (Ch. Crim.), 60-92.241, 7 Dec. 1961.

[752] Pierre-Yves Gautier, *Propriété littéraire et artistique* (Presses universitaires de France 2019), p. 131.

based on the assumption such photographic products would only gain potential notoriety and value with time. Some scholars also noted that the use of a photographic product, by either reproduction or exhibition, served precisely as the evidence of its documentary nature.[753] The logic of this statement comes from the fact that such photographic products merit their use due to the documentary content and the information these bear, which justifies their dissemination.

The documentary character of a photographic product was allowed to be assessed in accordance with both the subjective and objective criteria. The subjective criteria included elements related to the photographer themselves and their intrinsic motivation, such as their profession and the desire to create a document.[754] Objective criteria were related to an assessment of the subject or object captured and depicted in the photographic product, such as news and information or a scientific subject or object.[755] According to *Desbois*, therefore any assessment based on objective criteria would have to focus on the subject or object depicted, rather than on the execution of its depiction, as *Gendreau* quoted him.[756]

In general, it was the circumstances in which a photographic product was produced that confirmed its documentary character.[757] However, not only the situation or circumstances in which a photographic product was produced that confirmed its documentary character; the rarity or uniqueness of the object or subject depicted within the photographic product itself also gave a photographic product a documentary character, such as when a photographer captured a rare subject or object in special circumstances or situations.[758] Nonetheless, the main motive of a photographic product possessing the character of a documentary nature was that it would convey interesting information to the audience it reached, as *Heitland* quoted *Conseil d'État*, which summarized the legislative intentions on connection with the requirement of documentary character.[759] Therefore, a photographic product of documentary character was essentially defined as providing interesting information, due either to rarity or uniqueness of the depicted subject or object, or because of the circumstances in which it was produced.[760]

The reason that the French legislator introduced the documentary requirement was to eliminate situations in which a photographic product could be denied

753 Jean-Paul Oberthür, *Nouveau guide du droit d'auteur en photographie* (Annuaire de la photographie 1988), p. 14.

754 René Gouriou, *La photographie et le droit d'auteur* (Pichon et Durand-Auzias 1959), p. 24.

755 *Ibid.*

756 Ysolde Gendreau, *La protection des photographies en droit d'auteur français, américain, britannique et canadien* (LGDJ 1994), p. 58.

757 *Code de la propriété intellectuelle : annoté et commenté* (Dalloz, 23e édition ed. 2023), p. 49.

758 Pierre Frémond, *Le droit de la photographie, le droit sur l'image* (Publicness, 3rd ed. 1985), p. 57.

759 Horst Heitland, *Der Schutz der Fotografie im Urheberrecht Deutschlands, Frankreichs und der Vereinigten Staaten von Amerika* (C.H. Beck 1995), p. 165.

760 Jean-Paul Oberthür, *Nouveau guide du droit d'auteur en photographie* (Annuaire de la photographie 1988), p. 11.

protection solely due to its lack of artistic character.[761] This additional characteristic made it possible to recognize other photographic products that fell outside of the *artistic* standard. The documentary character was intended to include basically any photographic product documenting events, as well as those covering technical subjects.[762] In this sense, a photographic product possessing a documentary character could have the ultimate means of protection solely based on its purpose.[763] However, by doing so, the legislation created an obvious contradiction to the prohibition on considering the merit of a work. By introducing an obligatory assessment of the artistic or documentary character of a photographic product, the legislation opened the door to questions of merit. However, the documentary character could be seen in every photographic product, apart from those of artistic nature; by the virtue of their very existence, they represented a document.[764]

Another obvious contradiction was connected to the decisive criteria of documentary character. The circumstances in which the photographic product was produced give rise to the documentary character, but since there is almost no possibility for the photographer to influence these circumstances, their personality cannot be imprinted into such photographic products.[765] For this reason, it would never be possible for a finding of originality to be made, since the link between the originality of a photographic product and its documentary character could never be established. However, the French courts refused to admit this contradiction, which led to an almost unrestricted eligibility of photographic products for copyright protection.[766]

6.30.2.2 Artistic Character

According to the French jurisprudence at that time, any photographic product seeking anything else, or more, than a pure and simple representation of features would be considered artistic, and therefore possessing artistic character.[767] The artistic character of a photographic product was supposedly based on the choices made by the photographer, rather than on the circumstances in which such photographic product had been taken, as was the case with the photographic products of documentary character.[768]

---

761 Frédéric Pollaud-Dulian, *Le droit d'auteur : propriété intellectuelle* (Economica, 2nd ed. 2014), p. 220.

762 Frédéric Pollaud-Dulian, *Le droit d'auteur : propriété intellectuelle* (Economica, 2nd ed. 2014), p. 221.

763 Ysolde Gendreau, *La protection des photographies en droit d'auteur français, américain, britannique et canadien* (LGDJ 1994), p. 61.

764 Ysolde Gendreau, *La protection des photographies en droit d'auteur français, américain, britannique et canadien* (LGDJ 1994), p. 74.

765 Jean-Paul Oberthür, *Nouveau guide du droit d'auteur en photographie* (Annuaire de la photographie 1988), p. 15.

766 *Ibid.*

767 Pierre Frémond, *Le droit de la photographie, le droit sur l'image* (Publicness, 3rd ed. 1985), p. 37.

768 Pierre Sirinelli et al., *Code de la propriété intellectuelle* (Dalloz, 15th ed. 2015), p. 47.

Here too, the assessment process was not without obvious contradictions with the basic legal principles of the French copyright framework. The wording of Article 3 of the Act of 11 March 1957 referred to *caractère artistique* (artistic character) and not *artistic merit*. This wording reflects the prohibition on consideration of the artistic value of a product, which, as mentioned above, falls under the merit of a product. Nonetheless, even in such cases, this could be considered a contradiction, since a product's artistic or documentary character could easily be misunderstood for merit or value. Therefore, the assessment process of a product had to be devoid of these prohibited features enumerated in Article 2 of the Act of 11 March 1957, apparently except for the assessment of photographic products.[769] Still, the border between the required objective assessment of the potential artistic character of a photographic product and refraining from considering and appreciating its aesthetic merit might seem very thin.[770]

As already mentioned, the intention of the French legislator to introduce these two criteria was to limit the access of photographic products to copyright protection. This goal was, however, only achieved in one area of these two types of photographic products. The distinguishing of photographic products having an artistic character from other photographic products was successful. Nonetheless, other photographic products found their way into the realm of copyright protection through their documentary character by way of jurisprudence. In light of this, the introduction of these two additional criteria has, quite paradoxically, made copyright protection more accessible to more photographic products, since access to copyright protection became open via two paths.[771]

Without any further guidance from the French legislator, distinguishing between the two types of protectable photographic products proved to be difficult; excessive reliance on the courts in shaping the distinguishing criteria made them prone to arbitrariness and were easily misinterpreted due to incorrect characteristics and criteria in practice.[772] Artistic character seemed to be more closer to the traditional requirement of the presence of the author's personality, but the documentary character was harder to associate with any deeper involvement of the author, which would have resulted in the well-known *imprint*.[773] Statistically, however, French courts' rate of affirming copyright was higher in cases involving photographic products of an artistic character than those of documentary character.[774]

769 Pierre Frémond, *Le droit de la photographie, le droit sur l'image* (Publicness, 3rd ed. 1985), p. 35.

770 Pierre Frémond, *Le droit de la photographie, le droit sur l'image* (Publicness, 3rd ed. 1985), p. 36.

771 Ysolde Gendreau, *La protection des photographies en droit d'auteur français, américain, britannique et canadien* (LGDJ 1994), p. 61.

772 René Gouriou, *La photographie et le droit d'auteur* (Pichon et Durand-Auzias 1959), p. 34.

773 Caroline Carreau, *Mérite et droit d'auteur* (Librairie générale de droit et de jurisprudence 1981), p. 400.

774 Horst Heitland, *Der Schutz der Fotografie im Urheberrecht Deutschlands, Frankreichs und der Vereinigten Staaten von Amerika* (C.H. Beck 1995), p. 164.

6.30.3 The Period from 1985 onwards

The position of photographic products within the French copyright framework was revised again by an amendment of the Act of 11 March 1957 passed on 3 July 1985. The main goal of this amendment was to simplify the copyrightability-assessment process of photographic products.[775] The wording of the 3 July 1985 Act completely removed the two additional requirements based on either artistic or documentary character.[776] These requirements were no longer decisive for copyrightability.

In 1992, the French copyright framework witnessed yet another legislative amendment, this time via the CPI. The amendment resulted in the repeal of the amended Act of 11 March 1957 in its entirety, and the adoption of the currently effective CPI. However, since the amendment of 1992 did not alter the legal position of photographic products established by the amendment of Act of 3 July 1985, this section examines the two pieces of legislation together.

The removal of the two requirements was reflected in the amended wording of Article 3 of the Act of 11 March 1957. According to it, only *les œuvres photographiques* (photographic works)[777] and *œuvres celles réalisées à l'aide de techniques analogues à la photographie* (other works produced by techniques analogous to photography)[778] were to be eligible for copyright protection. The wording of Article 3 was also identically incorporated into Article L112-2 of the CPI.

After this amendment, the French copyright framework fully integrated photographic products into the list of protectable works without imposing any further requirements for their copyrightability, apart from the universal one applicable to all—originality.[779] The French legislator decided to establish a state of dogmatic unity in the treatment of photographic products and their overall position within the French copyright framework.[780] In the broadest of terms, the attention of copyright was shifted from the subject and content to the form of its depiction.[781] It is, however, worth noting that the removal of the two previous conditions (regarding

[775] Michel Vivant & Jean-Michel Bruguière, *Droit d'auteur et droits voisins* (Dalloz, 2nd ed. 2012), p. 178.

[776] Ysolde Gendreau, Axel Nordemann, & Rainer Oesch (eds.), *Copyright and photographs: an international survey* (Kluwer Law International 1999), p. 119.

[777] *Law No. 85-660, of July 3, 1985, on Author's Rights and on the Rights of Performers, Producers of Phonograms and Videograms and Audiovisual Communication Enterprises* (2. Sep. 2024), https://wipolex-res.wipo.int/edocs/lexdocs/laws/en/fr/fr001en.html.

[778] *Ibid.*

[779] Ysolde Gendreau, *La protection des photographies en droit d'auteur français, américain, britannique et canadien* (LGDJ 1994), p. 3.

[780] Horst Heitland, *Der Schutz der Fotografie im Urheberrecht Deutschlands, Frankreichs und der Vereinigten Staaten von Amerika* (C.H. Beck 1995), p. 171.

[781] Michel Vivant & Jean-Michel Bruguière, *Droit d'auteur et droits voisins* (Dalloz, 4th ed. 2019), p. 234.

the *artistic* or *documentary* character) was not retroactive, as *Linant de Bellefonds* quoted French case law on the subject.[782]

As already mentioned, as a consequence of the said amendment, the only requirement relevant to the potential eligibility of photographic products by copyright became their originality.[783] By shifting the prerequisite for copyrightability back to the imprint of the author's personality, the French legislator ensured a case-by-case individual assessment of photographic products. This approach inevitably necessitated detailed court assessments of the creative process and the production circumstances of photographic products.[784] The intention of the French legislator was to align the assessment process to determine the imprint of the author's personality and through it originality itself with other types of works. This alignment made the process of assessment of photographic products more rigorous, since the considerations of merit or other components related to a photographic product's artistic or documentary nature had become non-decisive.[785]

However, even though only the imprint of the author's personality became relevant for contested photographic products, courts have still been tempted to base its final decision on aesthetics, in spite of the prohibition in Article L112-1 of the CPI.[786] Nonetheless, since the amendment of 1985, all photographic products were subject to the same originality test as other potential works.[787]

Shortly after the amendment of 1985, French jurisprudence started applying the new, uniform criteria. Judicial decisions seem to have indeed adapted, although it was still feared the courts would nonetheless continue to apply the previous criteria.[788] Even so, the application of the new requirement in practice represents the overall approach of the French copyright framework towards photographic products—not every photographic product is eligible for copyright protection, as *Nordemann* quoted from case law of the *Cour de cassation*.[789]

Given the necessary reliance of the originality (and the assessment of it by examining the photographer's choices in depicting reality), the next step for French jurisprudence was to identify which choices could potentially demonstrate originality.

782 Xavier Linant de Bellefonds & Célia Zolynski, *Droits d'auteur et droits voisins* (Dalloz 2002), p. 95.

783 Stéphanie Carre, 'France'. In: Reto, M. Hilty (ed). *Balancing copyright: a survey of national approaches* (Springer 2012), p. 388.

784 Basile Ader, 'L'évolution de la notion d'originalité dans la jurisprudence,' 34 *LEGICOM* 43 (2005), p. 43.

785 Frédéric Pollaud-Dulian, *Le droit d'auteur : propriété intellectuelle* (Economica, 2nd ed. 2014), p. 221.

786 Michel Vivant & Jean-Michel Bruguière, *Droit d'auteur et droits voisins* (Dalloz, 2nd ed. 2012), p. 179.

787 Ysolde Gendreau, Axel Nordemann, & Rainer Oesch (eds.), *Copyright and photographs: an international survey* (Kluwer Law International 1999), p. 120.

788 Jean-Paul Oberthür, *Nouveau guide du droit d'auteur en photographie* (Annuaire de la photographie 1988), p. 18.

789 Axel Nordemann, *Die künstlerische Fotografie als urheberrechtlich geschütztes Werk* (Nomos 1992), p. 53.

For photographic products, originality was based on the effects of the photographer's choices such as lenses, film, lighting, framing, exposure time, shooting angle, pose of the photographed subject, contrast, colour, print technique, and contrast, as *Sirinelli* sums up the originality forming elements from French caw law.[790] All of these—as well as many more—serve as constituents of an original photographic work revealing the sensitivity of its author and reflecting their personality.[791] However, none of the manifestations of these choices in a photographic product are determinative on their own.[792] The availability of choices does not, by itself, give rise to originality.[793] Such available choices must be taken advantage of by the photographer in a creative way, and at the same time circumvent any possible technical constraints limiting their exercise. Based on the originality test's focus on the arbitrary choices of the photographer and the expression of their personality that these choices reveal, the originality test, as applied within the French copyright framework, is an open one.[794]

Photographic products which are not considered photographic works and therefore not eligible for copyright protection within the French copyright framework must be identified as such due to their extreme banality, as *Sirinelli* concluded from French case law.[795] Included among extremely banal photographic products are traditionally motor racing photographic products taken via *burst mode*, paparazzi, or aerial photographic products. From these examples, one can deduce that the circumstances of the production process of such photographic products do not allow their author, the photographer, to sufficiently take advantage of the choices through which their personality can be imprinted into the said photographic product. However, it must be noted that the reason for excluding such banal photographic products cannot be based on the banality of the subject or object depicted therein.[796] Instead, it is the banality of the creation process, or the banal treatment of the subject or object and the creation process by the photographer, that excludes such photographic products from copyright protection. The same must be said of unique or rare subject or object with respect to granting copyright protection. Since the amendment of Act of 3 July 1985, such characteristics do not automatically give rise to copyrightability. Within this context, the relevance of the subject or object is on the same level as that of an idea—it is not as such protectable by copyright.[797]

---

790 Pierre Sirinelli et al., *Code de la propriété intellectuelle* (Dalloz, 15th ed. 2015), p. 45.

791 Michel Vivant & Jean-Michel Bruguière, *Droit d'auteur et droits voisins* (Dalloz, 2nd ed. 2012), p. 251.

792 Ysolde Gendreau, Axel Nordemann, & Rainer Oesch (eds.), *Copyright and photographs: an international survey* (Kluwer Law International 1999), p. 120.

793 Antoine Latreille, 'L'appropriation des photographies d'œuvres d'art : éléments d'une réflexion sur un objet de droit d'auteur,' *Recueil Dalloz* 299 (2002), p. 299.

794 Lucie Tréguier & William van Caenegem, 'Copyright, Art and Originality: Comparative and Policy Issues,' 8 *Global Journal of Comparative Law* 95 (2019), p. 95.

795 Pierre Sirinelli et al., *Code de la propriété intellectuelle* (Dalloz, 15th ed. 2015), p. 46.

796 Antoine Latreille, 'L'appropriation des photographies d'œuvres d'art : éléments d'une réflexion sur un objet de droit d'auteur,' *Recueil Dalloz* 299 (2002), p. 299.

797 Antoine Latreille, 'La création photographique face au juge : entre confusion et raison,' 31 *LÉGIPRESSE* 139 (2010), p. 139.

The situation regarding photographic products of two-dimensional objects, such as paintings, drawings, or graphic works, is different in France, compared to the traditional approach in Germany. According to the opinion of the French jurisprudence, as *Sirinelli* concluded, such photographic products do not constitute a purely technical performance of a mere technical nature, and are thus eligible for copyright protection.[798] Even within this genre, the purpose of which is to create a reproduction as faithful as possible, the photographer is assumed to make a certain number of choices, which result in an original creation—a photographic work, as *Sirinerlli* concluded from French case law.[799]

By abandoning the documentary character introduced by the 1985 amendment, the scope of photographic products eligible for copyright narrowed slightly, while the abandoning of the artistic character did not have such effect, since photographic products considered artistic would have met the criteria imposed by the originality requirement anyway.[800] In sum, this means that most photographic products have continued to meet the criteria for copyright protection.

6.31 The Concept of a Photographic Work

As opposed to the notion of *photography*, the term *photographic work* suggests that it refers to a certain specific category within a wider spectrum of photographic products. The *overly general* nature of the term *photograph* was given as a reason by the French legislator for the introduction of a narrower term, *photographic work*.[801] The addition of the word *work* suggests its classification within the group of subject-matter eligible for copyright protection within the meaning of Article L112-1 of the CPI. Thus, status of a photographic work as a *work* is what makes it stand out from other categories of photographic products which are, for whatever reason, not eligible for copyright protection.

By establishing the concept of a *photographic work* as a singular reference to photographic products eligible for copyright protection within the French copyright framework, the French copyright framework also established a closer relationship to the provisions of the Berne Convention, which uses the same terminology.[802]

798 Pierre Sirinelli et al., *Code de la propriété intellectuelle* (Dalloz, 15th ed. 2015), p. 46.

799 Pierre Sirinelli et al., *Code de la propriété intellectuelle* (Dalloz, 15th ed. 2015), p. 46.

800 Horst Heitland, *Der Schutz der Fotografie im Urheberrecht Deutschlands, Frankreichs und der Vereinigten Staaten von Amerika* (C.H. Beck 1995), p. 174.

801 Pierre Frémond, *Le droit de la photographie, le droit sur l'image* (Publicness, 3rd ed. 1985), p. 34.

802 Ysolde Gendreau, *La protection des photographies en droit d'auteur français, américain, britannique et canadien* (LGDJ 1994), p. 21.

6.32 The Concept of 'Other Works Produced by Techniques Analogous to Photography'

Limiting copyrightability solely to photographic products fixed on traditional film or a via digital sensor (and thus excluding any other means of photographic production) would be contrary to the open approach of the French copyright framework.[803] Article L112-2 of the CPI includes types of works the French legislator specifically intended to be eligible for copyright protection at the time of the CPI's enactment.[804] The addition of *other works produced by techniques analogous to photography* in the French copyright framework serves to keep the state neutral and open to any future possible production processes similar to current ones. This technical neutrality allows the French copyright framework to shift its focus from the subject or object itself to its production process and any particular features of it.[805]

In order for a product produced by a technique or techniques analogous to photography to be classified as a (photographic work), it must meet certain requirements, which in turn allow it to benefit from copyright protection. The first requirement relates to the similarity of its production process to that of a photographic work, while the second, and the most important, is the requirement of fixation.[806] The requirement of production-process similarity is linked to the use of other types of radiation than light to create the image. If we assume that only visible-light radiation can be used to create a photographic work within the meaning of the CPI, then all other types of radiation would result in analogous works. The requirement of fixation precludes the image within a photographic product being of transitory nature. In other words, the image within a photographic product must be, to a certain degree, permanent. This permanence, however, does not have to be indefinite.

Given the requirements that an analogous work must meet, or better, which requirements reserved for *traditional* photographic works it would not meet, the number of potential analogous works might seem small. Nonetheless, despite the seemingly narrow room that analogous works might be accommodated in, the CPI still ensures that all works produced by techniques analogous to photography, currently or in the future, and that do not fall into the standard category reserved for photographic works, could still be covered by copyright protection. However, in the end, such categorization of a work is not necessarily important, given that the only requirement for its copyrightability is its originality.[807]

803 Ysolde Gendreau, *La protection des photographies en droit d'auteur français, américain, britannique et canadien* (LGDJ 1994), p. 34.

804 Pierre-Yves Gautier, *Propriété littéraire et artistique* (Presses universitaires de France 2019), p. 71.

805 Antoine Latreille, 'Images numériques et pratique du droit d'auteur,' 34 *LEGICOM* 51 (2005), p. 51.

806 Ysolde Gendreau, *La protection des photographies en droit d'auteur français, américain, britannique et canadien* (LGDJ 1994), p. 35.

807 Ysolde Gendreau, *La protection des photographies en droit d'auteur français, américain, britannique et canadien* (LGDJ 1994), p. 45.

The differentiation between photographic products and those produced by techniques analogous to photography is not clear. The French copyright framework, like the German one to a certain extent, relies on a type of a radiation source used throughout the production process. The importance of this differentiation should not be seen in differentiating between photographic works and those produced by techniques similar to photography, since the differentiation is irrelevant for the purposes of copyright law, as both types of photographic products are to be protected, nonetheless. However, the importance should rather be seen in the differentiation between subject-matter defined in Article 112-2 of the CPI as photographic works and works produced by techniques analogous to photography on the one hand, and the subject-matter of seemingly photographic nature on the other, since these would not be protectable within the meaning the Article L111-2 of the CPI.

6.33 Non-Original Photographic Products

However generous the French copyright framework might seem for photographic products, it too has limits. According to the opinion of one court, if the sole purpose of a photographic product is merely the faithful depiction of the photographed object, while the steps of the photographer and overall arrangements were justified by technical requirements, such photographic product cannot be eligible for copyright protection.[808] The production circumstances of this type of photographic product preclude the employment of creative steps by the photographer, thus making it impossible for the imprint of their personality to arise in such a photographic product.

In general terms, photographic products with a production process that can be reproduced by a large number of people with the identical result are not eligible for copyright protection.[809] In such cases, the exclusion from copyrightability is based on the product's averageness, or banality. The banality of such photographic products is based on their inability of being unique enough to stand out from other previous works of the same type and genre to a sufficient degree.[810]

The term *banality* can be defined as the exact opposite of the term *originality*.[811] Products of a banal nature preclude any existence of originality whatsoever. Banality in a product can be also defined as possessing a common everyday character, without any creative elements resulting from the author and also without any novelty distinguishing it from other previous products.[812] Nonetheless, one can make

808 Tribunal de grande instance de Grasse (1ère Ch. Civ.), 6 Mar. 2000, Dayez c/ Davin de Champclos. *Légipresse* 2000, p. 77.

809 Cour d'appel de Paris, 2003/19670, 29 Oct. 2004.

810 André Bertrand, *Droit d'auteur* (Dalloz, 3rd ed. 2010), p. 130.

811 Pierre-Yves Gautier & Nathalie Blanc, *Droit de la propriété littéraire et artistique* (LGDJ 2021), p. 42.

812 Nicolas Binctin, *Droit de la propriété intellectuelle : droit d'auteur, brevet, droits voisins, marque, dessins et modèles* (LGDJ, 7th ed. 2022), p. 80.

a positive finding of originality even in banal products, such as those of *la petit monnaie* nature. Therefore, the banality of a product does not automatically preclude a finding of originality. However, as mentioned on numerous occasions, individual assessment is still necessary.

Traditionally, photographic products produced automatically, such as by satellite, aerial means, or a photobooth, are considered non-original and therefore ineligible for copyright protection. However, if the mechanical process of the image fixation itself is excluded from the assessment of a photographic product to confirm the presumption of originality, the assessment focuses on the composition and expression stages.[813] Some have asserted that with such automatically produced photographic products, especially when assessing these two production stages, a finding of originality is possible.[814]

The main criterion for distinguishing photographic products capable of being *original* from those that are *non-original* is the intellectual involvement of the photographer. Intellectual involvement may result, as already mentioned, in the display of an imprint of their personality in a photographic product. The extent and depth of intellectual involvement required for an imprint relevant for the purposes of copyright law would be excluded in situations in which the photographer was precluded from or unable to involve themselves into the production process to such an extent so as to leave an imprint. Such situations might include, for example, photographic products taken very quickly,[815] unless, as with chance, the speed of the production process is deliberately employed and sufficiently governed by the photographer who, regardless of the speed, is still in control of the production process, and which still takes place in accordance with the photographer's pre-planned intentions.

What becomes of importance for the purposes of the eligibility of a photographic product for copyright protection within the French copyright framework is that a photographic product is not of extremely banal nature. Extreme banality itself may be derived from the aforementioned lack of mental involvement of the author throughout the production process. In borderline cases, the constraints on the photographer due to standardization requirements or exclusively technical imperatives must be thoroughly assessed, as *Caron* concluded from French case law.[816]

For example, some photographic products taken from an airplane, aerial photography, have been established as eligible for copyright protection.[817] The case is the same with the previously mentioned satellite-produced photographic products. If the preparations, focusing, and post-processing were made by a human being on Earth, the resulting photographic products should be eligible for copyright

[813] Horst Heitland, *Der Schutz der Fotografie im Urheberrecht Deutschlands, Frankreichs und der Vereinigten Staaten von Amerika* (C.H. Beck 1995), p. 175.

[814] Pierre Frémond, *Le droit de la photographie, le droit sur l'image* (Publicness, 3rd ed. 1985), p. 37.

[815] Christophe Caron, *Droit d'auteur et droits voisins* (LexisNexis, 6th ed. 2020), p. 147.

[816] Christophe Caron, *Droit d'auteur et droits voisins* (LexisNexis, 6th ed. 2020), p. 148.

[817] Emmanuel Pierrat, *Le droit d'auteur et l'édition* (Éditions du Cercle de la librairie, 4th ed. 2013), p. 58.

protection, as *Gautier* concluded from French case law.[818] These choices are referred to as personalized interventions required by the use of complex technology.[819]

The automaticity of the capture mechanism does not preclude the existence of the imprint of one's personality within a photographic product produced by such means.[820] It is for courts to assess the production process and the steps the photographer took during it on a case-by-case basis and in detail. For example, photographic products produced using the *burst mode* of an automatically triggered camera on board an aircraft were found not to be eligible for copyright protection due to the automaticity and lack of control over the creation process of the photographer.[821] Nonetheless, such automatically produced photographic products may be eligible for copyright protection if a photographer attempts to edit them during the post-process stage in a way that demonstrates originality, as *Caron* concluded from French case law.[822]

6.34 The Creation Process of a Photographic Product

Since *Desbois'* definition of the three-stage creation process of *idea, composition,* and *personal expression* was originally developed in connection with literary works, its application to photographic products has revealed various limits and differences. However, such differences only lie in the fact that the creation process of a photographic product has proven to be more demanding of certain skills.[823] This is, for example, due to the limited ability of photographers to perform later extensive or fundamental modifications of the structure of the already captured content. Nonetheless, if we apply the three-stage creation process to the production process of an original photographic product (a photographic work), it would follow the following steps to ensure the presence of an imprint of personality.

During the *idea* stage, a photographer thinks about depicting a certain object or a subject in a certain way. Therefore, whatever results as an outcome of this stage is equal to a mere idea, and as such not eligible for copyright protection in accordance with the *idea/expression dichotomy*.

During the *composition* stage, the actual creative steps are taken by the photographer, according to personal preference, the preceding idea, and the plan for its

818 Pierre-Yves Gautier & Nathalie Blanc, *Droit de la propriété littéraire et artistique* (LGDJ 2021), p. 102.

819 André Lucas, Valérie-Laure Benabou & Jean-Michel Bruguière, 'Droit d'auteur et droit voisins,' 26 *Propriétés Intellectuelles* 260 (2008), p. 260.

820 Pierre Frémond, *Le droit de la photographie, le droit sur l'image* (Publicness, 3rd ed. 1985), p. 62.

821 Tribunal de grande instance de Paris (3e Ch., 2e Sec.), 9 Oct. 2009. *RIDA.* 2010, p. 506.

822 Christophe Caron, *Droit d'auteur et droits voisins* (LexisNexis, 6th ed. 2020), p. 147.

823 Ysolde Gendreau, *La protection des photographies en droit d'auteur français, américain, britannique et canadien* (LGDJ 1994), p. 24.

realization. The preferred object or subject is found, the composition is prepared and selected, and the necessary technical equipment is selected, adjusted, and employed. All the steps in the second stage lead up to the actual fixation of the prepared image within the photographic work-to-be. Therefore, during the *composition* stage, the imprint of the photographer's personality can manifest itself through the creative and wilful steps of photographer that affect the arrangement and configuration of the depicted content within the photographic product. The content itself may be then depicted in an ordinary or unoriginal way, yet only composed originally.[824]

During the *personal expression* stage, which begins with the successful fixation of the prepared image within the selected medium, the photographic work is created. It is at this point that the photographic work takes the form of a personal expression of the photographer with an imprint of their personality, shaped and designed in accordance with their personal preferences. However, the photographic work might not yet be finished. Photographers most often need to develop the film as well as post-process and edit the photographic work, regardless of its analogue or digital form. This post-process stage thus also allows for the further imprint of a photographic work with one's personality. Therefore, during the personal expression stage, the imprint of the photographer's personality manifests itself through the creative and wilful steps of photographer affecting the way the captured content is depicted within the photographic product. Here, the captured content is depicted originally within the photographic product, while the composition is left unaffected by the photographer, leaving it unoriginal.[825] The imprint of photographer's personality can simultaneously present in a photographic product if both the composition of the content captured in the photographic product and also the way the captured content is depicted, were affected by wilful and creative steps of the photographer.[826]

However, it must be also noted that some photographic products do not possess originality at either of stages. If a given photographic product only depicts a subject or an object, reality itself does not appear to be *created*, but only faithfully *reproduced*.[827] Once again, in these cases, the product would not be eligible for copyright protection.

[824] Ysolde Gendreau, *La protection des photographies en droit d'auteur français, américain, britannique et canadien* (LGDJ 1994), p. 79.

[825] Ysolde Gendreau, *La protection des photographies en droit d'auteur français, américain, britannique et canadien* (LGDJ 1994), p. 80.

[826] *Ibid.*

[827] Antoine Latreille, 'L'appropriation des photographies d'œuvres d'art : éléments d'une réflexion sur un objet de droit d'auteur,' *Recueil Dalloz* 299 (2002), p. 299.

6.35 Requirements for Protection of Photographic Products

Any photographic product that the photographer wishes to protect by copyright within the meaning of the CPI must pass a two-step test. First, the photographic product must fall into one of the categories specified in Article L112-2 of the CPI. Such condition would certainly be met, since point 9 refers to *photographic works and works produced using techniques similar to photography*. Second, the photographic product must pass the assessment process focused on finding the imprint of the photographer's personality, thus having to qualify as a *work of the mind.*

In general terms, the second step of the test, the assessment process itself, can be further divided into two more steps. The first step would examine actions of the photographer before the actual fixation of the image—in other words, the actions leading towards the fixation itself. The second step would examine the fixation of the prepared image itself. The level of originality the photographer can demonstrate in both parts is directly proportional to the amount of the personal involvement therein.[828]

6.36 Originality in a Photographic Product

From the very beginnings of the introduction of the requirement of originality in connection with photographic products, the imprint of the author's personality—the manifestation of the originality itself, was found manifested in various ways within photographic products. At the end of the 19th century, the term *deeply personal touch* was first applied to justify eligibility of a photographic portrait for copyright protection.[829] As already mentioned, the requirement traditionally focused on the externalized form of the product;[830] French courts thus had to look for the externalization and manifestation of this deeply personal touch. Gradually, such manifestations came to include poses of the depicted subjects, arrangements of costumes, effects created by lighting, physiognomic expressions of the subjects, the choices of subject itself, the composition of subjects, and the angle of view, as *Gendreau* analysed French case law.[831] The courts considered these manifestations in combination, rather than individually.

---

828 Antoine Latreille, 'Images numériques et pratique du droit d'auteur,' 34 *LEGICOM* 51 (2005), p. 51.

829 Michel Vivant & Jean-Michel Bruguière, *Droit d'auteur et droits voisins* (Dalloz, 4th ed. 2019), p. 299.

830 Nicolas Binctin, *Droit de la propriété intellectuelle : droit d'auteur, brevet, droits voisins, marque, dessins et modèles* (LGDJ, 7th ed. 2022), p. 74.

831 Ysolde Gendreau, *La protection des photographies en droit d'auteur français, américain, britannique et canadien* (LGDJ 1994), p. 53.

Currently, the existence of originality itself should the need arise, must be demonstrated by identifying the original elements in the product, the photographic product, itself.[832] Photographers themselves, as the people most often directly responsible for the production of a particular photographic product, should be prepared to precisely identify any and all originality forming elements in the photographic product. The photographer, as the person who has made deliberate, free, and creative choices throughout the production process, with the aim of stamping it with an imprint of their personality, should be able to retrace these choices and describe them in detail. By retracing the individual steps, the photographer can also prove a direct personal link with their creation. It can be said originality arises from personal choices of the author, who evaded automaticity and restriction.[833] Ultimately, originality in a photographic product is created by the choices of the photographer, as *Gautier* concluded from French case law.[834] In general, the more a given photographic product is staged, the better the chances of it being original, as *Heitland* concluded from French case law.[835]

In order to fully understand the notion of originality in connection with photographic products, it also is useful to have a negative definition- in other words, which photographic products are not considered original and therefore ineligible for copyright protection. Photographic products where the production process is solely dictated or governed by technical considerations do not meet the threshold of originality, as *Caron* concluded from French case law.[836] As already mentioned, if the photographer does not circumvent these considerations, the production of an original photographic product is not possible. In other words, this type of photographic products is produced by means which do not allow deliberate and wilful interference from the creative choices of the photographer. It can be said the course of the production process of such nonoriginal photographic products is pre-set and cannot be changed beyond the prespecified borders. In sum, any and all photographic products the production of which was not a result of an arbitrary choice or choices of the photographer, or such production process was solely dictated by constraint are considered non-original within the French copyright framework.[837]

Unlike in Germany, where the final hypothetical question before the court is whether a photographic product should be designated as a *photographic work* or a *photograph*, in France the question asked is whether a photographic product is *original* or *non-original*. The difference between the two scenarios lies in the fact that in Germany, both photographic works and photographs are protected, with the

[832] Nicolas Binctin, *Droit de la propriété intellectuelle : droit d'auteur, brevet, droits voisins, marque, dessins et modèles* (LGDJ, 7th ed. 2022), p. 82.

[833] *Code de la propriété intellectuelle : annoté et commenté* (Dalloz, 23e édition ed. 2023), p. 36.

[834] Pierre-Yves Gautier, *Propriété littéraire et artistique* (Presses universitaires de France 2019), p. 129.

[835] Horst Heitland, *Der Schutz der Fotografie im Urheberrecht Deutschlands, Frankreichs und der Vereinigten Staaten von Amerika* (C.H. Beck 1995), p. 152.

[836] Christophe Caron, *Droit d'auteur et droits voisins* (LexisNexis, 6th ed. 2020), p. 92.

[837] *Ibid.*

only major difference being the term of protection. However, in France, a photographic product judged to be non-original would not attract any copyright or a related right type of protection whatsoever. A photographic product not meeting the originality criteria described below would not even be provided with the shorter term of protection that photographs within the German copyright framework would merit.

6.37 Constituents of Originality in a Photographic Product

The creative steps of photographers taken throughout the production process of a photographic product with the intention of producing an original photographic work can manifest themselves in many ways in such photographic works. Following are the examples of such creative steps grouped into four groups, according to their given place within the timeline of the production process of a photographic product.

6.37.1 The Choice of Subject or Object

The choice of the subject or object itself only serves as a prerequisite, that enables the future execution of ideas of the photographer in regard to the production of a photographic product. The nature of the subject or object and its features might, to a certain extent, presuppose the type, number, extent, and availability of author's creative steps. However, the choice of subject or object as such is still too ephemeral and thus not capable of being recognized as eligible for the purposes of copyright protection. Given its equality with an idea, one must rather focus on the form that the subject or object is given by the photographer, and the qualities implemented in the execution itself.[838] In other words, the choice of the subject or object does not, in itself, serve as a constituent of originality.

6.37.2 Arrangement or Pose of a Subject or Object

For the eligibility of a photographic product for copyright protection, it is not enough to only, so to speak, press the shutter button of a photographic apparatus. When feasible, the photographer must also arrange subject or object within the photographic product, so it reaches a state desired by the photographer.[839] Such arrangement

[838] René Gouriou, *La photographie et le droit d'auteur* (Pichon et Durand-Auzias 1959), p. 14.
[839] René Gouriou, *La photographie et le droit d'auteur* (Pichon et Durand-Auzias 1959), p. 14.

might, for example, ensure a balanced relationship of the depicted subject or object in the environment of the composition. However, outside of staged genres of photography, such as portraiture, the arrangement or pose of a subject or object may be impossible or unnecessary. Given its possible usability only in certain cases and circumstances, the arrangement or pose of a subject or object cannot be considered a universal criterion for the purposes of originality assessments. Nonetheless, where employed, the said arrangements may very well reveal wilful involvement of the photographer and their creative qualities.[840]

6.37.3 Choice of the Shooting Angle

The choice regarding the angle from which a given photographic product is taken, and therefore the image it bears will be depicted, can be considered to be an originality universal to all photographic products. The choice of angle itself determines the character of a photographic product.[841] The angle is a reflection and materialization of a photographer's creative choices, giving a specific character to a photographic product. However, even this criterion might be criticized, despite its universality. Some have claimed that every photographic product must be taken from at least some angle.[842] Therefore, in order to reflect the photographer's personality, the angle decision must be executed creatively and in a subjective way.

6.37.4 Retouching and Post-Processing

The photographer can take steps of a creative nature affecting the nature of a photographic product even in the period following the fixation of the image on whatever carrier chosen. This has gradually taken on even greater importance, given the availability and accessibility of digital technologies such as computers and software. The constant development, dissemination, and expansion of digital photography has enabled far more common and sophisticated retouching and post-processing activities. Creative steps taken by the photographer in the course of retouching and post-processing of a photographic product certainly entail wilful and intellectual conduct.[843] The possibility of employing additional aids, either of a mechanical or a software nature, only proves the versatility of the photographic medium and the scope of creative interventions it allows. If a photographer takes advantage of the space for creativity this potentially offers, they can enhance, edit, or add selected

840 *Ibid.*
841 René Gouriou, *La photographie et le droit d'auteur* (Pichon et Durand-Auzias 1959), p. 17.
842 René Gouriou, *La photographie et le droit d'auteur* (Pichon et Durand-Auzias 1959), p. 19.
843 René Gouriou, *La photographie et le droit d'auteur* (Pichon et Durand-Auzias 1959), p. 20.

features within a photographic product, thus making a stronger and more visible presence of the imprint of their personality.

In conclusion, the effort, external circumstances, choice of exposure, or employment of the motif are not considered manifestations of imprint of photographer's personality if they are not dependent on the choices of the photographer, as *Nordemann* quoted from French case law.[844] Also, the originality of a photographic product must be assessed independently of the subject or object it depicts.[845]

6.38 The Imprint of Personality in a Photographic Product and its Assessment Process

In 1986, French jurisprudence, the *Cour de cassation*, redefined the concept of originality, limiting it to a *mark of intellectual contribution* in a product, as *Lucas* quoted.[846] For photographic products, this meant demonstrating the imprint of the author's personality via the photographer's creative influence over choices, place, moments, framing, the position of objects or subjects and lighting, as *Bruguière* concluded from French case law.[847] All aspects had to be taken control of by the photographer in order for them to be able to bear an imprint of their personality.

With the emergence of new subject-matter seeking copyright protection, such as databases, computer programs, and photographic products, efforts were made to shift the classical originality test towards a higher level of abstraction by the following method: what activities of an author result in the visible presence of their personality in a product?[848] From the further development it can be deduced, that it was eventually settled that the difference between original and non-original products was achieved by the creative choices of the author, with the effects of these choices therefore serving as the distinguishing criteria.

The finding of the possible imprint of author's personality in a photographic product must be the result of creative research.[849] Such research must be conducted by courts, and it is up to them to explain why a particular product may be considered original.[850] If the result of such research is a finding confirming an imprint, the skill of the photographer leading to the creation of a photographic product could not be

844 Axel Nordemann, *Die künstlerische Fotografie als urheberrechtlich geschütztes Werk* (Nomos 1992), p. 53.

845 Antoine Latreille, 'L'appropriation des photographies d'œuvres d'art : éléments d'une réflexion sur un objet de droit d'auteur,' *Recueil Dalloz* 299 (2002), p. 299.

846 André Lucas, *Propriété littéraire et artistique* (Dalloz, 5th ed. 2015), p. 23.

847 *Code de la propriété intellectuelle 2022* (LexisNexis 2021), p. 215.

848 Daniel J. Gervais, *(Re)structuring Copyright: A Comprehensive Path to International Copyright Reform* (Edward Elgar Publishing 2017), p. 108.

849 Basile Ader, 'L'évolution de la notion d'originalité dans la jurisprudence,' 34 *LEGICOM* 43 (2005), p. 43.

850 Cour de Cassation (Ch. Comm.), 11 Mar. 1986, Gazette du Palais, 1986, p. 123.

considered purely mechanical or of mere generic know-how. Moreover, according to the *Cour de cassation*, the originality-assessment process may not be based on the artistic or commercial value of the work.[851] Such an approach would then be based on facts irrelevant for originality, making any assessment appear subjective and unusable for the purposes of French copyright law. Nonetheless, the requirement of originality is, based on its very nature, very subjective and never constant.[852] The subjectivity of the originality requirement comes from the very nature of personality itself—it is subjective to each who bears it: the individual. Therefore, one can say a personal imprint can only be identified subjectively, since every personality itself is original and subjective.

However, the manifestation of personality in the form of its imprint in a pure and clearly perceptible way is rare.[853] For this reason, the employment of subjective assessments might seem necessary. Nonetheless, the prohibition of such assessment, however correct, might prove difficult in practice as a result of courts being reluctant to dive deep into the assessment process out of fear of being accused of an overly subjective approach.[854] The imprint of one's personality might be incorrectly or mistakenly identified. The assessment process itself is therefore based on contradictory demands from the French legislator. The subjective assessment of the judge is prohibited, yet judges themselves are supposed to assess the imprint of a person's (subjective) personality.[855]

Closely connected to the concept of subjectivity is the aforementioned exclusion of merit or value from the assessment process. Judges can only make such assessments based on their own subjective reasoning.[856] Since judges are neither artists nor critics in the field of arts, they cannot include these features of a given product in their assessments. If taking into consideration of such criteria was not excluded from the assessment process, arbitrariness of the decisions of courts would prevail.[857] Naturally, this would preclude consistency of French jurisprudence on the subject.

The originality-assessment process of photographic products must be focused purely on the results of a creative process within the photographic product itself. This includes assessing the awareness of the photographer's actions and the consequences of them throughout the production process of a photographic product. According to *Frémond*, this therefore means closely assessing the individual phases of the production process, as *Nordemann* quoted him.[858] The purpose of doing so is to

---

851 Cour de Cassation (Ch. Crim.), 68-90.076, 13 Feb. 1969.

852 Pierre-Yves Gautier, *Propriété littéraire et artistique* (Presses universitaires de France 2019), p. 65.

853 Pierre-Yves Gautier & Nathalie Blanc, *Droit de la propriété littéraire et artistique* (LGDJ 2021), p. 53.

854 Pierre-Yves Gautier, *Propriété littéraire et artistique* (Presses universitaires de France 2019), p. 66.

855 Pierre Frémond, *Le droit de la photographie, le droit sur l'image* (Publicness, 3rd ed. 1985), p. 25.

856 Frédéric Pollaud-Dulian, *Le droit d'auteur: propriété intellectuelle* (Economica, 2nd ed. 2014), p. 186.

857 Pierre Frémond, *Le droit de la photographie, le droit sur l'image* (Publicness, 3rd ed. 1985), p. 26.

858 Axel Nordemann, *Die künstlerische Fotografie als urheberrechtlich geschütztes Werk* (Nomos 1992), p. 55.

exclude any photographic products taken mindlessly and therefore lacking the presence or display of the imprint of one's personality. The unpredictability of the form an imprint of one's personality may take within a product makes casuistry itself unpredictable as well.[859] The assessment process is therefore necessarily prone to the subjectiveness of the assessing individual. However, the necessity of such approach is underlined by the prohibition on consideration of the artistic or commercial value of the assessed photographic product.

Although explicitly prohibited by law, namely by Article L112-1 of the CPI, the form of expression can nonetheless be used as an aid to identify and demonstrate the presence of originality in a product.[860] The form of expression itself can be seen as a carrier carrying the imprint of personality of the author. The form of expression can be therefore used with the aim of identifying where the imprint of the author is present or expressed in a product. It is worth noting that a form can be protected by copyright on its own, but to do so it must by its nature, hypothetically, escape the ordinary and banal.[861] Moreover, even a banal work still remains a work and as such eligible for copyright.[862] However, the banality must not reach an extreme level.

Nonetheless, in practice, a judge may incorrectly employ the excluded criteria into the assessment process and still base their decision regarding the existence of originality on them.[863] Such conduct could entail two scenarios. The first scenario would involve an original product, the second a non-original one. In the former scenario, the presence of originality would be based on features non-decisive for its presence, and thus originality may be *disguised* behind different features. In the latter scenario, the presence of originality could be incorrectly or mistakenly identified, even where it was technically absent. In both cases, if a judge employed the excluded criteria (incorrectly or mistakenly), the finding of originality in a product would still be positive.

The general premise is that the originality cannot be presumed; it must be proved, as *Varnerot* quoted French case law.[864] However, in most cases, the courts implicitly presume that originality is present in a product in question, and it is only after its presence is contested that its author must try to prove the contrary.[865] Therefore, if the presence of originality is not questioned during a judicial proceeding, it can

859 Frédéric Pollaud-Dulian, *Le droit d'auteur: propriété intellectuelle* (Economica, 2nd ed. 2014), p. 204.

860 Frédéric Pollaud-Dulian, *Le droit d'auteur: propriété intellectuelle* (Economica, 2nd ed. 2014), p. 184.

861 Xavier Linant de Bellefonds & Christophe Caron, *Droits d'auteur et droits voisins: propriété littéraire et artistique* (Delmas, 2nd ed. 1997), p. 29.

862 Michel Vivant & Jean-Michel Bruguière, *Droit d'auteur et droits voisins* (Dalloz, 4th ed. 2019), p. 168.

863 Frédéric Pollaud-Dulian, *Le droit d'auteur: propriété intellectuelle* (Economica, 2nd ed. 2014), p. 187.

864 Valérie Varnerot, *Leçons de droit de la propriété littéraire et artistique* (Ellipses 2012), p. 57.

865 Patrick Tafforeau & Cédric Monnerie, *Droit de la propriété intellectuelle : propriété littéraire et artistique, propriété industrielle, droit international* (Gualino-Lextenso, 4th ed. 2015), p. 73.

be taken for granted, so to speak.[866] The situation is quite different when it comes to infringements. According to *Dreyer*, it is up to the party that believes its copyright has been infringed to prove that the infringing product is not original, which, if successful, implicitly proves the originality of the infringed work, as *Varnerot* quoted him.[867] Nonetheless, originality is presumed for *œuvres d'art pur* (*works of pure art*), whereas it must be proven for *œuvres d'art appliqué* (*works of applied art*).[868] In terms of photographic products, it is up to photographers themselves to demonstrate and prove the originality of their product within the product itself, as *Bruguière* concluded from French case law.[869] Such proof must clearly describe and provide evidence of arbitrary steps taken by the photographer resulting in a photographic product clearly distinguishable from similar products by others.[870]

The requirement of the imprint of the author's personality in a photographic product, and thus the finding of originality, is based on the rebuttable presumption of uniqueness of each personality in a human being. This uniqueness serves as the departure point for an author's visions regarding the creative alteration of banal and objective reality. If this presumption is correct, then if the author incorporated their mind sufficiently into their creation, the creation should be recognized as a work within the meaning of the CPI, and thus eligible for copyright protection. Incorporating a unique personality into a creation, should therefore result in its personal imprint therein. Therefore, if the original aspect of the work expresses the personality of the author, and if each personality is distinct from those of others, then the manifestation of such personality must be unique, and for that reason the work must be original.[871]

The significance of intellectual involvement for the purposes of distinguishing between original and non-original photographic products has been described above. Some have asserted that the expenditure of intellectual involvement of the author during the production process of a product must at least consist of their arbitrary own choices of a personal or artistic nature.[872] Such minimum involvement would in the eyes of the French copyright law ensure that the author of the photographic product employed choices originating from their independent personal preferences. This involvement, albeit minimum, would demonstrate to the assessing party that the photographic product in question was not taken automatically or without any considerations of the author.

As mentioned above, the attitude of the French copyright framework towards photographic products is formed in such a way as to preclude its limitation to

866 *Code de la propriété intellectuelle : annoté et commenté* (Dalloz, 23e édition ed. 2023), p. 36.

867 Valérie Varnerot, *Leçons de droit de la propriété littéraire et artistique* (Ellipses 2012), p. 57.

868 *Ibid.*

869 *Code de la propriété intellectuelle 2022* (LexisNexis 2021), p. 217.

870 Basile Ader, 'L'évolution de la notion d'originalité dans la jurisprudence,' 34 *LEGICOM* 43 (2005), p. 43.

871 Christophe Caron, *Droit d'auteur et droits voisins* (LexisNexis, 6th ed. 2020), p. 87.

872 Patrick Tafforeau & Cédric Monnerie, *Droit de la propriété intellectuelle : propriété littéraire et artistique, propriété industrielle, droit international* (Gualino-Lextenso, 4th ed. 2015), p. 70.

a specific subject or object, and instead focuses on the results and the nature of the production process. Within this context, giving too much credit to the author for their selection of photographic equipment is unsuitable for the purposes of originality assessment.[873] It is true that photographic equipment, to a certain extent, enables the photographer to materialise their creative vision in the way they choose, but it is still the photographer who must use the equipment; it is merely a tool or means for their creation. Even though the assessment process relies on the subjective assessment efforts of a judge, this approach necessarily ensures its neutrality.

To conclude, the French copyright system is focused on identifying the protected elements of a product. These bear the imprint of the author's personality, through the analysis and assessment of the creative process and the *idea, composition,* and *creative expression* stages that it consists of.[874] The focus is therefore on assessing the composition and the expression of the form, rather than on the *modus operandi* of the product itself.[875] The essential question underlining the originality assessment therefore consists more of what the form of a product is like, rather than how it was created.

[873] Christophe Caron, *Droit d'auteur et droits voisins* (LexisNexis, 6th ed. 2020), p. 145.

7 THE DEVELOPMENT OF ORIGINALITY STANDARD IN THE COPYRIGHT FRAMEWORK OF FORMER CZECHOSLOVAKIA

The Czechoslovak framework's choice and inclusion in the list of assessed national approaches towards the eligibility of photographic products for copyright protection were prompted by the different approaches towards copyrightability in central European jurisdictions. This specific approach, known as the requirement of *statistical uniqueness,* was not developed by Czechoslovak scholars. Instead, it was originally devised by *Alois Troller* and *Max Kummer* within the Swiss copyright framework. According to *Koukal*, it was later introduced into the Czechoslovak copyright framework.[876] The essence of this requirement, especially in comparison to the herein assessed approaches of the German, French and harmonized EU copyright frameworks, is a key feature that justifies its inclusion.

The overview begins with two copyright acts which preceded the existence of Czechoslovakia, but nonetheless remained effective for a significant period of time after the declaration of its independence on 28 October, 1918. This historical context sets the stage for the evolution of the copyright framework, a journey marked by significant changes and adaptations. Following are the copyright acts of independent Czechoslovakia, and finally copyright acts of Czech and Slovak Republics. Assessed separate national Czech and Slovak copyright acts are to show how the understanding of copyrightability of photographic products changed in each country in respect to their traditional national approaches, but most importantly in respect to the carried-out harmonization of the EU.

The assessment of the selected copyright acts, both prior to and after the carried-out harmonization of the EU, is a crucial aspect of this research. This assessment is not just a formality, but a key step in understanding the implications of the Czechoslovak copyright framework in the context of EU harmonization. It was done in order to demonstrate different approaches of both national copyright frameworks towards requirements for eligibility of products for copyright protection, and especially for copyrightability of photographic products.

---

[876] Pavel Koukal, *Autorské právo, public domain a lidská práva* (Masarykova univerzita, 2019), p. 39.

7.1 The Chapter's Relationship to the Selected Hypotheses and Research Questions

In terms of the outlined hypothesis No. 2 and No. 3 and the subsequent formulated Research Questions B and C, the purpose of this chapter is to prepare a theoretical knowledge framework representing the development of traditional approach towards qualification of photographic products for copyright protection within the national copyright frameworks of the Czech and Slovak Republics. The said prepared theoretical knowledge framework will then serve as basis, upon which the formulated Research Questions B and C will be confirmed or refuted in the chapter dedicated to the effects of the harmonization on the Czech and Slovak copyright framework.

7.2 1884. évi XVI. t törvénycikk a szerzői jogról

The Statutory Article 1884[877] protected works of literature, music, fine art, maps, plays, and photographic products. Unless otherwise stated, works protected under Statutory Article 1884 were protected for 50 years from the author's death.[878] Statutory Article 1884 was initially effective only in the Hungarian part of the Austro-Hungarian Empire. After the declaration of Czechoslovakia's independence on 28 October, 1918, Statutory Article 1884 remained effective, but only within the Slovak part of Czechoslovakia (formerly the Hungarian part of the Austro-Hungarian Empire), thus maintaining continuity.

Photographic products were traditionally subject to separate treatment. Statutory Article 1884 placed photographic products in a distinct provision, separate from other protectable works. According to Section 69, Statutory Article 1884 addressed the treatment of photographic products as follows:

'The mechanical reproduction, publication and placing on the market of works produced by photography, during the protection period established in Section 70, constitutes the exclusive right of the author of the original recording.'[879]

With regard to the potential definition of a photographic product or photography in general, Statutory Article 1884 provides only a reference in the form of *works produced by photography*. This is a rather generic definition; however, in being so, it may include a wide spectrum of works whose production involved photographic processes. The original recording should be understood as the initial fixation of the

[877] In English *'Statutory Article XVI/1884 on Copyright'*.
[878] § 11 of the Statutory Article XVI/1884 on Copyright.
[879] § 69 of the Statutory Article XVI/1884 on Copyright.

image onto the chosen light-sensitive layer. It should also be noted that Statutory Article 1884 was the first comprehensive copyright act to officially recognize photographic products (*works produced by photography*) not only in the Slovak part of Czechoslovakia but also throughout the Austro-Hungarian Empire.

Statutory Article 1884 conditions the copyrightability of photographic products under Section 69 by requiring that all copies made from the original recording include the name, company, place of residence of the author or publisher of the original recording, and the calendar year in which the photographic product was first published.[880] All photographic products under Section 69 of Statutory Article 1884 were protected for five years, beginning at the end of the calendar year in which the first authorized publication occurred.

Apart from being produced by photography and subject to formal requirements, photographic products were not required to meet any additional criteria to qualify for protection under Statutory Article 1884. Creative or artistic potential was not a deciding factor for their copyrightability under this statute.

7.3 Gesetz, betreffend das Urheberrecht an Werken der Literatur, Kunst und Photographie, RGBl. 197/1895

Although enacted before the formation of Czechoslovakia, the GbU[881] remained effective for six years after its establishment, until 1926. This situation mirrored that of the Slovak part of Czechoslovakia, as in both cases, a foreign-origin act continued to be effective until it was eventually replaced by a national Czechoslovak act. Notably, the GbU was effective solely in the Czech part of Czechoslovakia and marked the first legal act to officially recognize photographic works as eligible for copyright protection within what would become Czechoslovakia.[882] Section 1 of the GbU defined the notion of a *work* as follows:

'Literary, artistic and photographic works published in the country are protected by this law; furthermore, such works whose authors are Austrian citizens, whether the work was published in the country or abroad or whether not published at all.'[883]

[880] § 69 of the Statutory Article XVI/1884 on Copyright.

[881] In Czech: *'Zákon č. 197/1895 ř. z. o právu původském k dílům literárním, uměleckým a fotografickým'*; in English: *'Act No. 197/1895 Coll. On the Right of Origin for Literary, Artistic and Photographic Works'*.

[882] Markéta Klusoňová, *Vybrané otázky z art práva* (Masarykova univerzita 2017), p. 96.

[883] Sec. 1 of the Act No. 197/1895 Coll., On the Right of Origin for Literary, Artistic and Photographic Works.

The GbU did not yet include photographic products under the broader category of literary and artistic works; instead, it treated them separately, defining them as follows:

'All products in the production of which a photographic process has been used as a necessary auxiliary means shall be deemed to be photographic works within the meaning of this Act.'[884]

The definition of photographic products under the GbU encompassed all items produced by a photographic process. A product could be considered photographic only if it could not have been created without such a process. According to legal theory, photographic products were categorized as either *original* or *imitation/reproduction*.[885] Original photographic products included landscapes or portraits, while imitation/reproduction products encompassed photographic reproductions of artistic or literary works.

Original photographic products were eligible for copyright protection, with a term of 10 years under Section 48 of the GbU. In contrast, imitation/reproduction products could be subject to one of the following three conditions:

a) If an imitation/reproduction photographic product depicted a literary or artistic work protected under the GbU and was created with the consent of the original author, it would be eligible for an extended protection term of 30 years.
b) If an imitation/reproduction photographic product depicted a protected literary or artistic work but was created without the consent of the original author, it would not receive any protection.
c) If an imitation/reproduction photographic product depicted a literary or artistic work not protected under the GbU, the product would be eligible for the standard 10-year term of protection.[886]

The differentiation between original and imitation/reproduction photographic products likely stemmed from a desire to categorize these works based on their production process and the photographer's creative contribution, with corresponding protection terms.[887] Copyright protection, aside from portrait photographs, required the inclusion of certain information: the author's name or business name, address, and year of production.[888]

---

884 Sec. 4 of the Act No. 197/1895 Coll., On the Right of Origin for Literary, Artistic and Photographic Works.

885 Jaroslav Pospíšil, *Výklad zákona o právu autorském k dílům literárním, uměleckým a fotografickým* (Česká grafická akciová společnost Unie, 1905), p. 45.

886 Jaroslav Pospíšil, *Výklad zákona o právu autorském k dílům literárním, uměleckým a fotografickým* (Česká grafická akciová společnost Unie, 1905), p. 206.

887 Markéta Klusoňová, *Vybrané otázky z art práva* (Masarykova univerzita 2017), p. 99.

888 Sec. 40 of the Act No. 197/1895 Coll., On the Right of Origin for Literary, Artistic and Photographic Works.

Due to their categorization outside the realm of literary and artistic works, photographic works were subject to a shorter term of protection than the general 30-year term, which lasted throughout the author's life and expired 30 years posthumously.[889] Under Section 48 of the GbU, the term of protection for photographic works was limited to 10 years.[890] This period was calculated based on two separate events: first, the successful development and fixation of the image on a light-sensitive layer, and second, the first publication of the photographic product.

In the first stage, the item could not yet be considered a photographic product, as only the potential to create a positive print from its negative fixation existed. In the second stage, publication marked the beginning of public accessibility. This two-step calculation method meant a photographic product could potentially be protected for up to 20 years if it was produced and published for the first time in the 10th year after its initial fixation on the light-sensitive layer.[891]

In this framework, photographic products required only a *photographic process* to qualify for protection under the GbU, with no requirement for creative or artistic merit. Overall, the GbU treated photographic products differently depending on their production circumstances and the depicted object or subject. The photographer's rights were also subject to formal requirements, such as providing authorial information on each copy, except for portraits. Despite these complexities, the GbU offered a detailed regulatory framework for the rights of photographers.[892]

7.4 Zákon č. 218/1926 Sb., o původcovském právu k dílům literárním, uměleckým a fotografickým (o právu autorském)

The first purely Czechoslovak copyright act, ZoPA 1926,[893] definitively unified copyright regulation in Czechoslovakia. Until its enactment, copyright law was divided between the Czech part (formerly under Austrian law) and the Slovak part (formerly under Hungarian law). Thus, ZoPA 1926 eliminated this dual legal structure, which had originated from the Austro-Hungarian Empire's formation of a real union in 1867.

889 Sec. 43 of the Act No. 197/1895 Coll., On the Right of Origin for Literary, Artistic and Photographic Works.

890 Sec. 48 of the Act No. 197/1895 Coll., On the Right of Origin for Literary, Artistic and Photographic Works.

891 Jaroslav Pospíšil, *Výklad zákona o právu autorském k dílům literárním, uměleckým a fotografickým* (Česká grafická akciová společnost Unie, 1905), p. 231.

892 Karel Václav Adámek, *O právu autorském dle zákona ze dne 26. prosince 1895 č. 197 ř.z.* (Moravská knihtisk, 1898), p. 8.

893 In English: *'Act No. 218/1926 Coll. on the original right to literary, artistic and photographic works (on copyright)'*.

Not only can ZoPA 1926 be regarded as the first adopted Czechoslovak copyright act, but it also represents the first copyright law that aligns with modern standards. Regarding works protected under copyright, ZoPA 1926 provided the following definition:

'This Act protects literary, artistic (musical and visual), and photographic works published (Section 8(1) in the territory of the Czechoslovak Republic, as well as works by authors who are citizens of the Czechoslovak Republic, whether published or unpublished.'[894]

Regarding the aforementioned quoted provision, the ZoPA 1926 follows the Berne Convention in terms of the applicability of its provisions solely to works that can be affiliated with the literary and artistic spectrum. This traditional setting is still adhered to nowadays. What is interesting is the continuation of the separate referral to photographic works and their allocation outside of literary and artistic subject-matter that is qualified for copyright protection. To confirm this separate treatment, ZoPA 1926 also defines what is to be considered a photographic work within its meaning. The definition is identical to that used in the GbU and has the following wording:

'For the purposes of this Act, photographic works are all products and creations in which a photographic or similar process has been used as a necessary auxiliary means'.[895]

Photographic products were the only subject-matter within the meaning of the ZoPA 1926, where the author's personal creative activity or input was not to be considered a decisive criterion upon which such photographic product would be eligible for copyright protection.[896] The only requirement necessitating their copyrightability was the involvement of a *photographic or other similar process*.

The eligibility of photographic products for copyright protection was no longer subject to formalities related to the identification of the author on the copy of the photographic print. However, the differentiation between *original* and *imitation/reproduction* photographic products initially introduced by the GbU was transposed into the ZoPA 1926. The ZoPA 1926 also abolished the 10-year protection period, which was calculated depending on the event of successful development and fixation of the image on the light-sensitive layer. If no other specific term of protection would be applicable, the protection period could no longer exceed 10 years.

894 Sec. 1 of the ZoPA 1926.

895 Sec. 4 of the ZoPA 1926.

896 Jan Löwenbach, *Právo autorské: zákon ze dne 24. listopadu 1926, číslo 218. Sb. Z. a nař. s výkladem, judikaturou I prováděcími nařízením a hlavní normy mezinárodního a zahraničního práva původcovského* (Československý Kompas 1927), p. 41.

Photographic works were also subject to a separate, shorter term of protection in a duration of 10 years from their publication,[897] as opposed to the general one of 50 years,[898] which would, however, last throughout the author's life and expire 50 years after their death. The applicability of the shorter term of protection was the manifestation of the omission of recognition of personal creative activity or input of the author as a criterion for its copyrightability.[899] The dependence of copyrightability based only on the fulfilment of technical criteria was thus rewarded by a significantly shorter term of protection, a change that profoundly impacted the copyright landscape.

Although the ZoPA 1926 has adopted and continued the official recognition of photographic products eligible for copyright protection within its meaning as photographic works, just as the Statutory Article 1884 and GbU, it has refused to equal their position with other protected works. The most apparent manifestation of this inequality was the disproportionate term of protection available for photographic products.

7.5 Zákon č. 115/1953 Sb., o právu autorském

The next take on the regulation of copyright protection in Czechoslovakia was the ZoPA 1953.[900] ZoPA 1953 defined the subject-matter eligible for copyright protection within its meaning in the following way:

'The subject of copyright are literary, scientific and artistic works that are the result of the author's creative activity.'[901]

Section 2 (2) of the ZoPA 1953 further specifies the types of works by giving examples, including *díla fotografická* (photographic works). According to Section 69 of the ZoPA 1953, photographic works within the meaning of its Section 2 (1) were given a 10-year term of protection, beginning their publication,[902] as opposed to a general 50-year one applicable to other traditional types of works. The term of protection available for photographic works seems somewhat disproportionate, especially when compared to the term offered to *traditional* works. Nonetheless, such disproportionate treatment was still well within the then-current legal understanding of the photographic medium.

897 Sec. 41 of the ZoPA 1926.
898 Sec. 38 of the ZoPA 1926.
899 Jan Löwenbach, *Právo autorské: zákon ze dne 24. listopadu 1926, číslo 218. Sb. Z. a nař. s výkladem, judikaturou I prováděcími nařízením a hlavní normy mezinárodního a zahraničního práva původcovského* (Československý Kompas 1927), p. 41.
900 In English: *'Act No. 115/1953 Coll. Copyright Act'.*
901 Sec. 2 (1) of the ZoPA 1953.
902 Sec. 69 of the ZoPA 1953.

For a photographic product to be protected by copyright, two cumulative criteria explicitly stipulated in Section 2 (1) of the ZoPA 1953 must have been fulfilled: affiliation of the work with the three types of categories while simultaneously being the result of the author's creative activity. Another traditional criterion, that of being an expression perceptible by human senses, remains implicit.

The ZoPA 1953 was the first copyright act applicable in Czechoslovakia, which subjected photographic products to the condition of expenditure and display of creative activity. In other words, the technical nature of the photographic production process was now primarily decisive for the considerations regarding the eligibility of such produced photographic products for copyright protection.

7.6 Zákon č. 35/1965 Sb., o dílech literárních, vědeckých a uměleckých

The wording of the next Czechoslovak copyright act, the AutZ 1965[903], did not differ from its predecessors concerning photographic products. Its Section 2 (1) formulates the definition of an authorial work in the following way:

'The subject of copyright are literary, scientific and artistic works that are the result of the author's creative activity, in particular verbal, theatrical, musical, visual, including works of architectural art and works of applied art, cinematographic, photographic and cartographic works.'[904]

The quoted Section 2 (1) represents the so-called general clause upon meeting the criteria of which a product is to be copyrightable.[905] From the aforementioned quoted wording, the criteria of the general clause a product must meet in order for it to be considered a work within the meaning of Czechoslovak copyright law can be defined. With respect to this, such a product must be of a literary, scientific, or artistic nature and, at the same time, be the result of the author's creative activity.

The affiliation of the subject-matter seeking copyright protection with the literary, scientific, and artistic realm is traditional, stemming from the Berne Convention itself. The clarifying enumeration of specific types of potential works serves as a non-closed list to provide examples.

The AutZ 1965 did not, as such, include a legal definition of the author's notion of creative activity. What could have helped to define the notion was the zákon č. 36/1965 Sb. o dani z příjmů z literární a umělecké činnosti[906] which, quite bluntly, defined the creative activity in the following way:

903 In English: *'Act No. 35/1965 Coll., the Act on Literary, Scientific and Artistic Works'.*

904 Sec. 2 (1) AutZ 1965.

905 Ivo Telec, *Autorský zákon: komentář* (C.H. Beck 1997), p. 16.

906 In English: *'Act No. 36/1965 Coll., On Income Tax on Literary and Artistic Activities'.*

'Creative literary and artistic activity means an activity which results in a work that enjoys copyright protection.'[907]

Here, the mandatory interconnectivity of the creative activity with the literary and artistic nature of its result (the work) can be established. Therefore, only creative activity can give rise to a subject-matter (work) within the meaning of the AutZ 1965. Concerning this, it can be deduced that the AutZ 1965 continued in applying the requirement of expenditure and display of creative activity within a photographic product previously introduced by the ZoPA 1953.

Section 9 (1) of the AutZ 1965 conditions the protectability by copyright upon expression of the work in *any perceptible form*.[908] With respect to this, a third mandatory condition, that of being an expression perceptible in any perceptible form, can be formulated. The said condition seems natural for the enjoyment of any authorial work in general. Photographic products, as such, do not pose a challenging type of subject-matter for such requirements and are easily fulfilling them. However, considering the idea/expression dichotomy, it must nonetheless be repeatedly restated as a general rule for other types of subject-matter. The disproportionate state of affairs regarding the (shorter) term of protection available to photographic works was rectified by the inclusion of photographic products into the list of works to which the general 50-year term of protection was available.[909] The AutZ 1965 has, therefore, finally achieved elimination of the previously referred to disproportionate treatment of photographic products manifested through the different (shorter) available terms of protection.

---

[907] Sec. 2 (1) of the Act No. 36/1965 Coll., On Income Tax on Literary and Artistic Activities.
[908] Sec. 9 (1) of the Act No. 36/1965 Coll, On Income Tax on Literary and Artistic Activities.
[909] Sec. 33 (1) of the Act No. 36/1965 Coll., On Income Tax on Literary and Artistic Activities.

8 THE DEVELOPMENT OF ORIGINALITY STANDARD IN THE COPYRIGHT FRAMEWORK OF CZECH REPUBLIC

The chapter below is dedicated to the development of protection of photographic products within the Czech Republic's copyright framework. Its purpose is to provide chronological insight into the legislative development of the position of photographic products within the Czech copyright framework.

8.1 The Chapter's Relationship to the Selected Hypotheses and Research Questions

In terms of the outlined hypotheses No. 2 and No. 3 and the subsequent formulated Research Questions B and C, the purpose of this chapter is to prepare a theoretical knowledge framework representing the development of the traditional approach towards protectability of photographic products by copyright within the national copyright framework of the Czech Republic. The prepared theoretical knowledge framework would then serve as a basis upon which the formulated Research Questions B and C will be confirmed or refuted in the chapter dedicated to the effects of harmonization on the Czech copyright framework.

8.2 Zákon č. 121/2000 Sb. Zákon o právu autorském, o právech souvisejících s právem autorským a o změně některých zákonů

The AutZ 1965 remained effective throughout the rest of the existence of Czechoslovakia and well into the existence of the independent Czech Republic after the division of Czechoslovakia into Czech and Slovak Republics in 1993. Until its replacement by the new Copyright Act in 2000, it remained effective for 35 years. Nonetheless, its provisions were beginning to lag behind developments in the field of copyright. Although the Czech Republic would not officially become a member of the EU until 2004, the EU harmonization carried out prior to its joining in the field of copyright was also recognized within the national legislation by the Czech legislator. The outcome of the said efforts of approximating the Czech copyright legislation was the adoption of a new Copyright Act, the AutZ 2000.[910] Therefore, the AutZ 2000 represents the first national copyright act of the independent Czech Republic.

In terms of subject-matter protectable by copyright within its meaning, Section 2 (1) of the AutZ 2000 provides the following extensive definition of the notion of work:

'The subject of copyright is a literary work and other artistic and scientific work which is the unique result of the creative activity of the author and is expressed in any objectively perceptible form, including electronic form, permanently or temporarily, regardless of its scope, purpose or meaning (hereinafter referred to as work). In particular, work is a verbal work expressed in speech or writing, a musical work, a dramatic work and a work of music-drama, a choreographic work and a work of pantomime, a photographic work and a work expressed by a process similar to photography, an audiovisual work such as a cinematographic work, an artistic work such as a work of painting, graphic art, and sculpture, an architectural work including a work of urban design, a work of applied art and cartographic work.'[911]

Section 2 (2) of the AutZ 2000 adds the following:

'A work is also considered to be a computer program, a photograph, and a creation expressed by a process similar to a photograph, which is original in the sense that they are the author's own intellectual creation. A database, which is the author's own intellectual creation in the manner of selection or arrangement of its contents and the components of which are systematically or methodically arranged and individually made available electronically or in any other manner, is a work in the aggregate. Other criteria for determining the eligibility of a computer program and database for protection shall not apply.'

8.3 Definition of Works Within the Meaning of Section 2 (1) of the AutZ 2000

It can be seen that the first sub-section of Section 2 of the AutZ 2000 follows the structure and content (enumeration of types of works) of Section 2 of the Berne

[910] In English: *'Act No. 121/2000 Coll. The Act on Copyright, on Rights Related to Copyright and on Amendments to Certain Acts'.*

[911] Sec. 2 (1) AutZ 2000.

Convention. This has also been confirmed by the Explanatory memorandum to the draft Act on copyright, rights related to copyright, and amendments to certain acts (Copyright Act),[912] namely in its part dedicated to Section 2 of the AutZ 2000.[913] This interconnectedness through the identical classification of protectable subject-matter was also confirmed by others than the Czech legislator.[914] The list of the works in the first subsection is not definitive and is closed. Suppose a product is to be considered a work within the meaning of Section 2 (1) of the AutZ 2000. In that case, it has to cumulatively meet three criteria: uniqueness, being the result of the creative activity of its author, and being expressed in any objectively perceptible form.[915] Some also include the requirement of being a literary, artistic, or scientific work.[916]

8.4 Definition of Works Within the Meaning of Section 2 (2) of the AutZ 2000

The status of photographic products was previously governed by Section 2 (1) of the AutZ 1965. However, the said Section did not adhere to the specifically harmonized originality standard of photographic products within the meaning of Article 6 of the Term Directive I—*the author's own intellectual creation*. In respect to this, every photographic product seeking copyright protection within the meaning of Section 2 (1) of the AutZ 1965 was to possess characteristics of (statistical) uniqueness[917] rather than originality.[918] Regarding new subject-matter, only computer programs were included in Section 2 (1) of the AutZ 1965. The legitimate interests of photographers did not result in the inclusion of original photographic products into the wording of AutZ 1965, thus the copyright protection was not extended to non-statistically unique photographic products, let alone databases. The state of affairs was rectified by the creation of sub-section of Section 2 of the AutZ 2000.

Suppose a product is to be considered a work within the meaning of Section 2 (2) of the AutZ 2000. In that case, it has to cumulatively meet only two criteria: being the author's own intellectual creation and being expressed in any objectively

912 In Czech: '*Důvodová zpráva k návrhu zákona o právu autorském, o právech souvisejících s právem autorským a o změně některých zákonů (autorský zákon)*'.

913 § 2, Důvodová zpráva k návrhu zákona o právu autorském, o právech souvisejících s právem autorským a o změně některých zákonů (autorský zákon). Sněmovní tisk 443/0. Vládní návrh zákona o právu autorském – EU (1. Oct. 2024), https://www.psp.cz/sqw/historie.sqw?o=3&t=443.

914 Radim Polčák, Pavel Koukal & Rudolf Leška, *Autorský zákon: praktický komentář s judikaturou* (Leges 2020), p. 6.

915 Ivo Telec & Pavel Tůma, *Autorský zákon: komentář* (C.H. Beck, 2nd ed. 2019), p. 21.

916 Jiří Srstka et al., *Autorské právo a práva související: vysokoškolská učebnice* (Leges, 3rd ed. 2024), p. 72.

917 The requirement of statistical uniqueness will be elaborated on in more detail in its dedicated chapters, for example Chapter 8.5.1.

918 Ivo Telec, *Autorský zákon: komentář* (C.H. Beck 1997), p. 36.

perceptible form. The second sub-section of Section 2 provides for the enumeration of three types of subject-matter that do not fall under the so-called *general clause* formulated in its first sub-section.[919] Therefore, any product seeking copyrightability within the meaning of Section 2 (1) of the AutZ 2000 must meet the stipulated criteria.[920]

In other words, Section 2 (2) of the AutZ 2000 gives a closed list of three subject-matter that do not meet the criteria prescribed by the general clause of Section 2 (1) but are nonetheless considered works within the meaning of the AutZ 2000. Such eligibility of the three said subject-matter for copyright protection within the meaning of Article 2 (1) and its consideration and treatment as works are referred to as *fictional*.[921]

As will be elaborated on in more detail below, the second sub-section of Section 2 was added by the Czech legislator in order to account for subject-matter, which does not meet the strict, in the sense of statistical uniqueness, requirements for copyright protection. However, the Czech legislator only specified this later, specifically in 2016, as part of the Explanatory Memorandum to the Governmental draft amending Act on copyright, on rights related to copyright, and on amendments to certain acts (Copyright Act), which was later adopted as amendment No. 102/2017.[922] Therefore, under the influence of the carried out EU harmonization, a lower standard of originality is to be applied to this subject-matter—that of originality (being the *author's own intellectual creation*).[923] Traditional statistical uniqueness is replaced by originality based on the original relationship between the creator, the author, and their creation, the work. Therefore, concerning the aforementioned, the decisive delimitation criterion between works within the meaning of Section 2 (1) and Section 2 (2) is the (statistical) uniqueness of the former and the originality of the latter.

As to the term of protection, all works within the meaning of Section 2 (1) and (2) of the AutZ 2000 are to be protected by copyright during their author's life and 70 years after their death.[924] This represents the harmonized term of protection within the meaning of Term Directive II.

---

919 *Ibid.*

920 Irena Holcová et al., *Autorský zákon a předpisy související: (včetně mezinárodních smluv a evropských předpisů): komentář* (Wolters Kluwer 2019), p. 54.

921 Irena Holcová et al., *Autorský zákon a předpisy související: (včetně mezinárodních smluv a evropských předpisů): komentář* (Wolters Kluwer 2019), p. 71.

922 Bod 4, Důvodová zpráva k návrhu zákona o právu autorském, o právech souvisejících s právem autorským a o změně některých zákonů (autorský zákon). Sněmovní tisk 724/0. Vládní návrh zákona o právu autorském (1. Oct. 2024), https://www.psp.cz/sqw/historie.sqw?o=7&t=724.

923 Ivo Telec & Pavel Tůma, *Autorský zákon: komentář* (C.H. Beck, 2nd ed. 2019), p. 35.

924 Sec. 27(1) of the AutZ 2000.

8.5 General Clause Requirement

The *general clause* within the meaning of the Section 2 (1) of the AutZ 2000 represents a general requirement for the protectability of *traditional* products (works of art) by copyright. The said *general clause* consists of the following four conditions, which must be met cumulatively. It is the uniqueness, being the result of creative activity, being expressed in an objectively perceptible form and being a literary, artistic, or a scientific work.

8.5.1 Uniqueness

The requirement of uniqueness within the meaning of Section 2 is to be understood as a uniqueness of statistical nature, which entails the impossibility of the so-called *double creation*.[925] Uniqueness can also be characterized as a quantitative criterion of the volume of the invested creative individuality, as opposed to the qualitative criterion of having literary, artistic, or scientific qualities.[926] The uniqueness is also closely connected to the person and personality of the author. Such uniqueness directly extends and manifests the author's unique personality.[927]

Therefore, such an extensive interpretation of the requirement does not give room for recognizing the theoretical existence of two or more identical works. In other words, from the very nature of such a requirement, it is impossible to create two identical works simultaneously. Accordingly, two identical works cannot be protected within the meaning of the AutZ 2000 (that is, as a work within the meaning of Section 2 (1) of the AutZ 2000). The requirement of uniqueness can also be referred to as absolute individuality, which is based on the actual uniqueness of the work since it is presupposed that only one such work exists.[928]

8.5.2 Result of the Creative Activity

For the purposes of copyright law, the creative activity as such (identical to uniqueness) is closely related to the personal traits and personality of the creator—the author.[929] Therefore, the creative process is considered an activity of a unique and

[925] Helena Chaloupková & Petr Holý, *Autorský zákon: komentář* (C.H. Beck, 6th ed. 2023), p. 7.

[926] Ivo Telec & Pavel Tůma, *Autorský zákon: komentář* (C.H. Beck, 2nd ed. 2019), p. 19.

[927] Irena Holcová et al., *Autorský zákon a předpisy související: (včetně mezinárodních smluv a evropských předpisů): komentář* (Wolters Kluwer 2019), p. 55.

[928] Irena Holcová et al., *Autorský zákon a předpisy související: (včetně mezinárodních smluv a evropských předpisů): komentář* (Wolters Kluwer 2019), p. 56.

[929] Radim Polčák, Pavel Koukal & Rudolf Leška, *Autorský zákon: praktický komentář s judikaturou* (Leges 2020), p. 45.

absolute nature—as the personality.[930] Since it has such specific qualities and characteristics, it can be assumed that creative activity does not include copying, repetition, or mechanical routine.[931] From the very definition, it is evident that only activities of a creative nature can give rise to a product that is recognizable for AutZ 2000 and recognizable within its meaning.

According to the Czech Supreme Court, an author's creative activity is always considered an intellectual activity.[932] Therefore, any work within the meaning of the AutZ 2000 is also an intellectual creation. This consideration also bounds any creative activity solely to a human being. According to another decision of the Czech Supreme Court, creative activity depends on the author's personality traits, which is necessary for the creation of a work to be possible.[933] The decision defines *personality traits* as the ability to create within the literary, artistic, or scientific realms.[934]

8.5.3 Expressed in an Objectively Perceptible Form

The form in which the work is expressed must be perceivable by the senses of a human being—the potential spectator, thus making it a condition of a mandatory nature.[935] Without meeting this criterion, such an imperceptible product would fall outside the scope of copyright protection and its protectability due to, most probably, residing in the realm of ideas concerning the idea/expression dichotomy theory. It is worth noting, as the very wording of Subsection 1 of Section 2 states, that the form can be of a permanent or temporary nature. It is also irrelevant whether the work is perceivable only to a specific audience, such as text in braille for visually impaired individuals.[936]

Therefore, the work's expression represents the materialization of its originally immaterial form.[937] Within this context, it must be noted that the Czech copyright framework does not require the expressed material form to be fixed in whatever form. However, the said requirement is not met if the product only positively exists since its potential user/spectator must also have the option and availability to perceive it objectively.[938] Therefore, within this meaning, the requirement is connected to the nature of perceptibility rather than the nature of the existence of the assessed work.

930 Helena Chaloupková & Petr Holý, *Autorský zákon: komentář* (C.H. Beck, 6th ed. 2023), p. 8.
931 Ivo Telec & Pavel Tůma, *Autorský zákon: komentář* (C.H. Beck, 2nd ed. 2019), p. 17.
932 Supreme Court, 30 Cdo 4924/2007, 10 Nov. 2009.
933 Supreme Court, 30 Cdo 739/2007, 30 Apr. 2007.
934 Supreme Court, 30 Cdo 739/2007, 30 Apr. 2007.
935 Helena Chaloupková & Petr Holý, *Autorský zákon: komentář* (C.H. Beck, 6th ed. 2023), p. 8.
936 Irena Holcová et al., *Autorský zákon a předpisy související: (včetně mezinárodních smluv a evropských předpisů): komentář* (Wolters Kluwer 2019), p. 60.
937 Ivo Telec & Pavel Tůma, *Autorský zákon: komentář* (C.H. Beck, 2nd ed. 2019), p. 22.
938 Radim Polčák, Pavel Koukal & Rudolf Leška, *Autorský zákon: praktický komentář s judikaturou* (Leges 2020), p. 41.

8.5.4 Being a Literary, Artistic, or a Scientific Work

According to the Czech Supreme Court, the creative activity employed by the author throughout the production process must be done in a way that allows its result to be classified as literary, artistic, or scientific work.[939] Naturally, the said employed creative activity must also be of a literary, artistic, or scientific nature.

In other words, if the creative activity of an individual is to be recognized as having effects within the meaning of the AutZ 2000, such activity itself must be of a literary, artistic, or scientific nature. Therefore, the outcome of such creative activity must be able to be classified within the three said areas, or in other words, stay within their set conceptual boundaries.

8.6 Terminology Referring to Photographic Products Employed by the AutZ 2000

The terminology extracted from the wording of AutZ 2000 and elaborated on below does not have any practical implications relating to the protectability of photographic products referred to as such by copyright. The differentiation merely serves a theoretical purpose.

8.6.1 Fotografické dílo (photographic work)

A unique photographic product meeting the requirements of the general clause within the meaning of Section 2 (1) of the AutZ 2000 is, therefore, a work fully protectible by copyright within its meaning. Such a photographic product is the result of a standard photographic process.

8.6.2 Dílo vyjádřené postupem podobným fotografii (work expressed by a process similar to photography)

A unique photographic product meeting the requirements of the general clause within the meaning of Section 2 (1) of the AutZ 2000 is, therefore, a work fully eligible for copyright protection within its meaning. Such a photographic product is the result of a standard photographic process.

[939] Supreme Court, 30 Cdo 4924/2007, 10 Nov. 2009.

8.6.3 Fotografie (photograph)

An original photographic product meeting the requirements of the author's own intellectual creation of Section 2 (2) of the AutZ 2000 is considered a *fictitious work* but still fully protectable by copyright within the meaning of the AutZ 2000. Such a photographic product is not the result of a standard photographic process but a process of a similar nature, nonetheless still related to photography.

In respect to the aforementioned, all types of photographic products referred to above are fully qualified for copyright protection, regardless of their affiliation to either Section 2 (1) or 2 (2) of the Autz 2000 or their incorporation under one of the four types of photographic products.

8.7 Specificities of Photography Genre

The AutZ 2000 does not provide a legal definition of a photographic product, photographic subject-matter, or medium of photography in general. After reviewing several commentaries, a photographic product can be defined as follows:

> *'A photograph is a creative work in which an idea is expressed through an image, utilizing the artistic elements of shape, colour, light, and shadow, all made possible by photographic technology.'*[940]
>
> *'It is the product of capturing a moment in reality using technical optical means.'*[941]
>
> *'A work in which, according to doctrinal interpretations, the creator's thought is expressed through the image using the expression of shape and colour, otherwise also of light and shadow, using photographic techniques including digital.'*[942]

Within the meaning of the AutZ 2000, photographic products can be further divided into three main types—*jedinečné autorské dílo* (*photographic products which are unique authorial works*), *původní autorské dílo* (*photographic products which are original authorial works*) and *neautorské dílo* (*photographic products which are not authorial works*).[943] Therefore, one has to differentiate between artistic photographic products meeting the requirements within the meaning of Section 2 (1) of the AutZ 2000 (*photographic products which are original authorial works*), non-artistic photographic products meeting the requirements within the meaning of Section 2 (2) of the AutZ 2000 (*photographic products which are original authorial*

940 Helena Chaloupková & Petr Holý, *Autorský zákon: komentář* (C.H. Beck, 6th ed. 2023), p. 10.

941 Ivo Telec & Pavel Tůma, *Autorský zákon: komentář* (C.H. Beck, 2nd ed. 2019), p. 29.

942 Irena Holcová et al., *Autorský zákon a předpisy související: (včetně mezinárodních smluv a evropských předpisů): komentář* (Wolters Kluwer 2019), p. 65.

943 Helena Chaloupková & Petr Holý, *Autorský zákon: komentář* (C.H. Beck, 6th ed. 2023), p. 10.

works) and photographic products not meeting either of the two requirements, thus being of merely craft/artisan nature (*photographic products which are not authorial works*).[944]

8.7.1 Unique Authorial Photographic Products (Works)

A photographic product can be considered a unique authorial work; therefore, it is a photographic work, given that it meets the criteria prescribed by Section 2 (1) of the AutZ 2000. Amongst such criteria is *uniqueness*, which results from the creative activity and is expressed objectively. The most important and distinguishable feature of unique authorial photographic products is their uniqueness in the statistical sense. The *statistical uniqueness* makes photographic products possessing this feature comparable and equal with other works of (traditional) art for the purpose of AutZ 2000.[945] The said *statistical uniqueness* also relates not only to the uniqueness of time (moment of the production) but also to the uniqueness of the author's approach to the production process of the photographic product.[946] The *statistical uniqueness* must, therefore, be present within the author's approach to and throughout the production and post-process and also visible in the final photographic product. Statistically unique photographic products can also be considered absolutely individual, as it is presupposed that only one variant exists and will exist.[947] The said absoluteness is manifested in its recognised unique character. Within the meaning of the AutZ 2000, apart from photographic works, the term also includes works expressed by a process similar to photography.

In practice, photographic products of an artistic nature can be used as examples of unique authorial photographic works.[948] These can be considered to be works of art.[949] Unique photographic products are, therefore, not just the result of the author's creative activity but also the result of a unique and unrepeatable character.[950]

As already mentioned, the existence of a double creation is precluded for unique authorial works based on their expected nature and the *uniqueness* of their *statistical*

[944] Jiří Srstka et al., *Autorské právo a práva související: vysokoškolská učebnice* (Leges, 3rd ed. 2024), p. 80.

[945] Ivo Telec & Pavel Tůma, *Autorský zákon: komentář* (C.H. Beck, 2nd ed. 2019), p. 42.

[946] Martin Valoušek, *Fotografie a právo: autorské právo a ochrana osobnosti ve vztahu k fotografii* (Leges, 2nd ed. 2022), p. 14.

[947] Irena Holcová et al., *Autorský zákon a předpisy související: (včetně mezinárodních smluv a evropských předpisů): komentář* (Wolters Kluwer 2019), p. 56.

[948] Helena Chaloupková & Petr Holý, *Autorský zákon: komentář* (C.H. Beck, 6th ed. 2023), p. 10.

[949] Ivo Telec, 'Autorské právo k fotografiím podle nového autorského zákona,' *Právní rozhledy: časopis pro všechna právní odvětví* 539 (2000), p. 539.

[950] Martin Valoušek, *Fotografie a právo: autorské právo a ochrana osobnosti ve vztahu k fotografii* (Leges, 2nd ed. 2022), p. 14.

nature. Within the setting of unique authorial photographic products, only the creator of the earlier produced photographic product can be considered the author. In contrast, the creator of the later one can only be considered the creator of a reproduction of the first photographic product or a plagiarist.[951]

8.7.2 Original Authorial Photographic Products (Works)

An original authorial work is still fully qualified for copyright protection. However, it does not meet the condition of statistical uniqueness, as the statistically unique authorial works do. The exception from the general clause within the meaning of Section 2 (1) of the AutZ 2000 in the form of a lowered threshold for copyrightability is the result of the EU harmonization process.[952] The notion also includes creations expressed by a process similar to photography. As with Section 2 (1) and traditionally in general, such a setting ensures that photographic products can be protected by copyright, regardless of variations in their production process. Still, of course, such a production process must be of a (similar) photographic nature. By subsumption of original photographic products under a separate originality standard, the protectability of more photographic products within the national copyright framework of the Czech Republic was enabled.[953] Every photographic product, apart from those of artistic or purely mechanical nature, can nowadays qualify for copyright protection, given they fulfil the two prescribed requirements of being their author's intellectual creation and being expressed in an objectively perceptible form.

Some authors refer to original authorial works as fictitious works, which are still the author's intellectual creations; however, they display a lower degree of creativity.[954] The fictiveness some refer to is linked to the special nature of the three relatively novel types of subject-matter—databases, software, and photographic products. They are also three subject-matter types, each separately regulated in their dedicated directive by the EU legislator. The main criterion upon which the eligibility for copyright protection of such original photographic products is built is the existence of the photographer's creative intellectual activity.[955]

According to some scholars, an original photographic product is, therefore, neither a (statistically unique) photographic work nor (authorial) work since it does not fulfil the requirement of statistical uniqueness prescribed by the general clause

951 Jan Kříž (ed)., *Autorský zákon a předpisy související: komentář* (Linde 2005), p. 23.

952 Rudolf Leška, 'Czechia' In: Silke von Lewinski, *Copyright Throughout the World* (Thomson/West 2022), pp. 12–17.

953 Irena Holcová et al., *Autorský zákon a předpisy související: (včetně mezinárodních smluv a evropských předpisů): komentář* (Wolters Kluwer 2019), p. 81.

954 Helena Chaloupková & Petr Holý, *Autorský zákon: komentář* (C.H. Beck, 6th ed. 2023), p. 10.

955 Ivo Telec & Pavel Tůma, *Autorský zákon: komentář* (C.H. Beck, 2nd ed. 2019), p. 42.

of the AutZ 2000.[956] Unlike unique photographic products, original photographic products are only relatively individual.[957]

This approach exists because similar works are expected to exist. The relativity of individuality is reflected in its acknowledged original character, as opposed to uniqueness. Nonetheless, such *fictious works* are still (authorial) works within the meaning of AutZ 2000,[958] and they can still be accounted for due to the original relationship between the author and the work they have produced. However, considering the reduced expected input from the author's creative efforts in the work and the possibility of simultaneous protection for similar or identical works, the protection afforded to original works may be perceived as somewhat less robust compared to the protection granted to unique works.[959]

Through the said construct of *fictiveness*, the AutZ 2000 has adapted to the expansion of photographic products and photographic medium in general. The traditional requirement of (statistical) uniqueness prevented protection of most photographic products by copyright, thus also preventing adequate copyright protection for their authors—the photographers.[960]

Photographic products produced by tourists during sightseeing can be used as examples of original photographic works[961] or school photographic products depicting the pupils of the whole class.[962] Both types of photographic products cannot be considered traditional objects of copyright protection due to their lack of statistical uniqueness.[963]

The very concept of original (*fictious*) authorial works, as defined in Section 2(2) of the AutZ 2000, has lower requirements than those set for unique authorial works. Unique authorial works are those that represent the *author's own intellectual creation* expressed in a form that can be perceived objectively.[964] In contrast, the Czech legislator has partially lowered the uniqueness requirement to account for the specific characteristics of the photographic genre. Consequently, the idea of double creation is not inherently excluded for photographic works that are classified as original authorial works.[965]

---

[956] Ivo Telec, 'Autorské právo k fotografiím podle nového autorského zákona,' *Právní rozhledy: časopis pro všechna právní odvětví* 539 (2000), p. 539.

[957] Irena Holcová et al., *Autorský zákon a předpisy související: (včetně mezinárodních smluv a evropských předpisů): komentář* (Wolters Kluwer 2019), p. 56.

[958] Ivo Telec, 'Autorské právo k fotografiím podle nového autorského zákona,' *Právní rozhledy: časopis pro všechna právní odvětví* 539 (2000), p. 539.

[959] Ivo Telec & Pavel Tůma, *Autorský zákon: komentář* (C.H. Beck, 2nd ed. 2019), p. 35.

[960] Jan Kříž (ed)., *Autorský zákon a předpisy související: komentář* (Linde 2005), p. 23.

[961] Helena Chaloupková & Petr Holý, *Autorský zákon: komentář* (C.H. Beck, 6th ed. 2023), p. 13.

[962] Ivo Telec & Pavel Tůma, *Autorský zákon: komentář* (C.H. Beck, 2nd ed. 2019), p. 42.

[963] Ivo Telec, 'Autorské právo k fotografiím podle nového autorského zákona,' *Právní rozhledy: časopis pro všechna právní odvětví* 539 (2000), p. 539.

[964] Radim Polčák, Pavel Koukal & Rudolf Leška, *Autorský zákon: praktický komentář s judikaturou* (Leges 2020), p. 52.

[965] Helena Chaloupková & Petr Holý, *Autorský zákon: komentář* (C.H. Beck, 6th ed. 2023), p. 10.

To conclude, in practice, even a photographic product of a non-unique nature is still qualified for copyright protection, given that it is original, meaning it is the author's own intellectual creation. Therefore, such original photographic products are copyrightable in the same way as unique photographic products, however, based on different, lower criteria.[966]

8.7.3 Non-authorial Photographic Products

Non-authorial photographic products are those that do not meet the criteria for statistically unique or original authorial works. They can thus be referred to as *non-works* within the meaning of the AutZ 2000.[967] Such photographic products can also be called craft or artisan[968] or mere plain photographic recordings.[969] Amongst examples of non-authorial photographic products are ID photographic products produced by a machine (photobooth)[970] or a photocopy.[971] The examples show that the production process of non-authorial photographic products lacks work-related (statistically unique or original) creative human intervention and is fully governed by technical means and the purpose of the production. It can also be said that such non-authorial photographic products must be very simple, without any authorial and creative input from the author—the photographer.[972]

---

966 Polčák, R, Koukal, P, Leška, R. *Autorský zákon: praktický komentář s judikaturou*. Prahe: Leges, 2020, p. 53.

967 Ivo Telec, 'Autorské právo k fotografiím podle nového autorského zákona,' *Právní rozhledy: časopis pro všechna právní odvětví* 539 (2000), p. 539.

968 Jiří Srstka et al., *Autorské právo a práva související: vysokoškolská učebnice* (Leges, 3rd ed. 2024), p. 80.

969 Ivo Telec & Pavel Tůma, *Autorský zákon: komentář* (C.H. Beck, 2nd ed. 2019), p. 42.

970 Helena Chaloupková & Petr Holý, *Autorský zákon: komentář* (C.H. Beck, 6th ed. 2023), p. 10.

971 Ivo Telec & Pavel Tůma, *Autorský zákon: komentář* (C.H. Beck, 2nd ed. 2019), p. 42.

972 Martin Faloušek, *Fotografie a právo: autorské právo a ochrana osobnosti ve vztahu k fotografii* (Leges, 2nd ed. 2022), p. 13.

9 THE DEVELOPMENT OF ORIGINALITY STANDARD IN THE COPYRIGHT FRAMEWORK OF SLOVAK REPUBLIC

The chapter below is dedicated to the development of the protection of photographic products within the Slovak copyright framework. Its purpose is to provide chronological insight into the legislative development of position of photographic products within the Slovak copyright framework.

9.1 The Chapter's Relationship to the Selected Hypotheses and Research Questions

This chapter aims to establish a theoretical framework for understanding the traditional approach to the copyright protection of photographic products within the national copyright framework of the Slovak Republic, specifically addressing hypotheses No. 2 and No. 3, along with the related Research Questions B and C. The theoretical framework developed in this chapter will serve as a foundation for analysing the effects of harmonization on the Slovak copyright framework, allowing us to confirm or refute the formulated Research Questions B and C.

9.2 Zákon č. 383/1997 Z. z., autorský zákon

After the split of Czechoslovakia in 1993, AutZ 1965 remained effective in the territory of the Slovak Republic, thus mirroring the situation in the Czech Republic. The situation continued until 1997 when the Slovak legislator enacted the AZ 1997,[973] marking the beginning of the departure from the joint Czechoslovak copyright legislation. AZ 1997 represents the first modern and purely Slovak Act on copyright protection. Its section 6 defines the concept of work in the following way:

[973] In English: '*Act. No. 383/1997 Coll., Copyright Act*'.

'The subject of copyright is a literary, scientific or artistic work which is the result of the author's own intellectual activity, in particular... a photographic work.'[974]

The general clause outlined in Section 6 of the AZ 1997 states that a product must meet two criteria to be eligible for copyright protection as a work. First, it must qualify as a literary, artistic, or scientific work. Second, it must be the result of the author's own intellectual activity. The AZ 1997 also implies a third requirement: that the work must be perceivable by human senses. Since all three criteria mirror the current wording of the Slovak Copyright Act enacted in 2015, their definitions will be provided in the section dedicated to that Act below.

Section 5 (4) of the AZ 1997 defines a photographic product in the following way:

'A photographic work is a recording of light or other radiation on a medium on which an image is produced, irrespective of the manner in which the recording was made.'[975]

The definition of a photographic product, according to the AZ 1997, does not specify any additional requirements for its protection. Instead, it offers only a technical description of the production process. Therefore, all photographic products must comply with the criteria outlined in the general clause.

As to the term of protection, all works within the meaning of AZ 1997 are to be protected by copyright during their author's life and 70 years after their death, including photographic works.[976]

9.3 Zákon č. 618/2003 Z. z., o autorskom práve a právach súvisiacich s autorským právom

The second Slovak legislation governing copyright, the AZ 2003, was enacted in 2003 and replaced the AZ 1997. Its Section 7 (1) defined the notion of work in a manner identical to that of AZ 1997:

'The subject of copyright is a literary and other artistic work and a scientific work which is the result of the author's own intellectual activity, in particular... a photographic work.'[977]

---

974 Sec. 6 of the AZ 1997.
975 Sec. 5 (4) of the AZ 1997.
976 Sec. 18 (1) of the AZ 1997.
977 Sec. (7) (1) let (g) of the AZ 2003.

The AZ 2003 defined the concept of photographic work, which is consistent with the definition previously established by the AZ 1997.

'A photographic work is a recording of light or other radiation on a medium on which an image is produced, irrespective of the manner in which the recording was made.'[978]

Concerning this definition, such as the wording of the AZ 1997, the wording of AZ 2003 also provided only a technical definition of the said term, thus shifting the queries regarding the requirements governing the potential copyrightability to the *general clause* within the meaning of its Section 7 (1). Regarding this, only photographic products meeting the *general clause* within the meaning of Section 7 (1) of AZ 2003 could be protected by copyright. However, following Slovakia's accession to the EU in 2004, the *author's own intellectual creation* requirement was to be applied to photographic products to determine their eligibility for copyright protection. Subjecting photographic products to the general clause within the meaning of Section 7 (1) following 2004 would contradict the EU law.[979]

As to the term of protection, all works within the meaning of AZ 2003, including photographic works, are to be protected by copyright during their author's life and 70 years after their death.[980]

To conclude, within the meaning of the AZ 1997, mostly only artistic photographic products were traditionally recognised as being protected by copyright protection. Such artistic photographic products must have expressed a certain idea or message of the author, expressed their personality, and had the depicted image captured in a particular way with a certain meaning.[981]

9.4 Zákon č. 185/2015 Z. z., autorský zákon

When drafting this text, the most recent copyright legislation governing the Slovak national copyright framework is the AZ 2015.[982] Section 3 (1) provides the following definition of the notion of a work:

'The subject of copyright is a work of literature, art or science which is the unique result of the author's creative intellectual activity perceptible by the senses,

978 Sec. 5 (5) of the AZ 2003.

979 Martin Husovec, 'K európskemu prepisovaniu pojmových znakov autorského diela,' 4 *Duševné vlastníctvo* 24 (2011), p. 24.

980 Sec. 21 (1) of the AZ 2003.

981 Peter Vojčík, *Právo duševného vlastníctva* (Aleš Čeněk 2012), p. 108.

982 In English: '*Act No. 185/2015 Coll. Copyright Act*'.

irrespective of its form, content, quality, purpose, form of expression or degree of completion.'[983]

If a product seeks to be protected by copyright within the meaning of the AZ 2015, it must cumulatively fulfil three criteria stipulated in Section 3 (1):

a) Such a product must be affiliated with literature, art, or science.
b) It must be the unique result of the author's own creative intellectual activity.
c) It must be perceptible by human senses.

The three criteria can be considered to form the general clause for copyrightability within the Slovak copyright framework. I will now give the definition of each sub-criterion forming the said general clause.

9.4.1 Being a work of literature, arts, or science

The AZ 2015 follows the traditional requirement of affiliation of products recognisable as works within the meaning of copyright law initially put forward by the Berne Convention. The traditional *triumvirate* of literature, arts, and science is therefore formulated as the first amongst other criteria. Therefore, the provision of copyright protection is not bound to a particular type of work but rather to a wide range of works.[984] Nonetheless, a work within this range must still be affiliated with literature, arts, or science.

9.4.2 Being a unique result of the author's creative intellectual activity

The creative activity itself consists of two main sub-requirements. The first is that the product cannot be a mere copy of another, while the second is that the activity cannot be mechanical.[985] The requirement of creativity will, therefore, not be fulfilled if the production process of a product consists of mere copying of another previously existent product and it is at the same time purely mechanical, therefore governed solely by the technical/mechanical equipment employed.

Within the meaning of the AZ 2015, the requirement of uniqueness can take the form of either *statistical uniqueness* (*jedinečnosť*) or *original uniqueness* (*originalita*). The former is a type of uniqueness reserved for traditional works of art, which signifies a work's statistical uniqueness and absolute individuality.[986] In contrast,

[983] Sec. 3 (1) of the AZ 2015.

[984] Zuzana Adamová & Branislav Hazucha, *Autorský zákon: komentár* (C.H. Beck 2018), p. 22.

[985] Zuzana Adamová & Branislav Hazucha, *Autorský zákon: komentár* (C.H. Beck 2018), p. 31.

[986] In this respect, the said requirement of statistical uniqueness, referred to as *'jedinečnosť'*', is identical to the Czech concept of statistical uniqueness within the meaning of Section 2 para. 1 of the AutZ

the latter is the type of uniqueness applicable to more novel types of subject-matter claiming the eligibility for copyright protection. Amongst such novel subject-matter are also photographic products. The original unique works cannot claim their copyrightability via statistical uniqueness; instead, they can only claim their uniqueness via the original relationship between authors and their work. Therefore, the uniqueness of the author's intellectual creation must be assessed based on the subject-matter type and a case-by-case basis.[987]

However, the slight difference in wording regarding the requirement for protection between Section 7 of the AZ 2003 and Section 3 of the AZ 2015 must be highlighted. Whereas Section 7 of the AZ 2003 only refers to the result of the *author's own intellectual activity*, Section 3 of the AZ 2003 refers to the *unique result of the author's creative intellectual activity*.

According to the Explanatory Memorandum on the draft Act amending Act No. 618/2003 Coll. on copyright and rights related to copyright (Copyright Act) and amending and supplementing certain Acts,[988] the notion of the author's intellectual activity is to be interpreted within the meaning of authorial individuality.[989] Therefore, the implicit meaning of the notion from AZ 2003 was later amended in AZ 2015 by the addition of *unique* in order to sufficiently and explicitly reflect its meaning.

As previously mentioned, the requirement of *uniqueness*, as stipulated in the general clause of the AZ 2015, mirrors the Czech setting of the AutZ 2000. However, it is essential to note that this requirement of *uniqueness* was not part of the wording of the previous AZ 1997 and AZ 2003. Traditionally, the notion of uniqueness in connection with the subject-matter eligible for copyright protection was understood within the Slovak copyright framework as representing the requirement of uniqueness in terms of it being *statistical*.[990] With the harmonization of the EU and the replacement of statistical uniqueness with mere originality, the requirement seems rather redundant and obsolete, with no practical implications.

9.4.3 Being perceptible by human senses

The Slovak legislator has decided to include the requirement in the *general clause*. The previous wording of the AZ 1997 and AZ 2003 did contain the requirement in

2000.

[987] Zuzana Adamová & Branislav Hazucha, *Autorský zákon: komentár* (C.H. Beck 2018), p. 33.

[988] In Slovak: *'Dôvodová správa k návrhu zákona, ktorým sa mení a dopĺňa zákon č. 618/2003 Z. z. o autorskom práve a právach súvisiacich s autorským právom (autorský zákon) a o zmene a o doplnení niektorých zákonov'*.

[989] Dôvodová správa k návrhu zákona, ktorým sa mení a dopĺňa zákon č. 618/2003 Z. z. o autorskom práve a právach súvisiacich s autorským právom (autorský zákon) a o zmene a o doplnení niektorých zákonov (1. Oct. 2024), https://hsr.rokovania.sk/data/att/81512_subor.rtf.

[990] Jarmila Lazíková, *Autorský zákon: komentár* (Iura Edition 2013), p. 53.

general, only in connection with the emergence of the copyright based on the creation of the work itself.[991] The work must be perceptible immediately, directly, objectively and by subjects (potential audience) different from the author.[992] As already stated, the work does not have to be perceptible to all subjects, and it also does not have to be in a permanent form.

Section 3 of the AZ 2015 continues with enumerating examples of products that can be considered works within their meaning. The list is not closed or definitive, thus traditionally allowing other not-yet-known types of potential works within its meaning to be protected by copyright in the future. With such nature, the AZ 2015 follows the international trend set by the Berne Convention. Amongst such examples of products, it also provides a separate definition of the notion of a photographic work under its sub-section 5 in the following way:

'A photographic work is the capture of an image by means of a photographic technical device if it is the result of the creative intellectual activity of the author; no other conditions under paragraph 1 shall apply.'[993]

By the said separate provision, AZ 2015 excludes the applicability of the general clause within the meaning of Section 3 (1) to photographic products and subjects them to the fulfilment of separate conditions.[994] Therefore, the conditions a photographic product must meet in order for it to be recognized as a work within the meaning of the AZ 2015 and, as such, be subsequently protected by copyright are the following: being an image captured utilizing a photographic, technical device and being the result of the creative intellectual activity of the author. The character of the medium of photography also naturally fulfils one of the criteria of the general clause, that of being perceptible by human senses. It is given that in order for a photographic product to be enjoyed (viewed) by subjects (potential audience), the perceptibility by their senses (sight) is necessary.

The separate definition originated from Article 6 of the Term Directive II, and its wording is nearly identical to the national definition found in Section 3 (5) of the AZ 2015. As mentioned earlier, the previous versions of the AZ from 1997 to 2003 classified photographic products under the general clause applicable to traditional works of art, which required them to meet the requirement of *statistical uniqueness*. This meant that only artistic photographic products could qualify for copyright protection, as statistical uniqueness was *traditionally* expected for such photographic works. However, the current wording of the AZ 2015 no longer requires an assessment of photographic products for artistic qualities or *statistical uniqueness*.[995]

991 Jarmila Lazíková, *Autorský zákon: komentár* (Iura Edition 2013), p. 52.
992 Zuzana Adamová & Branislav Hazucha, *Autorský zákon: komentár* (C.H. Beck 2018), p. 34.
993 Sec. 3 (5) of the AZ 2015.
994 Jarmila Lazíková, *Autorský zákon č. 185/2015 Z.z: komentár* (Wolters Kluwer 2018), p. 39.
995 *Ibid.*

This change reflects the application of a lower *originality* threshold based on the EU's harmonized originality standard from Article 6 of the Term Directive II.[996]

Regarding the definitions of photographic works in the AZ 1997 and AZ 2003, the AZ 2015 introduced an important addition: it recognizes the result of the *author's creative intellectual activity*. This change marks a shift from a merely technical definition of a photographic work to a separate standard of originality that specifically applies to photographic products. The exclusivity of this harmonized EU originality standard clearly indicates the direction of the law, highlighted by the explicit exclusion of other conditions outlined in paragraph 1 (to be understood as Sub-section 1 of Section 3).

The lower harmonized originality standard for photographic products parallels that of the Czech AutZ 2000. Both national copyright acts maintained the reference to the requirement of uniqueness while acknowledging a lower originality standard for photographic products, as evidenced in dedicated sub-sections of the AZ 2015 and AutZ 2000. However, under the AZ 2015, a photographic product can only assert its copyrightability as a photographic work through Section 3 (5), unlike the AutZ 2000, which allows for a two-fold option via Section 2 (1) or Section 2 (2).

Concerning the term of protection, all works defined in Section 3 are protected by copyright during the author's life and for 70 years after their death.[997] This aligns with the harmonized term of protection established by the Term Directive I.

---

996 Rudolf Leška, 'Slovakia' In: Silke von Lewinski, *Copyright Throughout the World* (Thomson/West 2022), p. 32.

997 Sec. 32 (1) of the AZ 2015.

10 THE DEVELOPMENT OF ORIGINALITY STANDARD IN THE COPYRIGHT FRAMEWORK OF THE EUROPEAN UNION

According to *Bénabou*, the legislation of the EU has been traditionally rather discreet regarding the conditions for copyrightability of products within the copyright framework of the EU but has remained consistent on one condition—originality, as *Caron* quoted him.[998] The requirement of originality has been gradually harmonized, starting with an initial legislative definition through dedicated Directives. The initial legislative framework has been specified through jurisprudence of the CJEU. It is these two harmonization phases, the legislative and jurisprudential, that structure the following text.

10.1 The Chapter's Relationship to the Selected Hypotheses and Research Questions

The purpose of this chapter is to prepare an overview of theoretical knowledge presenting the development of requirements and criteria for eligibility of photographic products for copyright protection via both harmonization phases, known as the originality standard. This overview will then serve as the basis for confirming or rejecting Research Question A at the end of this chapter.

10.2 The First Harmonization Phase

In harmonization activities related to copyright, the EU legislator continues to favour directives, thus allowing, and indeed requiring, the Member States to amend their existing national copyright laws.[999] That being said, Article 288 of the TFEU states that a Member State is compelled to follow any Directive as to the result to be

[998] Christophe Caron, *Droit d'auteur et droits voisins* (LexisNexis, 6th ed. 2020), p. 89.

[999] Hayleigh Bosher & Eleonora Rosati (eds.), *Developments and directions in intellectual property law: twenty years of the IPKat* (Oxford University Press 2023), p. 130.

achieved, but the choice of the form and method of achieving this result is left to the discretion of the Member States. Directives are therefore not directly appliable in Member States, and for the applicability of their result to be achieved, the Member States must introduce their own legal instruments into their respective national legal systems.[1000]

Also, no Directive of the EU concerning matters of copyright contains an open list of recommended subject-matter to be considered eligible for copyright, such as, for example, Article 2 (1) of the Berne Convention. The only exception may be *computer programs*, *databases*, *photographs* and, however indirectly, certain kinds of *visual arts*.[1001] Nonetheless, these four types of subject-matter are scattered across different Directives along with their corresponding originality standard, rather than grouped into one designated Article of an EU legal act.

According to the Commission's Staff Working Paper on the Review of the EC Legal Framework in the Field of Copyright and Related Rights, *'the Community legislator has considered it necessary to take account of the special features or the special technical nature of the [three categories] subject-matter in question.'* This excluded them from the general mass of other works, and meant that the criteria for the assessment of their originality would be stipulated separately.[1002] Apart from the three special types of , determining the level (threshold) of originality a work must possess would be left to the discretion of the Member States, according to the said paper.[1003] Therefore, each Member State was free to employ different approaches regarding these categories of subject-matter, as *Griffiths* concluded from the Commission's Staff Working Paper.[1004]

The continental Member States have developed a traditional *sui generis* approach to the standard of originality, by basing their assessments on the intellectual input of authors, the *droit d'auteur* approach, rather than on their physical labour or effort.[1005] In the first phase of the copyright harmonization process, the EU developed an originality standard derived from these continental traditions. However, varied the copyrightable subject-matter might be, the basis of the originality standard would always be the *author's own intellectual creation*. This originality standard for works was then to be applied to every area of copyright harmonized under the corresponding Directive. As mentioned in the introduction, all Directives are

[1000] Morten Rosenmeier, Kacper Szkalej & Sanna Wolk, *EU Copyright Law: Subsistence, Exploitation and Protection of Rights* (Kluwer Law International 2019), p. 17.

[1001] Morten Rosenmeier, Kacper Szkalej & Sanna Wolk, *EU Copyright Law: Subsistence, Exploitation and Protection of Rights* (Kluwer Law International 2019), p. 32.

[1002] *European Commission Staff Working Paper on the Review of the EC legal framework in the field of copyright and related rights*, SEC(2004) 995, 19 Jul. 2004 (1 Oct. 2024), https://data.consilium.europa.eu/doc/document/ST-11634-2004-INIT/en/pdf

[1003] *Ibid.*

[1004] Irini A. Stamatoudi & Paul Torremans (eds.), *EU Copyright Law: a commentary* (Elgar 2014), p. 1103.

[1005] Annette Kur & Thomas Dreier, *European Intellectual Property Law: Text, Cases and Materials* (Edward Elgar 2013), p. 242.

consistent in their terminology: protection by copyright is provided only to works which are the *author's own intellectual creation.* Directives explicitly using this phrase include the Software Directive, the Database Directive, the Digital Single Market Directive and Term Directives I and II. So far, originality has only partially been harmonized via Directives, rather than in a more systematic manner.[1006]

Article 1 of the Software Directive stipulates that the author's work—in this case a computer program—is protected if it is original in the sense that it is the *author's own intellectual creation.* Other criteria are explicitly prohibited from being applied in order to determine a work's eligibility for copyright protection.[1007] Similarly to the diction used in the Software Directive, a database also must be the *author's own intellectual creation* to be eligible for copyright protection. [1008] Other criteria, especially those of aesthetic or qualitative nature, cannot be considered.[1009] The Digital Single Market Directive provides copyright protection to materials resulting from an act of reproduction of a work of visual art in the public domain, if the material is original in the sense that it is, again, the *author's own intellectual creation.*[1010] Finally, Term Directives I and II (in addition to stipulating the duration of copyright protection in general) govern the protection of original and non-original photographic products by copyright and related rights. It is for this reason the next sections cover their evolution in more detail.

10.2.1 Directive 93/98/EEC—Term Directive I

Term Directive I, as its name suggests, was an attempt to harmonize the term of protection of works in general. However, Term Directive I itself also specifically referred to a subject-matter of photographic products. The need to harmonize the term of protection arose from the various approaches Member States took in treating photographic products. Some allowed protection of photographic products by copyright, some by related rights, and some by both. This, naturally, resulted in different lengths of terms of protection.

Overall, Term Directive I did not attempt to harmonize matters of substantive law, especially the requirements for the copyrightability of products. Instead, it focused solely on harmonization (and particularly extension) of the term of protection. According to *von Lewinski,* such intentions can be considered positive, since the focus of harmonization was not put on how protection is provided, but

---

[1006] Irini A. Stamatoudi, 'Originality under EU Copyright Law' In: Paul Torremans, *Research Handbook on Copyright Law* (Edward Elgar Publishing 2017), p. 59.

[1007] Art. 1 (3) Software Directive.

[1008] Art. 3 (1) Database Directive.

[1009] Recital 16 Database Directive.

[1010] Art. 14 Database Directive.

simply on extending its duration.[1011] In other words, harmonization efforts did not interfere with the basic understanding of which subject-matter were eligible for copyright protection within the individual copyright frameworks of the Member States. However, the EU's intentions to extend the term of protection proved to be incompatible when dealing with the subject-matter of photographic products. Here, the superficial harmonization approach comprising of bypassing the national substantive laws of the Member States and extending the term of protection of all photographic products *en bloc* caused a backlash. This resulted in limiting harmonization to original photographic products, and thus leaving the term of protection of non-original photographic products unharmonized, therefore at the discretion of the Member States.

Term Directive I initially proposed a uniform term of protection applicable to all photographic products. This term of 70 years *post mortem auctoris* was to be applicable to all works eligible for copyright protection.[1012] However, this solution would have meant that all photographic products, regardless of their theoretical originality, would have benefited from the maximum term of protection, reserved only for products eligible for copyright protection.[1013] Such a scenario would have left the various national types of protection in force, but photographic subject-matter would be protected uniformly via harmonized EU law, regardless of its categorization within national copyright frameworks. In practice, national categorizations would have become redundant, and total harmonization would be achieved by such a legal bypass. The proposed term of protection would also cover photographic products, later labelled as *other photographs* eligible for protection by a related right type of protection within the meaning of Recital 17 and Article 6 of Term Directive I.

Nonetheless, the proposed uniform term of protection in regard to photographic products was not accepted and a two-tiered compromise solution was introduced instead. The proposed solution included granting copyright protection, along with its full corresponding term of protection, to photographic products original in the sense that they were the *author's own intellectual creation*. The second tier of the proposed solution gave Member States the option to protect *other photographs*, i.e., non-original photographic products. It is worth mentioning that the protection of *other* or *simple* photographic products is still not regulated at the EU or international levels.[1014] By creating this two-tiered system, the EU has abandoned the

[1011] Silke von Lewinski, 'Der EG-Richtlinienvorschlag zur Harmonisierung der Schutzdauer im Urheber- und Leistungsschutzrecht,' *GRUR Int.* 724 (1992), p. 724.

[1012] *Proposal for a Council Directive harmonizing the term of protection of copyright and certain related rights*, COM(92) 33 final – SYN 395, 23. Mar. 1992 (1. Oct. 2024), https://eur-lex.europa.eu/legal-content/EN/TXT/PDF/?uri=CELEX:51992PC0033.

[1013] Ramon C. Vallés, 'The requirement of originality' In: Estelle Derclaye (ed.) *Research handbook on the future of EU copyright* (Edward Elgar Publishing 2009), p. 124.

[1014] Mireille van Eechoud (ed.) *Harmonizing European copyright law: the challenges of better lawmaking* (Kluwer Law International 2009), p. 35.

harmonization of the term of protection applicable uniformly to for all photographic products, preferring to defer to the national interests of Member States.

The abandonment of full harmonization reached such an extent that EU legislator even gave up on harmonizing the minimum term of protection of *other photographs*. The position of non-original photographic products within national legal frameworks of the Member States was left fully to national legislators. Therefore, the possibility of enacting a parallel type of protection in the form of a related right was neither mandatory, nor harmonized.[1015]

In practice, therefore, a single photographic product might have different statuses in different Member States.[1016] A photographic product might be considered original, and therefore eligible for copyright protection in one Member State, but non-original in the other. These different national treatments in the Member States lead to differences in the lengths of the corresponding terms of protection. Looking at it from this perspective, the harmonization process failed to establish the uniform treatment of photographic products and thus their corresponding uniform position within the copyright framework of the EU.

Nonetheless, harmonization resulting from CJEU jurisprudence related to original photographic products, especially the lowering the applicable originality standard, has potentially mitigated the various national treatments of photographic products by the Member States.[1017] By lowering the originality threshold, the CJEU was able to encompass photographic products traditionally seen by Member States as non-original, thus also expanding its hypothetical *reach*.

Therefore, with the issuing of Term Directive I, original photographic products stood to benefit from the term of protection applicable to all standard original authorial works in the length of 70 years *post mortem auctoris*, thus making the, otherwise applicable minimum term of protection stipulated in the Berne Convention, inapplicable within the copyright framework of the EU. Since Article 7 (4) of the Berne Convention stated a minimum length of 25 years *from making* of a photographic product,[1018] the extension achieved by the harmonization was significant. The previously widely diverging situations in Member States regarding the eligibility of photographic products for either a copyright or related right type of protection (and with them connected their varying terms of protection), could not be seen as conflicting with the provisions of the Berne Convention,[1019] since the 25-year term

[1015] Michel M. Walter, 'Term Directive' In: Michel M. Walter & Silke von Lewinski, *European Copyright Law: A Commentary* (Oxford University Press 2010), p. 586.

[1016] Christina Angelopoulos, 'The Myth of European Term Harmonisation – 27 Public Domains for 27 Member States,' *IIC* 567 (2012), p. 567.

[1017] The effect of harmonization achieved by the CJEU through its jurisprudence will be further elaborated in Chapters Eleven to Thirteen.

[1018] Art. 7 (4) of the Berne Convention.

[1019] Richard Davis, Thomas St Quintin & Guy Tritton, *Tritton on Intellectual Property in Europe* (Sweet & Maxwell, 6th ed 2022), p. 671.

of protection only represented a minimum prescribed period of protection, which all Members States had been meeting anyway.

Due to these circumstances, apart from the harmonization of the term of protection, Term Directive I also attempted to harmonize the originality standard applicable to photographic products. These efforts can be seen as a continuation of the harmonization previously applied to the subject-matter of computer programs and databases. Article 6 subsequently set the requirements for the protection of photographic products by copyright and related rights.[1020] The harmonization of the originality standard applicable to photographic products via Term Directive I has been referred to by some as *accidental.*[1021] Indeed, its inclusion into a Directive not primarily dedicated to the harmonization of photographic products might give such an impression.

As mentioned above, the inclusion of the harmonization specifically aimed at the photographic products into Term Directive I was necessitated by their different treatment amongst the Member States, thus proving the status of a specific and ambiguous subject-matter. In other words, photographic products would simply stand out amongst other subject-matter *traditionally* eligible for copyright protection. The specific nature of the subject-matter caused its exclusion from the general text of this Directive, which was dedicated to protected subject-matter in general, and was instead included in a separate Recital and Article. Therefore, EU legislator has not only decided to harmonize the term of protection of original photographic products, but also specifically their applicable originality standard. To a certain extent, the harmonization of the originality standard of photographic products itself could be seen as a side-effect necessitated by the harmonization of the general term of protection.[1022] Nonetheless, this specific feature has not been fully overcome, as shown by the previously mentioned two-tiered system of protection, in which protection for (other) non-original photographic products are the competence of the Member States.

The originality standard within the meaning of Term Directive I applicable to photographic products is of a reduced level.[1023] This in part is due to the fact that photographic products are only subject to the requirement of being an *author's own intellectual creation*, omitting any other criteria from the originality assessment process. The said originality standard was later *refined* by the CJEU with the addition

[1020] Annette Kur, Thomas Dreier & Stefan Luginbühl, *European Intellectual Property Law: Text, Cases and Materials* (Edward Elgar Publishing 2019), p. 310.

[1021] Mireille van Eechoud, 'Along the Road to Uniformity: Diverse Readings of the Court of Justice Judgments on Copyright Work,' 3 *Journal of Intellectual Property, Information Technology and Electronic Commerce Law* 60 (2012), p. 60.

[1022] Stef van Gompel & Erlend Lavik, 'Quality, merit, aesthetics and purpose: An inquiry into EU copyright law's eschewal of other criteria than originality,' *RIDA* 100 (2013), p. 100.

[1023] Michel M. Walter, 'Term Directive' In: Michel M. Walter & Silke von Lewinski, *European Copyright Law: A Commentary* (Oxford University Press 2010), p. 586.

of requiring *personal touch.*[1024] In sum, since the adoption of Term Directive I, for copyright protection of a photographic product its originality is still required, however on a rather low level.

In terms of a character of photographic products eligible for copyright protection, the overall takeaway from Term Directive I is that a photographic product must be distinguishable from other photographic products.[1025] This must be achieved by the photographic product not being a mere copy of another photographic product, or being of banal or trivial nature.

The gradual expansion of the originality standard of *author's own intellectual creation* from the Software Directive to the Database Directive and finally to Term Directive I, should be understood as its *domestication* within the copyright framework of the EU. Although the subject-matter of photography seems to be different from those of computer programs and databases, it does share, to a certain extent, their hard conceptualization. This was probably initially the reason that EU legislator has decided to include the subject-matter of photography into their harmonization focus. The other rationale could have been the lack of any harmonization regarding related rights applicable to non-original (i.e., other) photographic products.[1026] The reduced, compromise originality standard of an *author's own intellectual creation* would easily cover most photographic products. As already mentioned, this solution would then be able to compensate for and substitute the lack of harmonization in non-original photographic products. Nonetheless, the ability of Member States to set conditions and requirements for the protection of non-original *other photographs*, still remains valid. Nevertheless, by introducing the *compromise* reduced originality standard while still leaving Member States the option to protect non-original photographic products effective, the EU significantly narrowed Member States' room for manoeuvre when regulating non-original photographic products.

The enacted equality of original photographic products within the meaning of Term Directive I with other copyrightable (original) subject-matter, seems to be a decision that has been both of dogmatically and objectively correct nature.[1027] As later proved by the jurisprudence of the CJEU in the *Painer* case, photographic products are perfectly capable of being original, and thus fully eligible for copyright protection.

[1024] Case C-145/10, *Eva-Maria Painer v. Standard VerlagsGmbH and Others, 1 December 2011*, ECLI:EU:C:2011:798, para. 92.

[1025] Michel M. Walter, 'Term Directive' In: Michel M. Walter & Silke von Lewinski, *European Copyright Law: A Commentary* (Oxford University Press 2010), p. 587.

[1026] Von Lewinski, S., Walter, M. M. Status of Harmonization. In: Walter, M. M, Lewinski, S. von, Walter, M. M. (eds.). *European copyright law: a commentary*. Oxford: Oxford Univ. Press, 2010, p. 1466.

[1027] Silke von Lewinski & Michel M. Walter, 'Status of Harmonization' In: Michel M. Walter & Silke von Lewinski, *European Copyright Law: A Commentary* (Oxford University Press 2010), p. 724.

10.2.1.1 Recital 17 of Term Directive I

The original proposal for what was later transformed into Recital 17 of Term Directive I had the following wording:

'Whereas under the Berne Convention photographic works qualify for a minimum term of protection of only 25 years from their making ; whereas, moreover, certain Member States have a composite system for the protection of photographic works, which are protected by copyright if they are considered to be artistic works within the meaning of the Berne Convention and protected under one or more other arrangements if they are not so considered ; whereas provision should be made for the complete harmonization of these differing terms of protection... '[1028]

Here, the reference to the Berne Convention, and only the assimilation of photographic works within its meaning to it, can be seen as a way to use it as a tool to distinguish (original) photographic works from (non-original) other photographs.[1029] However, photographic works within the meaning of the Berne Convention cannot be protected by a related-right type of protection, and only by copyright.

For this reason, Recital 17 later included the following (final) wording:

'Whereas the protection of photographs in the Member States is the subject of varying regimes; whereas in order to achieve a sufficient harmonization of the term of protection of photographic works, in particular of those which, due to their artistic or professional character, are of importance within the internal market, it is necessary to define the level of originality required in this Directive; whereas a photographic work within the meaning of the Berne Convention is to be considered original if it is the author's own intellectual creation reflecting his personality, no other criteria such as merit or purpose being taken into account; whereas the protection of other photographs should be left to national law... '[1030]

It is clear that Recital 17 of Term Directive I justifies harmonization in the field of photography by the need to provide protection to photographic products, particularly to those of *artistic* and *professional* character.[1031] Photographic products bearing such characteristics are considered to be important with respect to the internal market, and therefore the EU legislator highlights the economic role of these two types of photographic products, thus making these superior amongst other types of

[1028] *Proposal for a Council Directive harmonizing the term of protection of copyright and certain related rights*, COM(92) 33 final – SYN 395, 23. Mar. 1992 (1. Oct. 2024), https://eur-lex.europa.eu/legal-content/EN/TXT/PDF/?uri=CELEX:51992PC0033.

[1029] Mireille van Eechoud, 'Along the Road to Uniformity: Diverse Readings of the Court of Justice Judgments on Copyright Work,' 3 *Journal of Intellectual Property, Information Technology and Electronic Commerce Law* 60 (2012), p. 60.

[1030] Recital 17 of the Term Directive I.

[1031] *Ibid.*

photographic products due to their prioritised eligibility for copyright protection. It is also important to note that by doing so, EU legislator diverged from rationales regarding the eligibility for copyright protection outside of continental Europe, specifically that of the United Kingdom.[1032]

To some degree, the reference to *artistic or professional character* contradicts the statements prohibiting an assessment based on merit and purpose of a photographic work, as described above. It is hard to understand the descriptors *artistic* or *professional* other than as an indication of the context or aesthetic worth of the photographic work.[1033] It has been suggested that the decision of whether or not there is a sufficient amount of creative input may therefore depend, illogically, on the type of context in which the photographic work was taken.[1034] This contradiction was later amended by Term Directive II, which reworded what became Recital 16, and completely left out references to *artistic or professional character* as well as to the *importance within the internal market*, and thus declared a requirement of total objectivity when assessing the originality of a photographic product in accordance with the originality standard stated therein.

Still, the references to the *artistic* or *professional* character of photographic products, as well as to their potential value due to their importance for the internal market of the EU, had been inserted in the text of Term Directive I in part to satisfy the more utilitarian understanding of copyright protection by Member States outside of the continental EU.[1035] Also, the legislator's reference to the *level of originality* as well as the necessity of its definition, suggests there is more than one level of originality. In other words, the wording suggests that originality may be graded and is not only a matter of answering a yes-or-no question.[1036] These two contradictions—the first concerning the principles of merit and purpose, and the second concerning the level of originality—led to significant amending of Recital 17 before its transition to Term Directive II, as Recital 16.[1037]

On the other hand, the reference to the *author's own intellectual creation reflecting his personality* was part of the scheme satisfying the personality and author-centred understanding of copyright protection by Member States within the continental EU. Nonetheless, as stated above, these references satisfying the non-continental Member States were removed from the wording of Term Directive I, following the preparations for Term Directive II. These removals suggest an even closer inclination of EU legislator to the continental understanding of the originality standard.

1032 Horst Heitland, *Der Schutz der Fotografie im Urheberrecht Deutschlands, Frankreichs und der Vereinigten Staaten von Amerika* (C.H. Beck 1995), p. 62.

1033 Guy Tritton & Richard Davis, *Intellectual Property in Europe* (Sweet & Maxwell, 3rd ed. 2008), p. 519.

1034 *Ibid.*

1035 Michel M. Walter, 'Term Directive' In: Michel M. Walter & Silke von Lewinski, *European Copyright Law: A Commentary* (Oxford University Press 2010), p. 587.

1036 Ramon C. Vallés, 'The requirement of originality' In: Estelle Derclaye (ed.) *Research handbook on the future of EU copyright* (Edward Elgar Publishing 2009), p. 125.

1037 *Ibid.*

Also, the removal made it clear that any value judgements, and any decisions of copyrightability based on it, would be prohibited. Therefore, if a photographic product were to meet the originality requirement of being an *author's own intellectual creation reflecting his personality*, it would have to be treated in the same way as other works of authorship and benefit from the same term of protection.[1038]

Apart from highlighting the commitment towards the objective assessment of the originality of a photographic product, the exclusion of merit and purpose by stating *no other criteria, such as merit or purpose being taken into account* might reflect the materialisation of the need to treat photographic products as potentially artistic, thus applying a more traditional approach to assessing their originality.[1039] This can be confirmed by the fact that the Software and Database Directives also refer to the exclusion of aesthetic merits or criteria when it comes to the assessment of originality.

The exclusion of merit and purpose could be also seen as a reference to the practices related to granting copyright protection in national copyright frameworks of the Member States, especially France. Here, the eligibility of photographic products for copyright protection depended on a demonstration of their artistic or documentary character. Therefore, the explicit exclusion of the said criteria might be seen as both a warning and a reminder that the previous subjection to such, or any other additional or differing, criteria would no longer be applied in light of the conducted harmonization.[1040]

10.2.1.2 Article 6 of Term Directive I

The original proposal for Article 6, (initially Article 3), had the following wording:

> *'Protected photographs shall have the term of protection provided for in Article 1.'*[1041]

Article 1 of Term Directive I prescribed a mandatory protection of 70 years *post mortem auctoris*. Member States were thus forbidden to impose a shorter term of protection, such as the 25 years from the publication of the photographic product according to the Article 7 (4) of the Berne Convention for *protected photographs*. This proved to be an important step towards harmonization.[1042] What was to be

[1038] Mireille van Eechoud (ed.) *Harmonizing European copyright law: the challenges of better lawmaking* (Kluwer Law International 2009), p. 35.

[1039] Gunnar W. G. Karnell, 'European Originality: A Copyright Chimera,' *Intellectual Property* 73 (2002), p. 73.

[1040] Stef van Gompel & Erlend Lavik, 'Quality, merit, aesthetics and purpose: An inquiry into EU copyright law's eschewal of other criteria than originality,' *RIDA* 100 (2013), p. 100.

[1041] *Proposal for a Council Directive harmonizing the term of protection of copyright and certain related rights*, COM(92) 33 final – SYN 395, 23. Mar. 1992 (1. Oct. 2024), https://eur-lex.europa.eu/legal-content/EN/TXT/PDF/?uri=CELEX:51992PC0033.

[1042] Michel M. Walter, 'Term Directive' In: Michel M. Walter & Silke von Lewinski, *European Copyright Law: A Commentary* (Oxford University Press 2010), p. 586.

understood under the term 'protected photographs' was any and all photographic products that were protectable under the various national approaches applied by Member States. The Explanatory Memorandum confirmed this with the following:

'To secure proper harmonization of the term of protection, Article 3 provides that the term for photographic works is always to be seventy years, even though the actual substance of the right may be different, notably In Member States where there are different rules for different categories of photograph.'[1043]

Therefore, it was irrelevant whether a photographic product was eligible for protection under copyright or a related right; the duration of such protection would be 70 years *post mortem auctoris* in both cases. It was noted, however, that if a photographic product would not be of such a nature that would allow for its eligibility for a corresponding type of protection, it would not qualify as a *protected photograph* within the meaning of the proposed wording of Article 3.[1044] As already mentioned, the applicable narrative could be seen as harmonizing whatever terms of protection were present in national copyright frameworks of the Member States, without also harmonizing the criteria according to which such protection is granted. The proposed harmonization could be therefore seen as circumventing the national delimitation criteria between various types of protectable photographic products, but not to such an extent, as to affect the delimitation between protectable and non-protectable photographic products.

Article 3 remained unchanged in the proposal of Term Directive I and was not further amended by the Parliament or the Commission. It was apparently the Council that proposed the originality standard applicable to photographic products as we know it in its current wording of *author's own intellectual creation reflecting their personality.*[1045]

This formulation was preceded, or instigated, by the Council's concerns that the simple reference to *protected photographs*, as formulated in the proposed wording of Article 3, might not cover all photographic products as intended. The concern was especially aimed at *photographs of importance within the internal market*, which might fall below some national protection thresholds, thus not being eligible for copyright protection in all Member States.[1046] For this reason, the Council only proposed harmonization of the originality standard for original photographic

1043 *Proposal for a Council Directive harmonizing the term of protection of copyright and certain related rights*, COM(92) 33 final – SYN 395, 23. Mar. 1992 (1. Oct. 2024), https://eur-lex.europa.eu/legal-content/EN/TXT/PDF/?uri=CELEX:51992PC0033.

1044 *Ibid.*

1045 Mireille van Eechoud, 'Along the Road to Uniformity: Diverse Readings of the Court of Justice Judgments on Copyright Work,' 3 *Journal of Intellectual Property, Information Technology and Electronic Commerce Law* 60 (2012), p. 60.

1046 *Common Position of the Council of 22 July 1993 on the amended proposal for a Council Directive harmonizing the term of protection of copyright and certain related rights*, 7831/1/93 Rev 1.

products.[1047] It was this delimitation between photographic products which necessitated the definition of the originality standard applicable to (original) photographic products.

The final wording of Article 6 of Term Directive I was settled in the following way:

'Photographs which are original in the sense that they are the author's own intellectual creation shall be protected in accordance with Article 1. No other criteria shall be applied to determine their eligibility for protection. Member States may provide for the protection of other photographs.'[1048]

Article 6 of Term Directive I can be considered to be partially non-mandatory.[1049] In practice, the ambiguity is caused by the distinguishing of photographic products into *original photographs* and *other photographs*. The result of this process of distinguishing was the mandatory eligibility of *original photographs* for copyright protection, and the voluntary extension of a related right type of protection to *other photographs*. In this view, Member States were only obliged to cover original photographic products by copyright, if they met the harmonized originality criterion.

The overall takeaway from the wording of Article 6 is that only the distinctiveness of a photographic product, based on the quality of being an *author's own intellectual creation reflecting their personality* may be applied when assessing its originality. The parallel existence of the possibility of granting of protection to *other photographs* via a related right type of protection was not meant to indicate the possibility of introducing a requirement of a level of originality within the originality itself to (original) *photographs*.[1050] In other words, the discretion available to Member States in the realm of *other photographs* does not extend to original photographic products. Within the meaning of Article 6 of Term Directive I, a photographic product can either only be original or non-original.

10.2.2 Directive 2006/116/EC—Term Directive II

Term Directive II represented a consolidated version of Term Directive I, and indeed replaced it in its entirety. Term Directive II introduced further refinements of the requirements of the copyrightability of photographic products. These consisted of further approximation the EU harmonized copyright framework towards the copyright traditions of continental Europe. Since Term Directive II is the most relevant Directive for photographic products, and is also still in force at the time of writing

[1047] *Ibid.*

[1048] Art. 6 of the Term Directive I.

[1049] Gemma Minnero, 'The Term Directive' In: Irini A. Stamatoudi & Paul Torremans (eds.), *EU copyright law: a commentary* (Edward Elgar Publishing, 2nd ed. 2021), p. 202.

[1050] Gerhard Schricker, 'Farewell to the "Level of Creativity",' 26 *IIC* 41 (1995), p. 41.

of this text, the following pages focus on the evolution of this Directive, as well as the originality standard contained therein.

10.2.2.1 Recital 16 of Term Directive II

'The protection of photographs in the Member States is the subject of varying regimes. A photographic work within the meaning of the Berne Convention is to be considered original if it is the author's own intellectual creation reflecting his personality, no other criteria such as merit or purpose being taken into account. The protection of other photographs should be left to national law.'[1051]

The *varying regimes*, that Recital 16 of Term Directive II directly refers to were a consequence of Article 7 (4) of the Berne Convention.[1052] That Article only provided for a minimum term of protection: 25 years from the *making* of a *photographic work*. Conditions for the eligibility of photographic products by the corresponding type of protection were left at the discretion of the contracting parties of the Berne Convention. The omission of setting more conditions and specifying these in more detail might also demonstrate the complicated nature of the medium of photography itself. Given the historic variability of approaches towards the protection of photographic products, the Berne Convention simply did not touch upon the issue.

In order to fully comprehend its meaning and implications for its applicability to photographic products, it is necessary to first look at the definition of the originality standard of the *author's own intellectual creation reflecting his personality*, including definitions of its individual notions:

The first expression, *photographic work,* is an umbrella term used in both Term Directive I and Term Directive II for *photographs* and *other photographs*. The former is considered to be an original photographic product (i.e., a work) capable of being eligible for copyright protection, while the latter is not. However, the notion of a *photographic work* should always be understood within the meaning of the Berne Convention, according to both Directives. Direct referrals to the Berne Convention only emphasize the importance of this international treaty. It provides a global cornerstone framework for the protection of photographic works in Article 2 (1).[1053] All EU Member States are also its contracting parties. The photographic work must also be *original*, i.e., it must meet the prescribed harmonized originality standard, which means that a photographic work must possess the qualities recognizable as meeting the set originality standard.

For the purposes of copyright law, the fourth key term in the passage is that of the *author*, which signifies the originator or creator of a work.[1054] When

[1051] Recital 16 of the Term Directive II.

[1052] Michel M. Walter, 'Term Directive' In: Michel M. Walter & Silke von Lewinski, *European Copyright Law: A Commentary* (Oxford University Press 2010), p. 583.

[1053] Art. 2 (1) of the Berne Convention.

[1054] Peter Groves, *A Dictionary of Intellectual Property Law* (Edward Elgar 2012), p. 24.

photographic works are created, their author is called a *photographer*. Overly simplified, a photographer is thus a person who produces a photographic work using a process of photographic or similar nature. Closely connected to the person of the author is the fifth expression, that of the *own intellectual creation*. The adjective *intellectual* is meant as stemming from one's intellect. The notion of *intellect* can be defined as the from the ability to think in a logical way and understand things,[1055] or the faculty of reasoning and understanding objectively.[1056] The requirement of a photographer's intellectual input into the creation of a photographic work emphasizes the level of the originality standard, where abstract concepts in the photographer's mind are transformed into an objectively perceived medium: the photographic work. This input must be photographer's own and personal, as indicated in the formulation of the originality requirement. The resulting creation represents an act of making something that is new, causing something to exist that did not exist before,[1057] or especially showing artistic talent.[1058]

In addition, a photographic work must reflect its creator's personality. This sixth notion of *personality* can be defined as the various aspects of a person's character that combine to make that person different from other people,[1059] or combination of characteristics or qualities that form an individual's distinctive character.[1060]

Apart from the requirement of *own intellectual creation*, the photographic work must display its creator's personal distinctive touch. This part of the originality requirement ensures that the photographic work is distinguishable from the works of other photographers on the basis of uniqueness of personality of each photographer as a person. In respect to this, it is evident that the *author's own intellectual creation* on its own does not suffice for the copyrightability; a reflection of the photographer's personality must be also present.[1061]

The final seventh and the eighth notions are *merit* and *purpose*. In theory, these are not supposed to be taken into account when assessing the originality of a photographic work. Merit can be characterized as the quality of being good, so as to deserve praise, reward, or admiration.[1062] Purpose represents an objective, goal, or

1055 Albert Sydney Hornby & Sally Wehmeier (eds.) *Oxford advanced learner's dictionary of current English* (Oxford University Press, 7th ed. 2009), p. 807.

1056 Catherine Soanes (ed.), *Concise Oxford English Dictionary* (Oxford Univ. Press, 11. ed. 2006), p. 738.

1057 Albert Sydney Hornby & Sally Wehmeier (eds.) *Oxford advanced learner's dictionary of current English* (Oxford University Press, 7th ed. 2009), p. 360.

1058 Catherine Soanes (ed.), *Concise Oxford English Dictionary* (Oxford Univ. Press, 11. ed. 2006), p. 335.

1059 Albert Sydney Hornby & Sally Wehmeier (eds.) *Oxford advanced learner's dictionary of current English* (Oxford University Press, 7th ed. 2009), p. 1127

1060 Catherine Soanes (ed.), *Concise Oxford English Dictionary* (Oxford Univ. Press, 11. ed. 2006), p. 738.

1061 J. A. L. Sterling, *Sterling on World Copyright Law* (Thomson Reuters, 4th ed 2015), p. 1101.

1062 Albert Sydney Hornby & Sally Wehmeier (eds.) *Oxford advanced learner's dictionary of current English* (Oxford University Press, 7th ed. 2009), p. 960.

end,[1063] or in other words the aim or function for which something is done or created or for which something exists.[1064] Evaluating the merit and purpose of a photographic work can lead to assessments based on the reputation or popularity of the photographic work, the genre it belongs to, or its author's position in society or amongst other photographers. These factors can lead to biased decisions. For this reason, merit and purpose are excluded to prevent subjective assessments of the originality in photographic works. Instead, photographic works should be assessed without prejudice related to the reason behind their creation or to their creator as a person.

Like Recital 17 of Term Directive I, the wording of Recital 16 of Term Directive II also omitted references to the *need of harmonization, artistic* and *professional* character, or the *importance of photographic products within the internal market* of the EU. The reason for this deletion was most probably linked to the effort of making the text more comprehensive and compact, as well as less ambiguous, since especially in connection with the references to the artistic and professional character of the photographic products, the expressions proved to be redundant.[1065] Another reason for the said deletion, especially the references to the *artistic* and *professional* character, could have been the intention of further approximation of the EU copyright law towards the European continental understanding of copyright.

10.2.2.2 Article 6 of Term Directive II

Term Directive II also grants protection by copyright to all photographic products in Article 6, as lon as these are original in the sense that they are the *author's own intellectual creation*.[1066] The wording of Article 6 is as follows:

'Photographs which are original in the sense that they are the author's own intellectual creation shall be protected in accordance with Article 1. No other criteria shall be applied to determine their eligibility for protection. Member States may provide for the protection of other photographs.'[1067]

In order to ensure the eligibility for copyright protection even of photographic products of a more modest creative level, Term Directive II reintroduced a reduced level of originality applicable to photographic products—that of the *author's own intellectual creation*.[1068] Article 6 of Term Directive II also reintroduces the dual

[1063] Bryan A. Garner & Henry Campbell Black (eds.), *Black's Law Dictionary* (Thomson Reuters, 11th ed. 2019), p. 1493.

[1064] Catherine Soanes (ed.), *Concise Oxford English Dictionary* (Oxford Univ. Press, 11. ed. 2006), p. 1167.

[1065] Michel M. Walter, 'Term Directive' In: Michel M. Walter & Silke von Lewinski, *European Copyright Law: A Commentary* (Oxford University Press 2010), p. 584.

[1066] Art. 6 of the Term Directive II.

[1067] *Ibid.*

[1068] Michel M. Walter, 'Term Directive' In: Michel M. Walter & Silke von Lewinski, *European Copyright Law: A Commentary* (Oxford University Press 2010), p. 586.

subject-matter differentiation for photographic products—it explicitly divides photographic products into *photographs* and *other photographs*. Term Directive II leaves protection of the latter at the discretion of Member States, including the terms for that protection's, its establishment, conditions, duration, etc.[1069] According to *Gaubiac*, *Linder* and *Adams*, the separate terms of protection applicable to *other photographs* must be provided by a related right and based on conditions other than originality, as *Minnero* quoted them.[1070] If a Member State wishes to employ a related right type of protection , it must notify the Commission, including the basic reasoning behind the decision.[1071] Naturally, the length of the term of protection of *other photographs* differs amongst the Member States, which have decided on various differentiating measures between photographic products. Therefore, the protection of *other photographs* is neither mandatory nor harmonized.[1072] The conditions for eligibility of *other photographs*, therefore those photographic products of a non-original nature, are at the full discretion of Member States.[1073] The existence of such discretion is rightly considered a sign of incompleteness of harmonization within the field of photography.[1074]

From the wording of Article 6 of Term Directive II, it can be derived that *photographs* are considered original, while *other photographs* are not. One can then further deduce that the originality of a photographic product is the determining factor in whether it is to be eligible for copyright protection or not. What can also be derived from the wording of Article 6, and especially the reference to *other photographs*, is that the EU legislator implies assumes there are photographic products that are still worthy of protection—although not by copyright, but rather only by a related right type of protection.[1075]

Nonetheless, the practical importance and relevance of the standard of originality, as formulated in the first sentence of Article 6 of Term Directive II, is undermined by the given option to diverge from it in its third sentence.[1076] This is due to

---

1069 Michel M. Walter, 'Schutzdauer Richtlinie' In: Michel M. Walter & Silke von Lewinski (eds.), *Europäisches Urheberrecht: Kommentar ; insbesondere Software-, Vermiet- und Verleih-, Satelliten- und Kabel-, Schutzdauer-, Datenbank-, Folgerecht-, Informationsgesellschaft-Richtlinie, Produktpiraterie-Verordnung* (Springer 2001), p. 594.

1070 Gemma Minnero, 'The Term Directive' In: Irini A. Stamatoudi & Paul Torremans (eds.), *EU Copyright Law: a commentary* (Edward Elgar Publishing 2014), p. 277.

1071 Art 11 (1) of the Term Directive II.

1072 Michel M. Walter, 'Term Directive' In: Michel M. Walter & Silke von Lewinski, *European Copyright Law: A Commentary* (Oxford University Press 2010), p. 586.

1073 Michel M. Walter, 'Term Directive' In: Michel M. Walter & Silke von Lewinski, *European Copyright Law: A Commentary* (Oxford University Press 2010), p. 521.

1074 Achilles C. Emilianides, 'The Author Revived: Harmonisation Without Justification,' 26 *European Intellectual Property Review* 538 (2004), p. 538.

1075 Christian Handig, 'Wie viel Originalität braucht ein urheberrechtliches Werk?' 1 *Österreichisches Recht der Wirtschaft* 14 (2010), p. 14.

1076 Valérie-Laure Bénabou & André Françon, *Droits d'auteur, droits voisins et droit communautaire* (Bruylant 1997), p. 385.

a fact the options of the Member States related to the parameters of the protection applicable to *other photographs* are not regulated in any EU harmonized way.

10.3 Interim Conclusion on both Term Directives

The terminology used throughout both Term Directive I and II in connection with photographic products is *photographs*, *photographic works* and *other photographs*. *Photographic works* refer to photographic products within the meaning of the Berne Convention. In contrast, *other photographs* describe photographic products not meeting the prescribed work requirement within the meaning of Term Directive I and II, or the Berne Convention. The eligibility of these *other photographs* for protection is left to the discretion of individual Member States. While the term *photographs* seems to be used interchangeably in EU legislation or as a general (umbrella) term covering both *photographic works* as well as *other photographs*. However, it must be noted that neither *photographs* nor *photographic works* are standardized legal terms with definitions sufficiently and specifically clarifying their production process and through it their nature.[1077]

Moreover, neither Term Directive ever clearly defined the lower limit of protection for photographic works.[1078] With the vast number of potential variables, only the higher threshold of the author's own intellectual creation was successfully established by the EU legislator. In other words, it is not evident *until when* a photographic product may still be considered a photographic work, since only the *from when* is known. Neither of the two versions of Term Directives affected the requirements for the higher level of protection prescribed for photographic works.[1079] Therefore, the eligibility of photographic works for copyright protection remains unaffected. However, the requirements for the lower level were decreased even further, as described above. Nonetheless, both Term Directives have, in essence, restricted the imposition of exceptionally high requirements for the protection of photographic works by copyright.[1080]

To conclude, the concept of the *author's own intellectual creation* was adopted as a compromise formula during the first phase of the harmonization process between the relatively low originality threshold required as a precondition for copyright protection in the non-continental Member States and the higher standards used

[1077] Dana Ferchland, *Fotografieschutz im Wandel: Auswirkungen technischer, künstlerischer und rechtlicher Veränderungen auf den Urheberrechtsschutz von Fotografien* (Verlag Dr. Kovač 2018), p. 53.

[1078] Horst Heitland, *Der Schutz der Fotografie im Urheberrecht Deutschlands, Frankreichs und der Vereinigten Staaten von Amerika* (C.H. Beck 1995), p. 70.

[1079] Melanie Overbeck, *Der Lichtbildschutz gem. § 72 UrhG im Lichte der Digitalfotografie* (Lit 2018), p. 112.

[1080] Horst Heitland, *Der Schutz der Fotografie im Urheberrecht Deutschlands, Frankreichs und der Vereinigten Staaten von Amerika* (C.H. Beck 1995), p. 63.

throughout the Member States of the continental EU.[1081] Nonetheless at that time, the true meaning of this definition and its applicability remained rather unclear. Further clarification of the drafted originality standard was left to the CJEU through its jurisprudence. Such an approach was also presupposed by the official guide to the Berne Convention, which left the question of originality to be answered by courts.[1082] Indeed, in light of this, the copyright law of the EU has had to rely on further interpretation of Article 6 of Term Directives by the CJEU through its jurisprudence. This additional interpretation of legislation by the CJEU represents the second phase of the harmonization process.[1083]

10.4 The Second Harmonization Phase

As mentioned in the previous section, the harmonization of the originality standard concluded via Directives only touched on certain, select subject-matter. It was the case law of the CJEU that extended the application of the harmonized originality standard to other and all subject-matter beyond the dedicated Directives. The harmonization activities of EU legislator have set the scene for the CJEU, which has since assumed an increasingly active role in filling the existent legislative *vacancies*, as well as in interpreting EU legislation.[1084]

Through its case law, the CJEU not only interprets EU legislation and its various terminology, but has also tried to limit the room for possible national interpretations by the Member States (which however still remain substantial).[1085] Nevertheless, the decision-making activities of the CJEU not only serve the purpose of limiting the scope of legislative and jurisprudential autonomy of the Member States, but also provide further interpretation of EU legislation as well as its very own case law.[1086] Both purposes contribute to further harmonization of EU law.

It was 1992 when the CJEU first levelled judicial criticism on the EU level in connection with harmonization (or the lack thereof) in the field of intellectual property law, in its *Patricia (Phil Collins) case* decision.[1087] The case exposed what

1081 Irini A. Stamatoudi & Paul Torremans (eds.), *EU Copyright Law: a commentary* (Elgar 2014), p. 1103.

1082 World Organization for Intellectual Property (ed.), *Guide to the Berne convention for the protection of literary and artistic works: Paris Act, 1971* (WIPO 1978), p. 18.

1083 Thomas Margoni, *The Harmonisation of EU Copyright Law: The Originality Standard* (1 Sep. 2024), https://papers.ssrn.com/sol3/papers.cfm?abstract_id=2802327.

1084 Hayleigh Bosher & Eleonora Rosati (eds.), *Developments and directions in intellectual property law: twenty years of the IPKat* (Oxford University Press 2023), p. 140.

1085 Silke von Lewinski, 'Introduction: The Notion of Work Under EU Law,' *GRUR Int.* 1098 (2014), p. 1098.

1086 Eleonora Rosati, *Copyright and the Court of Justice of the European Union* (Oxford University Press 2019), p. 86.

1087 CJEU, Case C-92/92, *Phil Collins v Imtrat Handelsgesellschaft mbH and Patricia Im- und Export Verwaltungsgesellschaft mbH and Leif Emanuel Kraul v EMI Electrola GmbH*, 20 Oct. 1993,

issues different national terms of protection might cause. The situation involved the import of a product, a phonogram, from Member State 1, where its protection has already expired, to Member State 2, where the term of protection was longer, and thus not yet expired.

Such conduct by the CJEU very often has prompted the EU Commission to act, thus assuring the enactment of new legislation and further harmonization.[1088] Therefore, the role of the CJEU should not be underestimated. The CJEU has also proved to be flexible in terms of exploiting its room for manoeuvre in rephrasing questions of referrals by the national courts, in order to reach the intended goal.[1089] This means the CJEU might not always answer the referred questions as originally referred to it.

It can be therefore said that the CJEU has served as a catalyst and accelerator of the harmonization process.[1090] However, it must be noted that it is not only the CJEU that has played a significant role in the second harmonization phase judicial decisions. National courts of Member States, which begin the whole process through their referrals, also play a crucial role in the further development of EU law.[1091]

10.4.1 Selected Case Law of the Second Harmonization Phase

Interpretation of EU legislation by the CJEU has provided an additional significant source of information on the applicability of legal provisions and their approximation to actual situations. In the past, the CJEU had been asked to decide a number of cases related to originality and copyright. In terms of originality in particular, the CJEU has taken the initiative to define the legislative term of *author's own intellectual creation* in more detail in practice and has also expanded its applicability to all works eligible for copyright protection within the copyright framework of the EU.[1092] In doing so, the CJEU has assumed responsibility for a matter that had been intentionally kept unresolved by EU legislator, while also at the same time limiting the flexibility of Member States in assessing originality.[1093]

It must also be noted that the originality standard applicable within the copyright framework of the EU has been gradually developed through application of the

ECLI:EU:C:1993:847.

1088 Ana Ramalho, 'The Competence and Rationale of EU Copyright Harmonization' In: Eleonora Rosati, *The Routledge Handbook of EU Copyright Law* (Routledge 2021), p. 11.

1089 For example, the ruling of the CJEU in the Painer case.

1090 Christian Handig, 'Durch 'freie kreative Entscheidungen' zum europäischen urheberrechtlichen Werkbegriff,' *GRUR Int.* 965 (2012), p. 973.

1091 Matthias Leistner, 'Der europäische Werkbegriff,' *Zeitschrift für Geistiges Eigentum* 4 (2013), p. 4.

1092 Irini A. Stamatoudi, 'Originality under EU Copyright Law' In: Paul Torremans, *Research Handbook on Copyright Law* (Edward Elgar Publishing 2017), p. 62.

1093 Irini A. Stamatoudi & Paul Torremans (eds.), *EU Copyright Law: a commentary* (Elgar 2014), p. 1103.

requirement of the *author's own intellectual creation* to a diverse spectrum of subject-matter, including photographic products. It is the application of this originality standard to the subject-matter of photographic products by the CJEU in the *Painer* case, which in light of the relevance of this application for the research covered in this book, receives substantial attention below.

The cases discussed in the following sections frequently also dealt with matters outside the scope of this book; I have endeavoured to omit unrelated aspects of these cases.

10.4.1.1 The Infopaq case

The *Infopaq case*[1094] provided a foundation for the concept of originality within the copyright framework of the EU.[1095] In it, the CJEU had to elaborate on whether an extract from a newspaper article comprising of 11 words constituted an original work and was therefore eligible for copyright protection. It is worth noting that the original referral from the Danish court did not concern originality at all, but rather the right of reproduction for authorial works within the meaning of the Article 2 (a) of the InfoSoc Directive.[1096] In this case, the CJEU took the initiative, and adjusted the Danish referral, re-interpreting it, and then proceeded in three steps.

First, the CJEU held that the protection by copyright is only available for works which are the *author's own intellectual creation.*[1097] Second, no distinction between protection of the work as a whole and its part shall be made, according to the CJEU, as the parts share the originality of the whole work.[1098] Third, if these parts accommodate elements that can be considered expressions of the *author's own intellectual creation*, the parts shall be entitled to copyright protection as well.[1099] As a result, such elements must be original in the sense of having contributed to the work's authorial character.[1100]

What was not known with sufficient certainty at the time and only confirmed subsequently was whether the CJEU made the *author's own intellectual creation*

[1094] CJEU, Case C-5/08, *Infopaq International A/S v Danske Dagblades Forening*, 16 Jul. 2009, ECLI:EU:C:2009:465.

[1095] Irini A. Stamatoudi, 'Originality under EU Copyright Law' In: Paul Torremans, *Research Handbook on Copyright Law* (Edward Elgar Publishing 2017), p. 64.

[1096] Eleonora Rosati, 'Copyright at the CJEU: Back to the Start (of Copyright Protection)' In: Hayleigh Bosher & Eleonora Rosati, *Developments and Directions in Intellectual Property Law: Twenty Years of the IPKat* (Oxford University Press 2023), p. 218.

[1097] CJEU, Case C-5/08, Infopaq International A/S v Danske Dagblades Forening, 16 Jul. 2009, ECLI:EU:C:2009:465, para. 37.

[1098] CJEU, Case C-5/08, Infopaq International A/S v Danske Dagblades Forening, 16 Jul. 2009, ECLI:EU:C:2009:465, para. 38.

[1099] Eleonora Rosati, 'Copyright at the CJEU: Back to the Start (of Copyright Protection)' In: Hayleigh Bosher & Eleonora Rosati, *Developments and Directions in Intellectual Property Law: Twenty Years of the IPKat* (Oxford University Press 2023), para. 39.

[1100] Justine Pila & Paul Torremans, *European Intellectual Property Law* (Oxford University Press 2016), p. 302.

a standard of uniform nature to be applied to every subject-matter, thus replacing all local deviating standards of originality applicable in individual Member States.[1101] In other words, it was not still evident, at that time, to what extent the originality standard formulated by the CJEU was going to be applied in the various national copyright frameworks of Member States.[1102]

By taking these three steps, the CJEU de facto achieved full harmonization of the originality standard within the copyright framework of the EU.[1103] Before the *Infopaq* decision, it was understood that apart from photographic products, databases and computer programs, each Member State had autonomy in formulating separate national requirements for the eligibility of a product for copyright protection.[1104]

It is clear that the presence of intellectual input in a product or its part became the main determining factor when its originality and copyrightability was contested in the copyright framework of the EU. In other words, parts of a work are protected by copyright and may not be treated differently from the whole work which they are a part of, since these parts share the originality of the whole work.[1105] However, even these parts also must contain an element of the work that manifests the *author's own intellectual creation.*[1106]

By using 11-word excerpt of an article as an example of a subject-matter eligible for copyright protection, the CJEU had set the actual substantive requirement for copyrightability at the intermediate level of the (whole) *author's own intellectual creation.*[1107] The *intermediate* nature of the requirement lies in the fact that it is an excerpt—it constituted only part of the whole work (which was eligible for copyright), but it was elevated to a status of being eligible for copyright by itself, since it met the necessary prescribed criteria.

For any newspaper article, the *author's own intellectual creation* becomes materialized through its form, the manner in which the subject is presented, and the linguistic expression.[1108] The CJEU also noted the words that made up the article as a whole, could not be considered the *author's own intellectual creation* on their

[1101] Mireille van Eechoud, 'Along the Road to Uniformity: Diverse Readings of the Court of Justice Judgments on Copyright Work,' 3 *Journal of Intellectual Property, Information Technology and Electronic Commerce Law* 60 (2012), p. 60.

[1102] Matthias Leistner, 'Der europäische Werkbegriff,' *Zeitschrift für Geistiges Eigentum* 4 (2013), p. 4.

[1103] Eleonora Rosati, 'Originality in a Work, or a Work of Originality: the Effects of the Infopaq Decision,' 33 *European Intellectual Property Review* 746 (2011), p. 746.

[1104] Martin Husovec, 'Judikatórna harmonizácia pojmu autorského diela v únijnom práve,' 12 *Bulletin slovenskej advokácie* (2012), p. 16.

[1105] *Louis Theodor Christian Harms, 'Originality' and 'Reproduction' in Copyright Law with Special Reference to Photographs* (2 Sep. 2024), https://papers.ssrn.com/sol3/papers.cfm?abstract_id=2427669.

[1106] CJEU, Case C-5/08, *Infopaq International A/S v Danske Dagblades Forening*, 16 Jul. 2009, ECLI:EU:C:2009:465, para. 48.

[1107] Matthias Leistner, 'Der europäische Werkbegriff,' *Zeitschrift für Geistiges Eigentum* 4 (2013), p. 4.

[1108] CJEU, Case C-5/08, *Infopaq International A/S v Danske Dagblades Forening*, 16 Jul. 2009, ECLI:EU:C:2009:465, para. 44.

own.[1109] However, it is only through the choice, sequence, and combination of those words the author can demonstrate their creativity in an original style and achieve a result which can be considered an intellectual creation.[1110] Regarding this, the CJEU noted the following:

'Regarding the elements of such works covered by the protection, it should be observed that they consist of words which, considered in isolation, are not as such an intellectual creation of the author who employs them. It is only through the choice, sequence and combination of those words that the author may express his creativity in an original manner and achieve a result which is an intellectual creation.'[1111]

The significance of the *Infopaq* decision regarding originality lies in several aspects. First, the originality requirement previously exclusively reserved only for three specific subject-matter—photographic products, databases, and computer programs—was extended to all works falling under the EU's copyright framework.[1112] This in turn meant that all products, regardless of their nature or specific attributes, should be assessed equally in terms of originality. This harmonization was conducted by the CJEU despite the slight differences in wordings of the Software, Database, and Term Directives. Nonetheless, the requirements for protection stipulated by these three Directives were generalized to allow their application to other subject-matter.[1113] Second, the decision of the CJEU further made clear that the originality requirement is of qualitative, rather than quantitative nature.[1114] This means emphasis should not be put on the size of the work, in this case how much of the work has been copied, but rather on whether the work constitutes *author's own intellectual creation*. By equalling the work and its parts in front of the copyright through the requirement of *author's own intellectual creation*, the range of subject-matter eligible for copyright protection has significantly increased.[1115] In practice, such increase would be caused by the fact, that a work is now being officially recognized as capable of consisting of numerous sub-works, each of which is eligible for copyright protection in their own right, solely based on the fact they are their *author's own intellectual creation*. Third, the decision of the CJEU establishes the

[1109] CJEU, Case C-5/08, *Infopaq International A/S v Danske Dagblades Forening*, 16 Jul. 2009, ECLI:EU:C:2009:465, para. 45.
[1110] *Ibid.*
[1111] *Ibid.*
[1112] Irini A. Stamatoudi, 'Originality under EU Copyright Law' In: Paul Torremans, *Research Handbook on Copyright Law* (Edward Elgar Publishing 2017), p. 65.
[1113] Matthias Leistner, 'Der europäische Werkbegriff,' *Zeitschrift für Geistiges Eigentum* 4 (2013), p. 4.
[1114] Irini A. Stamatoudi, 'Originality under EU Copyright Law' In: Paul Torremans, *Research Handbook on Copyright Law* (Edward Elgar Publishing 2017), p. 66.
[1115] Justine Pila & Paul Torremans, *European Intellectual Property Law* (Oxford University Press, 2nd ed. 2019), p. 262.

originality as the sole criterion for protection by copyright.[1116] Therefore, any other criteria are to be excluded when copyrightability of a subject-matter is to be assessed. Fourth, the originality requirement shall be interpreted in a uniform and autonomous manner.[1117] In respect to this, the Member States must refrain from interpreting and defining the originality requirement through their national legal systems and their respective frameworks.

As a result of the CJEU's decision in the *Infopaq case*, any inconsistencies resulting from different approaches to products within national legal frameworks of Member States were to be eliminated, thus promoting harmonization in its second phase.[1118] However, from the reasoning of the CJEU in the said case, it was still not evident whether the notion of originality is to be understood in a subjective manner, as requiring the imprint of author's personality, or in a more objective manner.[1119]

Apart from the said full harmonization of the originality standard in the copyright framework of the EU, the CJEU has also achieved the introduction of the harmonized standard of infringement applicable to the right of reproduction attributed to the authors.[1120] In other words, the CJEU has reached its conclusion in regards to originality through the analysis of the reproduction itself. The CJEU has noted, that if there is a reproduction of a part of an original work, and that reproduced part is original itself, such reproduction constitutes reproduction within the meaning of Article 2 (a) of the InfoSoc Directive.[1121] In order for such a part of an original work to be protectable inherently, it must be the *author's own intellectual creation.*

At the time it was reached, the decision in the *Infopaq case* has also had an effect, although indirect, on photographic products. The point to be taken was, that if, figuratively speaking, mere *unoriginal* words which convey a mere *unoriginal* information can be arranged in an original manner, so can a photographer arrange *unoriginal* objects and subjects and capture them in an original manner.[1122] If the photographer employs choice, sequence and combination in a creative manner, just as the writer does with the words when writing an article, originality could be found via such choices in the resulting photographic product. It was therefore important that choices of such nature were found to be originality forming even for

[1116] Irini A. Stamatoudi, 'Originality under EU Copyright Law' In: Paul Torremans, *Research Handbook on Copyright Law* (Edward Elgar Publishing 2017), p. 66.

[1117] Irini A. Stamatoudi, 'Originality under EU Copyright Law' In: Paul Torremans, *Research Handbook on Copyright Law* (Edward Elgar Publishing 2017), p. 66.

[1118] Irini A. Stamatoudi & Paul Torremans (eds.), *EU Copyright Law: a commentary* (Elgar 2014), p. 1103.

[1119] Nicolas Berthold, 'L'harmonisation de la Notion D'originalité en Droit D'auteur,' 16 *Journal of World Intellectual Property* 58 (2013), p. 58.

[1120] Eleonora Rosati, 'Copyright at the CJEU: Back to the Start (of Copyright Protection)' In: Hayleigh Bosher & Eleonora Rosati, *Developments and Directions in Intellectual Property Law: Twenty Years of the IPKat* (Oxford University Press 2023), p. 219.

[1121] *Ibid.*

[1122] Benoît Michaux, 'L'originalité en droit communautaire après l'arrêt Infopaq,' 70 *Revue Lamy Droit de l'immatériel* 121 (2011), p. 121.

a seemingly unoriginal subject-matter, which was nonetheless also one of the questions at the heart of the future *Painer* decision.

Since its decision in the *Infopaq case*, the activities of the CJEU, within the meaning of content and effects of its decisions, are referred to as the *harmonization by stealth*, a notion first introduced by *Lionel Bently.*[1123] Such reference signifies the approach the CJEU has decided to take, especially in terms of its nature, towards the shaping of the requirement for protection of products by copyright in a form of the originality standard, as will be seen in the following selected case law.

10.4.1.2 The Bezpečnostní softwarová asociace case

In the second selected case, the *Bezpečnostní softwarová asociace* case,[1124] the CJEU held that a graphic user interface (GUI) of a computer program cannot be eligible for copyright protection under the Software Directive as a work, since it only constitutes an element through which users make use of the computer program itself.[1125] The issue to be resolved was how to assess a product for the possible presence of originality if the product itself clearly consisted of technical, functional, or other non-original elements. In certain cases, the CJEU noted that if a GUI represented its *author's own intellectual creation*, copyright protection would be granted under the InfoSoc Directive.[1126] The importance of this decision lies in two factors. First, the decision confirmed the harmonization of the originality standard from the *Infopaq* case.[1127] Second, the subject-matter differentiation of works became meaningless, given that a work may fall under copyright protection anytime it represents the *author's own intellectual creation.*[1128]

The CJEU also clarified that the term *creation*, as part of the formulated originality standard, presupposed an expenditure of creativity on the creator's—the author's—end, as *Rosati* quoted from the *Funke Medien case.*[1129] In other words, it is required by the standard of originality that the author expresses their creativity in an original manner.[1130] Here, the CJEU aligned the creativity with the freedom to

[1123] Lionel Bently. *Harmonization by Stealth: Copyright and the ECJ.* Fordham IP Conference. 2010, New York City (1. Oct. 2024), https://www.competitionlawassociation.org.uk/docs/harmonisation_bently_slides_01_05_12.ppt .

[1124] CJEU, Case C-393/09, *Bezpečnostní softwarová asociace – Svaz softwarové ochrany v Ministerstvo kultury*, 22 Dec. 2010, ECLI:EU:C:2010:816.

[1125] *Ibid.*, para. 41.

[1126] *Ibid.*, para. 51.

[1127] Eleonora Rosati, Originality in EU Copyright: *Full Harmonization through Case Law* (Edward Elgar Publishing 2013), p. 123.

[1128] *Ibid.*

[1129] Eleonora Rosati, 'Copyright at the CJEU: Back to the Start (of Copyright Protection)' In: Hayleigh Bosher & Eleonora Rosati, *Developments and Directions in Intellectual Property Law: Twenty Years of the IPKat* (Oxford University Press 2023), p. 220.

[1130] CJEU, Case C-393/09, *Bezpečnostní softwarová asociace – Svaz softwarové ochrany v Ministerstvo kultury*, 22 Dec. 2010, ECLI:EU:C:2010:816, para. 50.

choose from a range of options available to the author.[1131] However, the expression of the author's creativity must be permitted by the components of the GUI itself.[1132] This conclusion can be also further expanded to other subject-matter. The takeaway is that only a subject-matter which, due to its nature, is capable of being freely and creatively altered has any potential to become the *author's own intellectual creation*. In other words, the available or allowed methods of implementing the author's idea cannot be so limited, that the idea(s) that the author implemented into the product itself becomes indissociable with it.[1133] In such a scenario, the author's idea ceases to exist by merging with the product itself, and in such an environment, the room available to authors to freely and creatively express their personalities becomes too narrow to produce an *author's own intellectual creation*. The formulation is therefore a clear reference to the principle of the idea/expression dichotomy and the importance of adhering to it.

The CJEU's conclusion that the originality assessment process must omit such components of the GUI which were only differentiated by their technical function was based on Advocate General *Bot's* opinion, in which he stated that the criterion of originality cannot be met in such cases, since the various available ways of implementing an idea into such components is so limited that both, the idea and the expression, become indissociable from one another.[1134] Therefore, in these specific cases no creativity exists, which leads to the absence of a subject-matter that could be eligible for copyright protection.[1135] However, to possibly identify originality in a product containing such components, the assessment must perform a *dissection*.[1136] The outcome of such a *dissection* would be a clear differentiation between the choices of free and creative nature and those dictated by their functional or technical function.

In *Bezpečnostní softwarová asociace*, the CJEU continued to develop the formulated originality standard of *author's own intellectual creation* by specifying the circumstances for its application in practice. In the decision, it was particularly the necessity of omitting purely functional or technical elements of products from the originality assessment process, due to their inability to be processed through the author's free and creative choices.

1131 Irini A. Stamatoudi & Paul Torremans (eds.), *EU Copyright Law: a commentary* (Elgar 2014), p. 1104.

1132 CJEU, Case C-393/09, Bezpečnostní softwarová asociace – Svaz softwarové ochrany v Ministerstvo kultury, 22 Dec. 2010, ECLI:EU:C:2010:816, para. 50.

1133 Opinion of AG Bot in Case C-393/09, *Bezpečnostní softwarová asociace – Svaz softwarové ochrany v Ministerstvo kultury*, 14 Oct. 2010, para. 49.

1134 Opinion of AG Bot in Case C-393/09, *Bezpečnostní softwarová asociace – Svaz softwarové ochrany v Ministerstvo kultury*, 14 Oct. 2010, para. 75 and para. 76.

1135 Paul Torremans (ed.), Research handbook on copyright law (Edward Elgar 2017), p. 78

1136 Eleonora Rosati, 'Copyright at the CJEU: Back to the Start (of Copyright Protection)' In: Hayleigh Bosher & Eleonora Rosati, *Developments and Directions in Intellectual Property Law: Twenty Years of the IPKat* (Oxford University Press 2023), p. 222.

10.4.1.3 The Murphy case

Next, the *Murphy* case was brought before the CJEU to determine whether a sporting event (a football match), as the object of a satellite retransmission, could be protected by copyright.[1137] The CJEU answered this question in the negative. The main reasoning behind its answer was that sporting events could not be regarded as intellectual creations and therefore classifiable as works. The decision was reached by the following conclusion consisting of four steps.

First, the CJEU held that copyright protection could not be claimed because sporting events cannot be classified as works.[1138] Second, if sporting events were to be recognized as a subject-matter eligible for copyright protection, they would have to be original and therefore the *author's own intellectual creation.*[1139] Third, most sporting events are subject to the rules of the game, leaving no room for creative freedom for the purposes of eligibility for copyright protection (this is especially true for football matches).[1140] Last, it is indisputable that sporting events do not enjoy copyright protection on any other basis.[1141] Moreover, if athletes were able to claim copyright protection for their sports performances, it could lead to a potential monopoly on sports performance and the elimination of competition.[1142]

Protecting a sporting event by copyright and recognizing it as a *work* could be hardly imaginable even in countries with a loose understanding of originality criteria.[1143] However, the CJEU noted that sporting events as such could be protected as works within the national copyright frameworks of the Member States, if appropriate.[1144] This was feasible due to unique and original character that allowed the event to be transformed into a subject-matter, according to the CJEU.[1145]

[1137] CJEU, Case C-403/08, *Football Association Premier League Ltd and Others v QC Leisure and Others*, Case C-429/08, *Karen Murphy v Media Protection Services Ltd.,* 4 Oct. 2011, ECLI: EU:C:2011:631.

[1138] CJEU, Case C-403/08, *Football Association Premier League Ltd and Others v QC Leisure and Others*, Case C-429/08, *Karen Murphy v Media Protection Services Ltd.*, 4 Oct. 2011, ECLI: EU:C:2011:631, para. 96.

[1139] CJEU, Case C-403/08, *Football Association Premier League Ltd and Others v QC Leisure and Others*, Case C-429/08, *Karen Murphy v Media Protection Services Ltd.*, 4 Oct. 2011, ECLI: EU:C:2011:631, para. 97.

[1140] CJEU, Case C-403/08, *Football Association Premier League Ltd and Others v QC Leisure and Others*, Case C-429/08, *Karen Murphy v Media Protection Services Ltd.*, 4 Oct. 2011, ECLI: EU:C:2011:631, para. 98.

[1141] CJEU, Case C-403/08, *Football Association Premier League Ltd and Others v QC Leisure and Others*, Case C-429/08, *Karen Murphy v Media Protection Services Ltd.*, 4 Oct. 2011, ECLI: EU:C:2011:631, para. 99.

[1142] Stef van Gompel, 'Creativity, Autonomy, and Personal Touch' In: Mireille van Eechoud, Jostein Gripsrud & Lionel Bently, *Work of Authorship* (Amsterdam University Press 2015), p. 106.

[1143] Eleonora Rosati, Originality in EU Copyright: *Full Harmonization through Case Law* (Edward Elgar Publishing 2013), p. 137.

[1144] CJEU, Case C-403/08, Football Association Premier League Ltd and Others v QC Leisure and Others, Case C-429/08, Karen Murphy v Media Protection Services Ltd., 4 Oct. 2011, ECLI: EU:C:2011:631, para. 100.

[1145] *Ibid.*

The CJEU also introduced a new parameter into the originality assessment process—the creative freedom of the author.[1146] By putting emphasis on the creative nature of freedom, the CJEU highlighted its purpose as one of the constituents of copyright.[1147] The creative freedom of an author and the leeway in which it can be employed was also clearly given borders by the CJEU. In the CJEU's view, the rules (of the game) themselves served as the borders for creative freedom. From this, it can be deduced that a product eligible for copyright protection on the basis it represents the *author's own intellectual creation* can only exist within the meaning of the copyright law if it was produced by the actions of an author who was not solely bound by rules. In other words, the CJEU intentionally limited the definition of human creativity capable of producing products eligible for copyright protection with the aim of not only focusing on the leeway available to the author, but on the qualitative outcome this leeway.[1148] In light of this, the CJEU argued, one cannot speak of freedom and creativity if an individual is subject to imposed rules, constraints, or any other limitations affecting (i.e., limiting) their creative conduct.

The absence of any leeway to employ free and creative choices (as defined by the CJEU) might be considered the ultimate justification for the refusal of copyright protection, since it is the freedom and creativeness of a human being that the copyright law awards with its protection.[1149] This initiative of the copyright law, consisting of rewarding the free and creative conduct of human beings with protection, further encourages the production of products within the meaning of the copyright law. The expected effect of the requirement of the exercise of free and creative choices throughout the production process is the reflection of the author's personality in the final product. The expected different and various ways to employ these available free and creative choices help expose and express the personality of an author, and transfer this personality onto the product. It is also expected that only human beings with sufficient capacity to exploit the creative choices available in the leeway with their free character, will be able to become authors.

Therefore, the *Murphy* case led to two key points regarding creativity restrictions. First, if the activity of an individual is to put forth an effect to produce a product eligible for copyright protection, this effort must be conducted in an environment that allows for the existence of sufficient leeway for such activities. Second, such activities must not be bound by rules as such, thus allowing the communication of the author's own intellectual content in a form of their own intellectual creation;

1146 Irini A. Stamatoudi, 'Originality under EU Copyright Law' In: Paul Torremans, *Research Handbook on Copyright Law* (Edward Elgar Publishing 2017), p. 67.

1147 CJEU, Case C-403/08, Football Association Premier League Ltd and Others v QC Leisure and Others, Case C-429/08, Karen Murphy v Media Protection Services Ltd., 4 Oct. 2011, ECLI: EU:C:2011:631, para. 98.

1148 Matthias Leistner, 'Der europäische Werkbegriff,' *Zeitschrift für Geistiges Eigentum* 4 (2013), p. 4.

1149 Alain Strowel, *Le droit d'auteur européen en transition numérique: de ses origines à l'unification européenne et aux défis de l'intelligence artificielle et des Big Data* (Larcier 2022), p. 74.

otherwise, the product could be considered the creation of the person who made the rules.

10.4.1.4 The Football Dataco case

What is now referred to as the EU standard of originality was first referred to as such in the opinion by AG Mengozzi in connection with the *Football Dataco* case.[1150] In *Football Dataco*,[1151] amongst other considerations, the CJEU held that a database can be eligible for copyright protection—that is, if the database, by reason of the selection or arrangements of its contents, constituted the *author's own intellectual creation*.[1152] Following up on its previous decisions, the CJEU clearly designated the *author's free and creative choices* and *stamping of author's personal touch in the work* as originality-forming constituents in a product.[1153] The decision involved the following three central findings by the CJEU.

First, the expenditure of the intellectual effort and skill in creating the data must be excluded from the copyrightability assessment.[1154] Second, adding important special significance to that data by its selection or arrangement is irrelevant.[1155] Third, significant labour and skill cannot be basis for copyright protection, unless it somehow expresses originality in the selection or arrangement of the said data.[1156]

The decision demonstrates the difference in understanding of notion of originality between the continental part of the EU (*author's intellectual creation*) and UK (*intellectual effort and skill*).[1157] With the direct references towards *intellectual effort and skill*, the CJEU unequivocally rejected the originality concept as applied in the UK, which it replaced with the uniform originality concept widespread in the continental part of the EU—the *author's own intellectual creation*. In the end, originality in a product can only be claimed if its author exhibits their abilities in an original manner by making *free and creative choices* and by leaving their *personal touch* on the product in question.[1158]

[1150] Eleonora Rosati, 'Copyright at the CJEU: Back to the Start (of Copyright Protection)' In: Hayleigh Bosher & Eleonora Rosati, *Developments and Directions in Intellectual Property Law: Twenty Years of the IPKat* (Oxford University Press 2023), p. 220.

[1151] CJEU, Case C-604/10, *Football Dataco Ltd and Others v Yahoo! UK Ltd and Others*, 1 Mar. 2012, ECLI:EU:C:2012:115.

[1152] Eleonora Rosati, Originality in EU Copyright: *Full Harmonization through Case Law* (Edward Elgar Publishing 2013), p. 165.

[1153] Irini A. Stamatoudi, 'Originality under EU Copyright Law' In: Paul Torremans, *Research Handbook on Copyright Law* (Edward Elgar Publishing 2017), p. 74.

[1154] CJEU, Case C-604/10, *Football Dataco Ltd and Others v Yahoo! UK Ltd and Others*, 1 Mar. 2012, ECLI:EU:C:2012:115, para. 46.

[1155] *Ibid.*

[1156] *Ibid.*

[1157] Eleonora Rosati, Originality in EU Copyright: *Full Harmonization through Case Law* (Edward Elgar Publishing 2013), p. 168.

[1158] Irini A. Stamatoudi, 'Originality under EU Copyright Law' In: Paul Torremans, *Research Handbook on Copyright Law* (Edward Elgar Publishing 2017), p. 75.

10.4.1.5 The SAS case

According to the CJEU, neither the functionality of a computer program nor the programming language, amongst other elements, constitute a form of expression of that program, and both are therefore not capable of being copyrighted under the Software Directive.[1159] However, the CJEU's finding in the *SAS* case[1160] as such could not exclude copyrightability of such elements as works under the InfoSoc Directive, if these are their *author's own intellectual creation.*[1161] The exclusion of such elements from the form of expression of a computer program group is therefore without prejudice to their status as authorial works in their own right.[1162]

In his opinion, Advocate General *Bot* stated that a work (in this case the computer program) was protectable only from the point at which the selection and compilation of its elements were indicative of the creativity and skill of the author, and thus set their work apart from those of other authors.[1163] Even though this was related to the eligibility of computer programs for copyright protection, the remarks of Advocate General *Bot* have subsequently been nonetheless applicable to any product.

From this it can be derived, that the author must make actual choices throughout the production process and the result of such process—the work—must be individualized.[1164] Therefore, in order for a product to become an intellectual creation, two conditions must be met. First, creative choices must be employed during its production process. Second, the resulting product must possess an individualized character. The emphasis on the presence of both conditions is important. Cases when creative choices are employed, but the result is nevertheless not individualized, or when the result is individualized, but no creative choices were employed, might still occur.[1165] In the first example, creative freedom was available, but the product was produced by making obvious choices, that resulted in the absence of *personal touch*, although creative freedom was taken advantage of. In the second example, creative freedom was also available; however, the product was produced by an application of an arbitrary rule. Although this rule resulted in an individualized product, the product as such was not the result of freely made creative choices.

At the instigation of Advocate General *Bot*, the CJEU also once again brought forward the importance of compliance with the applicable idea/expression dichotomy.

1159 CJEU, Case C-604/10, *Football Dataco Ltd and Others v Yahoo! UK Ltd and Others*, 1 Mar. 2012, ECLI:EU:C:2012:115, para. 46.

1160 CJEU, Case C-406/10, *SAS Institute Inc. v World Programming Ltd.*, 2 May 2012, ECLI:EU:C:2012:259.

1161 CJEU, Case C-604/10, *Football Dataco Ltd and Others v Yahoo! UK Ltd and Others*, 1 Mar. 2012, ECLI:EU:C:2012:115, para. 45.

1162 Justine Pila & Paul Torremans, *European Intellectual Property Law* (Oxford University Press 2016), p. 278.

1163 Opinion of AG Bot in Case C-406/10, *SAS Institute Inc. v World Programming Ltd.*, 29 Nov. 2011, ECLI:EU:C:2011:787, para. 48.

1164 Lionel Bently et al., *Intellectual Property Law* (Oxford University Press, 6th ed 2022), p. 110.

1165 Lionel Bently et al., *Intellectual Property Law* (Oxford University Press, 6th ed 2022), p. 110.

The CJEU claimed that if elements of a functional nature were eligible for copyright protection, such eligibility would lead to the virtual monopolization of ideas.[1166] Therefore, apart from the lack of leeway for the expenditure of *free and creative choices*, the threat of the monopolization of ideas behind functional elements also led to their exclusion from copyrightability.

10.4.1.6 The Painer case

It was the CJEU's *Painer* case decision that initiated the beginning of efforts to change the treatment of photographic products under the copyright framework of the EU also in practice. This was achieved by unifying the status and treatment of all photographic products in terms of EU harmonized copyright law. Among the various conclusions reached by the CJEU in the case, the one with the broadest impact (not only for photographic products, but for all products eligible for copyright protection) was the *refined* standard of originality.

Eva-Maria Painer had worked for many years as a freelance photographer in Austria, focusing mainly on the subject of children, especially in kindergartens and schools. In the course of her work, she produced several photographic products of a pupil named *Natascha Kampusch*. As the CJEU noted in its preliminary remarks, the production process of these photographic products involved designing the background, deciding the position and facial expression of the subject, the development of the photographic products themselves (the photographic products were analogue, and produced in the 1990s), and finally stamping/labelling the final photographic products with her name.[1167]

Natascha Kampusch later became a victim of an abductor, whom she later successfully escaped from. Nonetheless, the abductor held her captive for almost eight years. The period shortly after her escape and before her first official public appearance was marked by intense public interest in her likeness, thus resulting in great demand for any photographic products depicting her. This is where the photographic product produced by *Eva-Maria Painer* of *Natascha Kampusch*, as the most recent photograph taken of her prior to her abduction, came into play.

As a preliminary remark, it must be noted that the case involved two types of photographic products. First, there were the *contested photos*, as referred to by Advocate General *Trstenjak*,[1168] or *contested photographs*, as referred to by the CJEU.[1169] Second, there was the *contested photo-fit*, a term used jointly by both

[1166] CJEU, Case C-406/10, *SAS Institute Inc. v World Programming Ltd.*, 2 May 2012, ECLI: EU:C:2012:259, para. 40.

[1167] CJEU, Case C-145/10, *Eva-Maria Painer v Standard VerlagsGmbH and Others*, 1 Dec. 2011, ECLI:EU:C:2011:798, para. 27.

[1168] Opinion of AG Trstenjak in Case C-145/10, *Eva-Maria Painer v Standard VerlagsGmbH and Others*, 12 Apr. 2011, ECLI:EU:C:2011:239, para. 22.

[1169] CJEU, Case C-145/10, *Eva-Maria Painer v Standard VerlagsGmbH and Others*, 1 Dec. 2011, ECLI:EU:C:2011:798, para. 27.

Advocate General *Trstenjak*[1170] and the CJEU.[1171] The first group included photographic products of the pupil *Natascha Kampusch*, originally produced by Eva-Maria Painer. The second group included a photo-fit—a photographic product produced by a graphic artist using computer software based on the *contested photo(graph)s*, intended to show the presumed current appearance of *Natascha Kampusch*. In other words, the *contested photo-fit* represented a facial composite traditionally used by law enforcement. The *contested photo-fit* was privately commissioned by the father of *Natascha Kampusch* himself, based on the photographic products originally produced by Eva-Maria Painer which had been acquired (purchased) by the *Kampusch* family from her.[1172]

Several Austrian and German magazines obtained *Painer's* photographic product of *Natascha Kampusch* and decided to publish it in print as well as online. *Eva-Maria Painer*, the sole creator and photographer, was neither asked for permission, nor credited for the use of her photographic product. Some of these magazines also decided to publish the contested photo-fit. Given this, *Eva-Maria Painer* decided to sue the publishers of these Austrian and German magazines in Austria for accounts, payment of appropriate remuneration, damages for her losses, and for a preliminary injunction against the publishers of the said Austrian and German magazines.[1173]

Referral of the Austrian Court

In essence, the Austrian Court sought clarification as to whether the originality standard applicable to photographic products (as defined in Article 6 of Term Directive II, and according to which copyright protection is vested in photographs which are their *author's own intellectual creation*, also included photographic products of portrait genre.[1174] If the answer to this question were affirmative, the follow-up question of the referring Austrian court was whether the threshold for protection should be higher than for other categories (genres) of photographic products, because of the allegedly minor degree of creative freedom such photographic products display.[1175] In other words, the referring Austrian court wanted to clarify if photographic products of the portrait genre were afforded *weaker* copyright protection or

[1170] Opinion of AG Trstenjak in Case C-145/10, *Eva-Maria Painer v Standard VerlagsGmbH and Others*, 12 Apr. 2011, ECLI:EU:C:2011:239, para. 29.

[1171] CJEU, Case C-145/10, *Eva-Maria Painer v Standard VerlagsGmbH and Others*, 1 Dec. 2011, ECLI:EU:C:2011:798, para. 36.

[1172] Mireille van Eechoud, 'Along the Road to Uniformity: Diverse Readings of the Court of Justice Judgments on Copyright Work,' 3 *Journal of Intellectual Property, Information Technology and Electronic Commerce Law* 60 (2012), p. 60.

[1173] CJEU, Case C-145/10, *Eva-Maria Painer v Standard VerlagsGmbH and Others*, 1 Dec. 2011, ECLI:EU:C:2011:798, para. 38.

[1174] Eleonora Rosati, *Originality in EU Copyright: Full Harmonization through Case Law* (Edward Elgar Publishing 2013), p. 151.

[1175] *Ibid.*

no copyright protection at all, due to their realistic nature and the correspondingly minor formative freedom of the photographer.[1176] The greatest factor emphasizing the importance of the referral, as well as the overall outcome of the case itself, was the genre of the photographic product in question, i.e., its nature as a portrait.[1177] The reason for this could be considered the prevalence and frequent use of the genre, thus possibly raising many practical issues and questions.

As already mentioned, the concerns regarding the realistic nature of the photographic product in question were sparked by its affiliation with the portrait genre. Seemingly, any photographer producing photographic products that belong to the genre of portraiture is bound by constraints (or even *standardization*) that characterize the genre as well as the photographic products belonging to it. Doubts were also raised in connection with the depicted subject (the pupil) as well as the circumstances in which the photographic product itself was produced, which would basically make the subject itself predetermined.[1178]

However, the referral of the Austrian court did not focus on clarifying the standards for subsistence of copyright in a photographic product, but rather sought interpretation of the limitations for quotations and for use in the interest of public security within the meaning of the InfoSoc Directive and the international standards of the Berne Convention. The question was further clarified in terms of *weaker protection or no protection at all* against any adaptations of photographic products of the portrait genre. As already mentioned, this was due to their allegedly realistic nature and minor degree of formative freedom available to the photographer. It was these questions that the referring Austrian court focused on with respect to the scope of protection of the photographic product in question.

What is important to note in regard to the content of the referral, is that it was also linked to a previous decision by the Austrian Supreme Court of Justice, which found that a photofit based on another photographic product was a new independent work, rather than an adaptation of the original portrait.[1179] The court held that this photofit was removed from the original portrait to such an extent that it could be considered a separate and independent work. The issue therefore lay in the fact that the original portrait met the low originality criterion for its copyrightability; nevertheless, the subsequent composite originating from it did not infringe on the copyright of the original portrait, but as already said, it was found to be a new individual work. This was due to the relatively low amount of creative interventions made by its author in the original portrait photographic product. By applying *the stronger the*

[1176] CJEU, Case C-145/10, *Eva-Maria Painer v Standard VerlagsGmbH and Others*, 1 Dec. 2011, ECLI:EU:C:2011:798, para. 43 (4).

[1177] Hans Peter Roth. 'EuGH, 01. 12. 2011 – C-145/10: Urheberrecht: Schutz von Portraitfo-tografien' 5 *EuZW* (2012), p. 182.

[1178] Andrea Wallace & Ellen Euler, 'Revisiting Access to Cultural Heritage in the Public Domain: EU and International Developments,' *IIC* 823 (2020), p. 823.

[1179] OGH, 4Ob170/07i, 11. Mar. 2008.

individuality, the stronger the protection equation, such narrow protection therefore resulted in no infringement of the copyright.[1180]

The conclusion of the Austrian Supreme Court of Justice seemed to be correct and in line with past (and subsequent) jurisprudence of the CJEU. However, such copying would be authorized only if the reproduced part of the composite was not the *author's own intellectual creation displaying their personality*. According to this reasoning, the InfoSoc Directive disallowed unauthorized copying of something that was original and therefore protected.[1181] Therefore, what was unknown at that time, was to what extent it was possible to copy from an original copyrighted photographic product, so that the copied part would still be considered infringing or non-infringing. In other words, the amount and nature of what could be taken out of a protected photographic product and not infringe it was not known.

The decisive factor in the case was the role of creative effort, especially its effects on the possible use of the photographic product.[1182] In other words, it was unclear to what extent the amount of creativity expressed and displayed in a photographic product affected third parties when using such photographic products. Simply put, the Austrian court wanted confirmation from the CJEU of the hypothesis that more invested and displayed creative effort equalled more protection against further use. This hypothesis can also be put in an inverted formulation: the more creative the photographic product is, the less free use it allows.[1183] Within this context, it would be only logical that the photographer would receive broader protection against the use of their photographic product or its parts based on its individual elements, from which the whole photographic products consists of, if these elements were their *author's own intellectual creation*.[1184] Therefore, the more elements which constitute their *author's own intellectual creation* the photographic product consists of, the more complex its protection against potential exploitation should be.

The Opinion of Advocate General Trstenjak

For the sake of preserving continuity, a breakdown of the Advocate General *Trstenjak's* opinion[1185] will be presented first. Advocate General *Trstenjak* rephrased the

1180 Mireille van Eechoud, 'Along the Road to Uniformity: Diverse Readings of the Court of Justice Judgments on Copyright Work,' 3 *Journal of Intellectual Property, Information Technology and Electronic Commerce Law* 60 (2012), p. 60.

1181 *Ibid.*

1182 Andrzej Matlak, 'Wyrok TSUE z 1. 12. 2011 r. w sprawie Eva-Maria Painer przeciwko Standard Verlags GmbH i in. (C-145/10)' In: Ewa Laskowska-Litak & Ryszard Markiewicz, *Prawo Autorskie: Komentarz do Wybranego Orzecznictwa Trybunału Sprawiedliwości UE* (Wolters Kluwer 2019, p. 182.

1183 Hans Peter Roth. 'EuGH, 01. 12. 2011 – C-145/10: Urheberrecht: Schutz von Portraitfo-tografien' 5 *EuZW* (2012), p. 182.

1184 Joachim Ungern-Sternberg, 'Verwendungen des Werkes in veränderter Gestalt im Lichte des Unionsrechts,' *GRUR* 533 (2015), p. 533.

1185 Opinion of AG Trstenjak in Case C-145/10, *Eva-Maria Painer v Standard VerlagsGmbH and Others*, 12 Apr. 2011, ECLI:EU:C:2011:239.

original referral of the Austrian Court and turned the focus to Article 6 of Term Directive II, thus putting the question of requirements of subsistence of copyright in a photographic product in the foreground. In other words, the CJEU focused, amongst other, on determining at what point a photographic product was considered an original work within the meaning of Term Directive II.

Amongst other considerations, *Trstenjak* noted that the creator of a portrait (as a photographic product) enjoys a relatively small degree of individual formative freedom, and thus the copyright protection of this kind of photographic product is accordingly narrow.[1186] For such a photographic product to be original in similar cases, a photographer must utilize the available formative freedom available to them.[1187] *Trstenjak* also noted that several aspects of a product, such as a particular degree of artistic quality or novelty, the purpose of creation, expenditure and costs, are irrelevant,.[1188] In other words, such aspects may not be taken into account for the purposes of assessment of copyright eligibility of a (photographic) product. Advocate General *Trstenjak* also noted, that according to Article 6 of Term Directive II, all results of human creativity are to be eligible for copyright protection, including those created by the use of various technical tools, photographic apparatuses notwithstanding. Therefore, the conditions for copyright eligibility in respect to the said Article were not particularly high.

According to Advocate General *Trstenjak*, the possibility of copyright protection of even a photo-fit is supposedly based on the presence of a personal intellectual creation.[1189] Therefore, if a personal intellectual creation originally embodied in the unedited photographic product is also still embodied in the edited photographic product, (the photo-fit) i.e., this *embodiment* was transferred to it, then such edited photographic product would be eligible for copyright protection.

Such an approach to copyrightability is based on the broad understanding the EU applies to the notion of *work*. The core of such understanding lies in the fact that the elements of an unedited work are considered works themselves and therefore *sub-works*.[1190] In case of an infringement of the edited *sub-work*, its relationship with the unedited work always *triggers* and establishes an infringement of the unedited work as well. Doing so means only a single author's rights are infringed.[1191]

1186 Opinion of AG Trstenjak in Case C-145/10, *Eva-Maria Painer v Standard VerlagsGmbH and Others*, 12 Apr. 2011, ECLI:EU:C:2011:239, para. 108.

1187 Opinion of AG Trstenjak in Case C-145/10, *Eva-Maria Painer v Standard VerlagsGmbH and Others*, 12 Apr. 2011, ECLI:EU:C:2011:239, para. 122.

1188 Opinion of AG Trstenjak in Case C-145/10, *Eva-Maria Painer v Standard VerlagsGmbH and Others*, 12 Apr. 2011, ECLI:EU:C:2011:239, para. 123.

1189 Opinion of AG Trstenjak in Case C-145/10, *Eva-Maria Painer v Standard VerlagsGmbH and Others*, 12 Apr. 2011, ECLI:EU:C:2011:239, para. 129.

1190 Moritz Finke, *Werk und Veränderung: Verwertungsrechte an veränderten Gestaltungen im Urheberrecht* (Mohr Siebeck 2022), p. 166.

1191 Starting from the next section, attention will be given only to the *contested photo(graph)s*—that is, the photographic products originally produced by *Eva-Maria Painer.* The issue of *contested photo-fit* will no longer be addressed by the author

Advocate General *Trstenjak* concluded her opinion by stating that due to the not *excessively high* criteria governing the copyright protection of photographic products in Term Directive II[1192], photographic products of the portrait genre may still be afforded copyright protection if they are an original intellectual creation of the photographer. This requires the photographer to have left their own *mark* by using the available formative freedom available to them.[1193] In a portrait, this *mark* can be left through the employment of photographer's creativity in, amongst other things, setting the angle, positioning the photographed subject, influencing the facial expression of the photographed subject, or adjusting the background, focus, lighting, and illumination.[1194] All these activities of the photographer must be done with the aim of producing a photographic product that displays the *personal character* of the photographer.[1195] However, it is worth noting that the statement by Advocate General *Trstenjak* regarding low criteria was left without a response or further reference by the CJEU in its subsequent decision. The aim of such *silence* was probably to avoid making any distinctions between the originality requirements already formulated for computer programs, databases, and photographic products, thus affirming the CJEU's uniform interpretation and future application to all products.[1196]

As mentioned above, what caused the ambiguity was the realistic nature of the photographic product in question, and with it connected the presumption of seemingly very narrow (or even non-existent) room for the employment and demonstration of creative steps of the photographer.[1197] Were this found to be true, the portrait's disputed use by third parties would have been considered non-infringing. Nonetheless, it is worth noting that the photographic product in question was indeed initially found to be protectable under Austrian copyright law. The further considerations related to the fact that a photographic product granted a corresponding type of protection, could enjoy a reduced extent of this protection; these findings are somewhat contradictory in essence.[1198] It was therefore first necessary to establish under what conditions a photographic product could be eligible for a corresponding type of protection

1192 Opinion of AG Trstenjak in Case C-145/10, *Eva-Maria Painer v Standard VerlagsGmbH and Others*, 12 Apr. 2011, ECLI:EU:C:2011:239, para. 124.

1193 Opinion of AG Trstenjak in Case C-145/10, *Eva-Maria Painer v Standard VerlagsGmbH and Others*, 12 Apr. 2011, ECLI:EU:C:2011:239, para. 215.

1194 Opinion of AG Trstenjak in Case C-145/10, *Eva-Maria Painer v Standard VerlagsGmbH and Others*, 12 Apr. 2011, ECLI:EU:C:2011:239, para. 124.

1195 Andrzej Matlak, 'Wyrok TSUE z 1. 12. 2011 r. w sprawie Eva-Maria Painer przeciwko Standard Verlags GmbH i in. (C-145/10)' In: Ewa Laskowska-Litak & Ryszard Markiewicz, *Prawo Autorskie: Komentarz do Wybranego Orzecznictwa Trybunału Sprawiedliwości UE* (Wolters Kluwer 2019), p. 184.

1196 Christian Handig, 'Durch 'freie kreative Entscheidungen' zum europäischen urheberrechtlichen Werkbegriff,' *GRUR Int.* 965 (2012), p. 973.

1197 Andrzej Matlak, 'Wyrok TSUE z 1. 12. 2011 r. w sprawie Eva-Maria Painer przeciwko Standard Verlags GmbH i in. (C-145/10)' In: Ewa Laskowska-Litak & Ryszard Markiewicz, *Prawo Autorskie: Komentarz do Wybranego Orzecznictwa Trybunału Sprawiedliwości UE* (Wolters Kluwer 2019), p. 193.

1198 Rafael Sánchez Aristi, Nieves I. Moralejo Imbernón & Sebastián López Maza, *La jurisprudencia del Tribunal de Justicia de la Unión Europea en materia de propiedad intelectual: análisis y comentarios* (Instituto Autor 2017), p. 395.

(in this case copyright protection), and second, what form and effects such protection would take in practice. The CJEU's task was to address these questions.

The Decision of the CJEU

The decision reached by the CJEU regarding the conditions for copyright protection of photographic products was based on the following question:

'Are Article 1(1) of Directive 2001/29 in conjunction with Article 5(5) thereof and Article 12 of the Berne Convention... particularly in the light of Article 1 of the First Additional Protocol to the European Convention for the Protection of Human Rights and Fundamental Freedoms [signed at Rome on 4 November 1950] and Article 17 of the Charter of Fundamental Rights of the European Union, to be interpreted as meaning that photographic works and/or photographs, particularly portrait photos, are afforded "weaker" copyright protection or no copyright protection at all against adaptations because, in view of their "realistic image", the degree of formative freedom is too minor?'[1199]

First, the CJEU accepted Advocate General *Trstenjak's* proposed rephrasing of the original referral above, and noted the following:

'Therefore, the referring court's question must be understood as asking, in essence, whether Article 6 of Term Directive I must be interpreted as meaning that a portrait photograph can, under that provision, be protected by copyright and, if so, whether, because of the allegedly too minor degree of creative freedom such photographs can offer, that protection, particularly as regards the regime governing reproduction of works provided for in Article 2(a) of Directive 2001/29, is inferior to that enjoyed by other works, particularly photographic works.'[1200]

In line with its previous case law on the subject, the CJEU held that for a photographic product to be eligible for copyright protection, it had to be the *author's own intellectual creation*[1201] provided that the author was able to express their creative abilities in its production by making *free and creative choices.*[1202] Choices of *free and creative* nature are those which can be isolated by a method of asking whether two authors would have been likely to produce essentially the same work in

[1199] CJEU, Case C-145/10, *Eva-Maria Painer v Standard VerlagsGmbH and Others*, 1 Dec. 2011, ECLI:EU:C:2011:798.

[1200] CJEU, Case C-145/10, *Eva-Maria Painer v Standard VerlagsGmbH and Others*, 1 Dec. 2011, ECLI:EU:C:2011:798, para. 86.

[1201] CJEU, Case C-145/10, *Eva-Maria Painer v Standard VerlagsGmbH and Others*, 1 Dec. 2011, ECLI:EU:C:2011:79, para. 87.

[1202] CJEU, Case C-145/10, *Eva-Maria Painer v Standard VerlagsGmbH and Others*, 1 Dec. 2011, ECLI:EU:C:2011:798, para. 89.

comparable circumstances.[1203] It is these creative choices that produce the protectable expression—an original work.[1204] It is true that every photographer necessarily makes choices throughout the production process of a photographic product.[1205] However, what is important and must be assessed, is the nature of these choices and the effect these have on the overall appearance of the captured image.

According to the CJEU, copyright-protected expression in the form of an original photographic work may manifest itself in several ways and at various points throughout its production:

In the preparation phase, the photographer can choose the background, the subject's pose and the lighting. When taking a portrait photograph, he can choose the framing, the angle of view and the atmosphere created. Finally, when selecting the snapshot, the photographer may choose from a variety of developing techniques the one he wishes to adopt or, where appropriate, use computer software.[1206]

Dividing the production process of a photographic product into three separate phases, the CJEU noted that the originality of a photographic product can be *imprinted* on the work and exist in it in three different stages, the said phases. This imprint of originality in the form of a *personal touch* can be imprinted and exist in each of the phases separately or cumulatively in multiple phases, as *Caron* concluded from French case law.[1207]

Also, by dividing the production process of a photographic product into three phases, the CJEU identified and determined the area(s) in which originality can reside and in which the photographer can *create* the said originality by employing *free and creative choices*.[1208] By doing so, the area(s) defined by the CJEU significantly widened, but not infinitely.[1209] Therefore, the assessing individual should know where to, figuratively speaking, look for original ways of expression of the photographer, and the photographer should know where originality can be formed, expressed or *imprinted.*

The Three Production Phases

When considering the *free and creative choices* photographers can make during the production process of a photographic product, the CJEU chronologically divided

[1203] Daniel J. Gervais & Estelle Derclaye, 'The Scope of Computer Program Protection after SAS: Are We Closer to Answers?' *European Intellectual Property Review* 565 (2012), p. 565.

[1204] *Ibid.*

[1205] André Lucas & Jean-Michel Bruguière, 'TGI Paris, 30 mai 2007, Claude Nuridsanz c/ Société d'Evian et autres,' 20 *Propriétés Intellectuelles* 309 (2007), p. 309.

[1206] CJEU, Case C-145/10, *Eva-Maria Painer v Standard VerlagsGmbH and Others*, 1 Dec. 2011, ECLI:EU:C:2011:798, para. 91.

[1207] Christophe Caron, *Droit d'auteur et droits voisins* (LexisNexis, 6th ed. 2020), p. 144

[1208] Rodrigo Bercovitz Rodríguez-Cano & Ignacio Garrote Fernández-Díez, *La unificación del derecho de propiedad intelectual en la Unión Europea* (Tirant lo Blanch 2019), p. 71.

[1209] Joëlle Verbrugge, 'Prouver l'originalité d'une ou plusieurs photographies,' *LÉGIPRESSE* 639 (2019), p. 639.

the production process of a photographic product into three distinct phases. The first phase, or the *preparation phase*, consists of a variety of choices related to lighting, the subject's pose, or the selection of a background.[1210] The next phase, the *taking phase* of the actual photographic product, provides room for creative choices when choosing the framing, angle of view, and the atmosphere created.[1211] The last phase, the *post process phase*, consists of the selection of a photographic product and allows photographers to choose from a variety of developing techniques or the use of computer editing software, where applicable.[1212]

John Adrian Lawrence Sterling used a different terminology to define the production process of a photographic product as consisting of three *stages*, but with largely similar contours. He asserted that the production process of a photographic product involves a pre-fixation, fixation, and post-fixation stage.[1213] The pre-fixation stage includes photographer's selection of object to be photographed, the angle of the shot and incidence of light and shadow.[1214] The second, fixation stage, covers the author's selection of photographic equipment, film, and aperture.[1215] Finally, the post-fixation stage involves decisions that affect the final appearance of the photographic product and its presentation.[1216] In the last stage, the photographer can make choices regarding the development, printing, enlargement, retouching, and other editing of the photographic product.[1217]

One can further elaborate on these three phases/stages, and the potentially available choices of photographers these comprise of, in more detail in the following way:

The first production phase/stage should entail free and creative choices related to the initial preparation of equipment, object or subject, the conditions, and the environment in which the actual photographic product is to be produced. In other words, all free and creative choices made throughout the first production phase/stage should set the ground for the execution (taking) of the photographic product itself.

The second production phase/stage should entail free and creative choices related to the final preparation of the equipment, object or subject, the conditions and the environment immediately preceding the execution, and the subsequent actual execution of the photographic product itself. In other words, all free and creative choices made throughout the second production phase/stage should have enabled

1210 CJEU, Case C-145/10, *Eva-Maria Painer v Standard VerlagsGmbH and Others*, 1 Dec. 2011, ECLI:EU:C:2011:798, para. 91.
1211 *Ibid.*
1212 *Ibid.*
1213 John A. L. Sterling, *World Copyright Law: Protection of Authors' Works, Performances, Phonograms, Films, Video, Broadcasts, and Published Editions in National, International, and Regional Law* (Sweet & Maxwell, 3rd ed. 2008), p. 312.
1214 *Ibid.*
1215 *Ibid.*
1216 *Ibid.*
1217 *Ibid.*

the actual execution of the photographic product itself resulting in its fixation on whatever radiation-sensitive material that the photographer chose.

The third production phase/stage should entail free and creative choices related to the finalization, customization, and post-processing of the executed (taken) and fixed photographic product. In other words, all *free and creative choices* made throughout the third production phase/stage should still allow for any last interventions, but at the same time should conclude the whole production process.

The final outcome of the three production phases/stages combined constitutes the final and original photographic work, which bears the expressed and materialized qualities that, in a form of a *personal touch* of the photographer, the expression and materialisation of which resulted from their *free and creative choices* in accordance with their idea and anticipated personal vision.

Whether the production process is divided into three *phases*, as defined by the CJEU, or into three *stages*, as expressed by *John Adrian Lawrence Sterling*, the aim is always to break the process down into smaller parts to make it more intelligible.[1218] Once this is done, each employed *free and creative choice* as well as its potential effect on the photographic product can be assessed individually and within the context of each separate production phase/stage. Breaking down the production process therefore allows for clearer identification of the elements potentially possessing a *personal touch*. This in turn plays a crucial role in the possible copyrightability of the assessed photographic product, and also the link of the *personal touch* to a particular *free and creative choice*.

The Composition of a Photographic Product

One cannot refer to *free and creative choices* without using and defining the term *composition*. Composition describes the way all the individual objects within the frame of view combine to form the final image depicted in a photographic product.[1219] More technically, composition describes the relationship of objects in a photographic product—the spaces between them, their relative size, and their placement within the photographed scene.[1220] According to *Prakel*, composition is basically everything that goes into the production process of a photographic product (image).[1221] He continues:

The process of image composition begins with consideration and exploration of the chosen subject. It involves selection and analysis of the subject in terms of its visual attributes, an appreciation of the subject itself and the process in light of one's personal feelings and motivations. Only then can all the elements be arranged

[1218] Hereafter, I use the term *'phase'* to refer to the production process of a photographic product.

[1219] Alexander Wrigley, *Beginners Guide to Photography Composition* (1 Sep. 2024), https://medium.com/photography-secrets/beginners-guide-to-photography-composition-88290d6c24ac.

[1220] Jason D. Little, *These Ideas on Perspective will Improve your Photography Composition* (1 Sep. 2024), https://www.lightstalking.com/ideas-perspective-will-improve-photography-composition/.

[1221] David Prakel, *The Visual Dictionary of Photography* (AVA Academia 2010), p. 72.

into a coherent, communicative and unique image. Photography cannot be a simple recording because photographers have to select part of the real world to frame. Composition becomes the expression of the photographer's personality.[1222]

One conclusion that can be drawn from this quote is that creative steps, first and foremost, relate to the composition, and subsequently to the further modification and customization of the rest of the elements of a photographic product. Composition therefore represents the cornerstone on which the rest of the photographic product is built and can be further freely and creatively modified to reflect the photographer's personality.

There are two basic types of composition, which differ in the required approach of the photographer and overall circumstances in which these can be created. The first is referred to as an *active* composition, while the second one as a *passive*.[1223] As the name suggests, the former represents photographers' significant and active creative involvement in the creation of the composition, in which they photographer has near-total control over the subjects and objects captured—the photographer assumes a completely active role. On the other hand, the latter presupposes a less active role of the photographer in terms of composition creation, which consists of selecting a situation and letting it unfold and compose itself—the photographer therefore assumes somewhat less active role.

Naturally, in an active composition, originality can be formed by the way of creating the composition, as well as in its fixation. In contrast, in passive composition, originality-forming choices may be shifted more towards fixation itself, rather than the *creation* of the composition. Nonetheless, in both situations, the photographer makes a decision to capture (fix) the composition at the moment when it corresponds to the idea of their intended result.[1224] The personality of the photographer can be imprinted onto the product (thus forming its originality) even via the fixation itself, since the captured composition also represents the materialization of an image form mentally anticipated by the photographer through their personal vision.[1225] As a result, it can be also said that the photographer does not reproduce objects or subjects, they reproduce the mentally anticipated *image* of these objects or subjects.[1226] This mental anticipation of what the fixed object or subject shall depict, shapes the production process, the free and creative choices applied throughout that process, and finally the final form of the photographic product itself.[1227] In sum, the photographer presents their personal perspective by image fixation.

[1222] David Prakel, *The Visual Dictionary of Photography* (AVA Academia 2010), p. 184.

[1223] Antoine Latreille, 'L'appropriation des photographies d'œuvres d'art: éléments d'une réflexion sur un objet de droit d'auteur,' *Recueil Dalloz* 299 (2002), p. 299.

[1224] *Ibid.*

[1225] Antoine Latreille, 'Une nouvelle œuvre de l'esprit (approche juridique),' 70 *Revue Lamy Droit de l'immatériel* 109 (2011), p. 109.

[1226] Yolande Finkelsztajn, 'Représentation et réalité,' 70 Revue Lamy Droit de l'immatériel 113 (2011), p. 113.

[1227] Philippe Gaudrat, 'Réflexions sur la forme des œuvres de l'esprit' In: Pierre Sirinelli et al. *Propriétés intellectuelles: mélanges en l'honneur de André Françon* (Dalloz 1995), p. 210.

The (Free and Creative) Nature of Choices Made through the Production Process

A photographic product is the result of human choices made by a photographer in a given situation.[1228] However, given the guidance of the CJEU, such choices must have certain prescribed specific features in order for these to be recognized under the EU harmonized copyright law. The choices made during the three production phases, which embed the photographer's emotion, impression or message in the captured image, must also go beyond simple know-how and reflect the photographer's specific approach.[1229] Such approach must be customized and adapted by the photographer in order for it to transform whatever the photographer wished to convey into the form of a captured image perceptible by human senses. According to *Susan Sontag* the photographer must already see the future photographic product in their mind.[1230]

Photography is not necessarily an art *per se*, or in all its forms. It is, however, a medium, through which art can be created and used for the purposes of creation, representation, and communication of its creator's statement.[1231] It is up to the author, the photographer, whether the photographic product will assume such a narrative role. It was in this context that *Susan Sontag* quoted *Ansel Adam's* definition of a *great* photographic product as a 'full expression of what one feels about what is being photographed in the deepest sense and is, thereby, a true expression of what one feels about life in its entirety.'[1232] What the photographer must also be aware of in this context is that the choices they have made throughout any or all of the phases must be justified by the emotion, impression, or message they wish to embody in the image captured in the photographic product.[1233] In other words, the choices must serve as means to express the photographer and their feelings, and this must emanate from the captured image as well. Whatever it was that the photographer wished to convey through the captured image, it must reflect their (free and creative) choices. According to *John Berger*, the degree to which the photographic product explains the message embodied in it, and therefore makes the photographer's choices transparent and comprehensible is what distinguishes a *work* from photographic products of a banal nature.[1234] Therefore, it is important to focus on both: the actual choices, and also their effect.[1235] However, merely identifying the

[1228] John Berger, *Understanding a Photograph* (Penguin Books 2013), p. 18

[1229] Pierre Pérot, 'Parodie d'une œuvre photographique : game over pour le Guerrillero Heroico,' *LÉGIPRESSE* 572 (2018), p. 572.

[1230] Susan Sontag, *On Photography* (Penguin Books 2008), p. 117.

[1231] Axel Nordemann, *Die künstlerische Fotografie als urheberrechtlich geschütztes Werk* (Nomos 1992), p. 227.

[1232] Susan Sontag, *On Photography* (Penguin Books 2008), p. 118.

[1233] Joëlle Verbrugge, 'Prouver l'originalité d'une ou plusieurs photographies,' *LÉGIPRESSE* 639 (2019), p. 639.

[1234] John Berger, *Understanding a Photograph* (Penguin Books 2013), p. 18.

[1235] Jean Vincent, 'L'Approche juridique pour la photographie et les autres formes d'expression,' 70 *Revue Lamy Droit de l'immatériel* 118 (2011), p. 118.

steps taken throughout the production process along with their technical parameters and peculiarities without also describing the effect these have had on the depicted image cannot be considered sufficient for the demonstration of originality.

Traditionally, the production process of photographic products is interpreted either as a precise act of conscious intelligence, or as an intuitive mode of encounter.[1236] The necessity of employing these interpretation approaches towards not only technically describing and mastering employed choices, but also how these are the means of materialisation and visualisation of photographer's thought processes resulting in their actual manifestation in the captured image, is the demonstration of author's conscious intellectual and personal involvement in the production process. This conscious involvement of the photographer must not be superficial, and must reach beyond the common and basic. The CJEU then chose the former interpretation of the nature of the production process.

The CJEU also noted that in the portrait genre, the remaining (available) room for creative choices, however limited, is nonetheless still sufficient to produce an original photographic work.[1237] Therefore, the creative choices, as described by the CJEU, can be conveniently executed by photographers in the context of production of a photographic product. However, the CJEU did not provide guidance on how much significance should be attributed to the creative part of the choices taken.[1238] Accordingly, as *Tritton* noted, whether or not the input in the form of creative choices is sufficient for a finding of originality depends on the context of a photographic product, as *Minnero* quoted him.[1239] Nonetheless, the final decision on the presence of the *personal touch* of a photographer in the photographic work must be determined by national courts on a case-by-case basis.[1240]

In fact, the available room for the production of an original photographic product within the portrait genre is truly limited, but apparently still sufficient for a photographic work to emerge.[1241] Due to the expectations of the family regarding the final photographic product depicting the pupil, it can be said that both the genre and the photographic products produced in it demand a certain degree of standardization. The adherence to certain, albeit minimal, rules of standardization is also necessitated by the capability of such photographic products to be monetized by their authors.[1242] All aspects and steps of the production process must follow the goal of depicting

[1236] Susan Sontag, *On Photography* (Penguin Books 2008), p. 116.

[1237] Christian Handig, 'The "Sweat of the Brow" is Not Enough!—More than a Blueprint of the European Copyright Term "Work",' European Intellectual Property Review 334 (2013), p. 334.

[1238] *Ibid.*

[1239] Gemma Minnero, 'The Term Directive' In: Irini A. Stamatoudi & Paul Torremans (eds.), *EU Copyright Law: a commentary* (Edward Elgar Publishing 2014), p. 278.

[1240] CJEU, Case C-145/10, *Eva-Maria Painer v Standard VerlagsGmbH and Others*, 1 Dec. 2011, ECLI:EU:C:2011:798, para. 94.

[1241] Christian Handig, 'Erste Umrisse eines europäischen Werkbegriffs,' 61 *Österreichische Blätter für gewerblichen Rechtsschutz und Urheberrecht* 4 (2012), p. 191.

[1242] Christian Handig, 'Durch 'freie kreative Entscheidungen' zum europäischen urheberrechtlichen Werkbegriff,' *GRUR Int.* 965 (2012), p. 973.

the subject in a certain (standardized) way. Any room available to the photographer outside of such standardization can be used for the employment of *free and creative choices*. This might then be the difference between original photographic products eligible for copyright protection and others of a non-original nature.

It is worth noting that employing choices of a free and creative nature can make the final photographic product more attractive and distinctive, thus making it prone to stand out among other photographic products belonging to the genre. It is due to this reason the CJEU identified and highlighted the existence and availability of freedom of (creative) choice as an essential constituent of originality.[1243] As already mentioned above, such *personalization* created through these choices can ensure, for example, easier monetization. However, the photographer's personalization must be built upon the standardized minimum, which would ensure the photographic product would still maintain its initial function—the depiction of the subject or object. Therefore, the standardized minimum must be preserved. Also, given the emphasis of the CJEU on *making free and creative choices*, the court followed the appeal by *Ansel Adams*, as quoted by *Susan Sontag*, and stopped referring to the production process of photographic products as *taking*, but rather as *making*.[1244]

By putting emphasis not only on the existence of the room in which *free and creative choices* can be made, but also on their actual exploitation and employment throughout the production process, the CJEU seemed to sanction any findings of originality based on the superficial assessment established solely on the existence of room for manoeuvre.[1245] Here, the CJEU merely implied the importance of the depth of the assessment process and identified what the focus of the assessment itself should be.

In regard to the extent of copyright protection and its proportionality based on the degree of available creative freedom, the CJEU stated the following:

> *'Nothing ... supports the view that the extent of such protection should depend on possible differences in the degree of creative freedom in the production of various categories of works.'*[1246]

This suggests that if the author took advantage of the creative freedom offered by the subject-matter, and this exploitation resulted in the imprint of their personality, then the result would be considered original within the meaning of the harmonized EU law. Therefore, no degrees of originality may be applied to different subject-matter: they are either original or not. No stronger or weaker originality exists.

1243 Rodrigo Bercovitz Rodríguez-Cano & Ignacio Garrote Fernández-Díez, *La unificación del derecho de propiedad intelectual en la Unión Europea* (Tirant lo Blanch 2019), p. 69.

1244 Susan Sontag, *On Photography* (Penguin Books 2008), p. 123.

1245 Stef van Gompel, 'Creativity, Autonomy, and Personal Touch' In: Mireille van Eechoud, Jostein Gripsrud & Lionel Bently, *Work of Authorship* (Amsterdam University Press 2015), p. 124.

1246 CJEU, Case C-145/10, *Eva-Maria Painer v Standard VerlagsGmbH and Others*, 1 Dec. 2011, ECLI:EU:C:2011:798, para. 97.

Moreover, it is not possible to base any potential categorization of the subject-matter on this. If a certain product meets the criteria prescribed for originality, it will be eligible for copyright protection in the same way as other original products, and thus enjoy the same extent of protection as those other original products.[1247] Also, by stating so, the CJEU merged the two separate requirements of being a *work* and being *original* into a single requirement.[1248] In other words, the assessment of product's potential copyrightability would therefore not begin with identification of the product as a work and subsequently its originality, but it would assume that the first presupposes the second and vice versa.

Creative Constraints

Portrait photography is a specific genre. The goal of a portrait as a photographic product is to display characteristic features of the portrayed subject and enable their perception by the audience in such a way that the portrayed subject would be easily recognizable. Putting emphasis on such specific portrayal to a certain extent limits a photographer's options to make *free and creative choices*.[1249] However, if the photographer nonetheless takes advantage of the said choices to specifically portray the subject, even in such a restricted environment, and utilizes their artistic freedom, the outcome should possess features that ensure the originality of a photographic product. This is exactly what the CJEU suggested in its enumeration of the free and creative choices available to the photographer within the three specified production phases.

Here, the—chosen—genre of portrait photography can be viewed as a deliberate constraint imposed by the photographer, *Eva-Maria Painer*, upon herself.[1250] The constraint lies in the relatively small formative freedom itself. Nonetheless, this does not automatically imply that the genre itself does not allow for *any* employment of *free and creative choices* and a subsequent development of originality. The constraint would make the employment more difficult and challenging, but not impossible. The photographer must simply show more creativity in overcoming such constraints. Nevertheless, photographic products belonging to the portrait genre—photographic products depicting another subject—can still be seen as *self-portraits* by *Dorothea Lange*, as quoted by *Susan Sontag*.[1251] According to this thinking,

[1247] Christian Handig, 'Durch 'freie kreative Entscheidungen' zum europäischen urheberrechtlichen Werkbegriff' *GRUR Int.* 965 (2012), p. 973.

[1248] Caterina Sganga, *The Notion of 'Work' in EU Copyright Law After Levola Hengelo: One Answer Given, Three Question Marks Ahead* (3 Sep. 2024), https://papers.ssrn.com/sol3/papers.cfm?abstract_id=3323011.

[1249] Stef van Gompel, 'Creativity, Autonomy, and Personal Touch' In: Mireille van Eechoud, Jostein Gripsrud & Lionel Bently, *Work of Authorship* (Amsterdam University Press 2015), p. 114.

[1250] Stef van Gompel, 'Creativity, Autonomy, and Personal Touch' In: Mireille van Eechoud, Jostein Gripsrud & Lionel Bently, *Work of Authorship* (Amsterdam University Press 2015), p. 110.

[1251] Susan Sontag, *On Photography* (Penguin Books 2008), p. 122.

personalization via a photographer's *free and creative choices* is in fact possible even in such a constrained photographic genre.

Given all this, some genres of photography are therefore, naturally, more restrictive than others. The restrictiveness of the genre depends on its expected or desired outcome and its submission to possible standardization. Also, certain (minimum) rules may be imposed to make sure authors remain within the genre and thus their creation remains in the form of a photographic product. As already noted above, such rules do not preclude the production of an original photographic product; these merely limit the photographer's freedom, but do not exclude it altogether.

In the realm of photography, authors may not only restrict themselves through the choices of the genre itself, but also through the choice of subject or object, medium, format, methods, circumstances, environment, and materials employed in the production process of a photographic product. These restrictions might serve as a commitment and a gateway to a specific type of manifestation of originality, inherent to the author themselves. It must be noted however, that the mere choice of these *restrictions* cannot by itself meet the requirement of creativity. The choice itself only opens possibilities to the actual and potential free and creative exploitation itself. Within this context, the choice itself only serves as one of the prerequisites for the production of an original product.

Functional and Technical Constraints

According to *Daniel J. Gervais*,

> *'A creative choice is one made by the author that is not dictated by the function of the work, the method or technique used, or by applicable standards or relevant good practice.'*[1252]

In another work, he noted that,

> *'Conversely, purely arbitrary or significant selection is insufficient. A conscious, human choice must have been made, even though it may be irrational.'*[1253]

In light of these considerations, choices or decisions which are limited by functional constraints or rules therefore cannot be considered as being of a creative nature. The eligibility of a product for copyright protection through its originality therefore does not cover mere technicalities, and their results, performed by the

1252 Daniel J. Gervais, *(Re)structuring Copyright: A Comprehensive Path to International Copyright Reform* (Edward Elgar 2017), p. 116

1253 Daniel J. Gervais, 'Feist Goes Global: A Comparative Analysis of the Notion of Originality in Copyright Law,' 49 *Journal of the Copyright Society of the U.S.A.* 949 (2002), p. 949.

author throughout the production process.[1254] If technical determinism serves as a factor excluding a product from copyrightability, then the medium of photography is indeed the best example by which such situations could be described in practice. The production process of a photographic product includes several necessary technical choices to be made by the photographer. It is not through these technical choices, or good photographic practices, that originality arises, but through the photographer's choices that are *not* so dictated.[1255] According to *Vilém Flusser*, the question then must be asked to what extent and by what methods has the photographer managed to overcome the technical device and its pre-set *program*.[1256]

Therefore, if photographers wish to produce an original, copyright-eligible photographic product, they must step outside the borders and the various restrictions set by the technical determinism of the photographic equipment and the common good photographic practices they employ—they must go beyond these borders via their *free and creative choices*. It is through such *free and creative choices* the photographer may bring a unique and individual perspective, despite the functional constraints, technological determinism or the complete banality of the photographed subject.[1257] From this example, it can be seen how such constraints governing most parts of the photographic production process can be overcome through the *free and creative choices* of the photographer and give rise to originality. Exactly these choices have allowed photographic products to gradually become recognized as potentially original works within the meaning of the EU harmonized law.[1258]

The Presence of Personal Touch

In *Painer*, the CJEU further developed previously introduced elements which serve as constituent parts of the criterion of originality, and it also introduced a new one—the author's personality, which must be manifested in stamping the work with a personal touch.[1259] In other words, by requiring the presence of a *personal touch* in a work, the CJEU refined its previously applied construction of the originality standard.[1260] This more specific criterion in the decision regarding additional *free and creative choices* and their expression in the form of a *personal touch* should not

[1254] David Pouchard, 'Le valorisation des fonds photographiques, ou comment concilier le droit d'auteur et l'accès au patrimoine culturel,' 36 *In Situ* 1 (2018), p. 8.

[1255] Daniel J. Gervais, *(Re)structuring Copyright: A Comprehensive Path to International Copyright Reform* (Edward Elgar 2017), p. 117.

[1256] Vilém Flusser et al., *Za filosofii fotografie* (Fra, 2nd ed. 2013), p. 53.

[1257] Dominique Sagot-Duvauroux, *L'Originalité et la Valeur de l'Image* (2 Sep. 2024), https://univ-angers.hal.science/hal-02528782/.

[1258] Lionel Bently et al., *Intellectual Property Law* (Oxford University Press, 6th ed 2022), p. 102.

[1259] Irini A. Stamatoudi, 'Originality under EU Copyright Law' In: Paul Torremans, *Research Handbook on Copyright Law* (Edward Elgar Publishing 2017), p. 70.

[1260] Eleonora Rosati, 'Copyright at the CJEU: Back to the Start (of Copyright Protection)' In: Hayleigh Bosher & Eleonora Rosati, *Developments and Directions in Intellectual Property Law: Twenty Years of the IPKat* (Oxford University Press 2023), p. 220.

be seen as a modification of its previous jurisprudence, but rather as the concretization of the criteria formulated in it.[1261] The additionality to the original requirement does not imply that only culturally significant works can be eligible for copyright, quite the contrary.[1262] The subject-matter at the heart of the *Painer* case, especially its nature, perfectly illustrates this. The additional requirement has been seen as a *paper declaration.*[1263] In this view, the *personal touch* would function as a mere formality, which would be met whenever the photographer has exercised any *free and creative choices*.

The CJEU's emphasis[1264] on the presence of a *personal touch* as the manifested outcome of an author's *free and creative choices* in a work, serves the purpose of clarifying the applicable sole criterion for originality—a combination of the author's personality and their own intellectual creation.[1265] This emphasis signified the emergence of a personalist approach to copyrightability of products, which was also confirmed by the subsequent jurisprudence by the CJEU itself.[1266] According to this reasoning, it would become necessary for the copyright law to cover, and thus protect, all products that might bear the author's personality, through which an author is psychologically dependent on such product.[1267] After all, as *Susan Sontag* put it quoting *Minor White*, 'The photographer projects himself into everything he sees, identifying himself with everything in order to know it and to feel it better.'[1268]

Additionally, the concept of personal touch itself serves as a convenient tool for differentiating between carefully composed photographic products, (i.e., works), and mere *point-and-shoot* snapshots.[1269] If a production process of a photographic product involved at least some attention to its outcome within the boundaries of the

[1261] Gunda Dreyer et al., *Urheberrecht: Urheberrechtsgesetz, Verwertungsgesellschaftengesetz, Kunsturhebergesetz* (C.F. Müller, 4th ed. 2018), p. 92.

[1262] Stef van Gompel, 'Creativity, Autonomy, and Personal Touch' In: Mireille van Eechoud, Jostein Gripsrud & Lionel Bently, *Work of Authorship* (Amsterdam University Press 2015), p. 95.

[1263] Ryszard Markiewicz, *Zabawy z Prawem Autorskim Dawne i Nowe* (Wolters Kluwer, 2nd ed. 2022), p. 258.

[1264] Here, it must be noted that the emphasis of the CJEU on the presence of a *personal touch* for the purposes of product's copyrightability strikingly resembles the condition required in the French copyright framework.

[1265] Eleonora Rosati, *Originality in EU Copyright: Full Harmonization through Case Law* (Edward Elgar Publishing 2013), p. 153.

[1266] Véronique Dahan & Charles Bouffier, 'Arrêt Painer du 1er décembre 2011 : la CJUE poursuit son œuvre d'harmonisation du droit d'auteur,' 80 *Revue Lamy Droit de l'immatériel* 14 (2012), p. 14.

[1267] Christian Gero Stallberg, *Urheberrecht und moralische Rechtfertigung* (Duncker & Humblot 2006), p. 147.

[1268] Susan Sontag, *On Photography* (Penguin Books 2008). p. 116.

[1269] Harn Lee, 'Case Comment: Photographs and the Standard of Originality in Europe: Eva-Maria Painer v Standard VerlagsGmbH, Axel Springer AG, Süddeutsche Zeitung GmbH, SPIEGEL-Verlag Rudolf AUGSTEIN GmbH & Co KG and Verlag M. DuMont Schauberg Expedition der Kölnischen Zeitung GmbH & Co KG (C-145/10),' 34 *European Intellectual Property Review* 290 (2012), p. 290.

three production phases specified and established by the CJEU, this should suffice for a photographic product to be considered original.[1270]

The presence of a *personal touch*, in the form of its imprint on a product, can also serve as a convenient indicator which can be employed to determine the extent of originality of various elements of the product. This imprint can be employed to assess whether the author (also unconsciously or subconsciously) borrowed, copied, or imitated from any pre-existing products.[1271] These 'borrowed, copied, or imitated' elements must also bear an imprint of personality of their author. Such an approach does not call into question the extent of originality for the purposes of product copyrightability, but merely aids in any infringement assessment.

In terms of a photographic product, the requirement of the presence of a *personal touch* represents the materialization of the main element of the *author's own intellectual creation*—choices of a free and creative nature.[1272] In other words, it is through the choices of the said nature, the personal touch is imprinted onto a product, which then becomes the *author's own intellectual creation.*

The Relationship between Free and Creative Choices and a Personal Touch

The personality of the photographer manifested via the presence of the *personal touch* can only be imprinted into the photographic product through *free and creative choices*.[1273] The stamp of a *personal touch* and its presence in a photographic product can therefore only be the direct consequence of the photographer's *free and creative choices*, conducted throughout the course of the production process of the photographic product itself. If no *free and creative choices* are employed, the photographer's personality simply cannot be present in a photographic product. The establishment of a direct causal link between the exercise of *free and creative choices* and the stamp of a *personal touch*, signifies the importance of those choices for the reflection of the author's personality. It is therefore the power and capability of the author to shape, edit and alter the surrounding world and its realities into a subject-matter of a creative nature, and as such is recognized as the most valuable and protected activity.[1274] In this view, the personality manifested via the *personal touch*

[1270] Justine Pila, 'The Authorial Works Protectable by Copyright' In: Eleonora Rosati, *The Routledge Handbook of EU Copyright Law* (Routledge 2021), p. 74.

[1271] Alain Strowel, *Le droit d'auteur européen en transition numérique : de ses origines à l'unification européenne et aux défis de l'intelligence artificielle et des Big Data* (Larcier 2022), p. 81.

[1272] Andreas Rahmatian, 'European Copyright Inside or Outside the European Union: Pluralism of Copyright Laws and the "Herderian Paradox",' *IIC* 912 (2016), p. 912.

[1273] Nathalie Martial-Braz, 'Cliché d'une harmonisation du droit d'auteur par la CJUE : du grand art!' *Recueil Dalloz* 471 (2012), p. 471.

[1274] Aurelija Lukoševičienė, 'On Author, Copyright and Originality: Does the Unified EU Originality Standard Correspond to the Digital Reality in Wikipedia?' 11 *Masaryk University Journal of Law and Technology* 215 (2017), p. 215.

must also depict the psychological characteristics of the author.[1275] The effect of this causal link is the establishment of originality, or in other words, the copyrightability.

Having established the causal link between *free and creative choices* and their manifestation in a form of a *personal touch* and the resulting originality, one can also use the *personal touch* to establish another causal link. The notion of *free and creative* choices as such does not specifically imply the unnecessary involvement of a human being. However, if these choices result in a *personal touch*, the necessary involvement of a human being—a person—is evident. Therefore, the *personal touch* can be used to establish the second causal link—that of a relationship between the author as a human being, the person, and their creation.

By putting emphasis on the choices, the author made throughout the production process of a photographic product, the CJEU simply stated that to create is to make choices.[1276] However, as with many other conclusions of the CJEU, this one is given certain limits and further corrections. It is worth noting that not every creation produced through choices made by the author can gain properties or qualities that are recognizable by the copyright law. Therefore, it is only the choices of a *free and creative* nature that have the possible effect of conferring the qualities of giving a *personal touch* to a product.

Regarding the relevance of choices for the possible finding of originality in a photographic product highlighted by the CJEU, it is possible, of course, to claim that all photographers necessarily make choices.[1277] To some, such statement can be seen as an unnecessary devaluing of the production process of a photographic product and the activities of photographers in general. However, what is important within this context is the intended general definition of the steps for these to be applicable to the production processes of all photographic products. Therefore, during the originality assessment process in a photographic product, it is crucial to look at the nature of these steps, how deeply a photographer can dive into their execution, and what mark or imprint they leave on the final photographic product.

This premise is supported by the assumption that every human being assuming the position of an author, is capable of leaving the stamp of their *personal touch* when exercising *free and creative choices* throughout the production process of a product.[1278] Therefore, if a product is to be eligible for copyright protection, it must be also unique. Uniqueness should be ensured by the stamping of the unique personality of an author onto the product. In other words, if every person and their

[1275] Christian Gero Stallberg, *Urheberrecht und moralische Rechtfertigung* (Duncker & Humblot 2006), p. 153.

[1276] Alain Strowel, *Le droit d'auteur européen en transition numérique : de ses origines à l'unification européenne et aux défis de l'intelligence artificielle et des Big Data* (Larcier 2022), p. 71.

[1277] Michel Vivant & Jean-Michel Bruguière, *Droit d'auteur et droits voisins* (Dalloz, 4th ed. 2019), p. 235.

[1278] Aurelija Lukoševičienė, 'On Author, Copyright and Originality: Does the Unified EU Originality Standard Correspond to the Digital Reality in Wikipedia?' 11 *Masaryk University Journal of Law and Technology* 215 (2017), p. 215.

personality is unique, the stamp of their personality must make the product itself unique as well, and therefore original and eligible for copyright protection.[1279] However, *Van Gompel* has argued that some see the requirement of a *personal touch* merely as the author's own individual way of expression, own to themselves, rather than an easily distinguishable and identifiable style, let alone the personal traits and individuality of the author.[1280] According to this perspective, the *personal touch* criterion would be reduced to merely proving the connection between the product and its author (the origination), omitting any kind of individuality of the author stemming from their personality. However, this is indeed the true harmonized meaning of the reduced originality standard. It was by emphasizing the presence of the *author's personality* and the *personal touch* in a photographic product that allowed the CJEU to shift towards the continental understanding of originality, and thus highlight the intellectual link (relationship) between the author and their creation.[1281]

The presence of the author's *personal touch* in a photographic product can only be used to prove or refute its originality based on this relationship. It cannot serve the purpose of proving the statistical uniqueness of a photographic product. Within this context it must be noted that not every photographic product can possess features created via *free and creative choices* of the author that would allow it to be easily distinguishable from other photographic products, or assigned to a specific individual author. Nonetheless, the emphasis put on the presence of the reflection of personality (individuality) of the author by the CJEU, and the important role that personality plays in the existence and identification of originality, underscores the importance of the individuality of a human being and its position within EU copyright law, as well as in an individual-centred democratic society more generally.[1282]

As already mentioned, the said approach of the CJEU is author-oriented. The individuality of an author and the uniqueness of their personality, and through it of their creation(s) as well, can be described by a quote by *Johann Gottlieb Fichte*, through which he defended the author's moral right to their creation, since only physical right has been generally recognised. Although made in regard to the work of a writer, it can be very well applied onto photographic processes, as well as to any other creative process:

'Everyone has their own idea process, their special way, to make up concepts and to connect them with each other: this is generally recognized and immediately recognized by everyone who understands it... Everything we are supposed to think, we have to think according to the analogy of our other way of thinking; and it is only

[1279] Ivo Telec & Pavel Tůma, *Autorský zákon: komentář* (C.H. Beck, 2nd ed. 2019, p. 18.

[1280] Stef van Gompel, 'Creativity, Autonomy, and Personal Touch' In: Mireille van Eechoud, Jostein Gripsrud & Lionel Bently, *Work of Authorship* (Amsterdam University Press 2015), p. 127.

[1281] Irini A. Stamatoudi, 'Originality under EU Copyright Law' In: Paul Torremans, *Research Handbook on Copyright Law* (Edward Elgar Publishing 2017), p. 70.

[1282] Alain Strowel, *Le droit d'auteur européen en transition numérique: de ses origines à l'unification européenne et aux défis de l'intelligence artificielle et des Big Data* (Larcier 2022), p. 74.

through this processing of foreign thoughts, according to the analogy of our way of thinking, that they become ours... It is more improbable than the most improbable that two people should think completely the same about an object. '[1283]

Some might claim that if contents of the aforementioned quote were to be applied universally, and without any further conditions, each creation of a human being having the qualities of their own intellectual creation, could be considered eligible for copyright protection. But such an approach would not be feasible. It is therefore why the individuality of each person in the position of an author only serves as a prerequisite for the further development of originality. This development is done through the *free and creative choices* within the (free and creative) room available to the author, as stated by the CJEU. In other words, the CJEU rejected any assessment of originality based on objective criteria such as novelty, and instead emphasized the need to focus on modifications resulting from the employment of the *free and creative choices*. It is these that help to establish a special relationship between the author and their creation.[1284] The two components of such relationship, the author's personality and their creation, must not be assessed separately, but rather jointly within the relationship they form.[1285] This is the only way originality can be sufficiently assessed. To assess originality, copyrightability must to be determined via the form of the product, particularly its alteration through *free and creative choices* made by the author within the available room. In light of this, the CJEU in its *Painer* case decision highlighted and preserved the possibility of copyrightability via *free and creative choices*.[1286]

This represented the first time that the CJEU officially confirmed the usage of the requirement of reflection of author's personality in their creation, in this case the photographic product, thus the subjective approach to originality as the decisive one.[1287] As said, this was achieved by establishing a direct and explicit link between the author as a human being and their creation.[1288] *Subjectivity* within the context of originality refers to the subjective nature of the author and the subjective nature of the relationship between the author and the product created by them.[1289] In respect to this, the subjectivity of the author and their relationship is transferred (imprinted) onto the created product, which then bears these subjective (personal) characteristics.

1283 Johann Gottlieb Fichte, *Johann Gottlieb Fichte's sämtliche Werke* (Verlag von Veit und Comp 1846), p. 227.

1284 Helmut Haberstumpf, 'Der europäische Werkbegriff und die Lehre vom Gestaltungsspielraum,' *GRUR* 1249 (2021), p. 1249.

1285 *Ibid.*

1286 Andrea Wallace & Ellen Euler, 'Revisiting Access to Cultural Heritage in the Public Domain: EU and International Developments,' *IIC* 823 (2020), p. 823.

1287 Nicolas Berthold, 'L'harmonisation de la Notion D'originalité en Droit D'auteur,' 16 *Journal of World Intellectual Property* 58 (2013), p. 58.

1288 Christophe Caron, *Droit d'auteur et droits voisins* (LexisNexis, 6th ed. 2020), p. 91.

1289 Antoine Latreille, 'Une nouvelle œuvre de l'esprit (approche juridique),' 70 *Revue Lamy Droit de l'immatériel* 109 (2011), p. 109.

Any *objective* treatment of such a relationship, and from it derived understanding of the EU harmonized concept of originality, is thus precluded. When discussing this subjective approach to originality, it must be differentiated from the subjective approach to its assessment by courts, which is prohibited. Currently, it seems that EU harmonization has so far perceived originality as being of subjective nature. However, the subjective nature is supposed to be assessed objectively by courts, and according to objective criteria. In fact, a subjective approach could affirm the definition of a photographic product as a manifestation of the individualised I.[1290]

Equal Treatment of Photographic Products

The CJEU's decision in the *Painer* case had an immense impact on the subject-matter categorization in general, in addition to photographic products.[1291] The decision lay down a general principle of equal treatment of all types of works in terms of their copyrightability, as long as they were original.[1292] The CJEU stressed the need to focus on the actual presence of originality in the photographic product, rather than on the photographic genre that the assessed photographic product belongs to.[1293] The refusal to find portraits to be inferior to other genres and types of photographic products was also extended to other subject-matter at the national levels of Member States, given that such subject-matter also met the requirements prescribed for their copyrightability.[1294] In other words, as already stated, no levels of originality within the product itself existed.[1295] The CJEU's conclusion was based on the absence of any prescribed dependence of the copyright protection of a photographic product (or any other product) on the existence of the possibility of creative interventions and their extent.[1296] The nonexistence of such dependence on this extent of intervention was also noted in EU legislation.[1297]

The decision of the CJEU in *Painer case* also proved that the medium of photography, regardless of genre or type, is of a nature that allows it to be creatively

[1290] Susan Sontag, *On Photography* (Penguin Books 2008), p. 119.

[1291] Marián Jankovič, 'How the Two Child Abuse Cases Helped to Shape the Test of Originality of Photographic Works' 17 *Masaryk University Journal of Law and Technology* 197 (2023), p. 197.

[1292] Nicolas Berthold, 'L'harmonisation de la Notion D'originalité en Droit D'auteur,' 16 *Journal of World Intellectual Property* 58 (2013), p. 58.

[1293] Andrea Wallace & Ellen Euler, 'Revisiting Access to Cultural Heritage in the Public Domain: EU and International Developments,' *IIC* 823 (2020), p. 823.

[1294] Sabine Büttler, 'Urheberrechtsschutz von Porträtfotografien, insbesondere bei der Verwendung als Fahndungsbild' *European Law Reporter* 82 (2012).

[1295] Here, a strong similarity to the French approach to originality in a product is evident. Within the French copyright framework, if a product is deemed original, it is recognized as such without further assessment of the degree or extent of its originality.

[1296] Hans Peter Roth. 'EuGH, 01. 12. 2011 – C-145/10: Urheberrecht: Schutz von Portraitfotografien' 5 *EuZW* (2012), p. 182.

[1297] For example, Recital 16 of the Database Directive (aesthetic or qualitative criteria); Recital 16 of the Term Directive (merit of purpose) and Recital 8 of the Software Directive (qualitative or aesthetic merits).

modified and edited to an extent that the personality of the photographer could be imprinted onto it. Therefore, basically any photographic product is perfectly capable of being eligible for copyright protection and may not be excluded from any possible eligibility for copyright protection simply based on its affiliation with the medium of photography as such. However, the CJEU omitted any considerations related to various creative constraints associated with the portrait genre, apart from the general recognition of a *relatively small degree of individual formative freedom*.[1298] In sum, the CJEU only focused on the positive definition and the enumeration of steps through which originality can be achieved.

Equal Treatment of Parts of Photographic Products

The photographic product at the centre of *Painer case* also clearly benefited from the principle of equating protected works with their parts, as first formulated in the *Infopaq case* decision. After that decision, *reproduction* or *reproduction in part* was understood as indivisible, and given autonomous and uniform interpretation in the copyright framework of the EU.[1299] Therefore, even though only a part of the original photographic product in the form of a *cropped image* was reproduced by the several Austrian and German magazines, the *cropped image* nonetheless still sufficiently met the criteria of being the *author's own intellectual creation*. In other words, the *cropped image* itself constituted a work in itself, and was therefore found to be eligible for copyright protection, due to the visible presence of the imprint of personality of its author. The *croppes image* was unambiguously identified as a *new and autonomous work protected by copyright*.[1300] In cases of infringements, the reproduction and reproduced parts would therefore have to be assessed from a qualitative point of view, rather than a quantitative one.[1301]

Such approach has been achieved by the conclusion of the CJEU, according to which it was impossible to make and identify distinctions between protectable original products, whether these are whole products or their parts.[1302] The court held that it was impossible to make and identify such distinctions due to the originality criterion of the *author's own intellectual creation reflecting their personality*, which bound the parts of an original work to the whole of the work, and thus its protection.

1298 Stef van Gompel, 'Creativity, Autonomy, and Personal Touch' In: Mireille van Eechoud, Jostein Gripsrud & Lionel Bently, *Work of Authorship* (Amsterdam University Press 2015), p. 124.

1299 Eleonora Rosati, *Copyright and the Court of Justice of the European Union* (Oxford University Press 2019), p. 87.

1300 CJEU, Case C-145/10, Eva-Maria Painer v Standard VerlagsGmbH and Others, 1 Dec. 2011, ECLI:EU:C:2011:798, para. 42.

1301 Sari Depreeuw, *The Variable Scope of the Exclusive Economic Rights in Copyright* (Kluwer Law International 2014), p. 203.

1302 Rafael Sánchez Aristi, Nieves I. Moralejo Imbernón & Sebastián López Maza, *La jurisprudencia del Tribunal de Justicia de la Unión Europea en materia de propiedad intelectual: análisis y comentarios* (Instituto Autor 2017), p. 396.

Therefore, in this case, the author was only required to demonstrate the reproduction of an authorial work, rather than claiming that part of the work was reproduced, as well as demonstrating that the work was eligible for copyright protection.[1303] Omitting these two steps made the process of establishing infringement easier and more straightforward for copyright holder(s). The omission of these two steps was also necessitated by the fact that since the *Infopaq* case decision, it became officially recognizable by the law that a work could consist of multiple *sub-works* in their own rights.

For example, in the case of photography, a single photographic product, depending on what it depicts and to what extent and quantity its elements creatively modified and edited by the author, could consist of many more photographic *sub-works* in their own rights. The only requirement for the eligibility of such *sub-works* for copyright protection would then be the imprint of the personality of their author. Therefore, the applicable criterion that emerged from the *Infopaq* case is more of a qualitative than quantitative nature.[1304] This is due to the emphasis put on the nature of the part of the work, rather than its size or the total proportion that it constitutes in the whole work.

If one wishes to venture into deeper analysis, the opinion of Advocate General *Kokott* delivered in connection with the *Football Dataco* case can shed further light on it. Although the case dealt with infringement related to the reproduction of video images, it can be used to understand the medium of photography better. In her opinion, Advocate General *Kokott* referred to *isolated items of colour for individual pixels* in individual video frames, as *single words* in literary works.[1305] Referring to the reasoning from the *Infopaq* case, pixels cannot be eligible for copyright protection, just as the individual words cannot be. However, if such pixels are brought together in a subject-matter (a photographic product) in a way that constitutes the *author's own intellectual creation* (reflecting their personality), copyrightability is possible.

The Universal Nature of the Formulated Originality Standard

The assessment of originality in a photographic product and the subsequent originality standard can be considered to be built upon the understanding and assessment processes of originality in the continental EU.[1306] It was especially the emphasis put on the author's personality and its imprint in the photographic product, as well

1303 Justine Pila & Paul Torremans, *European Intellectual Property Law* (Oxford University Press, 2nd ed. 2019), p. 262.

1304 Paul Torremans (ed.), *Research handbook on copyright law* (Edward Elgar 2017), p. 81.

1305 Opinion of AG Kokott in Case C-403/08, *Football Association Premier League Ltd and Others v QC Leisure and Others*, Case C-429/08, *Karen Murphy v Media Protection Services Ltd.*, 3 Feb. 2011, ECLI:EU:C:2011:43, para. 80.

1306 Irini A. Stamatoudi, 'Originality under EU Copyright Law' In: Paul Torremans, *Research Handbook on Copyright Law* (Edward Elgar Publishing 2017), p. 70.

as the reference to the presence of a *personal touch*, which assimilated the said originality standard within the continental part of the EU. This definition of the formulated originality standard, along with clarifying references, was the result of consensus found among the Member States.[1307]

The medium of photography played a key role in formulating what is now known as the universal originality standard—universal in terms of its application to all subject-matter eligible for copyright protection. It was photographic products and the requirement of originality originating from Article 6 of both Term Directives that caused this application of the standard to other subject-matter. Within this context, it must be noted that the originality standard was firstly formulated in the CJEU's *Infopaq* case decision, but the *Painer* case decision provided the addition of *reflecting his personality*. In other words, the decision in the *Painer* case created the requirement of the presence of a stamp of a *personal touch* of the author in the subject-matter.

At the time that the CJEU delivered its decision in the *Painer* case, no one realised the *universality* of the originality standard; it was still only assumed. Nonetheless, the formulation of the originality standard by the CJEU by clarifying its previous case law—and not as a deviation from it—supported assumption that the intention of the CJEU was in fact to establish the standard as universally applicable.[1308]

Effects of the Painer Case Decision

In conclusion, the CJEU's *Painer* case decision forced national courts to explore the potential of photography as a medium.[1309] National courts would have to assess photographic products in detail and investigate their production process in order to discover aspects where originality of such products might reside. The CJEU also affected photographers. Thereafter, they had a manual to ensure what steps they would need to take and what effects demonstrate in photographic products via the notion of a *personal touch* to hypothetically ensure originality and eligibility for copyright protection. Last but not least, the CJEU also influenced social perceptions about some photographic genres that had long been considered non-original.[1310] These also came to be seen as original, since simplicity is no longer considered a barrier to copyright protection.[1311] Nonetheless, the

[1307] Herman Cohen Jehoram, 'The EC Copyright Directives, Economics and Authors' Rights,' *IIC* 821 (1994), p. 821.

[1308] Axel Metzger, 'Der Einfluss des EuGH auf die gegenwärtige Entwicklung des Urheberrechts,' *GRUR* 118 (2012), p. 118.

[1309] Marián Jankovič, 'How the Two Child Abuse Cases Helped to Shape the Test of Originality of Photographic Works' 17 *Masaryk University Journal of Law and Technology* 197 (2023), p. 197.

[1310] Marián Jankovič, 'The Development and Harmonisation of Originality Standard of Photographic Works in the Copyright Framework of the European Union' 20 *Jusletter IT 30. März 2023* (2023), p. 1.

[1311] Justine Pila & Paul Torremans, *European Intellectual Property Law* (Oxford University Press, 2nd ed. 2019), p. 253.

positive manner in which the applicable originality standard was formulated by the CJEU, especially in connection with emphasis on the creative room exploitable by the author, leaves one under the impression that a finding of originality, and thus eligibility for copyright protection, cannot be simply denied by national courts.[1312]

10.4.1.7 The Renckhoff case

In the *Renckhoff* case,[1313] the originality of a photographic product was also touched upon amongst considerations related to an act of its communication to the public. The photographic product at the heart of this case, taken in the Spanish city of Cordoba by a German professional photographer, depicts a cityscape. In his opinion, Advocate General *Campos Sánchez-Bordona* expressed doubts whether the photographic product in question, a simple shot, satisfied the requirement for originality laid down in the *Painer* case.[1314] The Advocate General *Campos Sánchez-Bordona* thus made it clear that the originality represented an existent threshold, which still must be passed, regardless of how low it is set.

In the decision itself, the CJEU stated and recalled, in a form of a preliminary point, that a photographic product may be eligible for copyright protection only if it is the intellectual creation of the author reflecting their personality and at the same time expressing their free and creative choices employed throughout its production process.[1315] In accordance with this preliminary point, it may be assumed that the free and creative choices may also be expressed in a landscape or cityscape photograph.[1316] However, since the German copyright framework makes use of the figurative *back door*[1317] in Article 6 of Term Directive II and provides protection via a related right to *other photographs*, i.e., non-original photographic products, the doubt that the Advocate General *Campos Sánchez-Bordona* cast on the originality of this photographic product was unfortunately not further discussed by the CJEU,

[1312] Stef van Gompel, 'Creativity, Autonomy, and Personal Touch' In: Mireille van Eechoud, Jostein Gripsrud & Lionel Bently, *Work of Authorship* (Amsterdam University Press 2015), p. 124.

[1313] CJEU, Case C-161/17, *Land Nordrhein-Westfalen v Dirk Renckhoff*, 7 Aug. 2018, ECLI: EU:C:2018:634.

[1314] Opinion of AG Campos Sánchez-Bordona in Case C-161/17, *Land Nordrhein-Westfalen v Dirk Renckhoff*, 25 Apr. 2018, ECLI:EU:C:2018:279, para. 54.

[1315] CJEU, Case C-161/17, *Land Nordrhein-Westfalen v Dirk Renckhoff*, 7 Aug. 2018, ECLI: EU:C:2018:634, para. 14.

[1316] Tatiana Synodinou, *The Renckhoff Judgement: The CJEU Swivels the Faces of the Copyright Rubik's Cube (Part I)* (3 Sep. 2024), https://copyrightblog.kluweriplaw.com/2018/09/27/renckhoff-judgment-cjeu-swivels-faces-copyright-rubiks-cube-part.

[1317] The notion of the 'back door' is used by the author as a metaphor in the context of protection of non-original photographic works in terms of Article 6 of the Term Directive I and II. The said metaphor is to represent an option Member States can make use of in order to avoid explicitly expanding the copyrightability of photographic products and rather keep the system of a related-right type of protection in place.

apart from the said general preliminary point reference to the originality of photographic products and the *Painer* case.[1318]

Such omission of considerations related to originality of a photographic product might be what the *back door* in the form of a related right type of protection for *other photographs* achieves in practice. In this respect, any considerations regarding the originality of an assessed photographic product might be postponed until the expiry of the related right term of protection or omitted altogether. This process would be justified by the fact that the photographic product would be eligible for protection under a related right type of protection anyway. In such situations, the originality assessment would be rendered pointless. Any type of different treatment of photographic products, as opposed to other types of subject-matter eligible for copyright protection, or even different types of photographic products, would therefore not be objectively justified.[1319]

10.4.1.8 The Levola case

The question of whether the taste of a food product could be granted copyright protection was elaborated on by the CJEU in the *Levola* case.[1320] Having established the *author's own intellectual creation* as a universal requirement for copyrightability, it was clear that any product possessing such a link of psychological dependence on the author must be naturally eligible for copyright protection.[1321] However, everyday practice has shown that this requirement must be limited to a certain extent.

In *Levola*, the CJEU held that in order for a subject-matter to be classified as a work and eligible for copyright protection, two cumulative conditions had to be met.[1322] First, the subject-matter must be original in a sense it is the *author's own intellectual creation*.[1323] Second, for a creation to be classified as work, it must be the *expression* of the *author's own intellectual creation*.[1324] This case was the first time that the CJEU formulated this second condition in the form of an additional condition to the previously formulated and applied standard of originality.[1325]

[1318] CJEU, Case C-161/17, *Land Nordrhein-Westfalen v Dirk Renckhoff*, 7 Aug. 2018, ECLI:EU:C:2018:634, para. 14.

[1319] Hans Peter Roth. 'EuGH, 01. 12. 2011 – C-145/10: Urheberrecht: Schutz von Portraitfo-tografien' 5 *EuZW* (2012), p. 182.

[1320] CJEU, Case C-310/17, *Levola Hengelo BV v Smilde Foods BV*, 13 Nov. 2018, ECLI:EU:C:2018:899.

[1321] Christian Gero Stallberg, Urheberrecht und moralische Rechtfertigung (Duncker & Humblot 2006), p. 153.

[1322] CJEU, Case C-310/17, *Levola Hengelo BV v Smilde Foods BV*, 13 Nov. 2018, ECLI:EU:C:2018:899, para. 35.

[1323] CJEU, Case C-310/17, *Levola Hengelo BV v Smilde Foods BV*, 13 Nov. 2018, ECLI:EU:C:2018:899, para. 36.

[1324] CJEU, Case C-310/17, *Levola Hengelo BV v Smilde Foods BV*, 13 Nov. 2018, ECLI:EU:C:2018:899, para. 37.

[1325] Caterina Sganga, *The Notion of 'Work' in EU Copyright Law After Levola Hengelo: One Answer Given, Three Question Marks Ahead* (3 Sep. 2024), https://papers.ssrn.com/sol3/papers.cfm?abstract_id=3323011.

Therefore, copyright protection arises for instances of intellectual creation, and where that creation is accepted as a work.[1326] Insisting on copyright protection for *works* falling within the EU's concept would prevent protection by copyright of products that do not meet the criterion of being a *work* and at the same time prevent Member States from excluding works that indeed met the criterion for copyright protection.[1327] On this, the CJEU noted the following:

> *For there to be a 'work' as referred to in Directive 2001/29, the subject-matter protected by copyright must be expressed in a manner which makes it identifiable with sufficient precision and objectivity, even though that expression is not necessarily in permanent form.*[1328]

Given the previous focus on the shaping of the concept of originality, in the *Levola* case the CJEU shifted its attention to defining the term *work*. As presented by the CJEU, for a product to be recognized as a *work* for the purposes of EU copyright law, it must fully adhere to the principle of the *idea/expression dichotomy*, and also to the exclusion of the *fixation requirement*.[1329]

This definition will be broken down and assessed in more detail. The principle of the *idea/expression dichotomy* is represented by the term *expressed*. It implies that only an expressed product may be considered for copyright protection. The said fixation requirement, or the lack of, is represented by the phrase *not necessarily in permanent form*. Although borrowed from trademark law, the phrase *with sufficient precision and objectivity* is intended to preclude any subjective assessments;[1330] the assessment of a product must be done in an objective manner. Therefore, the main conclusion that can be taken from the decision of the CJEU is that for a product to be recognized as a *work*, it must be original and identifiable with sufficient precision and objectivity.[1331]

Another key element of the decision is that sight and hearing are, for the purposes of EU copyright law, senses of a superior nature.[1332] According to the CJEU, it is

---

[1326] Rosati E. The Levola Hengelo CJEU Decision: Ambiguities, Uncertainties ... and More Questions [online]. *Ipkitten.blogspot.com* 02. 09. 2024 [cit. 02. 09. 2024] http://ipkitten.blogspot.com/2018/11/the-levola-hengelo-cjeu-decision.html .

[1327] Eleonora Rosati, *Copyright and the Court of Justice of the European Union* (Oxford University Press, 2019), p. 128.

[1328] CJEU, Case C-310/17, *Levola Hengelo BV v Smilde Foods BV*, 13 Nov. 2018, ECLI:EU:C:2018:899, para. 40.

[1329] Eleonora Rosati, 'Copyright at the CJEU: Back to the Start (of Copyright Protection)' In: Hayleigh Bosher & Eleonora Rosati, *Developments and Directions in Intellectual Property Law: Twenty Years of the IPKat* (Oxford University Press 2023), p. 221.

[1330] *Ibid.*

[1331] Caterina Sganga, *The Notion of 'Work' in EU Copyright Law After Levola Hengelo: One Answer Given, Three Question Marks Ahead* (3 Sep. 2024), https://papers.ssrn.com/sol3/papers.cfm?abstract_id=3323011..

[1332] Alain Strowel, *Le droit d'auteur européen en transition numérique: de ses origines à l'unification européenne et aux défis de l'intelligence artificielle et des Big Data* (Larcier 2022), p. 74.

only through these two senses that identification with sufficient precision is currently possible. Therefore, olfactory or gustatory products cannot rely on their copyrightability simply because of their perceivability by smell or taste.[1333] The reliability of hearing can be contested as well; however, for the purposes of copyright law, it has continued to remain on the same figurative level as sight. Nonetheless, the CJEU noted that the impossibility to grant copyright protection to products based on their gustatory qualities is only due to the current state of scientific development, which does not allow the *precise and objective identification by technical means*.[1334] This implies that the CJEU considers the current state of affairs to be only temporary.

For the medium of photography, the decision of the CJEU reached in the *Levola* case did not affect the originality assessment test in any way.[1335] Given the reliance of the medium on perception solely by sight, any photographic product would surely pass the additional requirement for its potential copyrightability.

10.4.1.9 The Flos case

The referral of the Italian court regarding unregistered designs was, amongst other things, responded to by the CJEU in the *Flos* case.[1336] The CJEU stated that designs can be eligible for copyright protection if these were their *author's own intellectual creation*.[1337] This decision therefore settled the question of whether the *author's own intellectual creation* could be applicable to national unregistered designs. As a result, the CJEU's decision in the *Flos* case significantly narrowed the discretion of Member States for unregistered designs and the subsequent granting of copyright protection.[1338]

10.4.1.10 The Cofemel case

First, it must be noted that the CJEU's decision in the *Cofemel* case[1339] was based on a referral inspired by the *Flos* decision. The proceedings in *Cofemel* were initiated based on a referral by the Portuguese Supreme Court, which sought clarification

1333 Pavel Koukal, 'Reexamining Precision and Objectivity in Copyright Protection for Non-Traditional Creations' 21 *Jusletter IT 24. April 2024* (2024), p. 479.

1334 CJEU, Case C-310/17, *Levola Hengelo BV v Smilde Foods BV*, 13 Nov. 2018, ECLI:EU:C:2018:899, para. 43.

1335 Marián Jankovič, 'How the Two Child Abuse Cases Helped to Shape the Test of Originality of Photographic Works' 17 *Masaryk University Journal of Law and Technology* 197 (2023), p. 197.

1336 CJEU, Case C-168/09, *Flos SpA v Semeraro Casa e Famiglia SpA.*, 27 Jan. 2011, ECLI:EU:C:2011:29.

1337 Eleonora Rosati, 'Copyright at the CJEU: Back to the Start (of Copyright Protection)' In: Hayleigh Bosher & Eleonora Rosati, *Developments and Directions in Intellectual Property Law: Twenty Years of the IPKat* (Oxford University Press 2023), p. 222.

1338 Mireille van Eechoud, 'Along the Road to Uniformity: Diverse Readings of the Court of Justice Judgments on Copyright Work,' 3 *Journal of Intellectual Property, Information Technology and Electronic Commerce Law* 60 (2012), p. 60.

1339 CJEU, Case C-683/17, *Cofemel – Sociedade de Vestuário SA v G-Star Raw CV*, 12 Sep. 2019, ECLI:EU:C:2019:721.

and a clear definition of the conditions for copyrightability of works of applied art, industrial models, and designs. In its decision, the CJEU noted that in order for a product to be recognized as a *work* for the purposes of the copyright law, two cumulative conditions had to be met. First, the product must be of an original nature, i.e., an own intellectual creation of its author. Second, only elements which are the clear and objective expression of such intellectual creation can be considered works within the meaning of the EU copyright law.

The simplest conclusion of the *Cofemel* decision is that works of applied art are eligible for copyright protection under the same conditions as any other type of product, given that the prescribed conditions for this protection are met.[1340] Within this context, the decision can be also seen as a judicial solution to discrimination amongst different types of products.[1341] By extending copyright protection to works of applied art, given they also meet the conditions prescribed for originality, the CJEU ensured equality of access of such products to copyright protection.

The CJEU also noted that any requirements applicable to designs, such as aesthetic value, upon which their copyrightability would depend on, are contrary to the requirement of objectivity applicable within the copyright framework of the EU.[1342] Considerations based on aesthetic value are prohibited and not relevant for the purposes of possible copyrightability of a product.[1343] The elimination of the role of aesthetics in the originality assessment process serves two main purposes: first, it prevents subjecting the process to subjectivity, thus making the process more objective in nature, and second, it demonstrates that the harmonized originality standard serves as a figurative ceiling, which prohibits the application of any other criteria.[1344]

The decision of the CJEU in the *Cofemel* case also made it clear that originality represents a threshold that needs to be passed after a thorough examination, for a product to be eligible for copyright protection.[1345] In connection with the assessment process, the CJEU devised a negative version of its definition by referring to constraints of creative freedom. The CJEU noted that in order to rule out the presence of originality, context of the production process of a product must be assessed to such extent, that the room for making *free and creative choices* was not left

[1340] Eleonora Rosati, 'Copyright at the CJEU: Back to the Start (of Copyright Protection)' In: Hayleigh Bosher & Eleonora Rosati, *Developments and Directions in Intellectual Property Law: Twenty Years of the IPKat* (Oxford University Press 2023), p. 222.

[1341] Marianne Levin, 'The Cofemel Revolution – Originality, Equality and Neutrality' In: Eleonora Rosati, The *Routledge Handbook of EU Copyright Law* (Routledge 2021), p. 85.

[1342] CJEU, Case C-683/17, Cofemel – Sociedade de Vestuário SA v G-Star Raw CV, 12 Sep. 2019, ECLI:EU:C:2019:721, para. 55.

[1343] Analogously, the application of aesthetic criteria in order to determine the potential copyrightability of a database must also be excluded, according to the wording of Recital 16 of the Database Directive.

[1344] Koray Güven, 'Eliminating 'Aesthetics' from Copyright Law: The Aftermath of Cofemel', 71 *GRUR Int.* 213 (2022), p. 213.

[1345] Eleonora Rosati, 'Copyright at the CJEU: Back to the Start (of Copyright Protection)' In: Hayleigh Bosher & Eleonora Rosati, *Developments and Directions in Intellectual Property Law: Twenty Years of the IPKat* (Oxford University Press 2023), p. 223.

within the said context.[1346] In other words, if no leeway for making *free and creative choices* is available during the production process, the formation of originality is precluded by such absence.

10.4.1.11 The Brompton Bicycle case

The simplest conclusion of the *Brompton Bicycle*[1347] decision is that overlaps with other intellectual property laws are allowed, and at the same time that *functional shapes* can be in fact copyrighted if these display the effects of *free and creative choices* employed by the author during the production process.[1348] In other words, the copyright protection of functional shapes is possible, but the personality of the author must still be visible in such functional shapes dictated by technical considerations and not concealed by the functional/technical nature itself. Therefore, if the personality of the author, through the employed *free and creative choices*, has overcome the functionalities and technicalities of the product or its parts, the product or its parts is eligible for copyright protection.

What the CJEU applied in the *Brompton Bicycle* decision can be referred to as the *functionality exclusion*.[1349] This exclusion was achieved by conditioning the copyrightability on the author's *free and creative choices* made throughout the production process. If the functionality of a product prevails over its capability or capacity of accommodating the personality of its author (imprinted via their *free and creative choices*, copyrightability of such *functional* product is impossible.

Here again, the CJEU stated that in order for a product to be eligible for copyright protection, it is both necessary and sufficient that the product is a work, and original in the sense that it is its *author's own intellectual creation*, which resulted from their *free and creative choices*, and at the same time reflecting their personality.[1350]

1346 Alain Strowel, *Le droit d'auteur européen en transition numérique: de ses origines à l'unification européenne et aux défis de l'intelligence artificielle et des Big Data* (Larcier 2022), p. 73.

1347 CJEU, Case C-833/18, *SI and Brompton Bicycle Ltd v Chedech / Get2Get*, 11 Jun. 2020, ECLI:EU:C:2020:461.

1348 Eleonora Rosati, 'Copyright at the CJEU: Back to the Start (of Copyright Protection)' In: Hayleigh Bosher & Eleonora Rosati, *Developments and Directions in Intellectual Property Law: Twenty Years of the IPKat* (Oxford University Press 2023), p. 222.

1349 Marianne Levin, 'The Cofemel Revolution—Originality, Equality and Neutrality' In: Eleonora Rosati, *The Routledge Handbook of EU Copyright Law* (Routledge 2021), p. 96.

1350 Eleonora Rosati, 'Copyright at the CJEU: Back to the Start (of Copyright Protection)' In: Hayleigh Bosher & Eleonora Rosati, *Developments and Directions in Intellectual Property Law: Twenty Years of the IPKat* (Oxford University Press 2023), p. 224.

10.5 The Effects of Harmonization on Selected Segments of the EU Copyright Framework

As part of the first harmonization phase described above, EU legislator set up a general legislative framework. Part of this legislative framework included a requirement of originality, as the requirement for copyright protection provision; however, this legislation only directly dealt with the three subject-matter: computer programs, photographic products, and databases. Nonetheless, the requirement of the *author's own intellectual creation* was put to the test by its application in practice. In other words, the legislative framework prepared the ground for its practical application.

As is evident from the second harmonization phase, the institution which undertook this application in practice was the CJEU. However, it was not only the application in practice the CJEU has conducted. Since the application in practice also required adapting to various, and sometimes challenging, circumstances, the CJEU along the way *fine-tuned* the requirement of the *author's own intellectual creation* formulated by EU legislator. *Fine-tuning* consisted of formulating additional conditions to be applied jointly with the original requirement formulated in the EU legislation. The reason for this was that referrals by national Member-State courts to the CJEU entailed a variety of subject-matter seeking potential copyright protection. In light of this variety, slimming down the generally broad requirement of the *author's own intellectual creation* was certainly necessary.

The following sections further detail the effects of both the first and second harmonization phases on the selected segments and elements of the EU copyright framework. Special attention will be given to photographic products, where possible.

10.5.1 Directive (EU) 2019/790—the Digital Single Market Directive

One more piece of EU legislation exists as guidance on applying the originality standard to photographic products. Directive (EU) 2019/790—the Digital Single Market Directive was given room outside of both, the first and second harmonization phases, since it, to a certain extent, reflects not only the initial legislation adopted as part of the first harmonization phase, but also the case law of the CJEU, developed as part of the second harmonization phase. It was for these reasons; I have dedicated a specific section to this Directive.

Article 14 of the Digital Single Market Directive currently represents, the latest legislative codification of the originality standard of *author's own intellectual creation* developed by the CJEU in its jurisprudence.[1351] As a preliminary remark,

[1351] Eleonora Rosati, *Copyright and the Court of Justice of the European Union* (Oxford University Press, 2nd ed. 2023), p. 136.

it must be noted that the drafting of Article 14 was prompted by a decision by the German BGH in the *Museumsfotos* case[1352] that concerned photographic products of digitized works of visual art residing in the public domain.[1353] Article 14 of the Digital Single Market Directive refers to the subject-matter to be eligible for copyright protection within its meaning in the following way:

'Member States shall provide that, when the term of protection of a work of visual art has expired, any material resulting from an act of reproduction of that work is not subject to copyright or related rights, unless the material resulting from that act of reproduction is original in the sense that it is the author's own intellectual creation.'[1354]

Basically, the EU legislator made it clear that any reproduction of an unprotected *work of visual art* due to the expiration of its term of protection (in other words, residing in the public domain), cannot be eligible for copyright protection, unless the reproduction itself fulfilled the criteria for such protection. Simply put, the emergence of a (new) term of copyright protection in connection with *works of visual arts* for which the initial term has already expired, is not possible. Another aspect not possible is the granting of a term of copyright protection in connection with a photographic product that does not meet the requirements for its copyrightability.

The wording of Article 14 of the Digital Single Market Directive clearly stipulates that only photographic products which fulfil the criterion of being an *author's own intellectual creation* may be copyrighted. This therefore does not preclude, as Article 14 notes, such reproductions from attaining the qualities of photographic products eligible for copyright protection—the photographic works. In other words, reproduction photographic products can never be granted any other type of protection than copyright.[1355] This conclusion is well in line with the harmonized originality standard. Clearly, Article 14 of the Digital Single Market Directive presupposes that some photographic products produced in the course of reproduction of *works of visual art* can reach over the threshold reserved for photographic products eligible for copyright protection. In respect to this, the production of (original) photographic products within the meaning of EU copyright law is not excluded per se in the reproduction photographic genre.

The criterion of an *author's own intellectual creation*, especially the conditions of its fulfilment, has been already extensively detailed above. Nonetheless, the first

1352 AMG Nürnberg, 32 C 4607/15, 28. Oct. 2015; LG Berlin, 16 O 175/15, 31. May 2016; LG Berlin, 15 O 428/15, 31. May 2016; and LG Stuttgart, 17 O 690/15, 27. Sep. 2016.

1353 Giulia Dore & Pelin Turan, 'When Copyright Meets Digital Cultural Heritage: Picturing an EU Right to Culture in Freedom of Panorama and Reproduction of Public Domain Art,' *IIC* 37 (2024), p. 37.

1354 Art. 14 of the Digital Single Market Directive.

1355 Eleonora Rosati, *Copyright in the Digital Single Market: Article-by-Article Commentary to the Provisions of Directive 2019/790* (Oxford University Press 2021), p. 247.

question is whether the photographer has the room to make *free and creative choices* throughout the production process, and whether making choices of such nature is even desirable within the reproduction photographic genre. The follow-up question is whether choices made by photographers throughout the production process of a reproduction photographic product can be recognized as *free and creative*, and thus enabling its copyrightability.

If the production process of a reproduction photographic product is broken down into the three *production phases* defined in the CJEU's *Painer* decision, the nature of steps and choices made by the photographer in each phase can be assessed for the purposes of copyrightability. In regards to the third, *post-process* phase, UK Intellectual Property Office issued non-binding guidance. The agency stated that the copyrightability of a reproduction photographic product based on post-process retouching is unlikely, since *'There will generally be minimal scope for a creator to exercise free and creative choices if their aim is to make a faithful reproduction of an existing work.'*[1356] From this, it can be derived that any kind of post-processing aimed at enhancing natural features would most likely fail to adequately serve as the grounds for copyright protection of a reproduction photographic product. However, this would devoid most of the post-processing choices made within the reproduction genre of photography of originality forming potential. Even here, the more the production digitalization process is governed by technical factors and bound, if not restrained, by standardization policies and best practices, the less room there is left for the exercise of *free and creative choices*.[1357]

One of the effects of Article 14 of the Digital Single Market Directive was the removal of photographic products of the reproduction genre from the scope of national copyright frameworks, which had traditionally incorporated a related right type of protection for *other photographs* within the meaning of Article 6 of Term Directive II.[1358] This can be seen as a theoretical remedy to the dual system introduced by Article 6 of Term Directive II, since the wording of Article 14 of the Digital Single Market Directive did not offer any alternative protection to *other photographs*, as Article 6 did. This circumvention was to ensure that the public domain would not be devoid of photographic products that could be protected under national-level related right types of protection as *other photographs*, thus preventing any negative effects related to the volume of the public domain itself. Nonetheless, this loophole only applied to photographic products of the reproduction genre, within the meaning of Article 14 of the Digital Single Market Directive. Any other photographic products produced in circumstances different from the prescribed reproduction of *works of visual art* in public domain have continued to be governed by related rights within

---

1356 *Copyright Notice: Digital Images, Photographs and the Internet* (4 Oct. 2024), https://www.gov.uk/government/publications/copyright-notice-digital-images-photographs-and-the-internet/copyright-notice-digital-images-photographs-and-the-internet.

1357 Andrea Wallace & Ellen Euler, 'Revisiting Access to Cultural Heritage in the Public Domain: EU and International Developments,' *IIC* 823 (2020), p. 823.

1358 *Ibid.*

relevant national legal frameworks, if existent. This basically means that protection by related rights, if applicable, can only *intercept* photographic products produced outside of the said reproduction scenario. This arrangement prevents Member States from the introduction of any type of a related right type of protection applicable to reproduction photographic products, which in turn limits Member States' autonomy in connection to the protectability of photographic products within the meaning of Article 6 of Term Directive II.[1359] The very wording of Article 14 of the Digital Single Market Directive clearly presupposes such a scenario, since apart from excluding such photographic products from copyright protection, it also explicitly mentions the related rights type of protection as well.

The rise in the numbers of cases challenging the eligibility of photographic products by copyright that were produced under the circumstances presupposed by the provision of Article 14, can be expected.[1360] Naturally, this would stem from the need to subject such photographic products in question to the necessary assessment of originality to subsequently determine their eligibility for copyright protection. The possibility of such photographic products attracting copyright protection cannot be excluded per se based on their assignment to the *reproduction photography* genre. Nonetheless, this was also previously affirmed in the CJEU's decision in the *Painer* case, since here too, the subject depicted is pre-determined.[1361]

It is also worth noting that in the case of production of a reproduction of a photographic product already residing in the public domain, the recognition of this *mere* reproduction, as an original photographic product, would lead to restoration of copyright protection of the photographic product residing in the public domain. In other words, the copyright protection of the reproduced photographic product would be extended by another 70 years. In such a scenario, the photographic product residing in the public domain would be excerpted from it and returned to the hypothetical realm of copyright. In fact, if such conduct were approved by copyright law, protectability of, (not only) photographic products, would be practically perpetual.

To conclude, the question is still open on whether national courts will begin to recognize such reproduction photographic products as original, in light of the originality standard as formulated in the *Painer case* decision and take into considerations the steps taken by photographers during the three production phases. Naturally, for such photographic products to be found original, these steps taken throughout the three production phases would have to be recognized as originality forming.

1359 Eleonora Rosati, *Copyright in the Digital Single Market: Article-by-Article Commentary to the Provisions of Directive 2019/790* (Oxford University Press 2021), p. 248.

1360 Giulia Dore & Pelin Turan, 'When Copyright Meets Digital Cultural Heritage: Picturing an EU Right to Culture in Freedom of Panorama and Reproduction of Public Domain Art,' *IIC* 37 (2024), p. 37.

1361 Andrea Wallace & Ellen Euler, 'Revisiting Access to Cultural Heritage in the Public Domain: EU and International Developments,' *IIC* 823 (2020), p. 823.

10.5.2 The Concept of a Work

Protection by copyright only attaches to and accommodates a subject-matter capable of doing so. Such subject-matter is referred to as *works* or *authorial works* for the purposes of the EU copyright framework. In order to properly determine the boundaries and extent of application of copyright, it is necessary to assess and define the essential properties of a work, followed by determining to what extent a subject-matter must possess such properties.[1362] The outcome of any such assessment should be a clear delimitation between eligible for copyright and those that are not.

For the purposes of copyright law in general, a work is considered an original formal expression of human activity.[1363] Therefore, if a creation is to be considered a *work*, it must first and foremost become a form of expression. Second, this form of expression must somehow make it possible for the work to be perceptible by human senses. Such perceptibility, however, must be possible with sufficient precision and objectivity. Both concepts—that of *expression* and that of *sufficient precision and objectivity*—should therefore be understood as the latter merely developing the former, rather than as having synonymous meanings.[1364] It is only after these conditions are met in a product that the originality assessment process can commence.

In other words, if a product is to be considered eligible for copyright protection, it must first become a work, which then represents the physical materialization of expression of the author's idea.[1365] It is however worth noting that not every product classified as a *work* can automatically be considered original and therefore eligible for copyright protection. In other words, just because a product is not original, it does not mean it is precluded from acquiring the status of a *work*.[1366] However, if a product is original within the meaning of copyright law, it is presumed to have the status of a work, and if a product with the status of a work is not original, it can still be classified as a work.

The initial theoretical basis for harmonization of the concept of *work* can be traced back to a 1988 Green Paper[1367] that referred to the varying protection of different types of works within the national copyright frameworks of the Member States in the following way:

[1362] Justine Pila, 'The Authorial Works Protectable by Copyright' In: Eleonora Rosati, *The Routledge Handbook of EU Copyright Law* (Routledge 2021), p. 64.

[1363] Ramon C. Vallés, 'The requirement of originality' In: Estelle Derclaye (ed.) *Research handbook on the future of EU copyright* (Edward Elgar Publishing 2009), p. 114.

[1364] Pavel Koukal, 'New Developments in the EU Concept of Copyrighted Works' 20 *Jusletter IT 24. April 2023* (2023), p. 1.

[1365] Andreas Rahmatian, 'European Copyright Inside or Outside the European Union: Pluralism of Copyright Laws and the "Herderian Paradox",' *IIC* 912 (2016), p. 912.

[1366] Rodrigo Bercovitz Rodríguez-Cano & Ignacio Garrote Fernández-Díez, *La unificación del derecho de propiedad intelectual en la Unión Europea* (Tirant lo Blanch 2019), p. 48.

[1367] *Green Paper on Copyright and the Challenge of Technology—Copyright Issues Requiring Immediate Action.* COM (88) 172 final, 7 June 1988.

'Significant differences in the protection available to particular classes of copyright works can clearly fragment the internal market in those works in an undesirable way.'[1368]

Reading between the lines, it becomes apparent that the Commission (of the European Communities) had identified a threat to the internal market that would serve as the justification to initiate a harmonized definition of a *work* in the future.

It seems to confirm that for the purposes of EU copyright law, a work is a form of a creation/product that is already protected by copyright, and therefore original. In respect to this, some have claimed that the notion of an *original work* does represent a single concept, rather two separate notions.[1369] In other words, when referring to a work within the meaning of EU copyright law, one automatically refers to it as being original. It is true that the ways both the concepts of *work* and *originality* have been treated by the CJEU does not always allow for the clear separation of the two.[1370]

In order for there to be an (original) work within the meaning of EU copyright law, the originality-forming creative activity must be applied onto a subject-matter that is, not just capable of receiving and carrying such an intervention by the author, but also a subject-matter within the meaning of Article 2 (1) of the Berne Convention, which must be of a nature perceptible by human senses.[1371] Therefore, a subject-matter eligible for copyright must first be capable of being categorized as a *literary and artistic work* within the meaning of the non-exhaustive list of Article 2 (1) of the Berne Convention, and then also the *author's own intellectual creation* within the meaning of the EU harmonized law. The condition of being a *literary and artistic work* originates directly from the references of EU legislator as well as the CJEU. The EU legislation directs us outside of the EU jurisdiction into the international framework of the Berne Convention. By doing so, it demonstrates the significance of the Berne Convention itself for the copyright framework of the EU. However, some have claimed that the significance demonstrated by the CJEU is more superficial, and that the inspiration for copyrightability is drawn mostly from French copyright doctrine.[1372] This inspiration can be especially seen in the requirement of originality and its conditions.

It is worth noting, however, that the EU copyright framework does not automatically consider all works listed in Article 2 (1) of the Berne Convention as original

[1368] *Ibid.*

[1369] Andreas Rahmatian, 'European Copyright Inside or Outside the European Union: Pluralism of Copyright Laws and the "Herderian Paradox",' *IIC* 912 (2016), p. 912.

[1370] Rodrigo Bercovitz Rodríguez-Cano & Ignacio Garrote Fernández-Díez, *La unificación del derecho de propiedad intelectual en la Unión Europea* (Tirant lo Blanch 2019), p. 47.

[1371] Mireille van Eechoud, 'Along the Road to Uniformity: Diverse Readings of the Court of Justice Judgments on Copyright Work,' 3 *Journal of Intellectual Property, Information Technology and Electronic Commerce Law* 60 (2012), p. 60.

[1372] *Ibid.*

and therefore eligible for copyright protection. In respect to this, such works have the capability of being original or non-original. Photographic products are the prime example of this: to EU copyright framework makes a subsequent differentiation between original and non-original works. Only if a product is the *author's own intellectual creation* can it be provided with copyright protection as a work under the EU framework. This would therefore only prove the aforementioned assumption that if one refers to a work within the meaning of the EU copyright framework, it would automatically be considered to be original, even though the requirements for a work and *originality* are analytically separate.[1373]

As an example, photographic products are in fact listed in Article 2 (1) of the Berne Convention, under the definition of *photographic works to which are assimilated works expressed by a process analogous to photography*. Recital 17 of Term Directive I, now Recital 16 of Term Directive II, limited its applicability only to *photographic works within the meaning of the Berne Convention*. It is through this reference that the first necessary condition of falling under the list of Article 2 (1) of the Berne Convention is met. For the details on meeting the second condition, we must again turn to Recital 16 of Term Directive II. Here, the originality standard is listed and formulated exclusively in connection with photographic products. The Recital reads that in order for a photographic work to be considered original, and therefore eligible for copyright protection, it must be the *author's own intellectual creation reflecting their personality*. This would meet the second of the two prescribed conditions.

Apart from the legislation of the EU, the condition of being original was referred to as a requirement for being a work also by the CJEU itself. In its *Funke Medien*[1374] decision, the CJEU stated that in order for a subject-matter to be regarded as a *work* it must cumulatively meet two conditions. First, it must be the *author's own intellectual creation*, and second, it must be the *reflection of the author's personality*.[1375] However, the jurisprudence of the CJEU has added yet another condition over time, which must be applied to the concept of a work—*sufficient precision and objectivity*.[1376] This condition arose when the subject-matter in question identifiable by the sense of taste was to be delimitated from other works eligible for copyright protection.[1377] The criteria introduced by the CJEU for this delimitation were its identification with *sufficient precision and objectivity*. Therefore, for there to be a work within the meaning of EU copyright law, the subject-matter through which

[1373] Justine Pila, 'The Authorial Works Protectable by Copyright' In: Eleonora Rosati, *The Routledge Handbook of EU Copyright Law* (Routledge 2021), p. 71.

[1374] CJEU, Case C-469/17, *Funke Medien NRW GmbH v Bundesrepublik Deutschland*, 13 Nov. 2018, ECLI:EU:C:2019:623.

[1375] CJEU, Case C-469/17, *Funke Medien NRW GmbH v Bundesrepublik Deutschland*, 13 Nov. 2018, ECLI:EU:C:2019:623, para. 19.

[1376] CJEU, Case C-310/17, *Levola Hengelo BV v Smilde Foods BV*, 13 Nov. 2018, ECLI:EU:C:2018:899.

[1377] Pavel Koukal, 'Reexamining Precision and Objectivity in Copyright Protection for Non-Traditional Creations' 21 *Jusletter IT 24. April 2024* (2024), p. 479.

the work is expressed must be expressed in a manner that makes it identifiable with *sufficient precision and objectivity*, even if that expression is not necessarily in a permanent form.[1378]

The final outcome up to this point of the harmonization conducted by the CJEU in connection with the concept of a *work* eligible for copyright protection is the absolute lack of any freedom of Member States in determining the subject-matter, along with conditions for its copyrightability, whatsoever.[1379] Also, the absence of any reliance of the EU copyright law on categories of works (products) eligible for copyright protection, as well as the focus on the substantive protection requirement of *author's own intellectual creation* makes the harmonized concept of *work* an open one.[1380] Such a wide and open definition of this concept within the meaning of EU law, especially after having been gradually *refined* by the CJEU, is designed to ensure that any kind of subject-matter, regardless of its category or genre, will be assessed individually, equally, and according to the same standards.[1381] In sum, the concept of a *work* has officially became an autonomous concept of EU copyright law. Given this, all Member States are prevented from excluding works explicitly categorized by the EU legislation from copyright protection.[1382]

10.5.2.1 The Concept of an Author's Own Intellectual Creation

Closely connected to the notion of *work*, is the *author's own intellectual creation*. As is evident from the three types of subject-matter officially harmonized via dedicated Directives,[1383] any of such subject-matter requires a component of the *author's own intellectual creation* to be eligible for copyright protection.[1384] When referring to a work within the meaning of EU copyright, it is automatically assumed that such a work is the *own intellectual creation of its author*. This is also supported by the case law of the CJEU, according to which the expression must normally be given an autonomous and uniform interpretation throughout the Community.[1385] Nonetheless, the focus of the CJEU on originality still does not provide us with a comprehensive

---

[1378] CJEU, Case C-310/17, *Levola Hengelo BV v Smilde Foods BV*, 13 Nov. 2018, ECLI:EU:C:2018:899, para. 40.

[1379] Mireille van Eechoud, 'Along the Road to Uniformity: Diverse Readings of the Court of Justice Judgments on Copyright Work,' 3 *Journal of Intellectual Property, Information Technology and Electronic Commerce Law* 60 (2012), p. 60.

[1380] Matthias Leistner, 'Der europäische Werkbegriff,' *Zeitschrift für Geistiges Eigentum* 4 (2013), p. 4.

[1381] Justine Pila & Paul Torremans, *European Intellectual Property Law* (Oxford University Press, 2nd ed. 2019), p. 262.

[1382] Eleonora Rosati, 'Copyright at the CJEU: Back to the Start (of Copyright Protection)' In: Hayleigh Bosher & Eleonora Rosati, *Developments and Directions in Intellectual Property Law: Twenty Years of the IPKat* (Oxford University Press 2023), p. 222.

[1383] Computer programs, photographic products and databases.

[1384] Christian Handig, 'The Copyright Term "Work"—European Harmonisation at an Unknown Level,' 40 *IIC* 665 (2009), p. 665.

[1385] CJEU, Case C-306/05, *Sociedad General de Autores y Editores de España (SGAE) v. Rafael Hoteles SA.*, 7 Dec. 2006, ECLI:EU:C:2006:764, para. 31.

and persuasive definition of what the concept of a *work* really is.[1386] However, it is still given, that whatever subject-matter is eligible for copyright protection based on its qualities of *author's own intellectual creatio*n, it must first be a *work*.[1387] Also, the incorporation of creative freedom into the production process of a particular product usually means such creation will be considered an intellectual creation.[1388]

As already stated, EU legislator officially set the requirement for copyright protection—that of an *author's own intellectual creation* only for three types of subject-matter—computer programs, photographic products, and databases. We can therefore ask whether this requirement should also be applied to other subject-matter, or whether the EU legislator only intended to lower the requirements by harmonization for these three specific subject-matters. The answer can be found in the jurisprudence of the CJEU and its references to Article 6 of Term Directives. Demands by the CJEU for the uniform definition of a concept of *work* within the copyright framework of the EU have always been based on Article 6 of Term Directives.[1389] This could in fact mean that the harmonized *lowered* requirements are also intended to be applied also to other subject-matter outside of the three specified in the corresponding Directives.

Therefore, since we still lack a legislatively codified uniform definition of a *work*, we must turn to the jurisprudence of the CJEU. Through a string of case law, a definition of *author's own intellectual creation* emerged as a uniform requirement applicable to copyrightable products. Therefore, the CJEU has taken upon itself the formulation of a uniform concept of a *work* that would be applicable to all types of works, regardless of their classification, across the whole copyright framework of the EU.[1390] The concept can be seen as universal as possible in order to eliminate the previous reliance on set categories of works in national copyright acts. In respect to this, the CJEU has not limited itself by adhering to explicitly harmonized types of works, even though photographic products are among these.[1391]

10.5.2.2 The Concept and Requirement of Originality in the Copyright Framework of the EU

Regardless of the legal system and its corresponding copyright framework, originality constitutes a condition, in a form of a prerequisite for copyright protection, in

[1386] Mireille van Eechoud, 'Adapting the Work' In: Mireille van Eechoud, Jostein Gripsrud & Lionel Bently, *Work of Authorship* (Amsterdam University Press 2015), p. 162.

[1387] Eleonora Rosati, *Copyright and the Court of Justice of the European Union* (Oxford University Press, 2019), p. 91.

[1388] Lionel Bently et al., *Intellectual Property Law* (Oxford University Press, 6th ed 2022), p. 109.

[1389] Melanie Overbeck, *Der Lichtbildschutz gem. § 72 UrhG im Lichte der Digitalfotografie* (Lit 2018), p. 119.

[1390] Haimo Schack, Urheber- und Urhebervertragsrecht (Mohr Siebeck, 10th ed 2021), p. 107.

[1391] Artur-Axel Wandtke, Winfried Bullinger & Michael Bohne, *Praxiskommentar Urheberrecht: UrhG, UrhDaG, VGG, InsO, UKlaG, KUG, EVtr, InfoSoc-RL, Portabilitäts-VO* (C.H. Beck, 6th ed. 2022), p. 51.

all of them.[1392] The 2004 Commission staff working paper in the field of copyright referred to originality and its function in the copyright law in the following way:

'The notion of originality is one of the key concepts in copyright law and forms part of the underlying justification for the statutory system of copyright protection for authors. Originality corresponds to the independent creativity of the author as reflected in his or her literary or artistic creation'.[1393]

Prior to the harmonization of the originality standard, various national understandings in Member States provided for different solutions and requirements for its assessment in products. In particular, it was *how* products were assessed that formed the applicable originality standard.[1394] Traditionally, the general premise of the originality requirement does not lie in the statistical originality of a product, meaning such product must have never been produced before, but rather in the reflection of a certain level of creativity in the product itself.[1395] Within this meaning, originality must be seen as based on the notion of *origination*.[1396] Such origination must, however, lead back to the author of the product. It can be also said that originality refers to the original nature of the relationship between the author and their creation.

In terms of EU legislation, the conditions for meeting the originality standard were formulated for the three subject-matter as being their *author's own intellectual creation*, with no other criteria applicable to determine their eligibility for copyright protection. On the other hand, the Term Directives also stated that being original means being the *author's own intellectual creation*, while adding the addition of *reflecting his personality*. This would somehow suggest the originality requirement for photographic products is different, stricter, than those of the two other subject-matter.[1397]

The slight differences and variations between the three formulations can be attributed to the gradual refinement of the requirement, as well as less precision of the EU legislator.[1398] Nonetheless, any differences were found to be irrelevant for harmonization conducted by the CJEU in its later case law. This was achieved by a uni-

---

1392 Irini A. Stamatoudi, 'Originality under EU Copyright Law' In: Paul Torremans, *Research Handbook on Copyright Law* (Edward Elgar Publishing 2017), p. 57.

1393 *Commission Staff Working Paper on the Review of the EC legal framework in the field of copyright and related rights*, SEC(2004) 995, 19 Jul. 2004.

1394 Irini A. Stamatoudi, 'Originality under EU Copyright Law' In: Paul Torremans, *Research Handbook on Copyright Law* (Edward Elgar Publishing 2017), p. 57.

1395 Morten Rosenmeier, Kacper Szkalej & Sanna Wolk, *EU Copyright Law: Subsistence, Exploitation and Protection of Rights* (Kluwer Law International 2019), p. 42.

1396 Aurelija Lukoševičienė, 'On Author, Copyright and Originality: Does the Unified EU Originality Standard Correspond to the Digital Reality in Wikipedia?' 11 *Masaryk University Journal of Law and Technology* 215 (2017), p. 215.

1397 Gunnar W. G. Karnell, 'European Originality: A Copyright Chimera,' *Intellectual Property* 73 (2002), p. 73.

1398 Christian Handig, 'Durch "freie kreative Entscheidungen" zum europäischen urheberrechtlichen Werkbegriff,' *GRUR Int.* 965 (2012), p. 973.

form interpretation approach chosen by the CJEU, which accomplished that such inconsistencies were overcome. It was therefore CJEU jurisprudence that ensured the gradual extension of the said formulated requirement to other subject-matter.[1399]

The wording used also reveals the intention of the EU legislator with respect to photographic products to adhere to the stricter test of originality of the continental EU, which required a *personal expression* and not just *own intellectual creation.*[1400] The insistence on the presence of the additional feature, on top of the *author's own intellectual creation*, in a form of a *reflection of author's personality*, might suggest the intention of the EU legislator to adhere to the distinguishing between original photographic products (works) and simple photographic products, applied within several Member States.[1401] This additional feature in a form of a required presence of personality can be seen as a *final touch* of the personal approach of the continental Member States.[1402] Requiring the presence of the reflection of *author's personality* would exclude such *simple* photographic products or *other photographs* from the scope of Term Directive II, and copyrightability in general.

Such an approach originates from the continental part of the EU, the *droit d'auteur* Member States, and is the manifestation of how copyright protection was originally, and is still, provided on the basis of fairness, rather than usefulness.[1403] This approach proves that the orientation of such copyright frameworks is creator (person)-oriented. According to this approach, the focus of originality on authors and their personality is an evident outcome. Originality can be seen as evidence and materialization of authorship and also, at the same time, justification of eligibility for copyright protection of a product authored accordingly.[1404] This authorship, however, must materialize in a way and form that makes it sufficiently recognizable for the purposes of copyright law. Otherwise, the eligibility of a product for copyright protection based on its originality would not be possible.

This standard implies that in order to assess a product for the purposes of its originality, its author and the subjective choices they employ must be known.[1405] The need to identify the author and link them to their created product stems from the requirement of the *author's own intellectual creation*. The need to identify the em-

[1399] Morten Rosenmeier, Kacper Szkalej & Sanna Wolk, *EU Copyright Law: Subsistence, Exploitation and Protection of Rights* (Kluwer Law International 2019), p. 43.

[1400] Mireille van Eechoud, 'Object, Subject, and Duration of Protection' In: Mireille van Eechoud (ed.) *Harmonizing European Copyright Law: The Challenges of Better Lawmaking* (Kluwer Law International 2009), p. 41.

[1401] *Ibid.*

[1402] Herman Cohen Jehoram, 'The EC Copyright Directives, Economics and Authors' Rights,' *IIC* 821 (1994), p. 821.

[1403] Ramon C. Vallés, 'The requirement of originality' In: Estelle Derclaye (ed.) *Research handbook on the future of EU copyright* (Edward Elgar Publishing 2009), p. 109.

[1404] Ramon C. Vallés, 'The requirement of originality' In: Estelle Derclaye (ed.) *Research handbook on the future of EU copyright* (Edward Elgar Publishing 2009), p. 102.

[1405] Stef van Gompel, 'Creativity, Autonomy, and Personal Touch' In: Mireille van Eechoud, Jostein Gripsrud & Lionel Bently, *Work of Authorship* (Amsterdam University Press 2015), p. 128.

ployed subjective choices stems from the *reflection of personality*, because it is only through such choices that the author can stamp their personality onto the product. Nonetheless, the need to identify the author might also stem from the fact that only the author themselves can provide proper information regarding the production process and its particularities in general. In this respect, the originality requirement, as harmonized, is dependent on the act of the author, which must be of intellectual origin, thus highlighting the nature of copyright as an author's right.[1406] As already stated, the originality therefore essentially puts emphasis on the need for the existence of the said causal link between the author and their creation—the work.

The originality test through which the originality is to be determined, fulfils two roles. The first is to determine whether a product has the necessary qualities to be eligible for copyright, while the second determines the scope of actual protection.[1407] The former focuses on the fulfilment of the criterion of being an original intellectual creation, since the quality of being a mere intellectual creation does not necessarily imply originality. The latter then determines the extent of protection of the product, based on the amount of accumulated originality therein. Here too, the principle of *more displayed creativity equals more protection* is applicable, for example, in cases of infringements. As already stated, the extent of originality does not have any impact on its eligibility for copyright protection as such, since the product is either original or not. However, the amount of originality may determine the extent of protection against potential infringements.

The vagueness of the harmonized originality standard can be seen as both a curse and a blessing. If one sees the open and wide possibilities of copyright protection of various subject-matter as a positive feature, it is indeed a blessing. However, if one sees the ambiguity and openness to interpretation by national courts of Member States as a negative feature, it is indeed a curse. This vagueness has allowed originality to be referred to by some as nothing and everything at the same time; while individuals trying to assess and define *originality* oscillate all over this spectrum.[1408] Nonetheless, the requirement of originality, along with the nature of the test through which it is to be determined, ensures that if the assessed product is to be copyrighted, it will be done so based on the existence of a sufficient causal connection between the assessed product and its author.[1409]

[1406] Justine Pila, 'The Authorial Works Protectable by Copyright' In: Eleonora Rosati, *The Routledge Handbook of EU Copyright Law* (Routledge 2021), p. 74.

[1407] Mireille van Eechoud, 'Object, Subject, and Duration of Protection' In: Mireille van Eechoud (ed.) *Harmonizing European Copyright Law: The Challenges of Better Lawmaking* (Kluwer Law International 2009), p. 42.

[1408] John Vignaux Smyth, 'Originality in the Enlightenment and Beyond' In: Richard McGinnis, *Originality and Intellectual Property in the French and English Enlightenment* (Routledge 2009), p. 175.

[1409] Justine Pila, 'The Authorial Works Protectable by Copyright' In: Eleonora Rosati, *The Routledge Handbook of EU Copyright Law* (Routledge 2021), p. 74.

10.5.2.3 The Importance and Justification of Granting Protection via Originality

The construction of the originality standard and its focus on authors themselves, especially their personality, is capable of offering insights into how EU legislator, as well as the CJEU, have envisaged the relationship of authors vis-à-vis the rest of EU society. In such a setting, the author is being perceived as stationed at the centre, along with their ability to perform *free and creative choices* and stamping their personality on a product.[1410] The InfoSoc Directive, first and foremost, emphasized the high level of protection of an intellectual creation. According to the InfoSoc Directive, this high level of protection helps ensure the maintenance and development of creativity in the interests of authors,[1411] the continuation of creative and artistic work of authors through securing appropriate rewards,[1412] and to safeguard the independence and dignity of artistic creators.[1413]

This means that the creation (product) of the author—the original work as such—does not have to be of any practical use to EU society. This clearly demonstrates the different position in understanding the nature of a subject-matter, especially the irrelevance of its utilitarian nature. The EU copyright system is therefore clearly author oriented, with an emphasis on ensuring the existence of such conditions, which allow the existence of authors themselves as well as the continuation of their artistic and creative activities.

10.5.3 Conditions Excluded from the Assessment of Originality

The legislation of the EU also formulated what must be excluded from the originality assessment process; in other words, some *criteria applied to determine the eligibility for protection* must be avoided. These include tests as to the qualitative or aesthetic merits;[1414] aesthetic or qualitative criteria;[1415] or other criteria such as merit or purpose.[1416] However, apart from their enumeration, EU legislation does not provide any definitions of these excluded criteria. Nonetheless, it is clear that regardless of whatever criteria a court may want to apply, to determine the originality of a product, it must only be the *author's own intellectual creation* and nothing else.

[1410] Aurelija Lukoševičienė, 'On Author, Copyright and Originality: Does the Unified EU Originality Standard Correspond to the Digital Reality in Wikipedia?' 11 *Masaryk University Journal of Law and Technology* 215 (2017), p. 215.
[1411] Recital 9 of the InfoSoc Directive.
[1412] Recital 10 of the InfoSoc Directive.
[1413] Recital 11 of the InfoSoc Directive.
[1414] Recital 8 of the Software Directive.
[1415] Recital 16 of the Database Directive.
[1416] Recital 16 of the Term Directive II.

However, the different wording might still indicate that the excluded conditions might be interpreted differently, depending on the subject-matter in question and the corresponding Directive.

In practice, however, the prescribed exclusion of aesthetic, qualitative, merit-based or purpose-related criteria from the originality assessment process might be difficult to adhere to by national courts, especially in connection with products residing at the lower spectrum of originality.[1417] As *Eleonora Rosati* put it, jurisprudence of the CJEU affirming the exclusion of the criteria related to the aesthetic or artistic value has been acknowledged as well as refused by national courts of the Member States.[1418] When in doubt, especially in cases where the originality of the assessed product is not immediately and easily evident, national courts might resort to applying the excluded criteria as an aid to base their decision on. This could prove to be an easier approach for most courts. However, the excluded criteria might also lead to a refusal of copyrightability, if the courts focus on their presence, rather than on the presence of originality as such.

10.5.4 Conditions Irrelevant for the Assessment of Originality

10.5.4.1 Formalities

Both EU legislation and CJEU jurisprudence adhere to the principle stipulated in Article 5 (2) of the Berne Convention, which prohibits the subjection of enjoyment of author's rights in regard to their works to any formalities. Therefore, if a product meets the prescribed criteria, it is eligible for copyright at the moment of its creation.[1419] No additional formalities, such as registration with governmental or any other authorities, or the payment of a deposit or any kind of fees, are required.

10.5.4.2 Fixation requirement

The Berne Convention leaves the so-called *fixation requirement* at the discretion of its contracting parties, including all Member States. The continental Member States have traditionally not implemented this requirement into their national copyright frameworks.[1420] This traditional approach has been upheld in all Directives and was

1417 Stef van Gompel & Erlend Lavik, 'Quality, merit, aesthetics and purpose: An inquiry into EU copyright law's eschewal of other criteria than originality,' *RIDA* 100 (2013), p. 100.

1418 Eleonora Rosati, *Copyright and the Court of Justice of the European Union* (Oxford University Press, 2nd ed. 2023), p. 149.

1419 Morten Rosenmeier, Kacper Szkalej & Sanna Wolk, *EU Copyright Law: Subsistence, Exploitation and Protection of Rights* (Kluwer Law International 2019), p. 42.

1420 Antoine Latreille, 'From Idea to Fixation: A View of Protected Works' In: Estelle Derclaye, *Research Handbook on the Future of EU Copyright* (Edward Elgar Publishing 2009), p. 133.

later confirmed and harmonized by the jurisprudence of the CJEU.[1421] Nonetheless in reality, fixation proves the product actually exists.[1422] Fixation does indeed facilitate the existence of a product, proof of its eligibility for copyright protection and, last but not least, proof in case of infringement. Although not officially required, most products are fixed, and dependent on their existence for a certain type of carrier.

10.5.4.3 Novelty

Novelty is a requirement employable for the purposes of industrial property law, but not copyright. In respect to this, the importance of novelty as a requirement or determinant of the eligibility of a product for copyright protection is irrelevant, and the lack of novelty in a product may not be taken into account. *Novelty* most often refers to the transformation of an idea into a solution for a technical issue, whereas *originality* refers to creativity of an expression[1423] If one looks for novelty, the assessed product must be compared to what is already known. If one looks for originality, only the expression of a product must be assessed. For example, when comparing two photographic products of a portrait genre, these would not necessarily be novel, but certainly could be found to be eligible for copyright protection based on the originality of the way they are expressed. Therefore, the threshold for novelty is higher than that for originality. Nonetheless, the two requirements continue to cause confusion.

Also, if a product is novel in the sense that it is different or not identical to what was already known, it will most likely also be original as an *author's own intellectual creation reflecting their personality*.[1424] However, a product can also be original within the said meaning and still not be novel. Nonetheless, originality itself does imply a certain novelty of the product. It is for this reason that distinguishing between the two criteria must be made carefully.

1421 CJEU, Case C-310/17, *Levola Hengelo BV v Smilde Foods BV*, 13 Nov. 2018, ECLI:EU:C:2018:899, para. 40.

1422 Antoine Latreille, 'From Idea to Fixation: A View of Protected Works' In: Estelle Derclaye, *Research Handbook on the Future of EU Copyright* (Edward Elgar Publishing 2009), p. 140.

1423 Irini A. Stamatoudi, 'Originality under EU Copyright Law' In: Paul Torremans, *Research Handbook on Copyright Law* (Edward Elgar Publishing 2017), p. 57.

1424 Alain Strowel, *Le droit d'auteur européen en transition numérique: de ses origines à l'unification européenne et aux défis de l'intelligence artificielle et des Big Data* (Larcier 2022), p. 80.

10.6 Basic Principles Applicable to Subject-Matter Eligible for Copyright Protection Within the Copyright Framework of the EU

10.6.1 The Idea/Expression Dichotomy; Expression and Form

If the threshold for protectability of products by copyright based on the requirement of originality is harmonized and uniform, the boundary between ideas ineligible for copyright protection and the way they are expressed must be harmonized as well.[1425] It is a given that if a product aspires to be eligible for copyright protection, the idea must first be expressed, which allows it to be accessible to third parties through their perception, apart from the author themselves.[1426] This requires that a product takes on a form or a mode, which allows the formation of an object that is, figuratively speaking, graspable by human perception. In other words, the product must become *real*. We can therefore state that copyright does not protect mere ideas, but only their expressions. In other words, abstract parts of a product cannot be eligible for copyright protection, which rather focuses on the way these parts were expressed.[1427] The expression of a product itself guarantees that the product itself (the creation) is, figuratively speaking, aimed at human intellect.[1428] In respect to this, the expression allows the product to be perceived and enjoyed by the senses of another human being.

As mentioned above, the expression must take a certain form. Only a form that is developed and original can be eligible for copyright protection.[1429]

[1425] Christian Handig, 'Durch "freie kreative Entscheidungen" zum europäischen urheberrechtlichen Werkbegriff,' *GRUR Int.* 965 (2012), p. 973.

[1426] Antoine Latreille, 'From Idea to Fixation: A View of Protected Works' In: Estelle Derclaye, *Research Handbook on the Future of EU Copyright* (Edward Elgar Publishing 2009), p. 133.

[1427] Morten Rosenmeier, Kacper Szkalej & Sanna Wolk, *EU Copyright Law: Subsistence, Exploitation and Protection of Rights* (Kluwer Law International 2019), p. 42.

[1428] Antoine Latreille, 'From Idea to Fixation: A View of Protected Works' In: Estelle Derclaye, *Research Handbook on the Future of EU Copyright* (Edward Elgar Publishing 2009), p. 134.

[1429] Antoine Latreille, 'From Idea to Fixation: A View of Protected Works' In: Estelle Derclaye, *Research Handbook on the Future of EU Copyright* (Edward Elgar Publishing 2009), p. 135.

10.6.2 Free and Creative Choices, Creativity, and Creative Freedom

First and foremost, any choice made by the author throughout the production process of a product must be of a free (voluntary) nature. If the choice is of a free nature, it means the author has the discretion and the ability to associate and tie the choice to their intention to create and accordingly further adjust the nature of such choice. It is therefore only when a choice is of free and creative nature that it can become associated with a product eligible for copyright protection.[1430] However, it is equally important that the said choices of free and creative nature be made in a suitable environment. The available room for creative freedom itself has also been referred to as *Spielraum* (room to play) or *room to manoeuvre* (leeway).[1431] The nature of the choices and the environment must complement each other in their free, unrestricted, nature.

However, what is important in practice, is not to only focus on the determination of the actual creative freedom available, but also to what extent has the author exploited it, as well as to what extent the author has been restricted in their creative conduct within the available creative freedom.[1432] The availability of creative freedom as such does not ensure that the production process conducted under such conditions will automatically result in an *author's own intellectual creation.* The creative freedom only lays down suitable conditions for further exploitation by the author. The exploitation itself must be then made through the *free and creative choices*. Of course, these *free and creative choices* must not be restricted. In other words, the CJEU highlights both the available margin to manoeuvre, (which provides the opportunity to exercise *free and creative choices*), but also the free and creative choices themselves that originate from this environment.[1433]

The assessment based on the existence of *free and creative choices*, and their employment by the author throughout the production process of a product can be considered author-oriented. The originality standard based on such assessment is set at a relatively low level. If the level of the current originality standard was raised above the *author's own intellectual creation* and *stamp of personality*, which are both dependent on the exercise of *free and creative choices*, the core of the assessment process would likely shift towards a *higher* evaluation of novelty, aesthetics,

[1430] Philippe Gaudrat, 'Réflexions sur la forme des œuvres de l'esprit' In: Pierre Sirinelli et al. *Propriétés intellectuelles : mélanges en l'honneur de André Françon* (Dalloz 1995), p. 205.

[1431] Alain Strowel, *Le droit d'auteur européen en transition numérique: de ses origines à l'unification européenne et aux défis de l'intelligence artificielle et des Big Data* (Larcier 2022), p. 72

[1432] Stef van Gompel, 'Creativity, Autonomy, and Personal Touch' In: Mireille van Eechoud, Jostein Gripsrud & Lionel Bently, *Work of Authorship* (Amsterdam University Press 2015), p. 106.

[1433] Véronique Dahan & Charles Bouffier, 'Arrêt Painer du 1er décembre 2011 : la CJUE poursuit son œuvre d'harmonisation du droit d'auteur,' 80 *Revue Lamy Droit de l'immatériel* 14 (2012). p. 14.

and merit.[1434] It is for this reason that novelty, aesthetics, and merit are irrelevant for the purposes of copyrightability.

The free nature of choices suggests the existence of autonomy on the author's end is required. If one is not autonomous in their decisions and conduct, they cannot make choices of a free nature. The author must be able to maintain control over their self-expression, without which no autonomy is possible.[1435] Therefore, free actions must always be based on an author's authentic self. This means that these must come from them and be their own. The very same is applicable to one's creative freedom. Here, the stamp of one's personality on their own intellectual creation is conditioned by the free and creative exercise of available choices. In other words, only a free personality can create a product which reflects that personality. It is for this reason that the EU excludes products whose production process is dictated by technical or functional considerations[1436] or rules or constraints that leave no room for creative freedom.[1437] Examples in practice may entail situations in which the production process is bound by know-how, rules, standardization, etc. Therefore, if the creative freedom of the author is restricted, the resulting (restricted) activities of the author cannot give rise to an original product within the meaning of the EU copyright law. In such cases, the product is not eligible for copyright protection because the expression they offer to the potential audience is a mere useful characterizing of an objective reality, lacking any expression of the personality of their creator.[1438] In respect to this, all requirements and individual components of the originality standard are interconnected in their sequence. Therefore, the existence of each component is presupposed by the existence of another, previous, component or a condition. In other words, one component cannot exist without the previous existence of the preceding one, thus creating a figurative chain of dependence.

For photographic products, the technical, chemical, and electronic nature of the production process can be viewed as a constraint in itself, limiting the author's possibilities to make *free and creative choices*. However, such nature of the process can only be viewed as a necessary constraint, and only to a certain extent. The necessity of the constraint is predetermined by the very nature of the photographic process itself, and the amount of extent as a foundation of a bare minimum on which the employment and the use of the medium of photography can be based. Mastering the basic rules and nature of a photographic process only serves as a prerequisite for its further use. From this, we can deduce that only those who have learned to use and

1434 Stef van Gompel, 'Creativity, Autonomy, and Personal Touch' In: Mireille van Eechoud, Jostein Gripsrud & Lionel Bently, *Work of Authorship* (Amsterdam University Press 2015), p. 104.

1435 Christian Gero Stallberg, *Urheberrecht und moralische Rechtfertigung* (Duncker & Humblot 2006), p. 153.

1436 CJEU, Case C-393/09, *Bezpečnostní softwarová asociace – Svaz softwarové ochrany v Ministerstvo kultury*, 22 Dec. 2010, ECLI:EU:C:2010:816.

1437 CJEU, Case C-604/10, *Football Dataco Ltd and Others v Yahoo! UK Ltd and Others*, 1 Mar. 2012, ECLI:EU:C:2012:115.

1438 Philippe Gaudrat, 'Réflexions sur la forme des œuvres de l'esprit' In: Pierre Sirinelli et al. *Propriétés intellectuelles : mélanges en l'honneur de André Françon* (Dalloz 1995), p. 214.

operate the technology of photography according to its general and standard rules are able to introduce, develop, and employ deviations from those rules, including those of free and creative nature.[1439] It is these deviations, through the made *free and creative choices*, that give rise to the existence of originality in a photographic product.

However, it must be also highlighted that the fact an individual, assuming the role of the author, is highly skilled in their trade and masters its essential requirements, as well as any possible peculiarities, does not by itself ensure that a product produced in such a way would be eligible for copyright protection. Such approach, also confirmed by the CJEU, is a clear diversion from the EU non-continental (common law) understanding of copyright protection.[1440] In other words, the photographer cannot merely master the photographic trade itself, but must necessarily go beyond it if they wish to produce an original photographic product.

Using a speech as an example, *Stallberg* (quoted by *Helmut Haberstumpf*) argued that such deviations can be characterized in the following way:

> *'The concept of the intellectual work then encompasses those acts that partly elude the previous rules of the linguistic community, but nevertheless follow those rules to the extent that they are necessary to preserve the possibility of being considered a speech act at all. At the same time, this preserves the ability to connect to the new language rule that is implicitly opened up by the speaker breaking the rule.'*[1441]

Analogously, for a product to be recognized as a photographic work or a work produced by a process similar, it must be produced by a process that makes it recognizable as such. This production process has its minimal technical and other requirements, such as the use of radiant energy to form the image. If these minimal requirements were not met, we could not speak of a *photographic product* within the meaning of copyright law. Such requirements or rules must be followed to preserve the nature of a photographic product that allows it to be assimilated with other photographic products belonging to the said category. It is only when the said minimal conditions are met, and the rules followed to a minimal extent, the author can begin the deviation process by employing *free and creative choices* that might result in the production of their own intellectual creation displaying their personality.

Within this context it must be repeatedly highlighted, that not every deviation from the requirements and rules necessarily results in the production of a product,

[1439] Helmut Haberstumpf, 'Der europäische Werkbegriff und die Lehre vom Gestaltungsspielraum,' *GRUR* 1249 (2021), p. 1249.

[1440] Christian Handig, 'Durch "freie kreative Entscheidungen" zum europäischen urheberrechtlichen Werkbegriff,' *GRUR Int.* 965 (2012), p. 973.

[1441] Helmut Haberstumpf, 'Der europäische Werkbegriff und die Lehre vom Gestaltungsspielraum,' *GRUR* 1249 (2021), p. 1249.

which is associated with effects within the meaning of copyright law.[1442] In other words, any deviation must consist of the employment of *free and creative choices* that result in the alteration of a product, which is the *author's own intellectual creation* and that, with the result of a reflection of their personality.

It must be also noted, however, that the *deviation* does not have to be particularly extensive.[1443] For the purposes of copyright law, even minimal deviation from the standard processes and rules is sufficient for a finding of originality. In practice, this is confirmed by the existence of *small coin/change* subject-matter and its established copyrightability. However, the greater the deviation is, the more wholesome the protection and resistance of a product against possible infringement. Therefore, what suffices for the protection of a product by copyright might not suffice for the protection of the whole product against infringement.

The assessment process based on the creative freedom enables the identification of restraints, limitations, or rules of the production process from which the assessed product originated.[1444] Such restrictive elements predetermine the conduct of the author and allow them to only perform within the room provided and limited as such. As a result, authors are not able to make other interventions than those allowed. In such scenarios, the qualities of the resulting (unoriginal) product are predetermined.[1445] *Helmut Haberstumpf* quoted *Ludwig Wittgenstein's* comparison of following of rules and instructions to obeying an order—when a person always reacts in a certain trained way.[1446] In this analogy, obedience is naturally devoid of any free will and choice. Nonetheless, it must be noted that the existence of the rules themselves does not preclude the production of an original product.[1447] It is only by following them throughout the production process that has that effect.

The CJEU also established that for a certain type of a product to be successfully produced, a certain type of environment must be created or available. Also, if one wishes to produce a product eligible for copyright protection, certain additional conditions must be met. However, what must be also taken into consideration, is that not every product is produced solely for the authors themselves, but also for other people, their clients. The production process of such products might fall under expectations of the client stipulated in connection with the expected qualities the final product is to possess. The dependence of the final qualities of a product on the production environment, conditions, requirements, and instructions, in its own way functionally resembles rules, which are identified as constraints on the author's *free*

[1442] Helmut Haberstumpf, 'Der europäische Werkbegriff und die Lehre vom Gestaltungsspielraum,' *GRUR* 1249 (2021), p. 1249.

[1443] *Ibid.*

[1444] *Ibid.*

[1445] Rodrigo Bercovitz Rodríguez-Cano & Ignacio Garrote Fernández-Díez, *La unificación del derecho de propiedad intelectual en la Unión Europea* (Tirant lo Blanch 2019), p. 69.

[1446] Helmut Haberstumpf, 'Der europäische Werkbegriff und die Lehre vom Gestaltungsspielraum,' *GRUR* 1249 (2021), p. 1249.

[1447] Christian Handig, 'Durch "freie kreative Entscheidungen" zum europäischen urheberrechtlichen Werkbegriff,' *GRUR Int.* 965 (2012), p. 973.

and creative choices.[1448] This is also true for photographic products. Therefore, any assessment must not limit itself to identifying and analysing rules as such, but also all possible constraints, whatever their mode, structure, or form might be.

Given the reliance of the CJEU on the expenditure of *free and creative choices* by the author, products of obvious or trivial nature are excluded from the copyright protection based on their insufficient level of originality.[1449] It is reasonable to assert that if one willingly employs *free and creative choices* in the creation process, the outcome of such process must possess at least minimal manifestations of originality. However, a choice can be considered *creative* even when it is not *artistic*.[1450] As a result of this, the CJEU has rather focused on choices that alter the form of the work and only additionally on their *free and creative* nature.

10.6.3 The Harmonized Standard of Originality

The string of case law of the CJEU selected above is united by one common thread—the *author's own intellectual creation*. This notion itself is understood as consisting of *creative freedom*,[1451] *free and creative choices*[1452] and *personal touch*.[1453] In addition, the later case law of the CJEU added two more additional components. The fourth concerned being *perceivable with sufficient precision and objectivity*,[1454] and the fifth dealt with the *exclusion of functional elements*.[1455]

The CJEU case law suggests that Member States are precluded from applying any other standard of originality than that formulated by the CJEU itself.[1456] In other words, Member States are bound to apply the formulated originality standard horizontally, meaning to all products. Therefore, national courts must make a finding of originality in products by applying the CJEU's guidance, either as direct instructions or tests derived from its case law; this originality appears to be the sole requirement

[1448] *Ibid.*

[1449] Stef van Gompel, 'Creativity, Autonomy, and Personal Touch' In: Mireille van Eechoud, Jostein Gripsrud & Lionel Bently, *Work of Authorship* (Amsterdam University Press 2015), p. 100.

[1450] Lionel Bently et al., *Intellectual Property Law* (Oxford University Press, 6th ed 2022), p. 109.

[1451] CJEU, Case C-403/08, *Football Association Premier League Ltd and Others v QC Leisure and Others*, Case C-429/08, *Karen Murphy v Media Protection Services Ltd.*, 4 Oct. 2011, ECLI:EU:C:2011:631.

[1452] CJEU, Case C-604/10, *Football Dataco Ltd and Others v Yahoo! UK Ltd and Others*, 1 Mar. 2012, ECLI:EU:C:2012:115.

[1453] CJEU, Case C-145/10, *Eva-Maria Painer v Standard VerlagsGmbH and Others*, 1 Dec. 2011, ECLI:EU:C:2011:798.

[1454] CJEU, Case C-310/17, *Levola Hengelo BV v Smilde Foods BV*, 13 Nov. 2018, ECLI:EU:C:2018:899.

[1455] CJEU, Case C-833/18, *SI and Brompton Bicycle Ltd v Chedech / Get2Get*, 11 Jun. 2020, ECLI:EU:C:2020:461.

[1456] Eleonora Rosati, 'Copyright at the CJEU: Back to the Start (of Copyright Protection)' In: Hayleigh Bosher & Eleonora Rosati, *Developments and Directions in Intellectual Property Law: Twenty Years of the IPKat* (Oxford University Press 2023), p. 220.

qualifying a product for copyright protection as a work.[1457] The originality standard as formulated by the CJEU allows, if not even invites, national courts to protect even banal or trivial products by copyright by finding them *original*.[1458] Such effects of the harmonized originality standard might be seen as problematic, due to the overly lowered threshold, and at the same time widened scope of application.

10.7 The Harmonized Originality Assessment Test

Following the jurisprudence of the CJEU on the matter, the question of whether a product satisfies the requirement of being an *author's own intellectual creation* requires an assessment process consisting of two steps. The first step entails determining whether the assessed product is of such a nature that it creates room for the application of *free and creative choices*.[1459] It is only possible to move on to the second step if the question asked in the first one receives a positive answer. The second step then entails assessing the extent which the author took advantage of the available *free and creative choices* and exploited them in such a manner that the product bears their personal mark (an imprint of it).[1460] In other words, the person conducting the assessment must first establish whether they are in the presence of a product capable of being creatively modified, and if they are, then they must assess the extent of such creative modification and the mark it has left on the product.

Both steps are used to filter out original and non-original subject-matter. The first step of the test allows for the exclusion of *subject-matter incapable* of being altered in a way, with which the copyright law associates the effects of being protected by it.[1461] Such a subject-matter is incapable of carrying originality due to their very nature. The second step of the test allows for the exclusion of a subject-matter that offered scope for originality, but was not sufficiently altered by the author's steps of *free and creative nature*.[1462] Here, the subject-matter would be capable of carrying originality, but the author's conduct in connection with the production process was not of a nature that copyright law associates with the effects of originality. In other words, the author's conduct resulted in an absence of any imprint of their personality.

1457 Eleonora Rosati, *Originality in EU Copyright: Full Harmonization through Case Law* (Edward Elgar Publishing 2013), p. 188.

1458 Justine Pila, 'The Authorial Works Protectable by Copyright' In: Eleonora Rosati, *The Routledge Handbook of EU Copyright Law* (Routledge 2021), p. 75.

1459 Justine Pila & Paul Torremans, *European Intellectual Property Law* (Oxford University Press, 2nd ed. 2019), p. 252.

1460 *Ibid.*

1461 Justine Pila, 'The Authorial Works Protectable by Copyright' In: Eleonora Rosati, *The Routledge Handbook of EU Copyright Law* (Routledge 2021), p. 71.

1462 *Ibid.*

This two-step test is devised in such a way that only a few types of subject-matter, will fail to pass it with the outcome of not being eligible for copyright protection.[1463] Apart from ideas, the CJEU has excluded individual words and other building blocks of expression, sporting events, and works the expressive form of which is determined exclusively or predominantly by their nature, or purpose and tastes. However, it must be emphasized again that the exclusion of tastes from copyright protection was only done on the basis of the current state of scientific development, since this does not (currently) allow for their precise and objective identification.[1464] In respect to this, the exclusion of tastes might be considered only temporary, until the development in the field allows for the requirements stipulated by the CJEU to be met.

The originality of a product itself can also be determined by a four-step test, according to *Husovec*.[1465] The first step consists of isolating the functional elements of a work in which the idea and its expression coincide due to the narrow room they provide for realization of the idea.[1466] The second step consists of assessing the level of originality of a work's constituent parts that provide room for the author's *free and creative choices*.[1467] The third step consists of assessing the level of room for creativity and the extent of its exploitation by the author.[1468] The fourth and the final step consists of assessing the existence of the author's stamp of *personal touch* in the work.[1469]

10.8 Applying the Harmonized Originality Standard and Assessment Test to Photographic Products

The following pages outline the conditions a photographic product must meet for it to be eligible for protection within the copyright framework of the EU. This outline will be followed by an assessment test designed to show whether the existence of the relevant prescribed conditions can be confirmed or refuted. The objective of this test is to facilitate decisions regarding the eligibility of the assessed photographic product for copyright protection as a photographic work.

1463 Justine Pila & Paul Torremans, *European Intellectual Property Law* (Oxford University Press, 2nd ed. 2019), p. 252.

1464 CJEU, Case C-310/17, *Levola Hengelo BV v Smilde Foods BV*, 13 Nov. 2018, ECLI:EU:C:2018:899, para. 43.

1465 Martin Husovec, 'Judikatórna harmonizácia pojmu autorského diela v únijnom práve,' 12 *Bulletin slovenskej advokácie* (2012), p. 18.

1466 *Ibid.*

1467 *Ibid.*

1468 *Ibid.*

1469 *Ibid.*

10.8.1 Initial Conditions Prescribed by EU Legislation

Within the meaning of Term Directive II, a photographic product is eligible for copyright protection if it meets the condition of being a photographic work within the meaning of the Berne Convention, as well as being its *author's own intellectual creation reflecting their personality*. The precondition set by Term Directive II also means that a product must possess such qualities that would classify it under the umbrella term of *literary and artistic works* within the meaning of Article 2 (1) of the Berne Convention. For this, the product must be considered a product in a literary, scientific, or artistic domain. The last step consists of assigning the product to the final subject-matter category of *photographic works* or the assimilated but equal subject-matter category of *works expressed by a process analogous to photography*. The EU has established that all *literary and artistic works*, i.e., *productions* according to the wording of Article 2 (1) of the Berne Convention, including *photographic works to which are assimilated works expressed by a process analogous to photography*, are considered intellectual creations for the purposes of copyrightability.

However, whether a photographic product falls under the subject-matter category of *photographic works* or that of *works expressed by a process analogous to photography* is irrelevant for their copyrightability; nonetheless certain technical requirements must be met. The production process of both categories of photographic products must include radiant energy. In terms of *photographic works*, the production process must involve employment of light, whereas the production process of *works expressed by a process analogous to photography* must involve other kinds of radiant energy. Both production processes, regardless of the radiation source, must be of photographic, or to photography similar, nature.

After establishing that the qualities of the photographic product put it under the scope of the Berne Convention, the next step is to demonstrate the fulfilment of the condition of *author's own intellectual creation* and the *reflection of the author's personality*. Due to the lack of a legislative definition of either term, it is necessary to turn to the case law of the CJEU on the matter.

10.8.2 Initial Conditions Prescribed by the Case Law of the CJEU

The relevant case law of the CJEU established that an *author's own intellectual creation (reflecting one's personality)* consists of several implicit and explicit components. These include conditions related to author as such, the production process, itself and the qualities that result from the production process. These components are used to complete and define the expression within the context of the EU's copyright framework.

Implicit conditions include the one related to the author. The requirement of *intellectual nature* of the resulting creation clearly implies the involvement of (human) intellect. It is therefore implicitly established that the notion presupposes only involvement of a human being in the position of the author. This excludes any other subjects from being recognized as authors for the purposes of EU copyright law, be it animals, artificial intelligence, robots, machines, etc.

Amongst the explicit conditions related to the production process are those related to *creative freedom* and *free and creative choices*. In the first place, the production process itself must be conducted in an environment that is free, i.e., not constrained in any way, especially creatively. It is only in such environment the author can make actual *free and creative choices*. It is only through these choices that the qualities of the resulting product can be affected to the extent that the product becomes eligible for copyright protection.

Explicit conditions related to the qualities of the final product—the work—include those related to the presence of a *personal touch* and *being perceivable with sufficient precision and objectivity*. The presence of a *personal touch*, the manifested outcome of the employment of *free and creative choices* during the production process, signifies the presence of the unique personality of the author in a photographic product. The condition of being perceivable with sufficient precision and objectivity does not pose any practical issues for photographic products due to their perceptibility by sight;[1470] similarly, the functionality exclusion is irrelevant since a photographic product as such does not possess functional parts.

10.8.3 Applying the Originality Assessment Test to Photographic Products in Practice

It is a given that photographic products are capable of being creatively modified, and therefore original. Because of this, the assessment process must also omit considerations regarding identification of being perceptible with sufficient precision and objectivity as well as possible absorption of a *personal touch* by functionality of a product's element. Therefore, the originality assessment process of a photographic product (which confirms or refutes the existence of the conditions prescribed by EU legislation and jurisprudence of the CJEU) should consist of the following steps, including corresponding questions, the assessing individual must take and ask in the following order:

1. Was the assessed product cumulatively produced using light or other radiant energy and by photographic or similar process, so that the assessed product can

[1470] Marián Jankovič, 'The Development and Harmonisation of Originality Standard of Photographic Works in the Copyright Framework of the European Union' 20 *Jusletter IT 30. März 2023* (2023), p. 1.

be labelled as a *photographic work,* or a *work expressed by a process analogous to photography* within the meaning of Article 2 (1) of the Berne Convention?
2. Is the subject claiming authorship of the assessed photographic product a human being, so that the subject can be considered the author-photographer?
3. Did the subject claiming authorship of the assessed photographic product sufficiently govern its production process, so that the subject can be considered the author-photographer?
4. Was the environment in which the photographic product was produced free of constraints that would preclude the existence of creative freedom?
5. Were any of the potentially existing constraints overcome by the photographer through *free and creative choices* they themselves made?
6. What choices were made by the photographer during the three production phases and can these choices be characterized as being *free and creative*?
7. Did at least one of the *free and creative choices* made during the three production phases manifest itself in the assessed photographic product as a *personal touch*?
8. Can causality be established between a *free and creative choice* and its corresponding *personal touch*?
9. Does the *personal touch* manifest an emotion, feeling, or a message of the photographer?
10. Can causality be established between the personal touch and the corresponding manifested emotion, feeling, or a message of the photographer?

Apart from the initial establishment of the subject-matter and the nature and the role of the author, the rest of the aforementioned assessment test can be summed up as substantiating a) what choices the photographer made; b) why the photographer made such choices; c) with what intended purpose the photographer made such choices; d) what effects resulted from the photographer's choices and e) whether the photographer achieved the intended outcome of such choices as anticipated.

If a photographic product passes this 10-step test[1471]—in other words, if every question of the test can be answered in affirmative, it will be considered original within the meaning of the harmonized EU copyright law. However, it must be noted that such findings may sometimes not be made, due to a lack of sufficient cooperation and substantiation from the photographer. This may be due to the lack of substantiation of the photographer's choices made throughout the production process, and the nature and effect of these choices on the overall appearance of the photographic product. This could also demonstrate the insufficient intellectual involvement of the photographer into the production process, which could subsequently preclude the production and existence of a photographic work within the meaning of harmonized EU law. However, sometimes the intellectual involvement might not be visible or evident, even if present. In such cases, without the photographer's or an

[1471] Hereinafter only referred to as the '10-step test'.

expert's clarification, a sufficiently substantiated decision on the originality of the assessed photographic product may be impossible to reach.

10.9 Interim Conclusion

The path towards the originality standard as we know it now—uniformly interpreted and applied throughout the copyright framework of the EU—began in EU directives and has continued throughout the case law of the CJEU. It is still relatively unknown whether the originality standard, as formulated at the time of drafting of this text, should be considered final. Given the content of the current referrals concerning matter of originality pending before the CJEU, its definitiveness is doubtful.[1472] In respect to this, we might expect yet another series of *fine-tuning* shaping of its employment in practice, further interpreting and formulating of potential additional restrictions and rules related to its use. The need for *fine-tuning* inevitably arises from the open and vague nature of the originality standard itself. Due to this starting position set by the EU legislation, the role that the CJEU has taken on via referrals from Member State courts is irreplaceable in the current set-up. Nonetheless for now, following the assessed EU legislation and case law of the CJEU above, the definition of the devised originality standard and its application to subject-matter in practice can be summed up in the following five steps:

First, the originality standard is an autonomous concept and as such should be applied within all national copyright frameworks of the Member States.

Second, the originality standard is applicable to all subject-matter capable of being a work, and not only limited to the three types of works officially harmonized within the meaning of EU Directives.

Third, the prerequisite of existence of originality in a work is that it is its *author's own intellectual creation*, and displays an *imprint of their personality* that is the result of their *free and creative choices*.

Fourth, the originality standard is also applicable to parts of the work, regardless of their size and the share of the work as a whole.

Fifth, the originality standard is applicable only to subject-matter that can be perceived with *sufficient precision and objectivity*.

[1472] Referrals such as in the CJEU Case C-580/23, *Mio and Others*, and Case C-795/23, *konektra*.

11 THE EFFECTS OF HARMONIZATION ON THE COPYRIGHT FRAMEWORK OF GERMANY

The following three chapters attempt to assess the potential effects the harmonization process on the four selected national copyright frameworks, specifically regarding the position and treatment of photographic products and their potential eligibility for copyright protection. From the author's perspective, the pivotal event from which these potential effects will be assessed is the decision of the CJEU in the *Painer case*. This case was chosen as the focal point for analysis due to its significance in confirming the previous legislative harmonization initiated by the EU legislator during the first harmonization phase. The *Painer* decision is also critical for the role it played in unifying the requirements for copyright protection of photographic products and also for symbolically concluding the harmonization process related to photographic products.

However, this assessment of the *Painer case* decision's effect and the potential adjustment of the national courts in practice, will be accompanied by two additional areas of focus. First, it will include an examination of the potential impact of the EU legislation itself—specifically, Term Directive I—resulting from the first harmonization phase, on relevant national legislative provisions concerning photographic products and originality in general. Second, it will be followed by assessment of the potential impact on selected national concepts related to photographic products and originality in general.

With regard to the chosen methodological approach, the assessment of potential effects will be conducted in three consecutive parts, covering national legislation, case law and selected concepts. This assessment structure is designed to provide a comprehensive insight into the anticipated effects related to both harmonization phases.

11.1 The Chapter's Relationship to the Selected Hypotheses and Research Questions

As previously stated, the purpose of this chapter is to confirm or refute Research Questions B and C within the scope of hypotheses No. 2 and No. 3. This analysis will rely on assessing the potential effects of both harmonization phases on selected aspects of the German national copyright framework. The theoretical framework established earlier will serve as a reference point against which the post-harmonization state of the German copyright framework will be compared. This comparison aims to highlight the anticipated changes resulting from both harmonization phases.

11.2 The Effects of Term Directives on the Position of Photographic Products

Within the German copyright framework, the shift in perception—and consequently the status—of photographic products as potential *photographic works* eligible for copyright protection was, somewhat unexpectedly, driven by the adoption and subsequent transposition of Term Directive I. For this reason, the analysis of German case law will use the adoption of Term Directive I, rather than the *Painer case* decision of the CJEU, as the point from which this shift will be examined.

With regard to photographic products, the framework for approximating German copyright law to that of EU harmonized was outlined in Recital 17 of Term Directive I. This recital introduced the requirement that the personality of the author must be reflected—and therefore recognizable—in photographic works within its meaning.[1473] This requirement is viewed as a prerequisite for the copyright protection of a photographic product. However, the Explanatory section of the 1995 amendment to the UrhG[1474] explicitly states that recognizing the author from their work through their personality or through their mark left in the work is not necessary.[1475] Although this may seem contradictory, the German legislator did not transpose this requirement into the UrhG. The reasoning was that the UrhG already included the requirement of *author's personal intellectual creation*, which the German legislator considered sufficient. Thus, it was deemed unnecessary by the German legislator to separately stipulate the recognizability of the author's personality in the wording of the UrhG, as it was already implicitly expressed from their work itself.[1476] Moreover, the requirement of author' personality to be reflected and recognized in a photographic product is not explicitly stated in the Article 6 of Term Directive I. This Article only requires that a photographic product be the *author's own intellectual creation* to qualify for copyright protection.

[1473] Recital 17 of the Term Directive I.

[1474] *Entwurf eines Vierten Gesetzes zur Änderung des Urheberrechtsgesetzes. Deutscher Bundestag – 13. Wahlperiode. Drucksache 13/781* (1. Oct. 2024), https://dserver.bundestag.de/btd/13/007/1300781.pdf

[1475] *Entwurf eines Vierten Gesetzes zur Änderung des Urheberrechtsgesetzes. Deutscher Bundestag – 13. Wahlperiode. Drucksache 13/781* (1. Oct. 2024), https://dserver.bundestag.de/btd/13/007/1300781.pdf, p. 8.

[1476] Dana Ferchland, *Fotografieschutz im Wandel: Auswirkungen technischer, künstlerischer und rechtlicher Veränderungen auf den Urheberrechtsschutz von Fotografien* (Verlag Dr. Kovač 2018), p. 122.

In relation to photographic products, the situation prior to the amendment of Term Directive I was characterized by a focus on meeting the requirement of individuality set for a work (photographic work) at an above-average degree.[1477] According to *Schricker* and *Loewenheim*, this approach led to the exclusion of *kleine Münze* photographic products from copyright protection, even though under this doctrine, such photographic products should be traditionally located at the lower level of copyright protection, but nonetheless in the realm of copyright protection still, as *Overbeck* quoted them.[1478] As a result, photographic products were often denied classification as *photographic works* and, consequently, were not granted copyright protection. Such photographic products were judicially recognized as *photographs*, thus becoming eligible for protection by a related right type of protection only.

11.3 Reflections of the First Harmonization Phase in the German National Legislation

The first harmonization phase within the German national legislation was realised through the *Reform of 1995* of the UrhG. As previously mentioned, this reform was primarily driven by the universal extension of the copyright protection period, as outlined in Article 1 of Term Directive I. Additionally, German legislation adopted the official distinction between *photographic works* and *other photographs*, incorporating it into German legislation, the UrhG. Regarding photographic products, the effects of the first harmonization phase can be summarized in two main areas of their materialization in practice.

First, the protection period for photographic products eligible for copyright protection, specifically *Lichtbildwerke*, was extended to 70 years *post mortem auctoris*. In this regard, it can be said that the photographic works, *Lichtbildwerke*, have clearly benefited from this extension, as a photographic subject-matter eligible for copyright protection. Second, the requirement to recognize qualities of *documenting contemporary history* in photographic products eligible for a related-right type of protection was eliminated. This change unified photographic products previously labelled formerly as *photographs documenting contemporary history* and *other photographs* under the concept of *Lichtbilder* within the meaning of the UrhG. The concept of *Lichtbilder* can thus be seen as a direct consequence and representation of the term *other photographs* within the meaning of Term Directive I.

Regarding the originality standard of *author's own intellectual creation* applicable to photographic products, as formulated in Article 6 of Term Directive I, the

[1477] Melanie Overbeck, *Der Lichtbildschutz gem. § 72 UrhG im Lichte der Digitalfotografie* (Lit 2018), p. 108.
[1478] *Ibid.*

German legislator has not found it necessary to incorporate it explicitly into the UrhG. This decision is likely justified, most probably, by the presence of a similar term, *persönliche geistige Schöpfungen* (*personal intellectual creation*), officially translated as *author's own intellectual creation*, which has been part of the UrhG since its adoption in 1965.

In light of the above, the *Reform of 1995*, as a direct legislative consequence of adopting Term Directive I, significantly impacted the scope of related-right type of protection. In this regard, distinguishing between photographic products eligible for related-right type of protection has become more coherent due to their unification under the category of *Lichtbilder*. Nonetheless, the *schism* between *Lichtbildwerke* and *Lichtbilder* persisted, as Term Directive I permitted the recognition of *other photographs*—a category under which *Lichtbilder* fall—allowing the German copyright framework to maintain this distinction.

11.4 Case Law After the Adoption of Term Directive I

The following examples illustrate the shift in understanding and assessment of photographic products for their eligibility for copyright protection by German courts. The figurative threshold for copyright protection of photographic products was clearly lowered, resulting in more photographic products being classified as *photographic works* and, consequently, eligible for copyright protection.

In a judgement of the OLG Hamburg,[1479] the question of copyright protection for a photographic product depicting a surfacing submarine was addressed. The OLG Hamburg decided that the photographic product could be classified as a *photographic work* due to its particularly well-captured mood, which transcended mere objective depiction.[1480] According to the OLG Hamburg, the photographer achieved this effect by choosing the ideal moment for the exposure to expose the image. This mood was of threatening nature and possessed atmospheric density, while the elements of the photographic work itself had a creative effect. The OLG Hamburg has also made a direct reference to Term Directive I when assessing the photographic product in question for the characteristics of a work.

Similarly, in the *Freiburger Münster*[1481] judgement, the LG Mannheim decided that when a photographer creates a composition that goes beyond a purely technically correct representation, the resulting photographic product meets the requirements for copyright protection. In the *TV-MAN*[1482] judgement, the LG Düsseldorf, decided that the photographer's creative achievement is expressed in the meaning

[1479] OLG Hamburg, 5 U 159/03, 3 Mar. 2004, *ZUM-RD*. 2004, p. 303.

[1480] *Ibid.*

[1481] LG Mannheim, 7 S 2/03, 14 Jul. 2006.

[1482] LG Düsseldorf, 12 O 34/05, 8 Mar. 2006.

of a photographic product, thus rendering the craftsmanship of the photographer irrelevant. In light of this, the photographic product in question was protected by copyright as a photographic work. The Higher regional court in Cologne, in the *Clamp Pose*[1483] judgement, further emphasized that the requirements for copyright protection were fulfilled by a posture of the subject depicted, which gave the photographic product artistic characteristics. Additionally, in *Wagner family photos*,[1484] the OLG Hamburg ruled that the composition depicted in the photographic products was deliberately designed, which gave it individual expression. In the *Beuys photographs*[1485] judgement, the OLG Düsseldorf considered the nature of three types of photographic products—photographic products depicting exhibition rooms, photographic products depicting exhibits and photographic products depicting the artist himself—portraits. All three were found to be meeting the requirements set for photographic works on the grounds of high level of creative achievement due to the light chosen and structure of their composition.[1486]

The BGH also confirmed this lowered threshold, ruling that the assessment of photographic products for their copyrightability should not focus on their displayed above-average quality, but rather on the presence of the minimal intellectual effort of the author.[1487] Thus, the transposition of Term Directive I into German copyright framework has significantly lowered the traditional requirement for copyright protection of photographic products to such an extent, that even the expenditure of minimal intellectual effort by the photographer, traditionally associated with *photographs*, became sufficient for copyrightability. With the threshold now lowered, it has become considerably easier for photographic products to reach the quality level prescribed for works within the meaning of the UrhG.[1488] This change is especially relevant for *photographs* within the meaning of Section 72 of the UrhG, as the minimal intellectual effort was previously considered to be a requirement for this photographic subject-matter.

Clearly, it was therefore Term Directive I which enabled German national courts to also include photographic products of traditionally non-copyrightable genres due to their nature, into the realm of copyright protection.[1489] However, such inclusion is possible only provided that a photographic product possesses individuality given to it by its author.

The *Painer case* decision of the CJEU did not significantly alter approach of German courts in this regard. It is true, that the CJEU has introduced a mandatory

[1483] OLG Köln, 6 U 189/97, 5 Mar. 1999. 'Klammerpose', *GRUR*. 2000, p. 43.

[1484] OLG Hamburg, 3 U 175/98, 5. Nov. 1998. 'Wagner-Familienfotos', *GRUR*. 1999, p. 717.

[1485] OLG Düsseldorf, 20 U 115/95, 13. Feb. 1996, 'Beuys-Fotografien', *GRUR*. 1997, p. 49.

[1486] Matthias Leistner, 'Von Joseph Beuys, Marcel Duchamp und der dokumentarischen Fotografie von Kunstaktionen,' *ZUM 468* (2011), p. 468.

[1487] BGH, I ZR 55/97, 3. Nov. 1999, 'Werbefotos' *GRUR*. 2000, p. 343.

[1488] Melanie Overbeck, *Der Lichtbildschutz gem. § 72 UrhG im Lichte der Digitalfotografie* (Lit 2018), p. 112.

[1489] Melanie Overbeck, *Der Lichtbildschutz gem. § 72 UrhG im Lichte der Digitalfotografie* (Lit 2018), p. 109.

addition to the requirement of *author's own intellectual creation*—the *personal touch*. However, this addition can be easily translated into the German concept of *individuality*. Within this meaning, the individuality can therefore be seen as a manifestation of something of a strictly personal nature.[1490]

Within the German copyright framework, the requirement of individuality is met if a product reflects individuality of its author. This means that the author has contributed something to the product based on their individual (personal) traits. According to German traditional perspective, individuality can be viewed as representing an additional clarifying requirement to personal intellectual creation. Nonetheless, the result of EU harmonization is that any product (creation) is considered personal (individual) if it possesses the personal touch (stamp) of its author.[1491] For the purposes of comparison, the notions of *personal* and *individual* can be regarded as identical. Therefore, in respect to harmonization, the requirement of *personal touch* aligns with the traditional German concept of *individuality*.

11.5 The Effects of Harmonization on the Selected German Concepts

11.5.1 The Concept of Lichtbildwerk

According to the Article 6 of both Term Directives, copyright protection is granted only to photographic products which are *'original in the sense they are the author's own intellectual creation, with no other criteria to be applied to determine their eligibility for protection'*. Here, the EU legislator expressed a clear intent not to subject photographic products to a condition of particular level of design.[1492] Based on this, the introduced originality standard can be seen as reduced compared to other traditionally applicable requirements.[1493] As a result, the applied criterion of superiority of *photographic works*, the *Lichtbildwerke*, to *photographs*, the *Lichtbilder*, based on the presence of higher-than-average level of design of the former, was abandoned.

In other words, the level of design is no longer specifically assessed in photographic products as a result of the legislative harmonization in the field. Instead, the criterion itself has been fully subsumed under the requirement of *author's own*

[1490] Karl-Nikolaus Peifer, '"Individualität" or Originality? Core Concepts in German Copyright Law,' *GRUR Int.* 1100 (2014), p. 1100.

[1491] *Ibid.*

[1492] Ulrich Loewenheim, *Handbuch des Urheberrechts* (C.H. Beck, 3rd ed. 2021), § 6 Rn. 16.

[1493] Artur-Axel Wandtke, Winfried Bullinger & Michael Bohne, *Praxiskommentar Urheberrecht: UrhG, UrhDaG, VGG, InsO, UKlaG, KUG, EVtr, InfoSoc-RL, Portabilitäts-VO* (C.H. Beck, 6th ed. 2022), p. 1429.

intellectual creation. Accordingly, the standard of originality applicable to photographic products within the German copyright framework was expressly defined and harmonized as of July 1, 1995. Therefore, by way of precedence of the EU law, the application of the relevant Sections of the UrhG relevant to photographic products must be made in accordance with the Article 6 of then, Term Directive I. This also includes eligibility of photographic products for copyright protection within the meaning of the said standard.

In general, after the coming of Term Directive I and its Article 6 into force, the general requirement for copyrightability of photographic products became relatively low, resulting in the removal of the previously applicable requirement of the minimum level of design.[1494] As a result, photographic products that did not display sufficient minimum level of design can therefore be considered for copyright protection after the introduction of Term Directive I. The said shift was continuously confirmed by German courts.[1495]

Also, given the explicit exclusion of other criteria for the eligibility of photographic products for copyright protection, Article 6 allows even for everyday and simple photographic products to be protected by copyright as photographic works within its meaning. This is made possible by the relatively low requirements for individuality in a photographic work, through which the own intellectual activity and creation of the author is manifested.[1496] According to *Schricker*, the requirement of individuality alone now serves as the determining factor for the copyrightability of a photographic product, as *Ricke* quoted him.[1497]

The continual decrease in requirements at the lower level of copyright protection threshold has expanded the scope of eligibility of photographic products for copyright protection under Section 2 of the UrhG.[1498] Such setting, therefore, allows more *photographs* to cross the figurative border and be recognized as photographic works within the meaning of the UrhG. According to *von Lewinski* and *Schricker*, given the traditionally higher requirements for protection of photographic products compared to other types of works within the German copyright framework, the intention behind introducing Term Directive I could, in fact, be characterized as lowering the originally applicable requirements for copyrightability, as *Ricke* quoted them.[1499]

1494 Thomas Dreier & Gernot Schulze, *Urheberrechtsgesetz: Urheberrechts-Diensteanbieter-Gesetz, Verwertungsgesellschaftengesetz, Nebenurheberrecht, Kunsturhebergesetz: Kommentar* (C.H. Beck, 7th ed. 2022), p. 160.

1495 For example in OLG Düsseldorf, I-20 U 143/07, 15. Apr. 2008, *ZUM.RD*. 2008, p. 524.

1496 Ilva Johanna Schiessel, *Reichweite und Rechtfertigung des einfachen Lichtbildschutzes gem. § 72 UrhG* (Nomos 2020), p. 43.

1497 Stefan Ricke, *Entwicklung des rechtlichen Schutzes von Fotografien in Deutschland* (Lit 1998), p. 152.

1498 Melanie Overbeck, *Der Lichtbildschutz gem. § 72 UrhG im Lichte der Digitalfotografie* (Lit 2018), p. 121.

1499 Stefan Ricke, *Entwicklung des rechtlichen Schutzes von Fotografien in Deutschland* (Lit 1998), p. 152.

11.5.2 The Concept of Lichtbild

The notion of *photographs* (*Lichtbilder*) is to be interpreted, for the purposes of harmonized EU law, as *other photographs* within the meaning of the Article 6 of both Term Directives. Based on the described two-tier system applicable within the German copyright framework, it can be inferred that the wording of Article 6 of Term Directive I presupposes exact such situations within the national copyright frameworks of Member States. In other words, *photographs* fall under the exception that allows Member States to grant them a related-right type of protection, different form copyright, at their discretion.[1500]

The expanded scope of eligibility of photographic products for copyright protection under Section 2 of the UrhG has led to its more frequent application to photographic products previously classified as *other photographs*.[1501] This shift has directly affected and limited the applicability of Section 72 of the UrhG to a number of photographic products that were previously eligible for protection under related right-type of protection.

In light of this, one might question whether the existence of Section 72 of the UrhG remains justified, given the harmonization activities of the EU and lowering of the requirements for copyrightability. Regardless of the eventual fate of Section 72 and protection of *photographs*, some argue that abolishing Section 72 of the UrhG could finally equalize the protection of photographic products with that of other classical works of art.[1502] According to *Walter*, the legislative status of *photographs* within the UrhG nonetheless remains unchanged, as the reference to *other photographs* within the meaning of Article 6 of Term Directives I & II suggests that the two-tier system of protection continues to apply across the entire copyright framework of the EU, not just within that of Germany, as *Nordemann* quoted him.[1503]

11.5.3 The Effects of the Digital Single Market Directive on the Concept of Lichtbild

In Article 14, the Digital Single Market Directive excludes photographic products produced in the course of reproducing works of visual art in the public domain not only from copyright protection but also from any form of related-right type of protection. This exclusion applies only if the photographic product does not fulfil the

[1500] Art. 6 of the Term Directive II.

[1501] Melanie Overbeck, *Der Lichtbildschutz gem. § 72 UrhG im Lichte der Digitalfotografie* (Lit 2018), p. 191.

[1502] Melanie Overbeck, *Der Lichtbildschutz gem. § 72 UrhG im Lichte der Digitalfotografie* (Lit 2018), p. 196.

[1503] Wilhelm Nordemann et al. *Urheberrecht: Kommentar zum Urheberrechtsgesetz, Verlagsgesetz, Urheberrechtswahrnehmungsgesetz* (W. Kohlhammer, 10th ed. 2008), p. 1227.

criterion of *author's own intellectual creation* as defined by harmonized EU law. In this context, Article 14 of the Digital Single Market Directive specifically affects only those photographic products within the German copyright framework that would traditionally be classified as *photographs (Lichtbilder)*. Such photographs, if produced during the reproduction of a work of visual art in the public domain, would not be eligible for protection by a related-right type of protection under Section 72 of the UrhG.

Traditionally, within the German copyright framework, any reproduction photographic product that did not reach over the threshold required for copyright protection would still be eligible for a related-right type of protection under Section 72 of the UrhG.[1504] Previous German case law on the reproduction photographic products of works of visual art was substantial—such reproduction photographic products were deemed eligible for a related-right type of protection under Section 72 of the UrhG; i.e., recognized as a *Lichtbild* at minimum. The last manifestation of this approach was a string of case law involving the use of photographic products of works of visual art in the possession of the *Reis-Engelhor Museen* institution in Germany (*REM*), known collectively as the *Museumsfotos*, which included a total of four cases.[1505] All reproduction photographic products depicting works of visual art in the public domain, as the subject-matter of these four cases, were found to be eligible for a related-right type of protection as *Lichtbilder* under Section 72 of the UrhG.

This string of cases clearly demonstrates that reproduction photographic products traditionally enjoyed a related-right type of protection under Section 72 of the UrhG. This protection has undoubtedly influenced the further dissemination of the reproductions of works of visual art in the public domain, whose copyright protection has expired, as the authors of such reproduction photographic products can continue to exploit them even after expiration.[1506] Nonetheless, the cases also clearly show that these reproduction photographic products do not meet the threshold reserved for original photographic products, the *Lichtbildwerke*, under Section 2 of the UrhG.

The analysed case law also demonstrates that reproduction photographic products of works of visual art, in this case the paintings, are neither original photographic products nor copies but occupy an intermediary category, meeting the characteristics of a photographic product under Section 72 of the UrhG—the *Lichtbild*.[1507]

[1504] Andrea Wallace & Ellen Euler, 'Revisiting Access to Cultural Heritage in the Public Domain: EU and International Developments,' *IIC 823* (2020). 2020, p. 823.

[1505] AMG Nürnberg, 32 C 4607/15, 28. Oct. 2015; LG Berlin, 16 O 175/15, 31. May 2016; LG Berlin, 15 O 428/15, 31. May 2016, LG Stuttgart, 17 O 690/15, 27. Sep. 2016.

[1506] Mathilde Pavis, *Digitized Images of Works in the Public Domain: What Rights Vest in Them? Analysis of the Recent BGH Reiss-Engelhorn Judgement—Part 1* (1 Sep. 2024), https://ipkitten.blogspot.com/2019/02/digitized-images-of-works-in-public.html.

[1507] Andrea Wallace & Ellen Euler, 'Revisiting Access to Cultural Heritage in the Public Domain: EU and International Developments,' *IIC 823* (2020). 2020, p. 823.

The harmonization conducted in the area of photographic reproductions of works of visual art in the public domain through Article 14 of the Digital Single Market Directive aims to limit the manoeuvring area of Member States; i.e. limit their discretion in granting protection by stipulating that such subject-matter can only be eligible for copyright protection if recognized as an *author's own intellectual creation.*

Article 14 of the Digital Single Market Directive was transposed into the UrhG as Section 68, with the following wording, which fully complies with the harmonized wording and revises the traditional understanding of such photographic subject-matter:

'Reproductions of works of visual arts in the public domain are not protected by related rights under Parts 2 and 3.'[1508]

Through this transposition, the entire genre of reproduction photography (of works of visual art in the public domain) was removed from the scope of Section 72 of the UrhG and the related-right type of protection it provided. As a result, authors of such reproduction photographic products can no longer claim a related-right type of protection intended for photographs.

11.6 Compliance with the Conditions of the 10-step Test

It has been sufficiently demonstrated that the German national copyright framework has successfully adapted to the conclusions and subsequent intended effects of both harmonization phases. This is especially evident in the application of the lowered standard of originality to photographic products. However, this adjustment has been implemented gradually since the adoption of Term Directive I, thus preceding the formulation of the additional conditions related to the *author's own intellectual creation,* particularly the requirement of a *personal touch.* As noted, the required presence of a *personal touch* began to be interpreted and applied, through German jurisprudence, as a substitute for the traditional requirement of *individuality.* While this informal approach may be beneficial and straightforward, there is a risk that the very essence and content of this informally interpreted and adjusted to notion could be lost in the process.

In terms of compliance with the conditions of the 10-step test, it can be concluded that the German national copyright framework adheres to it, albeit informally. In other words, this assessment test, upon which the eligibility of a photographic product for copyright protection shall be determined, is applied with the intended purpose and goal in mind, though not in the formal entirety of its all successive

[1508] Sec. 68 of UrhG.

steps. This approach may be particularly relevant in understanding the significant relationship represented by the dependence of the *personal touch* on the expenditure of *free and creative choices*.

11.7 Interim Conclusion

The general effect of the EU harmonization within the German copyright framework concerning photographic products can be characterized by a continuous lowering of requirements for their protection. The gradual lowering of requirements for copyright protection of photographic products, initiated legislatively by Term Directive I and later concluded and confirmed judicially by the *Painer case* decision, has affected the position of both *photographic works* and *photographs*. In this context, the *Painer case* decision represented a *mere* confirmation of the traditional German requirement of individuality, which was replaced by the harmonized *personal touch*—albeit with the identical meaning and effect. It was therefore the transposition of Term Directive I that marked this shift in perception and position of photographic products, facilitating their access to copyright protection. This has been achieved through the uniform application of the requirement of *author's own intellectual creation* to all photographic products, which represents a lower requirement for protection by copyright.

The more the requirements for the lower level of protection of photographic products are decreased, the less relevant the related-right type of protection under Section 72 of the UrhG becomes.[1509] This is due to the broader scope of copyright protection capabilities at its lower levels. However, it is safe to assume that such protection cannot extend below the *kleine Münze* photographic works, as this subject-matter is already *barely protectable* by copyright due to its nature.[1510] Therefore, by decreasing the requirements for the lower level of photographic products eligible for copyright protection, this lowered threshold pushes downward even lower and overlaps with the requirements for higher level of protection of photographs, thereby decreasing them. One can imagine a figurative situation in which copyright presses on the related right, constantly reducing its scope.

In this context, the number of *photographic works* eligible for copyright protection appears to be increasing at the expense of *photographs* eligible only for a related-right type of protection. The continuation of this general approach of the EU legislator seems to be confirmed and manifested as a trend through the treatment of photographic products depicting works of visual art in the public domain, as specified in Article 14 of the Digital Single Market Directive. Since only copyright

[1509] Melanie Overbeck, *Der Lichtbildschutz gem. § 72 UrhG im Lichte der Digitalfotografie* (Lit 2018), p. 118.

[1510] Melanie Overbeck, *Der Lichtbildschutz gem. § 72 UrhG im Lichte der Digitalfotografie* (Lit 2018), p. 120.

protection is permissible for such photographic products as *photographic works*, *other photographs*, as defined in Article 6 of Term Directive II, appear to be sidelined by the EU legislator.

Nonetheless, despite the intention to achieve full harmonization in this area, the final codified version of both Term Directives still maintains a definitional distinction between *photographic works* and *photographs*.[1511] Thus, the harmonization focused solely on *photographic works* and, from the perspective of the EU harmonized law, left *photographs* unregulated. Consequently, the EU legislator has not yet taken the opportunity to eliminate the ambiguities surrounding the distinguishing between *photographic works* and *photographs* within the German copyright framework.

[1511] Horst Heitland, *Der Schutz der Fotografie im Urheberrecht Deutschlands, Frankreichs und der Vereinigten Staaten von Amerika* (C.H. Beck 1995), p. 60.

12 THE EFFECTS OF THE HARMONIZATION ON THE COPYRIGHT FRAMEWORK OF FRANCE

12.1 The Chapter's Relationship to the Selected Hypotheses and Research Questions

As previously stated, the purpose of this chapter is to confirm or refute Research Questions B and C within the scope of outlined hypotheses No. 2 and No. 3. This confirmation or refutation will be based on an assessment of the potential effects that both harmonization phases may have had on the selected aspects of the French national copyright framework. The previously established theoretical knowledge framework will serve as a point of reference, against which the post-harmonization state of the French national copyright framework will be compared, thereby creating a potential contrast that highlights the anticipated changes resulting from both harmonization phases.

12.2 The Presence of Originality in a Photographic Product

Case law of the CJEU, beginning with the *Infopaq case* decision, has positively affected the reduction of the proof of originality resting on authors. For photographers, this effect was particularly achieved by the *Painer case* decision. The CJEU has provided a broader and more objective interpretation of originality, thereby making it easier to establish in cases where originality is contested. This intervention by the CJEU has been made at a time when the French copyright framework, through its case law, was becoming increasingly stringent and demanding regarding the burden of proof for originality.[1512] However, some argue that the French national case law has never traditionally shown significant rigor in its approach to granting copyright protection.[1513]

In light of such contradictory statements, it is essential to consider that case law related to photographic products within a specific copyright framework is often as diverse as the medium of photography itself.[1514] Given the variety of circumstances of case law and creative opportunities that the medium of photography offers, this diversity is inevitable.

As previously mentioned, a photographer can create an imprint of their personality in a photographic product throughout three distinct phases—*before, during and after*, according to the CJEU. Such originality can be displayed either alternatively in each phase, or cumulatively in two or three of them.[1515] The clear enumeration of these three phases, along with a clear indication of the associated creative steps, has facilitated the work of judges, including those in France.[1516] However, these phases and the steps involved were part of the French copyright framework before they were explicitly formulated by the CJEU in its *Painer case* decision.[1517]

Apart from the said facilitation, these phases also act as defined boundaries that a judge should not exceed during the assessment process of a photographic product. For instance, the Court of Versailles stated that the free and creative choices of a photographer may be employed before taking of the image, at the moment of its actual taking or at the time of development of the image.[1518] The first phase may include staging, posing or lighting. The second phase may include choice of framing, angle of shot or the atmosphere created. The third phase may include various development techniques. Ultimately, however, the choices of the photographer deemed relevant for the actual potential finding of originality within a photographic product—and thereby justifying its protection, are at the judge's discretion.[1519]

Through the *Painer case* decision, the assessment of author's choices and their impact on originality became omnipresent in the French copyright framework, as *Vivant* and *Bruguière* concluded from French case law.[1520] In other words, the declared relevance of author's (photographer's) choices for finding of originality

[1512] Florence Gaullier, 'La preuve de l'originalité : mission impossible ?' 70 *Revue Lamy Droit de l'immatériel* 126 (2011), p. 126.

[1513] Michel Vivant & Jean-Michel Bruguière, *Droit d'auteur et droits voisins* (Dalloz, 4th ed. 2019), p. 235.

[1514] Christophe Caron, *Droit d'auteur et droits voisins* (LexisNexis, 6th ed. 2020), p. 144.

[1515] *Ibid.*

[1516] Michel Vivant & Jean-Michel Bruguière, *Droit d'auteur et droits voisins* (Dalloz, 4th ed. 2019), p. 235.

[1517] Christophe Caron, 'Droit d'auteur de l'Union européenne : des photographies et des exceptions,' 14 *Communication – Commerce Électronique* 26 (2012), p. 26.

[1518] Cour d'appel de Versailles, 16/02894, 26 Jan. 2018.

[1519] Michel Vivant & Jean-Michel Bruguière, *Droit d'auteur et droits voisins* (Dalloz, 4th ed. 2019), p. 331.

[1520] *Ibid.*

in photographic products was also extended to other, meaning all, subject-matter within the French copyright framework.

12.3 Reflections of the First Harmonization Phase in the French National Legislation

The last national legislative reform affecting photographic products has been carried out in 1985. Similar to the German *Reform of 1995*, this French reform eliminated the legislative recognition of requirements of artistic and documentary character, upon the fulfilment of which the eligibility of photographic products for copyright protection had previously depended. As a result, photographic products became subject only to the fulfilment of the requirement of being a *work of the mind*, in order to be considered for protection by copyright. It should also be noted that the French legislator has never implemented a related-right type of protection for photographic products. Therefore, traditionally, the only recognized type of protection has been copyright.

Therefore, in terms of French national legislation regarding photographic products, the state of affairs just prior to the adoption of Term Directive I can be characterized by the following three points. First, only photographic products that can be labelled as *works of the mind* are eligible for copyright protection. Second, only photographic works are recognized as protectable photographic subject-matter (eligible for copyright protection). Third, the term of protection applicable to photographic works was fifty years *post mortem auctoris*.

Since the French legal framework did not introduce the option to protect photographic products through a related-right type of protection, the possibility of allocating certain types of photographic products from the mass of all photographic products, due to their failure to meet the criteria for photographic works, as *other photographs* within the meaning of the Article 6 of Term Directive I, was irrelevant to the French legislator.

Regarding the traditional notion of *work of the mind*, the French legislator did not modify its wording to bring it closer to the EU harmonized standard of originality of *author's own intellectual* creation, which was then applicable to photographic products. The omission of any modification of this notion in connection with the adoption of Term Directive I, as seen with the German UrhG, may perhaps suggest that the French legislator felt such modification was unnecessary due to the identical or very similar substantive meaning of both notions.

In this context, the only legislative adjustment which can be considered as reflecting the first harmonization phase within French national legislation was the adoption of the *Loi n° 97-283 du 27 mars 1997 portant transposition dans le code de la propriété intellectuelle des directives du Conseil des Communautés européennes nos 93/83 du 27 septembre 1993 et 93/98 du 29 octobre 1993 (1) ('ACT No. 97-283 of 27 March 1997 transposing into the Intellectual Property Code Council Directives 93/83 of 27 September 1993 and 93/98 of 29 October 1993 (1)').* In terms of its effects on photographic products, the only change introduced by the said Act was the extension of the protection period to seventy years *post mortem auctoris*, previously introduced by Term Directive I.

12.4 Case Law Prior to the *Painer Case* Decision

Shortly before the *Painer case* decision, the overall approach of the French copyright framework toward eligibility of photographic products for copyright protection could be described as focused on originality as a central element with the necessity of proving evidence of its presence.[1521] The central position of originality and the burden of proof consisting of proving its existence resting with the author, thus allowing the court to make its assessment, was formulated by the *Tribunal de grande instance de Paris* in 2008.[1522] Also, the direction of this development was later confirmed by the case law of the CJEU.

Amongst photographic products traditionally found to be original, and therefore eligible for copyright protection, were also those depicting static objects, such as paintings or antique objects. For instance, between 1996 and 2008, choosing the angle and lighting was sufficient for findings of originality in such cases.[1523] This approach was also confirmed by a 2001 decision of the Paris Court of Appeal, where photographic products depicting paintings by *Pablo Picasso* were found to be original, as *Pierrat* quoted it.[1524] Similarly, in 2007, a court deemed a sequence of photographic products depicting a blooming of a poppy to be original, based on the following criteria: the choice to photograph a complete sequence, choices of lighting, lens, film, aperture, shutter speed and angle of shots, focus on details, choices of neutral and uniform background, all of which gave the photographic products in question a particular character carrying the imprint of their author's personality.[1525]

Photographic products found not to be original, and therefore not eligible for copyright protection, include those depicting candidates participating in municipal elections. In a 1989 decision by a court in Lyon, these photographic products were found not to be eligible for copyright protection due to photographer remaining as

[1521] André Lucas, Valérie-Laure Benabou & Jean-Michel Bruguière, 'TGI Paris, 13 mars 2009, p. Bazin c/ T. Bouët et Grands magasins de la Samaritaine (en attente),' 32 *Propriétés Intellectuelles* 260 (2008), p. 260.

[1522] Tribunal de grande instance de Paris, 08/01490, 9 Sep. 2008.

[1523] Mathilde Pavis, *Forgive My French: Copyright 'A La Carte' for Photographic Works* (1 Sep. 2024), https://the1709blog.blogspot.com/2015/07/forgive-my-french-copyright-la-carte.html.

[1524] Emmanuel Pierrat, *Le droit d'auteur et l'édition* (Éditions du Cercle de la librairie, 4th ed 2013), p. 57.

[1525] André Lucas & Jean-Michel Bruguière, 'TGI Paris, 30 mai 2007, Claude Nuridsanz c/ Société d'Evian et autres,' 20 *Propriétés Intellectuelles* 309 (2007), p. 309.

neutral as possible in their depiction, as *Linant de Bellefonds* quoted it.[1526] Similarly, in 2007, the Paris Court of Appeal found paparazzi photographic products depicting a skiing couple not to be original, and therefore ineligible for copyright protection, due to their lack of possessing the qualities of author's own intellectual creation and the lack of display of photographer's personality.[1527]

In 2009, the *Tribunal de grande instance de Paris* ruled that aerial photographic products produced in automatically triggered bursts by photographic devices mounted on an airplane fuselage were found not to be original due to not bearing imprint of photographer's personality.[1528] In this case, the photographer was regarded by the court as a mere technician who, if replaced by another, would achieve the same result under identical conditions.

12.5 Case Law After the *Painer* Case Decision

The shift in the perception of assessing originality in photographic products within the French copyright framework, particularly the necessary emphasis on the results of the free and creative choices, can be illustrated by a case with circumstances similar to those of *Painer case*. In a 2015 case involving a photographic product depicting musician *Jimi Hendrix*, the French national approach, compliant to that of EU harmonized, had to be confirmed by the court of higher instance, the *Cour d'Appel Paris*.

After the court of the previous (lower) instance refused to recognize its originality, the photographic product's originality was ultimately recognized based on the information provided by the applicant, describing the photographer's choices employed throughout the production process and their effect on the final captured image. The court of higher instance supported its decision, by which the originality was recognized, with the following considerations regarding the photographer's actions: guiding and directing subject during the shooting, asking the subject to take the pose captured, choosing the black and white film in order to give the subject more attitude and seriousness, choosing a specific type of a lens in order to achieve a wide effect, topped by choosing the decor, lighting angle of view and the frame.[1529] The said court concluded with the following:

1526 Xavier Linant de Bellefonds & Célia Zolynski, *Droits d'auteur et droits voisins* (Dalloz 2002), p. 96.

1527 André Lucas, Valérie-Laure Benabou & Jean-Michel Bruguière, 'Droit d'auteur et droit voisins,' 26 *Propriétés Intellectuelles* 260 (2008), p. 206.

1528 Christophe Caron, 'Droit d'auteur de l'Union européenne: des photographies et des exceptions,' 14 *Communication – Commerce Électronique* 26 (2012), p. 22.

1529 Michael A. Weiss, *Paris Court of Appeals: Photograph of Jimi Hendrix is Original and Thus Protected by French Copyright* (1 Sep. 2024), https://www.linkedin.com/pulse/paris-court-appeals-photograph-jimi-hendrix-original-thus-weiss/.

'That these elements, added to the fact, uncontested and established by evidence, that Mr. Mankowitz, an internationally recognized photographer, notably for having been the photographer of the Rolling Stones, whose photographs enjoy a high reputation, establish that the photograph at stake is the result of free and creative choices made by the photographer which reflect the expression of his personality.'[1530]

It appears that the higher court has also considered and acknowledged the internationally well-known persona of the photographer—a criterion that should be excluded from the originality assessment process. Additionally, the court stated that *'the work must present a unique physiognomy evidencing an aesthetic parti pris and reflecting the stamp of personality of its author'*.[1531] Emphasizing aesthetics and its relevance for determining originality is also in breach of established national jurisprudence.[1532] Nonetheless, the choices made by the photographer and their effect were sufficiently explained to the court by the applicant.[1533]

In 2018, the *Cour d'Appel Versailles* found that the photographic product depicting the famous image of *Ernesto 'Che' Guevara* taken by *Alberto Korda*, was original. The court established the originality of the photographic product based on the presence of the reflection of its author's personality. Among the recognized originality forming choices employed by the photographer were the following: deliberately opting for the *Ernesto 'Che' Guevara* among other subjects due to his intense gaze embracing the crowd, choosing a low angle shot accentuating the messianic aspect of the portrait and bringing out the emotion and timelessness of the moment by choosing a new composition by reframing the chosen subject.[1534] All these elements, created by the said choices, reveal an aesthetic research and a personal contribution of the photographer, all of which goes beyond simple know-how.[1535] These choices helped to highlight the intensity of the character, independently of the depicted subject of *Ernesto 'Che' Guevara*, stamping the photographic product with the personality of its author, the photographer, via the personal touch.

One could also argue that the photographic product documented only characteristics of the depicted subject, which do not result from choices of free and creative nature employed by the photographer. However, in this case, originality arises from the photographer's desire to capture a certain object or subject, which the intended audience might find of interest.[1536] It is also worth noting that, through the aforemen-

[1530] Cour d'appel de Paris (8e Ch.), 16/14758, 13 Jun. 2017.

[1531] *Ibid.*

[1532] Mathilde Pavis, *Hendrix's Portrait Is Original Afterall Say Paris Court of Appeal* (1 Sep. 2024), https://ipkitten.blogspot.com/2017/06/hendrixs-portrait-is-original-afterall.html?m=0.

[1533] Benoît Spitz, *France: Mankowitz's Photo of Jimi Hendrix is Finally Protected by Copyright in Appeal* (1 Sep. 2024), https://copyrightblog.kluweriplaw.com/2017/08/18/france-mankowitzs-photo-jimi-hendrix-finally-protected-copyright-appeal/.

[1534] Cour d'Appel de Versailles, No. 16/08909, 7 Sep. 2018.

[1535] *Ibid.*

[1536] Pierre Pérot, 'Parodie d'une œuvre photographique : game over pour le Guerrillero Heroico,' *LÉGIPRESSE* 572 (2018), p. 572.

tioned choices, the photographer has highlighted the subject's characteristics and offered a new perspective on these traits as well as on the photographed subject in general.

The decisions of the French courts in the two given examples, both of which involved positive findings of originality in the assessed photographic products, are linked by the necessity of proving the existence of a personal touch and its origin in, as well as their connection to, the free and creative choices made by the author throughout the production process. The required establishment of this origin and connection directly follows the guidance provided by the CJEU in its *Painer case* decision.

12.6 The Effects of Harmonization on the Selected French Concepts

12.6.1 The Presence of a Personal Touch

The traditional French requirement of originality, with its condition of reflecting the author's personality, corresponds to the requirement set out by the CJEU in its *Painer case* decision. In this context, the requirement of presence of a *personal touch* can be considered synonymous with the *imprint of one's personality*.[1537] Therefore, it can be said that the CJEU followed the traditional concept of the French copyright framework, which focuses on the expression of author's personality and based its formulated requirement of the said *personal touch* on it.[1538]

12.6.2 The Free and Creative Choices

The harmonization of the EU may have left the nature and meaning of the originality requirement unchanged, yet it has affected the degree sufficient for finding of originality and subsequent protection by copyright.

Under the EU harmonization tendencies, the focus shifts to demonstrating the author's intellect, the manifestation of which is to be done through *free and creative choices*. This approach suggests that the originality assessment process based on the presence of a *personal touch* became more prone to objectivization, thus rendering the requirement to a mere style clause.[1539] Any objectivization general-

[1537] *Code de la propriété intellectuelle: annoté et commenté (Dalloz, 23e édition ed. 2023)*, p. 36.

[1538] Véronique Dahan & Charles Bouffier, 'Arrêt Painer du 1er décembre 2011 : la CJUE poursuit son œuvre d'harmonisation du droit d'auteur,' 80 *Revue Lamy Droit de l'immatériel* 14 (2012), p. 14.

[1539] Céline Castets-Renard, 'L'originalité en droit d'auteur européen : la CJUE creuse le sillon,' 82 *Revue Lamy Droit de l'immatériel* 6 (2012), p. 6.

ly aims to exclude any subjective elements from the assessment process—such as merit, purpose, artistic value, etc. Naturally, the choices leading to the imprint of author's personality must be of free and creative nature, rather than dictated by technical means or simply dictated in general.

Therefore, the traditional French understanding gave way to the harmonized approach introduced by the CJEU. Consequently, the proper and notable visual effect, traditionally recognized within the French copyright framework, was replaced by emphasis on the manifestation of free and creative choices, even if the production process of such a product was dictated by technical means.[1540] The decisive criterion in this harmonized approach is whether the author was still able to reflect their personality in the product through the *personal touch*.

In summary, the attachment of originality has shifted from the exteriorized form of the product to the intellectual approach of the author during its production process. In this context, it is always essential to disassociate the form from the substance during the originality assessment process.[1541]

12.6.3 The 'Other Photographs'

Regarding the potential granting of copyright protection to *other photographs* within the meaning of Article 6 of Term Directive II, France has never implemented this option.[1542] Implementing such an option into the French copyright framework would be contrary to the traditionally established approach to originality, which either grants copyright protection to a photographic product due to its original character or finds the photographic product non-original and therefore ineligible for copyright protection.

12.7 Compliance with the Conditions of the 10-step Test

It has been sufficiently demonstrated that the French national copyright framework has been able to adapt to the conclusions and subsequent intended effects of both harmonization phases. This is especially true for the application of the lowered standard of originality to photographic products.

1540 Nicolas Binctin, *Droit de la propriété intellectuelle: droit d'auteur, brevet, droits voisins, marque, dessins et modèles* (LGDJ, 7th ed. 2022), p. 79.

1541 *Code de la propriété intellectuelle: annoté et commenté* (Dalloz, 23e édition ed. 2023), p. 30.

1542 Antoine Latreille, 'La création photographique face au juge : entre confusion et raison,' 31 *LÉGIPRESSE* 139 (2010), p. 139.

In contrast with Germany, this adjustment began in France primarily only after the *Painer case* decision. The formulation of the additional condition to the *author's own intellectual creation*—specifically, the requirement of a *personal touch*—did not require extensive (re)interpretation by the French courts. The required presence of a *personal touch* began to be interpreted and applied by French courts as a substitute for the traditional requirement of an *imprint of one's personality*. In this context, the application of this informal approach may avoid many of the negative aspects observed in the German copyright framework with respect to the same approach.

Therefore, in terms of compliance with the conditions of the 10-step test, it can be concluded that the French national copyright framework adheres to it, albeit informally. In other words, this assessment test, which determines the eligibility of a photographic product for copyright protection, is applied with the intended purpose and goal in mind, though not in the formal entirety of all its successive steps. The only part disrupting this formal completeness is represented by the emphasis on *free and creative choices*. Based on this, the French copyright framework complies with the 10-step test almost entirely.

In this context, the emphasis on the required presence of a *personal touch* through the EU harmonization fully adheres to the French understanding of this requirement. Therefore, the only addition needed in the 10-step test is the emphasis on *free and creative choices* and their relevance in establishing the relationship between these and the *personal touch*.

12.8 Interim Conclusion

The traditional and unified French requirement of originality might seem similar to the one introduced by the CJEU in its jurisprudence. With only slight difference in the emphasis placed on the *free and creative choices*, this is in fact the case. In this context, it can be said that the CJEU adopted and adjusted the traditional French requirement of originality. Consequently, access to copyright protection might therefore not seem so unfamiliar to French lawyers.[1543]

The harmonization activities of the CJEU through its case law have not had any significant impact on the traditional understanding and application of the requirement of originality concerning photographic products, since the harmonized originality standard is considered to be identical to that of traditional French origin, as *König* concluded from opinions of various scholars.[1544] In other words, for finding of originality in a product, French courts use and apply the same criteria as those introduced by the CJEU. Consequently, it can be stated that the harmoni-

[1543] Christophe Caron, *Droit d'auteur et droits voisins* (LexisNexis, 6th ed. 2020), p. 90.

[1544] Eva-Marie König, *Der Werkbegriff in Europa: eine rechtsvergleichende Untersuchung des britischen, französischen und deutschen Urheberrechts* (Mohr Siebeck 2015), p. 246.

zation of the EU in the field of originality of photographic products did not affect the overall understanding of originality or necessitate modification of French copyright law.[1545]

According to *Dommering*, harmonization has rendered originality a meaningless criterion, incapable of performing its traditional function of serving as a distinguishing tool between original (and thus copyright-protectable) and non-original (and thus copyright- unprotectable) products, as *Lucas* quoted him.[1546] As a result, some advocate for stricter assessment of originality, as the French copyright framework appears to have become less restrictive in this process, making it comparable to copyright jurisdictions abroad.[1547]

Nonetheless, in line with the application practice of the CJEU, originality within the French copyright framework remains a criterion of great variability and accessibility to a large variety of products. The reason behind such approach is the pragmatic nature of copyrightability, based on the presence of an imprint of a personality of their author in the form of a *personal touch*.[1548]

[1545] Christophe Caron, 'Droit d'auteur de l'Union européenne : des photographies et des exceptions,' 14 *Communication – Commerce Électronique* 26 (2012), p. 26.

[1546] André Lucas et al., *Traité de la propriété littéraire et artistique* (LexisNexis, 5th ed. 2017), p. 162.

[1547] *Ibid.*

[1548] Eva-Marie König, *Der Werkbegriff in Europa: eine rechtsvergleichende Untersuchung des britischen, französischen und deutschen Urheberrechts* (Mohr Siebeck 2015), p. 260.

13 THE EFFECTS OF THE HARMONIZATION ON THE COPYRIGHT FRAMEWORKS OF CZECH AND SLOVAK REPUBLICS

The biggest challenge in applying the principles resulting from the harmonization in the area of photographic products was overcoming the traditional requirements and understandings of (statistical) uniqueness in its statistical sense and replacing it with the harmonized requirement of the author's own intellectual creation. The necessity of carrying out this replacement stemmed from the need of application of the mentioned reduced harmonized standard of originality in both Czech and Slovak copyright frameworks. The following sections assess the extent to which, if at all, this goal of harmonization has been achieved.

13.1 The Chapter's Relationship to the Selected Hypotheses and Research Questions

The purpose of this chapter is to confirm or refute the Research Questions B and C in relation to hypotheses No. 2 and No. 3. This confirmation or refutation will be based on an evaluation of the potential effects that both phases of harmonization may have had on specific aspects of the Czech and Slovak national copyright frameworks. The theoretical knowledge frameworks established earlier will serve as a reference point against which the post-harmonization state of the Czech and Slovak national copyright frameworks will be compared. This comparison aims to highlight the anticipated changes resulting from both harmonization phases.

13.2 Reflections of the First Harmonization Phase in the Czech National Legislation

Regarding photogaphic products, the Czech copyright framework, as outlined in the AutZ 2000, presents a somewhat dual approach. Section 2(1) of the AutZ 2000 recognizes photographic works as authorial works of a *unique* nature. Simultaneously, it introduces a separate subsection that classifies certain photographic products as *original* authorial works. This distinction was necessitated by the harmonized requirements of the EU.[1549]

While this framework acknowledges the special qualities of photography, it also retains the traditional Czech view of authorial works and their inherent uniqueness.[1550] However, the current framework's differentiation of photographic products into these two categories needs to be reconciled with the broader harmonization efforts.

The Czech legislator's decision to categorize *original* photographic products in the new subsection of the AutZ 2000 significantly impacts provision of copyright protection. This change streamlines the process by eliminating the need for lengthy proving of the statistical uniqueness of photographic products.[1551] As a result, a wider range of photographic works can be protected by copyright with less cumbersome justification, highlighting the practical advantages of this legislative update.

The distinction between unique or original photographic products does not affect their copyright protection; rather, it only influences their theoretical classification. The introduction of the second subsection of Section 2 in the AutZ 2000 was intended to officially recognize the *original* status of certain photographic products and comply with EU harmonization efforts. Consequently, these *original* photographic products are subject to the lowered originality standard established by the EU legislator and the CJEU.

However, the Explanatory memorandum to the draft Act on copyright, on rights related to copyright and on amendments to certain acts (Copyright Act), brings much-needed clarity. It does not consider the addition of the option to appropriate *original* photographic products under copyright as a significant change. Instead, it clarifies the notional distinction between *unique* and *original* photographic products, thereby dispelling any ambiguity. This distinction is based on a mark of originality, which does not fulfil the requirement of a unique result of creative activity, as *unique* photographic products do.[1552]

It can also be said that by introducing copyright protection for *original* or non-unique photographic products, the AutZ 2000 universally covered all photographic products existing within the Czech Republic's copyright framework and eliminated the need to demonstrate their protectability by copyright via expert opinions and the ambiguity related to the authorial nature of photographic products in general.[1553]

[1549] Ivo Telec, 'Autorské právo k fotografiím podle nového autorského zákona,' *Právní rozhledy: časopis pro všechna právní odvětví* 539 (2000), p. 539.

[1550] Martin Valoušek, *Fotografie a právo: autorské právo a ochrana osobnosti ve vztahu k fotografii* (Leges, 2nd ed. 2022), p. 13.

[1551] Jan Kříž (ed)., *Autorský zákon a předpisy související: komentář* (Linde 2005), p. 53.

[1552] Důvodová zpráva k návrhu zákona o právu autorském, o právech souvisejících s právem autorským a o změně některých zákonů (autorský zákon). Sněmovní tisk 443/0. Vládní návrh zákona o právu autorském – EU (1. Oct. 2024), https://www.psp.cz/sqw/historie.sqw?o=3&t=443, § 2.

[1553] Ivo Telec, 'Autorské právo k fotografiím podle nového autorského zákona,' *Právní rozhledy: časopis pro všechna právní odvětví* 539 (2000), p. 539.

The said effect is also confirmed by the wording of Section 106 (4) of the AutZ 2000, which also enables the eligibility for copyright protection of products which were not protected under the previous regulations or whose content of protection was different from the one under AutZ 2000.[1554]

Also, the extension of the copyright term of protection within the meaning of Article 1 of the Term Directive I have been taken into account, and the original national term of protection, which was 50 years *post mortem auctoris*, has been extended to 70 years *post mortem auctoris* in order to adhere to EU harmonization.

13.3 Reflections of the Second Harmonization Phase in the Czech National Case Law

Before the adoption of the AutZ 2000 in 2000, all photographic products seeking copyright protection were required to meet a general criterion of statistical uniqueness. This requirement has also been reflected in Czech national case law. Although the relevant case chosen to demonstrate this was decided in 2006, the determination of a photographic product's eligibility for copyright protection had to comply with the provisions of the AZ 1965, meaning the assessment process was based on the legislation in effect at the time the photographic product was created. In this context, statistical uniqueness needed to be confirmed or refuted through an expert opinion, which concluded that the photographic product in question exhibited the necessary qualities, making it eligible for copyright protection as a photographic work.[1555]

The period leading up to the CJEU's decision in the *Painer case*, as well as prior to the adoption of AutZ 2000, was characterized by a trend emphasizing the necessity of determining the potential protectability of photographic products based on the requirement of statistical uniqueness. As already stated, the confirmation or refutation of this uniqueness was to rely on expert opinions.

In a 2020 case, the Regional Court in České Budějovice stated that a work's uniqueness cannot be interpreted merely as a statistical uniqueness. Instead, it should reflect the creator's personality. In this context, a work is seen as an expression of the author's personality and creative imagination, thereby qualifying it as *statistically unique*.[1556]

However, this Czech court eventually took a different stance, emphasizing the importance of statistical uniqueness. It argued that the reflection of the author's personality in a product should not justify its protection based solely on this statistical uniqueness. Rather, it should be assessed according to originality as defined by harmonized EU law. The Regional Court aligned its reasoning with guidance from the

1554 Sec. 106 (4) of the AutZ 2000.

1555 Supreme Court, 30 Cdo 1051/2006, 21 Dec. 2006.

1556 Regional Court in České Budějovice, 12 C 14/2020, 21 Jan. 2021.

Supreme Court, which is appropriate. Nonetheless, the court employed this reflection of personality to support an objective understanding of statistical uniqueness rather than focusing on the subjective originality required within the EU framework to establish the necessary connection between the author and their work.

In a 2021 case involving the unauthorized use of photographic products during an award ceremony, the High Court in Prague addressed their status as potential works. It concluded that a photographic product, as defined in Article 2(1) of the AutZ 2000, is considered either *unique* or *original*.[1557] However, it clarified that a photographic product cannot be both *unique* and *original* at the same time; instead, it can meet one of these criteria but not both cumulatively. This distinction raises interpretative challenges regarding the protectability of photographic products under Czech copyright law. Nevertheless, in practice, it should not matter whether a product is classified as unique or original; it should be subject to copyright protection either way.

In a 2022 ruling, the High Court in Prague determined that photographic products depicting the use of mobile phones are not eligible for copyright protection under the AutZ 2000. The Court cited the requirement of uniqueness as a key factor in determining whether a product can be protected by copyright. It explained that uniqueness corresponds to the concept of unreproducibility, indicating that the work does not need to possess absolute uniqueness, but rather a uniqueness that approaches absolute uniqueness.[1558]

In a 2023 case concerning the copyrightability of a dramatic play's name, the Supreme Court emphasized the requirements for copyright protection, including the notion of *statistical uniqueness*. According to the Court, a work's uniqueness relates to its unrepeatability. This definition suggests that copyright does not require a work to be 100% individual but rather to possess a nearly absolute level of *uniqueness*.[1559] The Supreme Court's stance affirms the necessity of considering *statistical uniqueness* when evaluating copyright protectability.

Subsequent case law following the CJEU's decision in the *Painer case* consistently highlights the importance of meeting the requirement of statistical uniqueness in determining the potential copyrightability of various products. However, such conclusions, particularly regarding photographic products after the *Painer decision*, are deemed unacceptable and contradictory to EU law's lowered originality standard. Although the Czech legislator has officially acknowledged this harmonization, it has done so in a limited manner that includes only original photographic products, leaving unique photographic works unaffected. However, this recognition is largely superficial, as it is not successfully applied in practice by Czech courts, which diverge from the intended effects of the EU harmonization, highlighting the need for more substantial changes.

[1557] High Court in Prague, 3 Co 170/2021, 19 Apr. 2022, para. 7.
[1558] High Court in Prague, 3 Co 79/2022, 17 Oct. 2023, para. 6.
[1559] Supreme Court, 27 Cdo 2023/2019, 24 Mar. 2021, para. 26.

13.4 Reflections of the First Harmonization Phase in the Slovak National Legislation

The previous chapters clearly demonstrate that the Czech legislator has opted to classify photographic products as having a *fictitious work* status. This approach aims to ensure that these products can be protected by copyright while also imposing a separate standard of originality. In contrast, the Slovak legislator has directly granted photographic products a work status, while still subjecting them to a separate originality standard. Despite these differing methods, both approaches share a common goal: achieving legislative conformity with EU harmonization.

However, one issue remained unresolved. Shortly after the introduction of the AZ 2015, some have pointed out the potential conflict between the requirement of *uniqueness* contained in it and the concept of *the author's own intellectual creation*. According to *Husovec*, the future development in this area depends on two factors. First, to what extent will the CJEU apply the originality standard based on *the author's own intellectual creation*?[1560] Second, how will Slovakian courts interpret the requirement of (statistical) *uniqueness*? As a result, it appears that the Slovak legislator did not clearly distinguish between the requirements of *uniqueness* and *originality* in the AZ 2015.[1561]

It is now established that the notion of *uniqueness* within the meaning of the AZ 20215 is to be understood as *original* within the meaning of harmonized EU law.[1562] This significant reinterpretation means that the traditional statistical type of uniqueness to which the notion referred to is no longer applicable for the purposes of fulfilling the requirement for a product's eligibility for copyright protection. As a result, the new interpretation of the notion of *uniqueness* for the purposes of AZ 2015 renders the introduction of the requirement of *uniqueness* in the wording of AZ 2015 seemingly redundant in practice.

In terms of photographic products, the harmonization activities surrounding the standard of originality have impacted Slovakia's copyright framework to a significant degree. It has become essential to recognize the copyrightability of photographic works, even if they are not *statistically unique*. This shift allows for a greater number of photographic products to be theoretically protected by copyright, broadening the scope of what can be considered *original*. By adopting this approach, the traditional requirement of *statistical uniqueness* has been rendered inapplicable. Consequently, in the realm of photographic products, Slovakia's established requirement of uniqueness has been replaced, both judicially and legislatively, by

1560 Martin Husovec, *Slovakia Adopts a New Copyright Act: It's a Mixed Bag—Part I* (1 Sep. 2024), https://copyrightblog.kluweriplaw.com/2016/02/29/slovakia-adopts-a-new-copyright-act-its-a-mixed-bag-part-i/

1561 Jarmila Lazíková, *Autorský zákon: komentár* (Iura Edition 2013), p. 53.

1562 Zuzana Adamová, *Právo duševného vlastníctva* (TINCT 2020), p. 30.

the requirement of originality. This aligns with the lower EU-standard of originality defined as *the author's own intellectual creation.*[1563]

The harmonization has not only improved the standard of originality but has also simplified the traditional process of proving the artistic qualities and statistical uniqueness of photographic products. This simplification has been achieved by legally subjecting photographic products to a lower originality standard, defined as *the author's own intellectual creation.* Additionally, judicial guidance has provided examples of photographer's choices that may be determinative for the formation of originality. As a result, the requirement for expert opinions to demonstrate a photographic product's eligibility for potential copyright protection has been eliminated, relieving the photographic industry of unnecessary bureaucratic obstacles.

In terms of the extension of copyright term of protection, the AZ 2015 has simply continued in the application of the extended term from the AZ 2003, thus reflecting the stability and continuity in this aspect of the law. The Slovak legislator had already taken into account the EU harmonization conducted in the area in the earlier national legislation. The introduction of the term of copyright protection in duration of 70 years *post mortem auctoris* has therefore not represented a significant novelty.

Since the CJEU has consistently applied the standard of *author's own intellectual creation* as a universally applicable and harmonized requirement for originality for all works, in the Slovak copyright framework, the requirement of (statistical) *uniqueness* has been effectively aligned with the harmonized EU standard of *author's own intellectual creation*, thereby replacing the traditional emphasis on (statistical) *uniqueness*. However, within the Slovak copyright framework, it was first the Slovak judiciary that has set the conditions for the secondary adjustments of national legislation.

13.5 Reflections of the Second Harmonization Phase in the Slovak National Case Law

Traditionally, the distinction between photographic products that could be protected by copyright and those that could not has relied on case law and legal theory. The determination of potential copyrightability often required expert assessments.[1564] Additionally, the level of creative effort exerted by the author and its expression in the product was not considered determinative for this differentiation.[1565] The current landscape, however, is characterized by relatively high requirements for copyright protection in relation to photographic products. It has been judicially acknowledged[1566] that the traditional criterion of *uniqueness* necessitates a higher standard

[1563] Jarmila Lazíková, *Autorský zákon č. 185/2015 Z.z: komentár* (Wolters Kluwer 2018), p. 40.
[1564] Jarmila Lazíková, *Autorský zákon č. 185/2015 Z.z: komentár* (Wolters Kluwer 2018), p. 39.
[1565] Peter Vojčík, *Právo duševného vlastníctva* (Aleš Čeněk 2012), p. 101.
[1566] Constitutional Court, III. ÚS 651/2016, 28. Nov. 2017.

for copyright eligibility. This higher standard was notably recognized in the decision made by the Slovak Constitutional Court (SCC) in the *'Tank Man'* case,[1567] which will be further explained in the following sections.

The defendant, a newspaper publishing company, was sued by the heirs of the photographer who captured a famous scene on 21 August, 1968, in Bratislava, now Slovakia, during the invasion of Czechoslovakia by the Warsaw Pact armies. The photograph at the centre of the dispute shows a bare-chested man in pyjamas standing in protest in front of a Soviet tank. The defendant published this photograph multiple times in 2003 and 2005 without crediting the author, Mr. *Bielik*, and without obtaining a licence. They also cropped and edited the image, thereby infringing on his personal and economic rights. All three general courts—the District Court, the Regional Court, and the Supreme Court—ruled in favour of Mr. *Bielik's* heirs. The defendant has now appealed to the final national judicial instance, the SCC.

To evaluate the protectability of the photographic product in question, we must use criteria defined by the AutZ 1965 that was in effect at the time of its creation. The Constitutional Court pointed out that for a product to be protected by copyright under AutZ 1965, it must primarily meet the requirement of *uniqueness*. This requirement signifies that the work results from a *'unique and unrepeatable intellectual and creative effort by the author, reflecting the author's personality and abilities'*.[1568]

Some argue that the photographic product in question was granted copyright protection largely due to the emotions it conveys, rather than its composition, which would typically be the determining factor.[1569] This perspective was supported by the Regional Court, which emphasized the impact of the emotions depicted on the observer's emotional perception. However, the author's prompt response also received acknowledgment. From further analysis by the SCC, it can be inferred that the photographer's compositional choices played a crucial role in conveying those emotions. In this context, it is important to recognize that emotions are a vital characteristic of a photographic product and represent one of the expressions of *free and creative choices*. The photographer skilfully adjusted the composition of the image to effectively capture the unfolding situation, thereby creating a conducive environment for the expression and transmission of emotions to various potential audiences.

The SCC has confirmed that the photographic product in question is protectable under copyright according to (Czecho) Slovak law. However, it has also made a statement regarding its potential protection under EU law. The SCC noted that the *statistical uniqueness* of a photographic work is no longer the key factor for copyright protectability, following the ruling of the CJEU in the *Painer case*.

[1567] Constitutional Court, II. ÚS 647/2014, 30. Sep. 2014.

[1568] Constitutional Court, II. ÚS 647/2014, 30. Sep. 2014, para 33.

[1569] Ryszard Markiewicz, *Zabawy z Prawem Autorskim Dawne i Nowe* (Wolters Kluwer, 2nd ed. 2022), p. 264.

Additionally, the SCC stated that the photographic product would certainly meet the conditions set by the EU's harmonized *originality* standard.

The SCC concludes that even if the photographic product in question is not deemed eligible for copyright protection under the AZ 1965, it may still be qualified for retroactive copyright protection based on its potential originality as defined by harmonized EU law.[1570] This ruling illustrates the possibility of obtaining copyright protection through harmonized EU law and the standard of originality it sets. In light of the SCC's findings, the photographic product was determined to possess characteristics that would secure its copyright protection.

As previously mentioned, the decision of the SCC, reached on 30 September, 2014, occurred before the adoption of the currently effective Copyright Act, the AZ 2015, which included an updated definition of works and photographic products. However, this decision was made after the CJEU's ruling in the *Painer case*. Consequently, the decision serves primarily as a judicial confirmation of the harmonized EU law but also establishes the necessary direction for future national treatment of photographic products within the Slovak copyright framework.

In this context, the decision of the SCC, issued by the highest judicial authority in the Slovak Republic, provides guidance for lower Slovak courts regarding the treatment of photographic products. Therefore, the wording of Section 3 (5) of the AZ 2015 codifies the legal principles established by this decision and the preceding case law.[1571]

In a 2015 case decided at the Regional Court in Žilina, provisions of the AZ 2003 had to be applied to determine the photographic product's protectability by copyright. Given the said Regional Court's decision, the AZ 2003 and its *statistical uniqueness* had to be applied. Regarding this, the photographic product in question was subject to the fulfilment of the traditional requirement of *statistical uniqueness*. Therefore, the photographic product had to fulfil the requirement for its protectability by copyright within the meaning of the general clause reserved for traditional works of art. The photographic product in question was found ineligible for copyright protection because it was taken in a usual manner, without the author's distinctive creativity. According to the Regional Court, the distinctive creativity must result from the creativity of an unmistakable unique character dependent on the individual personal characteristics of the author, thus making it distinguishable from other photographic products taken by other persons with, more or less, the same result.[1572] The said Regional Court has focused on the statistical *uniqueness* of the photographic product rather than on its *originality*.

In a 2015 case decided by the Regional Court in Žilina, the provisions of the AZ 2003 were applied once again to assess the eligibility for copyright protection

[1570] Constitutional Court, II. ÚS 647/2014, 30. Sep. 2014, para 34.

[1571] Martin Husovec, *Slovakia Adopts a New Copyright Act: It's a Mixed Bag—Part I* (1 Sep. 2024), https://copyrightblog.kluweriplaw.com/2016/02/29/slovakia-adopts-a-new-copyright-act-its-a-mixed-bag-part-i/

[1572] Regional Court in Žilina, 7 Co 335/2015, 23. Sep. 2015.

of a photographic product. The Regional Court began its analysis by referencing the harmonized EU originality standard, which requires that a work demonstrates *the author's own intellectual creation reflecting their personality* and includes *the expression of free and creative choices*, in line with the *Painer case* decision. The court then discussed the criteria of *uniqueness* and *inimitability*, citing the traditional requirement for statistical uniqueness as a way to distinguish between photographic products that can be protected by copyright as original works and those that do not meet these criteria. As a result, the latter cannot be protected by copyright. Ultimately, the Regional Court noted that the applicant had not adequately specified why their photographic product should be considered *unique and inimitable* or how it *reflects their personality as the author*.[1573]

The Regional Court conflates two distinct frameworks: traditional copyright protectability requirements and those established by EU harmonization. The former is indicated by references to *uniqueness* and *inimitability*, while the latter is captured in the concept of the *reflection of the author's personality*. As a result, it remains unclear which set of requirements the Regional Court intended to apply—whether traditional or EU harmonized standards.

This example illustrates the potential confusion that can arise from the use of non-harmonized terminology in practice. It is now widely accepted, as previously noted, that the traditional requirement of uniqueness should be interpreted in line with the EU's harmonized originality standard, rather than as a measure of statistical uniqueness. However, the ongoing use of this notion by Slovakian courts continues to lead to further ambiguity.

In a case analogous to the *Infopaq* decision, the SCC faced the task of determining whether the online copying and dissemination of magazine articles constitutes infringement of copyright under the laws of the Slovak Republic.[1574] While one might assume that the answer would be straightforward given the jurisprudence of the CJEU, previous national judicial instances had responded negatively to this question. The key issue at stake was whether the harmonized EU standard of originality could be applied to magazine articles, thereby taking precedence over the traditional requirement of statistical uniqueness.

The SCC acknowledged that it is the responsibility of national courts to interpret Section 3 (1) of the AZ 2015, which outlines the general clause for the copyrightability of works, in alignment with harmonized EU law—essentially, in a euro-conformist manner.[1575] With this conclusion, it became clear that preference would be given to the interpretations established by the CJEU, marking a shift away from the traditional Slovak approach to copyright protectability.

The Constitutional Court continued to enumerate the jurisprudence of the CJEU, highlighting the requirement of *author's own intellectual creation* as a universal

[1573] *Ibid.*
[1574] Constitutional Court, III. ÚS 651/2016, 28. Nov. 2017.
[1575] Constitutional Court, III. ÚS 651/2016, 28. Nov. 2017, para. 31.

harmonized EU standard for originality. According to the SCC, this body of CJEU case law demonstrates that the traditional Slovak doctrine of statistical uniqueness—understood in the context of Section 3 (1) of the AZ 2015—is much stricter than the originality standard established by harmonized EU law.[1576] Consequently, EU harmonization has effectively overcome the higher threshold of statistical uniqueness. This acknowledgement, issued by the highest judicial authority of the Slovak Republic and aligned with the conclusions of the CJEU, is binding across the entire Slovak copyright framework. However, as evidenced by subsequent case law following both decisions of the SCC, the elimination of the concept of statistical uniqueness and the application of the lower originality threshold continue to present challenges.

In a 2019 case decided by the Regional Court in Bratislava, the status of photographic works under AZ 2015 was called into question. The Regional Court stated that the quality of *uniqueness* or *unrepeatability* in photographic products distinguishes them as authorial works rather than mere craft products.[1577] Moreover, the Regional Court noted that the *uniqueness* concerning these photographic products cannot be regarded as absolute uniqueness; instead, it should be understood as an 'almost' absolute uniqueness.[1578]

This perspective sheds light on how the requirement of *uniqueness* is applied to photographic products. It cannot therefore be interpreted in its strict statistical sense, reserved solely for traditional works of art, but rather in a relative sense or as being nearly unique. Importantly, the requirement for uniqueness, as articulated in the general clause of AZ 2015, does not apply to photographic products. Instead, these products are subject only to the specific standard of originality defined in Section 3 (5) of AZ 2015: the *author's own intellectual creation*.

In this particular case, the Regional Court determined that the photographic products at hand were not subject to copyright protection. The court justified its decision by stating that the applicant failed to demonstrate an individual contribution to the photographic products that would render them unique, unmistakable, and distinguishable from others.[1579] According to the Regional Court, the applicant did not adequately trace the steps taken throughout the production process; where they attempted to do so, their explanation did not meet the court's standards for establishing the work's status.

The problematic aspect of the Regional Court's decision lies in its confusing references to the requirement of *uniqueness*. According to the Term Directives I & II, the *Painer case*, and provisions of the AZ 2015, photographic works are not subject to any requirements beyond that of an *author's own intellectual creation*, which reflects their personality. This concept of uniqueness should not be interpreted as

[1576] *Ibid.*

[1577] Regional Court in Bratislava, No. 5Co/239/2019, 10 Dec. 2019, para. 6.

[1578] Regional Court in Bratislava, No. 5Co/239/2019, 10 Dec. 2019, para. 14.

[1579] Regional Court in Bratislava, No. 5Co/239/2019, 10 Dec. 2019, para. 22.

statistical uniqueness or a form approaching absolute uniqueness; doing so would contradict the lower originality standard applicable to photographic works, as most do not meet such a stringent requirement.

Instead, the uniqueness referenced in the AZ 2015 should emphasize the photographer's distinct personality, authorial status, and moral rights accompanying it. The EU legislator introduced the lower *originality* standard precisely to eliminate the need to prove statistical uniqueness, aiming to prioritize acknowledging the author's unique personality rather than the statistical distinctiveness of their works. Consequently, photographic products should not be held to a standard that requires them to differentiate features that set them apart from the works of other photographers.

13.6 Confusing Translations and Usage of Terminology in the Slovak Copyright Framework

The Slovak legislator introduced the term *unique* (*jedinečný*) for the first time in the amendment of the current Copyright Act, the AZ 2015. This development was somewhat surprising, given that the term had not appeared in any of the previous versions of Slovak copyright acts.

In the official Slovak translation of the Term Directive II, the term *original* found in Recital 16 and Article 6 is translated as *pôvodný*.[1580] However, the Slovak legislator did not adopt *pôvodný* in the wording of the AZ 2015. Conversely, while the official translation does not include *jedinečný* (*unique*), the AZ 2015 does. This discrepancy indicates a lack of consistency in translations[1581] between *original* and its Slovak equivalents, *originálny* and *pôvodný*. Given that *jedinečný* (*unique*) is to be interpreted as *original* under harmonized EU law,[1582] there is significant potential for confusion regarding the meanings of these terms. Nonetheless, both *originálny* and *pôvodný* refer to the definition of *author's own intellectual creation*, which is identically translated in both the Term Directive II and the AZ 2015.

Regarding the copyright protectability of photographic products, Section 3 (1) of AZ 2015 should be considered *lex generalis*, while Section 3 (5) serves as *lex specialis*. Therefore, the copyrightability of photographic products should not rely on the broad stipulations of the former section but should instead be governed by the specific originality standard laid out in the latter section. Mandating that photographic products meet the requirements of the general clause would contradict EU

[1580] See the Slovak version of the Term Directive II.

[1581] Martin Husovec, 'Judikatórna harmonizácia pojmu autorského diela v únijnom práve,' 12 *Bulletin slovenskej advokácie* (2012), p. 18.

[1582] Zuzana Adamová, *Právo duševného vlastníctva* (TINCT 2020), p. 30.

harmonized law. Consequently, the requirement of *uniqueness* should not apply to photographic products at all.

13.7 On the Necessity of Displaying Personal Touch and its Relationship to Statistical Uniqueness

As a preliminary remark, the requirement of statistical uniqueness, as an ontological concept in copyright understanding, originated in Switzerland and was initially introduced into the former Czechoslovak copyright framework by *Karel Knap.*[1583] This concept was subsequently incorporated into the distinct copyright frameworks of the two successor states of Czechoslovakia: the Czech Republic and the Slovak Republic. In light of the harmonization efforts undertaken thus far, the Czech Republic and the Slovak Republic have adopted varying approaches to this traditional concept, which will be explored in greater detail below.

The traditional statistical uniqueness requirement within the Slovak and Czech copyright frameworks is relatively stringent. It mandates that all works seeking copyright protection demonstrate *'creativity of an unmistakable special character dependent on the individual personal qualities of the author.'*[1584] The conclusion reached by Advocate General Trstenjak prior to the CJEU's *Painer case* decision regarding the *'not excessively high'*[1585] requirements governing the copyright protection of photographic works in accordance with Article 6 of the Term Directive II may seem somewhat contradictory. However, it is crucial to note that this aspect of the requirements was not referenced or discussed in the CJEU's ruling.

As articulated by the CJEU in the *Painer case* decision, a photographic work eligible for copyright must not only satisfy the now-universal harmonized originality standard but also reflect the author's personality through a *personal touch*. The CJEU specifically referred to the existence of the personal touch in connection with photographic works, and this reflection of the author's personality has since been integrated into the originality standard. This integration marks a significant evolution in copyright law. However, as noted, this is not explicitly conveyed as a distinct mark of *personal touch.*

As argued previously, the necessity of displaying a personal touch—representing the reflection of author's personality through *free and creative choices*—is essential in establishing the *originality* of the photographic work. Thus, *originality*

1583 Pavel Koukal, *Autorské právo, public domain a lidská práva* (Masarykova univerzita 2019), p. 47.

1584 Martin Husovec, 'Judikatórna harmonizácia pojmu autorského diela v únijnom práve,' 12 *Bulletin slovenskej advokácie* (2012), p. 19.

1585 Opinion of AG Trstenjak In Case C-145/10, *Eva-Maria Painer v Standard VerlagsGmbH and Others*, 12 Apr. 2011, ECLI:EU:C:2011:239, para. 124.

should indicate the author's and their creation's intrinsic connection or relationship. However, considering the additional requirement of a *personal touch*, the initial intent to lower the originality standard of photographic works—by emphasizing the relationship between the author and their creation—may have inadvertently resulted in a heightened requirement, comparable to that of *statistical uniqueness*.

Suppose the assertion holds that every individual assuming the role of an author or photographer possesses a unique personality and that this personality must be manifested in their photographic work as a *personal touch*. In that case, it can be argued that the originality standard has been raised rather than lowered. This is because achieving *statistical uniqueness* in photographic products is inherently more challenging, though not impossible. Such a perspective supports the notion that the criteria for copyright protection of photographic works should not be set at a low level.[1586] However, this view contrasts the actions of the EU legislator and the CJEU regarding EU copyright law, particularly as they continue to broaden the scope of what can be considered eligible for copyright protection.

Thus, examining the extent and level at which national courts in the Member States will enforce this requirement and its significance is crucial. A vital question arises: What is the relationship between the EU's harmonized standard of *author's own intellectual creation* and Slovakia's national criteria of *creativity of unmistakable special character* or *statistical uniqueness*? This question is not only pertinent but also requires careful exploration and clarification.[1587]

In relation to the adoption and application of the *personal touch* requirement within national copyright frameworks, its threshold must be appropriately calibrated to align with the intended lower EU standard of originality. The additional requirement to reflect the author's personality through this *personal touch* is somewhat misguided.[1588] While the originality requirement, as defined by the harmonized standard, should remain in effect, however it must not be set excessively high or too low.

The rationale behind introducing the requirement to *reflect the author's personality*, as articulated by the EU legislator and later applied by the CJEU through the concept of *personal touch*, may stem from concerns that the primary criterion of an author's own intellectual creation might not adequately differentiate copyrightable photographic works from those that are not.[1589] In this context, the *personal touch* could function as a figurative handbrake—a tool to separate purely mechanical photographic products, or those constrained solely by technical limitations, from works with prominent human and personal elements. However, the requirement of *au-*

1586 Christian Handig, 'Was ist eine "eigene geistige Schöpfung der Urhebers"?: Der auslegungsbedürftige Werkbegriff des europäischen Urheberrechts,' *UFITA* 55 (2009), p. 55.

1587 Peter Sokol, *Podali sme amicus curiae pred Ústavným súdom* (1 Sep. 2024), https://eisionline.org/2012/03/13/podali-sme-amicus-curiae-pred-ustavnym-sudom/

1588 Christian Handig, 'Was ist eine "eigene geistige Schöpfung der Urhebers"?: Der auslegungsbedürftige Werkbegriff des europäischen Urheberrechts,' *UFITA* 55 (2009), p. 14.

1589 *Ibid.*

thor's own intellectual creation alone should be sufficient without the need for the additional *personal touch* criterion.

Regarding *uniqueness*, the concept of *personal touch* is intended to represent this attribute in a photographic work. Uniqueness pertains not only to the uniqueness of personality of the photographer but also to the statistical uniqueness of the photographic product in a philosophical sense. Nevertheless, in the context of EU harmonization, both legal theory and practice have made concessions, indicating that the *personal touch* requirement cannot serve as a means to establish the statistical uniqueness of the photographer's personality. Doing so would contradict the lowered originality standard of the *author's own intellectual creation.*

In this sense, the requirements of *personal touch* and *statistical uniqueness* would aim not merely to differentiate works (allowing for the possibility of similar creations) but to establish a level of distinction such that the photographic product is unique from a statistical perspective. This shift moves the focus from fundamental distinctiveness—where another photographer might produce a similar work differently—to true statistical uniqueness, which posits that no other photographer could have created the photographic product in the same way.[1590]

The requirement of a personal touch should be understood as a reflection of the photographer's *free and creative choices*. Whenever a photographer exercises their creativity, they do so in alignment with their unique personality, which should be evident in the final photographic product. In essence, the imprint of the photographer's personality, manifested as a personal touch, is expressed through these free and creative choices.

The assessment of this personal touch revolves around recognizing the nature of the relationship between the photographer and their work. The term *personal* here pertains to the author's personality and signifies the connection between the photographer and their photographic product. As *Susan Sontag* quoted *Harry Callahan*, it is about an individual expressing themselves in a distinctive manner through this relationship—not merely for the sake of being different.[1591]

13.8 Compliance with the Conditions of the 10-step Test

In examining the outcomes of both harmonization phases, it is evident that the national copyright frameworks of the Czech Republic and the Slovak Republic started from an identical position, characterized by the necessity to address the traditional requirement of statistical uniqueness. Both copyright frameworks have been

[1590] Christian Handig, 'Was ist eine "eigene geistige Schöpfung der Urhebers"?: Der auslegungsbedürftige Werkbegriff des europäischen Urheberrechts,' *UFITA* 55 (2009), p. 8.

[1591] Susan Sontag, *On Photography* (Penguin Books 2008), p. 118.

demonstrated to have adapted to the conclusions and intended effects arising from these harmonization phases. However, the nature of these adjustments and their implications remain the subject of debate, particularly regarding applying a lowered standard of originality to photographic works.

In the Czech Republic, introducing an additional requirement—specifically, the need for a *personal touch*—to the definition of an author's intellectual creation has not yet achieved a significant jurisprudential response. Nevertheless, it can be anticipated that the requirement of absolute uniqueness within the Czech copyright framework will lead to a broad, informal approach by Czech jurisprudence in both the introduction and subsequent reinterpretation of its established concepts. As previously mentioned, the requirement of statistical uniqueness stands out as a potential focal point for this (re)interpretation.

Regarding compliance with the conditions of the 10-step test, it can be concluded that the Czech national copyright framework still needs to meet this standard adequately. In other words, the assessment test designed to determine the copyrightability of photographic works needs to be applied effectively in line with its intended purpose.

Conversely, the Slovak Republic's approach has diverged notably from that of the Czech Republic. Here, the additional condition of a *personal touch* has received appropriate jurisprudential attention. The SCC has established the presence of the *personal touch* as a required standard of originality of photographic works. Subsequently, Slovak jurisprudence has come to interpret this requirement as a substitute for the traditional standard of statistical uniqueness. However, this landmark decision and its establishment have yet to be consistently understood and applied correctly by lower Slovak courts.

The Slovak national copyright framework is obliged to adhere to the 10-step test, as mandated by the jurisprudence of the SCC. Nevertheless, lower-instance courts often need help in applying this test correctly, sometimes confusing it with the traditional requirement of *statistical uniqueness*, which complicates the assessment of copyrightability of photographic works.

13.9 Interim Conclusion on the Comparison of Acknowledgements of Harmonization in Czech and Slovak Copyright Frameworks

From adopting Term Directive I, it became clear that photographic products would be exempt from the varying national treatments in the Member States, which made them subject to various standards of originality and thresholds. This exemption was reaffirmed in Article 6 of Term Directive II and further solidified by the CJEU's decision in the *Painer case*. Subsequently, this exemption was extended to all subject-matter eligible for copyright protection under the *originality* standard defined as an *author's own intellectual creation*, including additional elements such as a *personal touch*.

The Slovak copyright framework has adapted to this harmonization, as evidenced by two decisions from its Constitutional Court. However, it remains for the lower courts to align fully with this shift and begin to reject the traditional (higher) originality requirement of statistical uniqueness in practice. In essence, the Slovak copyright framework has moved from an objective understanding of originality to a more subjective perspective.

The requirement of statistical uniqueness can illustrate the distinction between objective and subjective perceptions of originality. The traditional expectation of uniqueness from a statistical standpoint reflects the objective understanding of originality; it necessitates that a work is objectively unique when compared to other creations. Conversely, the subjective understanding views *originality* as rooted in the author's relationship with their intellectual creation. In this context, the assessment of originality—and consequently, the potential for copyright protectability—does not extend beyond this individual relationship. Given the narrower scope of assessment, the requirements are inherently lower, resulting in a more passable threshold. Thus, within the Slovak copyright framework, uniqueness should be interpreted as being original within the meaning of the harmonized EU law.

In contrast, the Czech copyright framework still needs to address the consequences of EU harmonization in this area adequately. Unlike Slovakia's judicial recognition, the Czech framework has not followed suit. As a result, the Czech Republic continues to adhere to the requirement of statistical uniqueness, subjecting photographic products and other works to a higher threshold of originality and thereby denying potential copyright protection to potential works. This approach contravenes the obligation of a euro-conformist interpretation of EU law.

Regarding photographic products, the Czech copyright framework is thus awaiting a pivotal ruling akin to the *Tank Man* decision, which would officially shift away from the traditional understanding of conditions for copyright protectability—namely, the statistical uniqueness requirement—and align it with the fully harmonized EU standard of an author's own intellectual creation that reflects their personality.

14 INTERIM CONCLUSION ON THE HYPOTHESES AND RESEARCH QUESTIONS

14.1 Hypothesis No. 1 and Research Question A

To address Hypothesis No. 1 and provide an answer to Research Question A, the following conclusion is presented:

Based on the conducted research, it has been sufficiently demonstrated that, as a result of both harmonization phases, an originality standard of *author's own intellectual creation* has been established as the sole requirement for copyright protection eligibility of photographic products within the copyright framework of the EU. This originality standard has undergone numerous judicial refinements and interpretations, leading to its clearer meaning and establishment of firmer boundaries for its practical application.

It can be therefore stated with reasonable certainty that, for a photographic product to be eligible for copyright protection within the copyright framework of the EU, it must be capable of characterization as the *author's own intellectual creation.* This requires a production process that allows *creative freedom* to a sufficient extent, enabling the incorporation of *free and creative choices*. A photographic product resulting from such production process must also bear the author's *personal* touch, be capable of *being perceptible with sufficient precision and objectivity*, and must be *excluded of any functional elements*.

Only when the aforementioned conditions are met in a final photographic product, can the effect in a form of copyrightability within the meaning of the harmonized EU law be associated with such photographic product.

14.2 Hypothesis No. 2 and Research Question B

To address Hypothesis No. 2 and provide an answer to Research Question B, the following conclusion is presented:

Research into the national copyright frameworks of the four selected Member States has demonstrated that approaches to adjusting to the conclusions and subsequent intended effects of both harmonization phases are not uniform. In terms of reception of these conclusions and subsequent intended effects, the four assessed national copyright frameworks can be categorized into two categories.

The first category includes the German and French copyright frameworks, where the conditions for copyright protection of photographic products did not necessitate amendments of the respective national copyright legislation. The second category includes the Czech and Slovak copyright frameworks, where the conditions for copyright protection of photographic products did require amendments of the respective national copyright legislation.

The first category of national copyright frameworks, Germany and France, employed an informal approach, characterized by EU-conforming interpretation of the existing national requirements and concepts, without formal amendments. The second category of national copyright frameworks, Czech and Slovak Republics, by contrast, employed a formal approach, characterized by formal amendments of the existing national requirements and concepts. This formal approach resulted only in the formal recognition of photographic products as a subject-matter eligible for copyright protection based on the reduced EU harmonized originality standard. However, in addition to this formal approach, both national copyright frameworks also incorporated the informal approach. The second category therefore represents a mix of both, the formal and informal, approaches towards the reception of the conclusions and subsequent intended effects of both harmonization phases. This mixed approach was necessitated by the traditional application of the requirement of statistical uniqueness.

In summary, it can be said that approaches towards the reception of the conclusions and subsequent intended effects of both harmonization phases of national copyright frameworks of the Member States vary. However, the common goal remains adaptation to harmonization.

14.3 Hypothesis No. 3 and Research Question C

To address Hypothesis No. 3 and provide an answer to Research Question C, the following conclusion is presented:

Based on the conducted research, it has been sufficiently demonstrated that the effect of both harmonization phases has been an increase in the number of photographic products potentially eligible for copyright protection within the entirety of copyright framework of the EU. This is due to the establishment of the originality standard of the *author's own intellectual creation* as the sole requirement for copyrightability.

This increase in copyright-eligible photographic products is also supported by case law in the national copyright frameworks of Germany, France, and Slovakia. The increase of potentially copyright protectable photographic products has also led to an increase of total number of protectable photographic products, however only within the French and Slovak copyright frameworks. This is because Germany still provides a related-right type of protection to non-original photographic products. Such photographic products, while now eligible for copyright protection, remained and still remain protected under a related right type of protection.

Certain national copyright frameworks of the Member States have shown resistance to the conclusions and subsequent intended effects of both harmonization phases. In the Czech Republic, for instance, the increase in number of copyright protectable photographic products is merely anticipated by legislatively set conditions, since the Czech courts still continue to apply the traditional requirement of statistical uniqueness.

Due to the absence of a settlement with the applicability of the requirement of statistical uniqueness by the highest Czech jurisprudential authorities, this traditional requirement seems to remain valid, in practice at least. Only the national copyright framework of Slovakia has succeeded in dealing with the said *heritage* in the form of the requirement of statistical uniqueness; however, even in Slovakia, where the matter was settled by the SCC—the court of the highest judicial instance, courts of lower instances seem to continue to apply the traditional requirement, sometimes event jointly with the EU harmonized one, leading to much confusion.

In conclusion, the lowered nature of the formulated originality standard of the *author's own intellectual creation* is also recognized at the national levels of copyright frameworks of the Member States. However, in one of the assessed national copyright frameworks, this recognition remains largely formal so far.

15 CONCLUSION

The analysis of national and EU perspectives on the copyright treatment of photographic products demonstrates that the medium of photography is firmly established. Legal regulations concerning copyright have not hindered the advancement or distribution of photographic technology. Moreover, copyright has consistently found ways to protect photographic works, though this protection comes with limitations—specifically, the requirement of originality.

As noted in the introduction, within the copyright framework of the EU, copyright protection focuses primarily on the creator—the photographer, rather than on their creation.[1592] In this context, every creation reflecting its author's personality indirectly obtains copyright protection through this reflection. For photographic products, this reflection takes the form of an additional element: a *personal touch*. Referring to *personal touch* as an additional element underscores that it was not the first formulated and solely applicable requirement for copyright protection within the copyright framework of the EU. The initial foundational requirement was that of the author's own intellectual creation. Later, through the jurisprudence of the CJEU, other additional criteria were introduced, including *creative freedom, free and creative choices, perceptibility with sufficient precision and objectivity*, and the *exclusion of functional elements*. However, the last two criteria seem largely irrelevant for photographic products.

Upon closer examination, the applicable requirements of the *author's own intellectual creation* and *personal touch*, as part of the harmonized EU originality standard formulated during both harmonization phases, might initially seem to disqualify a significant number of photographic products from copyright protection. However, the research indicates that establishing originality through a combination of the *author's own intellectual creation* and *personal touch* criteria is achievable in most cases. This combination has been found present in photographic products across most genres. Consequently, the lowered threshold for copyright protection has led to an increase in copyrightable photographic products within the copyright framework of the EU.

However, the formulated harmonized originality standard, particularly its later form *enhanced* through additional elements formulated through the jurisprudence of the CJEU, must have been practically applied within the national copyright frameworks of the Member States. This approach was intended to be implemented primarily by national legislators and, more importantly, national courts. However, as

[1592] Andreas Rahmatian, 'Originality in UK Copyright Law: The Old "Skill and Labour" Doctrine Under Pressure,' 44 *IIC* 4 (2013).

the research results show, not all Member States adhered to the harmonization to the same extent or in the same way. The adherence to and reception of the harmonized originality standard of the *author's own intellectual creation* has been destined to be most effectively executed and comprehended within the national copyright framework of France. This smooth transition and reception can likely be attributed to the substantial similarities between the traditional French requirement of originality and the EU-harmonized originality standard, particularly given the emphasis on reflecting the author's personality in photographic products. For this reason, it is advisable to examine the traditional aspects of the French copyright framework related to originality when seeking the origins and foundations of the EU harmonized standard of originality.

As previously mentioned, the positive way the CJEU has constructed the room for creativity available to photographers—allowing them to make *free and creative choices* during the production process—suggests that national courts should always make a finding of originality and cannot simply deny copyright protection.[1593] Nonetheless, this finding and its substantiation by national courts might still depend on various factors, such as how the facts are presented to the court, the circumstances of the case, and, most importantly, the argumentation of lawyers.[1594] Additionally, as previously noted, the active cooperation of photographers themselves should not be considered negligible.

Nonetheless, if photographers present focused, technically accurate arguments, most of their photographic products could be recognized as photographic works protectable by copyright.[1595] If a photographer consciously incorporates *free and creative choices* into the production process of a photographic product, manifesting as their personal touch, it should clearly qualify as a photographic work within the meaning of the EU-harmonized originality standard, thus making it eligible for copyright protection. After all, photographers have traditionally been required to explain what they are doing and why it is valuable.[1596] In this context, such explanations will become more focused on substantiating the conditions required to meet the harmonized originality standard. Most photographic products possess this personal touch, and in such cases, it only needs to be substantiated.

This is ensured by the established subjective nature of originality, which depends on the *free and creative choices* of the photographer. In this context, the photographer must maintain a conscious intellectual presence regarding the free and creative choices made during the production process; otherwise, substantiating the presence of their personal touch may prove problematic or even impossible.

1593 Stef van Gompel, 'Creativity, Autonomy, and Personal Touch' In: Mireille van Eechoud, Jostein Gripsrud & Lionel Bently, *Work of Authorship* (Amsterdam University Press, 2015), p. 124.

1594 Stef van Gompel, 'Creativity, Autonomy, and Personal Touch' In: Mireille van Eechoud, Jostein Gripsrud & Lionel Bently, *Work of Authorship* (Amsterdam University Press, 2015), p. 130.

1595 Melanie Overbeck, *Der Lichtbildschutz gem. § 72 UrhG im Lichte der Digitalfotografie* (Lit 2018), p. 122.

1596 Susan Sontag, *On Photography* (Penguin Books, 2008), p. 115.

Nonetheless, it remains to be seen whether the subjective approach will continue to be applied within the EU copyright framework, especially in light of the two recent referrals to the CJEU.[1597] Both referrals, among other things, seek to answer the question of whether the originality assessment process and its potential findings should be based on the author's subjective perspective or an objective standard—that is, whether the author's subjective approach and perspective should prevail over the objective perception and criteria. However, both national referring courts lean towards an objective standard.

To conclude, within the current harmonized framework—with unambiguously and comprehensibly identified constituents of originality in photographic products, as well as clearly defined and set boundaries for applying the EU harmonized originality standard, including the originality assessment process—national courts in the Member States are obliged to proceed in a manner conforming with the EU harmonized law. Given that the harmonization in the field of originality standard has been achieved via Directives and jurisprudence of the CJEU, Member States have a twofold approach available. However, both aim toward the same end.

First, national copyright frameworks may abandon their traditional norms and replace them entirely with new ones, harmonized by the EU—a method known as the formal approach. Second, national copyright frameworks may choose to interpret their traditional norms in a way that would ensure their conformity and alignment with the EU harmonized law—a method known as the informal approach. It has been observed and established that Member States creatively apply these approaches depending on the characteristics of their national copyright frameworks, particularly in terms of rigidity and resistance to external, foreign influences. A combination of both approaches is sometimes applied within a single framework.

Still, harmonization in the field of copyright seems far from complete. Rather, it appears to be a continuously evolving and expanding process, and the originality standard of an *author's own intellectual creation* shares these characteristics as well. In this regard, we can anticipate further *refinements* from the CJEU in the form of setting figurative borders of application in practice and further clarifications regarding its meaning.

Photography itself is also constantly evolving—not only in its technological aspects but also in its social and legal status. The effects of harmonization, in both of its phases, have had a significant impact on this evolution. These effects have contributed to a more precise definition of the conditions upon the fulfillment of which a photographic product can attain the legal status of a photographic work eligible for copyright protection. Through attaining such legal status, the social status of this photographic product also advances, becoming more embedded and accepted within society. This embedding and acceptance further extend to the entire medium of photography.

[1597] CJEU Case C-580/23, *Mio and Others*, and Case C-795/23, *konektra*.

In light of the above, both phases of harmonization have considerably contributed to greater equalization of photographic products with other *traditional* works of art, as well as to their stronger establishment within the realm of harmonized EU copyright law. Finally, we can expect further illumination of the photographic production process and specificities of photographic products, thus revealing the nature of photography as a medium to a broader public.

BIBLIOGRAPHY

Books and Monographs

1. Paul Abel, *Urhebervertragsrecht: Handbuch* (Nomos 2022).
2. Karel Václav Adámek, *O právu autorském dle zákona ze dne 26. prosince 1895 č. 197 ř.z.* (Moravská knihtisk 1898).
3. Zuzana Adamová & Branislav Hazucha, *Autorský zákon: komentár* (C.H. Beck 2018).
4. Zuzana Adamová, *Právo duševného vlastníctva* (TINCT 2020).
5. Robert Stephen Paul Beekes & Lucien van Beek, *Etymological Dictionary of Greek* (Brill 2010).
6. Valérie-Laure Bénabou & André Françon, *Droits d'auteur, droits voisins et droit communautaire* (Bruylant 1997).
7. Lionel Bently et al., *Intellectual Property Law* (Oxford University Press, 6th ed. 2022).
8. Lionel Bently & Brad Sherman, *Intellectual Property Law* (Oxford University Press, 4th ed. 2014).
9. Rodrigo Bercovitz Rodríguez-Cano & Ignacio Garrote Fernández-Díez, *La unificación del derecho de propiedad intelectual en la Unión Europea* (Tirant lo Blanch 2019).
10. Christian Berger & Sebastian Wündisch (eds.), *Urhebervertragsrecht: Handbuch* (Nomos, 3rd ed. 2022).
11. John Berger, *Understanding a Photograph* (Penguin Books 2013).
12. André Bertrand, *Droit d'auteur* (Dalloz, 3rd ed. 2010).
13. Nicolas Binctin, *Droit de la propriété intellectuelle: droit d'auteur, brevet, droits voisins, marque, dessins et modèles* (LGDJ, 7th ed. 2022).
14. Marcel Bisges, *Die Kleine Münze im Urheberrecht: Analyse des ökonomischen Aspekts des Werkbegriffs* (Nomos 2014).
15. Nicolas Bouche, *Intellectual Property Law in France* (Wolters Kluwer, 3rd ed. 2017).
16. Hayleigh Bosher & Eleonora Rosati (eds.), *Developments and directions in intellectual property law: twenty years of the IPKat* (Oxford University Press 2023).
17. Georg Hendrik Christiaan Bodenhausen (ed.), *Guide to the Berne Convention for the Protection of Literary and Artistic Works* (BIRPI 1968).
18. Christophe Caron, *Droit d'auteur et droits voisins* (LexisNexis, 6th ed. 2020).
19. Caroline Carreau, *Mérite et droit d'auteur* (Librairie générale de droit et de jurisprudence 1981).
20. Helena Chaloupková & Petr Holý, *Autorský zákon: komentář* (C.H. Beck, 6th ed. 2023).
21. Karel Císař, *Co je to fotografie?* (Herrmann & synové 2004).
22. Code de la propriété intellectuelle 2022 (LexisNexis, 23rd ed. 2021).
23. Code de la propriété intellectuelle: annoté et commenté (Dalloz, 23rd ed. 2023).

24. Mélanie Clément-Fontaine, *Synthèse. 70 Revue Lamy Droit de l'immatériel* (2011).
25. William R. Cornish & David Llewelyn, *Intellectual Property: Patents, Copyright, Trade Marks and Allied Rights* (Sweet & Maxwell, 6th ed. 2007).
26. Paul p. Craig & Carol Harlow (eds.), *Lawmaking in the European Union* (Kluwer Law International 1998).
27. Jean-Luc Daval, *Photography: History of an Art* (Skira/Rizzoli, R. F. M. 1982).
28. Richard Davis, Thomas St Quintin & Guy Tritton, *Tritton on Intellectual Property in Europe* (Sweet & Maxwell, 6th ed. 2022).
29. Sari Depreeuw, *The Variable Scope of the Exclusive Economic Rights in Copyright* (Kluwer Law International 2014).
30. Estelle Derclaye (ed.), *Research handbook on the future of EU copyright* (Edward Elgar 2009).
31. Henri Desbois, *Le droit d'auteur en France* (Dalloz, 3rd ed. 1978).
32. Thomas Dreier & Gernot Schulze, *Urheberrechtsgesetz: Urheberrechts-Diensteanbieter-Gesetz, Verwertungsgesellschaftengesetz, Nebenurheberrecht, Kunsturhebergesetz: Kommentar* (C.H. Beck, 7th ed. 2022).
33. Thomas Dreier & Gernot Schulze, *Urheberrechtsgesetz: Verwertungsgesellschaftengesetz, Kunsturhebergesetz: Kommentar* (C.H. Beck, 6th ed. 2018).
34. Gunda Dreyer et al., *Urheberrecht: Urheberrechtsgesetz, Verwertungsgesellschaftengesetz, Kunsturhebergesetz* (C.F. Müller, 4th ed. 2018).
35. František Drtikol, *Oči široce otevřené* (Svět 2002).
36. Bernard Edelman, *Le droit saisi par la photographie suivi de Le personnage et son double La rue et le droit d'auteur L'oeil du droit, nature et droit d'auteur* (Flammarion 2001).
37. Mireille van Eechoud (ed.), *Harmonizing European copyright law: the challenges of better lawmaking* (Kluwer Law International 2009).
38. Mireille Van Eechoud, Jostein Gripsrud & Lionel Bently, *Work of Authorship* (Amsterdam University Press 2015).
39. Jan Eichelberger, Thomas Wirth, & Fedor Seifert (eds.), *UrhG Urheberrechtsgesetz: UrhG, UrhDaG, VGG: Handkommentar* (Nomos, 4th ed. 2022).
40. Dana Ferchland, *Fotografieschutz im Wandel: Auswirkungen technischer, künstlerischer und rechtlicher Veränderungen auf den Urheberrechtsschutz von Fotografien* (Verlag Dr. Kovač 2018).
41. Ysolde Gendreau, Axel Nordemann, & Rainer Oesch (eds.), *Copyright and photographs: an international survey* (Kluwer Law International 1999).
42. Johann Gottlieb Fichte, *Johann Gottlieb Fichte's sämmtliche Werke* (Verlag von Veit und Comp 1846).
43. Moritz Finke, *Werk und Veränderung: Verwertungsrechte an veränderten Gestaltungen im Urheberrecht* (Mohr Siebeck 2022).
44. Vilém Flusser et al., *Za filosofii fotografie* (Fra, 2nd ed. 2013).
45. André Françon, *Cours de propriété littéraire, artistique et industrielle* (Les Cours de droit 1999).
46. Pierre Frémond, *Le droit de la photographie, le droit sur l'image* (Publicness, 3rd ed. 1985).
47. Bryan A. Garner & Henry Campbell Black (eds.), *Black's Law Dictionary* (Thomson Reuters, 11th ed. 2019).

48. Pierre-Yves Gautier, *Propriété littéraire et artistique* (Presses universitaires de France, 11th ed 2019).
49. Pierre-Yves Gautier & Nathalie Blanc, *Droit de la propriété littéraire et artistique* (LGDJ 2021).
50. Ysolde Gendreau, *La protection des photographies en droit d'auteur français, américain, britannique et canadien* (LGDJ 1994).
51. Ysolde Gendreau, Axel Nordemann, & Rainer Oesch (eds.), *Copyright and photographs: an international survey* (Kluwer Law International 1999).
52. Daniel J. Gervais, *(Re)structuring Copyright: A Comprehensive Path to International Copyright Reform* (Edward Elgar Publishing 2017).
53. Paul Goldstein & Marketa Trimble, *International Intellectual Property Law: Cases and Materials* (Foundation Press, 5th ed. 2019).
54. Stef van Gompel, *Formalities in Copyright Law: An Analysis of their History, Rationales and Possible Future* (Wolters Kluwer 2011).
55. René Gouriou, *La photographie et le droit d'auteur* (Pichon et Durand-Auzias 1959).
56. Peter Groves, *A Dictionary of Intellectual Property Law* (Edward Elgar Publishing 2012).
57. Horst Heitland, *Der Schutz der Fotografie im Urheberrecht Deutschlands, Frankreichs und der Vereinigten Staaten von Amerika* (C.H. Beck 1995).
58. Georg Herbst (ed.), *Festschrift für Rainer Klaka* (J. Schweitzer Verlag 1987).
59. Reto M. Hilty, Christophe Geiger, & Valérie-Laure Benabou (eds.), *Impulse für eine europäische Harmonisierung des Urheberrechts* (Springer 2007).
60. Irena Holcová et al., *Autorský zákon a předpisy související* (Wolters Kluwer 2019).
61. Albert Sydney Hornby & Sally Wehmeier (eds.), *Oxford Advanced Learner's Dictionary of Current English* (Oxford University Press, 7th ed. 2009).
62. Heinrich Hubmann, Alexander Peukert & Manfred Rehbinder, *Urheberrecht und verwandte Schutzrechte: ein Studienbuch* (C. H. Beck, 19th ed. 2023).
63. Robin Earle Kelsey, *Photography and the Art of Chance* (Belknap Press 2015).
64. Markéta Klusoňová, *Vybrané otázky z art práva* (Masarykova univerzita 2017).
65. Eva-Marie König, *Der Werkbegriff in Europa: eine rechtsvergleichende Untersuchung des britischen, französischen und deutschen Urheberrechts* (Mohr Siebeck 2015).
66. Walter Koschatzky, *Die Kunst der Photographie: Technik, Geschichte, Meisterwerke* (Deutscher Taschenbuch Verlag 1987).
67. Pavel Koukal, *Autorské právo, public domain a lidská práva* (Masarykova univerzita 2019).
68. Jan Kříž (ed.), *Autorský zákon a předpisy související: komentář* (Linde 2005).
69. Annette Kur & Thomas Dreier, *European Intellectual Property Law: Text, Cases and Materials* (Edward Elgar Publishing 2013).
70. Annette Kur, Thomas Dreier & Stefan Luginbühl, *European Intellectual Property Law: Text, Cases and Materials* (Edward Elgar Publishing, 2019).
71. Hugh Ian Lang Laddie, Peter Prescott & Mary Vitoria, *The Modern Law of Copyright and Designs* (LexisNexis, 4th ed. 2011).
72. Reto M. Hilty (ed.), *Balancing copyright: a survey of national approaches* (Springer 2012).
73. Jarmila Lazíková, *Autorský zákon č. 185/2015 Z.z: komentár* (Wolters Kluwer 2018).
74. Jarmila Lazíková, *Autorský zákon: komentár* (Iura Edition 2013).

75. Valérie Varnerot, *Leçons de droit de la propriété littéraire et artistique* (Ellipses 2012).
76. Silke von Lewinski, *International Copyright Law and Policy* (Oxford University Press 2008).
77. Silke von Lewinski, *Copyright throughout the World* (Thomson/West 2022).
78. Xavier Linant de Bellefonds & Christophe Caron, *Droits d'auteur et droits voisins: propriété littéraire et artistique* (Delmas, 1997).
79. Xavier Linant de Bellefonds & Célia Zolynski, *Droits d'auteur et droits voisins* (Dalloz 2002).
80. Ulrich Loewenheim et al., *Urheberrecht: UrhG, KUG, VGG: Kommentar* (C.H. Beck, 6th ed. 2020).
81. Ulrich Loewenheim et al., *Urheberrecht: Kommentar* (C.H. Beck, 5th ed. 2017).
82. Ulrich Loewenheim, *Handbuch des Urheberrechts* (C.H. Beck, 3rd ed. 2021).
83. Jan Löwenbach, *Právo autorské: zákon ze dne 24. listopadu 1926, číslo 218. Sb. Z. a nař. s výkladem, judikaturou I prováděcími nařízením a hlavní normy mezinárodního a zahraničního práva původcovského* (Československý Kompas 1927).
84. André Lucas et al., *Traité de la propriété littéraire et artistique* (LexisNexis, 5th ed. 2017).
85. André Lucas, *Propriété littéraire et artistique* (Dalloz, 5th ed. 2015).
86. Ryszard Markiewicz, *Zabawy z Prawem Autorskim Dawne i Nowe* (Wolters Kluwer, 2nd ed. 2022).
87. Reginald McGinnis (ed.), *Originality and intellectual property in the French and English Enlightenment* (Routledge 2009).
88. Petrus S. R. F. Mathijsen, *A Guide to European Union Law* (Sweet & Maxwell, 9th ed. 2007).
89. Lucia Moholy, *Sto let fotografie: 1839-1939* (Kunsthalle 2024).
90. Philipp Möhring et al. (eds.), *Urheberrecht: UrhG, KUG, UrhWahrnG, VerlG; Kommentar* (C.H. Beck, 3rd ed. 2014).
91. Axel Nordemann, *Die künstlerische Fotografie als urheberrechtlich geschütztes Werk* (Nomos 1992).
92. Axel Nordemann et al., *Urheberrecht: Kommentar zum Urheberrechtsgesetz, Verlagsgesetz, Urheberrechtswahrnehmungsgesetz* (W. Kohlhammer, 11th ed. 2014).
93. Wilhelm Nordemann et al., *Urheberrecht: Kommentar zum Urheberrechtsgesetz, Verlagsgesetz, Urheberrechtswahrnehmungsgesetz* (W. Kohlhammer, 10th ed. 2008).
94. Wilhelm Nordemann et al., *Urheberrecht: Kommentar zum Urheberrechtsgesetz und zum Urheberrechtswahrnehmungsgesetz: Mit den Texten der Urheberrechtsgesetze der DDR, Österreichs und der Schweiz* (V. Kohlhammer, 7th ed. 1988).
95. Wilhelm Nordemann et al., *Urheberrecht: Kommentar zum Urheberrechtsgesetz und zum Urheberrechtswahrnehmungsgesetz* (W. Kohlhammer, 8th ed. 1994).
96. Wilhelm Nordemann et al., *Urheberrecht: Kommentar zum Urheberrechtsgesetz und zum Urheberrechtswahrnehmungsgesetz* (W. Kohlhammer, 9th ed. 1998).
97. Jean-Paul Oberthür, *Nouveau guide du droit d'auteur en photographie* (Annuaire de la photographie 1988).
98. Melanie Overbeck, *Der Lichtbildschutz gem. § 72 UrhG im Lichte der Digitalfotografie* (Lit 2018).
99. Emmanuel Pierrat, *Le droit d'auteur et l'édition* (Éditions du Cercle de la librairie, 4th ed. 2013).

100. Justine Pila & Paul Torremans, *European Intellectual Property Law* (Oxford University Press 2016).
101. Eugène Pouillet, *Traité des dessins et modèles de fabrique* (Imprimerie et libraire générale de jurisprudence 1884).
102. Thomas Platena, *Das Lichtbild im Urheberrecht: gesetzliche Regelung und technische Weiterentwicklung* (P. Lang 1998).
103. Philine Pohlhausen, *Das Original in der Fotografie im Lichte des Urheberrechts* (Nomos 2021).
104. Radim Polčák, Pavel Koukal & Rudolf Leška, *Autorský zákon: praktický komentář s judikaturou* (Leges 2020).
105. Frédéric Pollaud-Dulian, *Le droit d'auteur: propriété intellectuelle* (Economica, 2nd ed. 2014).
106. Jaroslav Pospíšil, *Výklad zákona o právu autorském k dílům literárním, uměleckým a fotografickým* (Česká grafická akciová společnost Unie, 1905).
107. David Prakel, *The Visual Dictionary of Photography* (AVA Academia 2010).
108. Petr Rezek, *Tělo, věc a skutečnost v umění šedesátých a sedmdesátých let* (Jan Placák-Ztichlá klika, 2nd ed. 2010).
109. Stefan Ricke, *Entwicklung des rechtlichen Schutzes von Fotografien in Deutschland* (Lit 1998).
110. Sam Ricketson & Jane C. Ginsburg, *International Copyright and Neighbouring Rights. 2* (Oxford Univ. Press, 2nd ed. 2006).
111. Sam Ricketson & Jane C. Ginsburg, *International Copyright and Neighbouring Rights: The Berne Convention and Beyond* (Oxford University Press, 3rd ed. 2022).
112. Eleonora Rosati, *Copyright and the Court of Justice of the European Union* (Oxford University Press 2019).
113. Eleonora Rosati, *Copyright and the Court of Justice of the European Union* (Oxford University Press, 2nd ed. 2023).
114. Eleonora Rosati, *Copyright in the Digital Single Market: Article-by-Article Commentary to the Provisions of Directive 2019/790* (Oxford University Press 2021).
115. Eleonora Rosati, *Originality in EU Copyright: Full Harmonization through Case Law* (Edward Elgar Publishing 2013).
116. Morten Rosenmeier, Kacper Szkalej & Sanna Wolk, *EU Copyright Law: Subsistence, Exploitation and Protection of Rights* (Kluwer Law International 2019).
117. Eleonora Rosati (ed.), *The Routledge handbook of EU copyright law* (Routledge 2021).
118. Rafael Sánchez Aristi, Nieves I. Moralejo Imbernón & Sebastián López Maza, *La jurisprudencia del Tribunal de Justicia de la Unión Europea en materia de propiedad intelectual: análisis y comentarios* (Instituto Autor 2017).
119. Haimo Schack, *Kunst und Recht: Bildende Kunst, Architektur, Design und Fotografie im deutschen und internationalen Recht* (Mohr Siebeck, 3rd ed. 2017).
120. Haimo Schack, *Urheber- und Urhebervertragsrecht* (Mohr Siebeck, 9th ed. 2019).
121. Haimo Schack, *Urheber- und Urhebervertragsrecht* (Mohr Siebeck, 10th ed. 2021).
122. Ilva Johanna Schiessel, *Reichweite und Rechtfertigung des einfachen Lichtbildschutzes gem. § 72 UrhG* (Nomos 2020).
123. Pierre Sirinelli et al. *Propriétés intellectuelles: mélanges en l'honneur de André Françon* (Dalloz 1995).

124. Pierre Sirinelli et al., *Code de la propriété intellectuelle* (Dalloz, 15th ed. 2015).
125. Pierre Sirinelli, *Propriété littéraire et artistique* (Dalloz, 2nd ed. 2004).
126. Catherine Soanes (ed.), *Concise Oxford English Dictionary* (Oxford Univ. Press, 11. ed. 2006).
127. Susan Sontag, *On Photography* (Penguin Books 2008).
128. Brad Spitz, *Guide to Copyright in France: Business, Internet and Litigation* (Kluwer Law International 2015).
129. Jiří Srstka et al., *Autorské právo a práva související: vysokoškolská učebnice* (Leges 3rd ed. 2024).
130. Christian Gero Stallberg, *Urheberrecht und moralische Rechtfertigung* (Duncker & Humblot 2006).
131. J. A. L. Sterling, *Sterling on World Copyright Law* (Thomson Reuters, 4th ed. 2015).
132. J. A. L. Sterling, *World Copyright Law* (Sweet & Maxwell 2008).
133. Alain Strowel, *Le droit d'auteur européen en transition numérique* (Larcier 2022).
134. Patrick Tafforeau & Cédric Monnerie, *Droit de la propriété intellectuelle* (Gualino-Lextenso éditions, 4th ed. 2015).
135. Ivo Telec, *Autorský zákon: komentář* (Beck 1997).
136. Ivo Telec & Pavel Tůma, *Autorský zákon: komentář* (C.H. Beck, 2nd ed. 2019).
137. Paul Torremans (ed.), *Research handbook on copyright law* (Edward Elgar Publishing 2017).
138. Guy Tritton & Richard Davis, *Intellectual Property in Europe* (Sweet & Maxwell, 3rd ed. 2008).
139. Martin Valoušek, *Fotografie a právo: autorské právo a ochrana osobnosti ve vztahu k fotografii* (Leges, 2nd ed. 2022).
140. Valérie Varnerot, *Leçons de droit de la propriété littéraire et artistique* (Ellipses 2012).
141. Michel Vivant & Jean-Michel Bruguière, *Droit d'auteur et droits voisins* (Dalloz, 2nd ed. 2012).
142. Michel Vivant & Jean-Michel Bruguière, *Droit d'auteur et droits voisins* (Dalloz, 4th ed. 2019).
143. Michel Vivant, Jean-Louis Navarro & Jean-Louis Bilon, *Code de la propriété intellectuelle 2012* (LexisNexis, 13th ed. 2012).
144. Peter Vojčík, *Právo duševného vlastníctva* (Aleš Čeněk 2012).
145. Endress Wanckel, *Foto- und Bildrecht* (C.H. Beck, 5th ed. 2017).
146. Artur-Axel Wandtke et al., *Praxiskommentar Urheberrecht: UrhG, VGG, InsO, UKlaG, KUG, EVtr, InfoSoc-RL* (C.H. Beck, 5th ed. 2019).
147. Artur-Axel Wandtke, Winfried Bullinger & Michael Bohne, *Praxiskommentar Urheberrecht: UrhG, UrhDaG, VGG, InsO, UKlaG, KUG, EVtr, InfoSoc-RL, Portabilitäts-VO* (C.H. Beck, 6th ed. 2022).
148. Michel M. Walter & Silke von Lewinski (eds.), *Europäisches Urheberrecht: Kommentar* (Springer 2001).
149. Michael M. Walter & Silke von Lewinski (eds.), *European copyright law: a commentary* (Oxford Univ. Press 2010).
150. Julia Werner, *Die Reformbedürftigkeit des Lichtbildschutzes nach Paragraph 72 UrhG aus rechtsökonomischer Perspektive* (Peter Lang 2023).
151. World Organization for Intellectual Property (ed.), *Guide to the Berne convention for the protection of literary and artistic works: Paris Act, 1971* (WIPO 1978).

Chapters in Collective Monographs and Edited Books

1. Mireille van Eechoud, 'Adapting the Work' In: Mireille van Eechoud, Jostein Gripsrud & Lionel Bently, *Work of Authorship* (Amsterdam University Press 2015).
2. Mireille van Eechoud, 'The European Concern with Copyright and Related Rights' In: Mireille van Eechoud (ed.), *Harmonizing European Copyright Law: The Challenges of Better Lawmaking* (Kluwer Law International 2009).
3. Mireille van Eechoud, 'Object, Subject, and Duration of Protection' In: Mireille van Eechoud (ed.), *Harmonizing European Copyright Law: The Challenges of Better Lawmaking* (Kluwer Law International 2009).
4. Yves Gaubiac, Brigitte Lindner & John N. Adams, 'Duration of Copyright' In: Estelle Derclaye, *Research Handbook on the Future of EU Copyright* (Edward Elgar Publishing 2009).
5. Philippe Gaudrat, 'Réflexions sur la forme des œuvres de l'esprit' In: Pierre Sirinelli et al., *Propriétés intellectuelles: mélanges en l'honneur de André Françon* (Dalloz 1995).
6. Stef van Gompel, 'Creativity, Autonomy, and Personal Touch' In: Mireille van Eechoud, Jostein Gripsrud & Lionel Bently, *Work of Authorship* (Amsterdam University Press 2015).
7. Antoine Latreille, 'From Idea to Fixation: A View of Protected Works' In: Estelle Derclaye, *Research Handbook on the Future of EU Copyright* (Edward Elgar Publishing 2009).
8. Rudolf Leška, 'Czechia' In: Silke von Lewinski, *Copyright Throughout the World* (Thomson/West 2022).
9. Rudolf Leška, 'Slovakia' In: Silke von Lewinski, *Copyright Throughout the World* (Thomson/West 2022).
10. Marianne Levin, 'The Cofemel Revolution – Originality, Equality and Neutrality' In: Eleonora Rosati, *The Routledge Handbook of EU Copyright Law* (Routledge 2021).
11. Silke von Lewinski & Michel M. Walter, 'Status of Harmonization' In: Michel M. Walter & Silke von Lewinski, *European Copyright Law: A Commentary* (Oxford University Press 2010).
12. Maria Martin-Prat, 'Twenty Years After – the State of EU Copyright Law' In: Hayleigh Bosher & Eleonora Rosati, *Developments and Directions in Intellectual Property Law: Twenty Years of the IPKat* (Oxford University Press 2023).
13. Andrzej Matlak, 'Wyrok TSUE z 1. 12. 2011 r. w sprawie Eva-Maria Painer przeciwko Standard Verlags GmbH i in. (C-145/10)' In: Ewa Laskowska-Litak & Ryszard Markiewicz, *Prawo Autorskie: Komentarz do Wybranego Orzecznictwa Trybunału Sprawiedliwości UE* (Wolters Kluwer 2019).
14. Gemma Minnero, 'The Term Directive' In: Irini A. Stamatoudi & Paul Torremans, *EU Copyright Law: A Commentary* (Edward Elgar Publishing 2021).
15. Gemma Minnero, 'The Term Directive' In: Irini A. Stamatoudi & Paul Torremans (eds.), *EU Copyright Law: a Commentary* (Edward Elgar Publishing, 2nd ed. 2021).
16. Gemma Minnero, 'The Term Directive' In: Irini A. Stamatoudi & Paul Torremans (eds.), *EU Copyright Law: a Commentary* (Edward Elgar Publishing 2014).
17. Axel Nordemann, 'Germany' In: Ysolde Gendreau, Axel Nordemann & Reto Oesch, *Copyright and Photographs: An International Survey* (Kluwer Law International 1999).

18. Justine Pila, 'The Authorial Works Protectable by Copyright' In: Eleonora Rosati, *The Routledge Handbook of EU Copyright Law* (Routledge 2021).
19. Ana Ramalho, 'The Competence and Rationale of EU Copyright Harmonization' In: Eleonora Rosati, *The Routledge Handbook of EU Copyright Law* (Routledge 2021).
20. Eleonora Rosati, 'Copyright at the CJEU: Back to the Start (of Copyright Protection)' In: Hayleigh Bosher & Eleonora Rosati, *Developments and Directions in Intellectual Property Law: Twenty Years of the IPKat* (Oxford University Press 2023).
21. Claudia Schlüter, 'Harmonisierung ohne Harmonie? Das Infopaq v. DDF-Urteil des EuGH und der europäische Werkbegriff' In: Horst-Peter Götting, Dieter Stauder & Christoph Schlüter, *Nourriture de l'esprit: Festschrift für Dieter Stauder zum 70. Geburtstag* (Nomos 2011).
22. Gernot Schulze, 'Der Schutzumfang des Urheberrechts in Deutschland' In: Reto M. Hilty, Christophe Geiger & Valérie-Laure Benabou, *Impulse für eine europäische Harmonisierung des Urheberrechts: Urheberrecht im deutsch-französischen Dialog* (Springer 2007).
23. Pierre Sirinelli & Alexandra Bensamoun, 'France' In: Silke von Lewinski, *Copyright Throughout the World* (Thomson/West 2022).
24. John Vignaux Smyth, 'Originality in the Enlightenment and Beyond' In: Richard McGinnis, *Originality and Intellectual Property in the French and English Enlightenment* (Routledge 2009).
25. Irini A. Stamatoudi, 'Originality under EU Copyright Law' In: Paul Torremans, *Research Handbook on Copyright Law* (Edward Elgar Publishing 2017).
26. Dorothee Thum, 'Germany' In: Silke von Lewinski, *Copyright Throughout the World* (Thomson/West 2022).
27. Ramon C. Vallés, 'The requirement of originality' In: Estelle Derclaye (ed.), *Research Handbook on the Future of EU Copyright* (Edward Elgar Publishing 2009).
28. Andrea Wallace & Ellen Euler, 'Revisiting Access to Cultural Heritage in the Public Domain: EU and International Developments,' In: *IIC* 823 (2020).
29. Michel M. Walter, 'Term Directive' In: Michel M. Walter & Silke von Lewinski, *European Copyright Law: A Commentary* (Oxford University Press 2010).
30. Michel M. Walter, 'Schutzdauer Richtlinie' In: Michel M. Walter & Silke von Lewinski, *Europäisches Urheberrecht: Kommentar* (Springer 2001).
31. Michel M. Walter, 'Schutzdauer Richtlinie' In: Michel M. Walter & Silke von Lewinski (eds.), *Europäisches Urheberrecht: Kommentar* (Springer 2001).

Journal Articles

1. Basile Ader, 'L'évolution de la notion d'originalité dans la jurisprudence,' 34 *LEGICOM* 43 (2005).
2. Christina Angelopoulos, 'The Myth of European Term Harmonisation – 27 Public Domains for 27 Member States,' *IIC* 567 (2012).
3. Nicolas Berthold, 'L'harmonisation de la Notion D'originalite en Droit D'auter,' 16 *Journal of World Intellectual Property* 58 (2013).
4. Marcel Bisges, 'Der europäische Werkbegriff und sein Einfluss auf die deutsche Urheberrechtsentwicklung,' *ZUM* 357 (2015).

5. Sabine Büttler, 'Urheberrechtsschutz von Porträtfotografien, insbesondere bei der Verwendung als Fahndungsbild,' *European Law Reporter* 82 (2012).
6. Christophe Caron, 'Droit d'auteur de l'Union européenne : des photographies et des exceptions,' 14 *Communication - Commerce Électronique* 26 (2012).
7. Céline Castets-Renard, 'L'originalité en droit d'auteur européen : la CJUE creuse le sillon,' *82 Revue Lamy Droit de l'immatériel* 6 (2012).
8. Melanie Clément-Fontaine, 'Synthèse,' 70 *Revue Lamy Droit de l'immatériel* 137 (2011).
9. Véronique Dahan & Charles Bouffier, 'Arrêt Painer du 1er décembre 2011 : la CJUE poursuit son œuvre d'harmonisation du droit d'auteur,' 80 *Revue Lamy Droit de l'immatériel* 14 (2012).
10. Giulia Dore & Pelin Turan, 'When Copyright Meets Digital Cultural Heritage: Picturing an EU Right to Culture in Freedom of Panorama and Reproduction of Public Domain Art,' *IIC* 37 (2024).
11. Achilles C. Emilianides, 'The Author Revived: Harmonisation Without Justification,' *26 European Intellectual Property Review* 538 (2004).
12. Yolande Finkelsztajn, 'Représentation et réalité,' *70 Revue Lamy Droit de l'immatériel* 113 (2011).
13. Jan Franzen & Albrecht Götz von Olenhusen, 'Lichtbildwerke, Lichtbilder und Fotoimitate: Abhängige Bearbeitung oder freier Benutzung?' *UFITA* 435 (2007).
14. Friedrich Karl Fromm, 'Der Apparat als geistiger Schöpfer,' *GRUR* 304 (1964).
15. Florence Gaullier, 'La preuve de l'originalité : mission impossible ?' 70 *Revue Lamy Droit de l'immatériel* 126 (2011).
16. Christophe Geiger, 'Liberté de l'image et droit d'auteur,' 26 *LÉGIPRESSE* 84 (2005).
17. Ysolde Gendreau, 'La protection des photographies en droit d'auteur français, américain, britannique et canadien,' *LGDJ* 80 (1994).
18. Daniel J. Gervais & Estelle Derclaye, 'The Scope of Computer Program Protection after SAS: Are We Closer to Answers?' *European Intellectual Property Review* 565 (2012).
19. Daniel J. Gervais, 'Feist Goes Global: A Comparative Analysis of the Notion of Originality in Copyright Law,' 49 *Journal of the Copyright Society of the U.S.A.* 949 (2002).
20. Koray Güven, *Eliminating 'Aesthetics' from Copyright Law: The Aftermath of Cofemel,* 71 *GRUR Int.* 213 (2022).
21. Helmut Haberstumpf, 'Der europäische Werkbegriff und die Lehre vom Gestaltungsspielraum,' *GRUR* 1249 (2021).
22. Christian Handig, 'The "Sweat of the Brow" is Not Enough! – More than a Blueprint of the European Copyright Term "Work",' *European Intellectual Property Review* 334 (2013).
23. Christian Handig, 'Durch "freie kreative Entscheidungen" zum europäischen urheberrechtlichen Werkbegriff,' *GRUR Int.* 965 (2012).
24. Christian Handig, 'Erste Umrisse eines europäischen Werkbegriffs,' 61 *Österreichische Blätter für gewerblichen Rechtsschutz und Urheberrecht* 4 (2012).
25. Christian Handig, 'Lauter Lichtbildwerke!' 58 *Österreichische Blätter für Gewerblichen Rechtsschutz und Urheberrecht* 8 (2009).
26. Christian Handig, 'The Copyright Term "Work" - European Harmonisation at an Unknown Level,' *40 IIC* 665 (2009).

27. Christian Handig, 'Was ist eine "eigene geistige Schöpfung der Urhebers"? : Der auslegungsbedürftige Werkbegriff des europäischen Urheberrechts,' *UFITA* 55 (2009).
28. Christian Handig, 'Wie viel Originalität braucht ein urheberrechtliches Werk?' 1 *Österreichisches Recht der Wirtschaft* 14 (2010).
29. Thomas Hoeren, 'Urheberrechtliche Probleme des Dokumentarfilms,' *GRUR* 145 (1992).
30. Martin Husovec, 'Judikatórna harmonizácia pojmu autorského diela v únijnom práve,' 12 *Bulletin slovenskej advokácie* (2012).
31. Martin Husovec, 'K európskemu prepisovaniu pojmových znakov autorského diela,' 4 *Duševné vlastníctvo* 24 (2011).
32. Marián Jankovič, 'The Development and Harmonisation of Originality Standard of Photographic Works in the Copyright Framework of the European Union' 20 *Jusletter IT 30. März 2023* (2023).
33. Marián Jankovič, 'How the Two Child Abuse Cases Helped to Shape the Test of Originality of Photographic Works' 17 *Masaryk University Journal of Law and Technology* 197 (2023).
34. Herman Cohen Jehoram, 'The EC Copyright Directives, Economics and Authors' Rights,' *IIC* 821 (1994).
35. Gunnar W. G. Karnell, 'European Originality: A Copyright Chimera,' *Intellectual Property* 73 (2002).
36. Pavel Koukal, 'New Developments in the EU Concept of Copyrighted Works' 20 *Jusletter IT 24. April 2023* (2023).
37. Pavel Koukal, 'Reexamining Precision and Objectivity in Copyright Protection for Non-Traditional Creations' 21 *Jusletter IT 24. April 2024* (2024).
38. Antoine Latreille, Images numériques et pratique du droit d'auteur, 34 *LEGICOM* 51.
39. Antoine Latreille, 'L'appropriation des photographies d'œuvres d'art: éléments d'une réflexion sur un objet de droit d'auteur,' *Recueil Dalloz* 299 (2002).
40. Antoine Latreille, 'La création photographique face au juge : entre confusion et raison,' 31 *LÉGIPRESSE* 139 (2010).
41. Antoine Latreille, 'Une nouvelle œuvre de l'esprit (approche juridique),' 70 *Revue Lamy Droit de l'immatériel* 109 (2011).
42. Harn Lee, 'Case Comment: Photographs and the Standard of Originality in Europe: Eva-Maria Painer v Standard VerlagsGmbH, Axel Springer AG, Süddeutsche Zeitung GmbH, SPIEGEL-Verlag Rudolf AUGSTEIN GmbH & Co KG and Verlag M. DuMont Schauberg Expedition der Kölnischen Zeitung GmbH & Co KG (C-145/10),' 34 *European Intellectual Property Review* 290 (2012).
43. Matthias Leistner, 'Der europäische Werkbegriff,' *Zeitschrift für Geistiges Eigentum* 4 (2013).
44. Matthias Leistner, 'Von Joseph Beuys, Marcel Duchamp und der dokumentarischen Fotografie von Kunstaktionen,' *ZUM* 468 (2011).
45. André Lucas, Valérie-Laure Benabou & Jean-Michel Bruguière, 'Droit d'auteur et droit voisins,' 26 *Propriétés Intellectuelles* 260 (2008).
46. André Lucas, Valérie-Laure Benabou & Jean-Michel Bruguière, 'TGI Paris, 13 mars 2009, p. Bazin c/ T. Bouët et Grands magasins de la Samaritaine (en attente),' 32 *Propriétés Intellectuelles* 260 (2008).

47. André Lucas & Jean-Michel Bruguière, 'TGI Paris, 30 mai 2007, Claude Nuridsanz c/ Société d'Evian et autres,' 20 *Propriétés Intellectuelles* 309 (2007).
48. Aurelija Lukoševičienė, 'On Author, Copyright and Originality: Does the Unified EU Originality Standard Correspond to the Digital Reality in Wikipedia?' 11 *Masaryk University Journal of Law and Technology* 215 (2017).
49. Nathalie Martial-Braz, 'Cliché d'une harmonisation du droit d'auteur par la CJUE : du grand art!' *Recueil Dalloz* 471 (2012).
50. Axel Metzger, 'Der Einfluss des EuGH auf die gegenwärtige Entwicklung des Urheberrechts,' *GRUR* 118 (2012).
51. Benoît Michaux, 'L'originalité en droit communautaire après l'arrêt Infopaq,' 70 *Revue Lamy Droit de l'immatériel* 121 (2011).
52. Axel Nordemann & Friedrich Nicolaus Heise, 'Urheberrechtlicher Schutz für Designleistungen in Deutschland und auf europäischer Ebene'. *ZUM* 128 (2001).
53. Wilhelm Nordemann, 'Lichtbildschutz für fotografisch hergestellte Vervielfältigungen,' *GRUR* 15 (1987).
54. Karl-Nikolaus Peifer, 'Individualität' or Originality? Core Concepts in German Copyright Law,' *GRUR Int.* 1100 (2014).
55. Pierre Pérot, 'Parodie d'une œuvre photographique : game over pour le Guerrillero Heroico,' *LÉGIPRESSE* 572 (2018).
56. David Pouchard, 'Le valorisation des fonds photographiques, ou comment concilier le droit d'auter et l'accés au patrimoine culturel,' 36 *In Situ* (2018).
57. Andreas Rahmatian, 'European Copyright Inside or Outside the European Union: Pluralism of Copyright Laws and the 'Herderian Paradox', *IIC* 912 (2016).
58. Andreas Rahmatian, 'Originality in UK Copyright Law: The Old 'Skill and Labour' Doctrine Under Pressure,' 44 *IIC* 4 (2013).
59. Eleonora Rosati, 'Originality in a Work, or a Work of Originality: the Effects of the Infopaq Decision,' *33 European Intellectual Property Review* 746 (2011).
60. Hans Peter Roth, 'EuGH, 01. 12. 2011 - C-145/10: Urheberrecht: Schutz von Portraitfotografien,' 5 *EuZW* (2012).
61. Gerhard Schricker, 'Farewell to the 'Level of Creativity', 26 *IIC* 41 (1995).
62. Ernst H. Stefan, 'BGH, 20. 11. 1986 – I ZR 160/84: 'Werbepläne', 6 *GRUR* 360 (1987).
63. Ivo Telec, 'Autorské právo k fotografiím podle nového autorského zákona,' *Právní rozhledy: časopis pro všechna právní odvětví* 539 (2000).
64. Lucie Tréguier & William van Caenegem, 'Copyright, Art and Originality: Comparative and Policy Issues,' *8 Global Journal of Comparative Law* 95 (2019).
65. Joachim Ungern-Sternberg, 'Verwendungen des Werkes in veränderter Gestalt im Lichte des Unionsrechts,' *GRUR* 533 (2015).
66. Mireille van Eechoud, 'Along the road to uniformity: diverse readings of the Court of Justice judgements on copyright works,' *3 Journal of Intellectual Property, Information Technology and Electronic Commerce Law* 60 (2012).
67. Stef van Gompel & Erlend Lavik, 'Quality, merit, aesthetics and purpose: An inquiry into EU copyright law's eschewal of other criteria than originality,' *RIDA* 100 (2013).
68. Joëlle Verbrugge, 'Prouver l'originalité d'une ou plusieurs photographies,' *LÉGIPRESSE* 639 (2019).

69. Jean Vincent, 'L'Approche juridique pour la photographie et les autres formes d'expression,' 70 *Revue Lamy Droit de l'immatériel* 118 (2011).
70. Silke von Lewinski, 'Der EG-Richtlinienvorschlag zur Harmonisierung der Schutzdauer im Urheber- und Leistungsschutzrecht,' *GRUR Int.* 724 (1992).
71. Silke von Lewinski, 'Introduction: The Notion of Work Under EU Law,' *GRUR Int.* 1098 (2014).
72. Andrea Wallace & Ellen Euler, 'Revisiting Access to Cultural Heritage in the Public Domain: EU and International Developments,' *IIC* 823 (2020).

Electronic and Other Sources

1. *Common Position of the Council of 22 July 1993 on the amended proposal for a Council Directive harmonizing the term of protection of copyright and certain related rights*, the Council's reasons, 7831/1/93 REV 1 ADD 1, Brussels, 10 August 1993.
2. *Copyright Notice: Digital Images, Photographs and the Internet* (4 Jan. 2021), https://www.gov.uk/government/publications/copyright-notice-digital-images-photographs-and-the-internet/copyright-notice-digital-images-photographs-and-the-internet.
3. Dominique Sagot-Duvauroux, *L'Originalité et la Valeur de l'Image* (2 Sep. 2024), https://univ-angers.hal.science/hal-02528782/.
4. *Dôvodová správa k návrhu zákona, ktorým sa mení a dopĺňa zákon č. 618/2003 Z. z. o autorskom práve a právach súvisiacich s autorským právom (autorský zákon) a o zmene a o doplnení niektorých zákonov* (1 Oct. 2024), https://hsr.rokovania.sk/data/att/81512_subor.rtf.
5. *Důvodová zpráva k návrhu zákona o právu autorském, o právech souvisejících s právem autorským a o změně některých zákonů (autorský zákon). Sněmovní tisk 443/0. Vládní návrh zákona o právu autorském – EU* (1 Oct. 2024), https://www.psp.cz/sqw/historie.sqw?o=3&t=443.
6. *Důvodová zpráva k návrhu zákona o právu autorském, o právech souvisejících s právem autorským a o změně některých zákonů (autorský zákon). Sněmovní tisk 724/0. Vládní návrh zákona o právu autorském* (1 Oct. 2024), https://www.psp.cz/sqw/historie.sqw?o=7&t=724.
7. Eleonora Rosati, *The Levola Hengelo CJEU Decision: Ambiguities, Uncertainties ... and More Questions* (2 Sep. 2024), http://ipkitten.blogspot.com/2018/11/the-levola-hengelo-cjeu-decision.html.
8. *Entwurf eines Gesetzes zur Änderung von Vorschriften auf dem Gebiet des Urheberrechts Drucksache 10/837, Drucksache 10/3360* (1. Nov. 2024), https://dserver.bundestag.de/btd/10/033/1003360.pdf.
9. *Entwurf eines Vierten Gesetzes zur Änderung des Urheberrechtsgesetzes. Deutscher Bundestag - 13. Wahlperiode. Drucksache 13/781* (1 Oct. 2024), https://dserver.bundestag.de/btd/13/007/1300781.pdf.
10. *European Commission Staff Working Paper on the Review of the EC legal framework in the field of copyright and related rights*, SEC(2004) 995, 19 Jul. 2004 (1 Oct. 2024), https://data.consilium.europa.eu/doc/document/ST-11634-2004-INIT/en/pdf.
11. *Intellectual Property Code* (1 Sep. 2024), https://wipolex-res.wipo.int/edocs/lexdocs/laws/en/fr/fr467en.html.

12. Jason D. Little, *These Ideas on Perspective will Improve your Photography Composition* (1 Sep. 2024), https://www.lightstalking.com/ideas-perspective-will-improve-photography-composition/.
13. Lionel Bently, *Harmonization by Stealth: Copyright and the ECJ. Fordham IP Conference* (2010), New York City (1 Oct. 2024), https://www.competitionlawassociation.org.uk/docs/harmonisation_bently_slides_01_05_12.ppt.
14. Louis Theodor Christian Harms, *Originality and Reproduction in Copyright Law with Special Reference to Photographs* (2 Sep. 2024), https://papers.ssrn.com/sol3/papers.cfm?abstract_id=2427669.
15. Martin Husovec, *Slovakia Adopts a New Copyright Act: It's a Mixed Bag – Part I* (1 Sep. 2024), https://copyrightblog.kluweriplaw.com/2016/02/29/slovakia-adopts-a-new-copyright-act-its-a-mixed-bag-part-i/.
16. Thomas Margoni, *The Harmonisation of EU Copyright Law: The Originality Standard* (1 Sep. 2024), https://papers.ssrn.com/sol3/papers.cfm?abstract_id=2802327.
17. Mathilde Pavis, *Digitized Images of Works in the Public Domain: What Rights Vest in Them? Analysis of the Recent BGH Reiss-Engelhorn Judgement – Part 1* (1 Sep. 2024), https://ipkitten.blogspot.com/2019/02/digitized-images-of-works-in-public.html.
18. Mathilde Pavis, *Forgive My French: Copyright "A La Carte" for Photographic Works* (1 Sep. 2024), https://the1709blog.blogspot.com/2015/07/forgive-my-french-copyright-la-carte.html.
19. Mathilde Pavis, *Hendrix's Portrait Is Original Afterall Say Paris Court of Appeal* (1 Sep. 2024), https://ipkitten.blogspot.com/2017/06/hendrixs-portrait-is-original-after-all.html?m=0.
20. Caterina Sganga, *The Notion of "Work" in EU Copyright Law After Levola Hengelo: One Answer Given, Three Question Marks Ahead* (3 Sep. 2024), https://papers.ssrn.com/sol3/papers.cfm?abstract_id=3323011.
21. Peter Sokol, *Podali sme amicus curiae pred Ústavným súdom* (1 Sep. 2024), https://eisionline.org/2012/03/13/podali-sme-amicus-curiae-pred-ustavnym-sudom/.
22. Benoît Spitz, *France: Mankowitz's Photo of Jimi Hendrix is Finally Protected by Copyright in Appeal* (1 Sep. 2024), https://copyrightblog.kluweriplaw.com/2017/08/18/france-mankowitzs-photo-jimi-hendrix-finally-protected-copyright-appeal/.
23. Tatiana Synodinou, *The Renckhoff Judgement: The CJEU Swivels the Faces of the Copyright Rubik's Cube (Part I)* (3 Sep. 2024), https://copyrightblog.kluweriplaw.com/2018/09/27/renckhoff-judgment-cjeu-swivels-faces-copyright-rubiks-cube-part/.
24. Michael A. Weiss, *Paris Court of Appeals: Photograph of Jimi Hendrix is Original and Thus Protected by French Copyright* (1 Sep. 2024), https://www.linkedin.com/pulse/paris-court-appeals-photograph-jimi-hendrix-original-thus-weiss/.
25. *Proposal for a Council Directive harmonizing the term of protection of copyright and certain related rights*, COM(92) 33 final – SYN 395, 23 Mar. 1992 (1 Oct. 2024), https://eur-lex.europa.eu/legal-content/EN/TXT/PDF/?uri=CELEX:51992PC0033.
26. Sanne Taekema, *Theoretical and Normative Frameworks for Legal Research: Putting Theory into Practice* (1 Sep. 2024), https://papers.ssrn.com/sol3/papers.cfm?abstract_id=3123667.
27. Alexander Wrigley, *Beginners Guide to Photography Composition* (1 Sep. 2024), https://medium.com/photography-secrets/beginners-guide-to-photography-composition-88290d6c24ac.

INDEX

www.ingramcontent.com/pod-product-compliance
Lightning Source LLC
LaVergne TN
LVHW020001031026
849161LV00023B/805